The Halloween Encyclopedia
SECOND EDITION

ALSO BY LISA MORTON
AND FROM MCFARLAND

Savage Detours: The Life and Work of Ann Savage (2010)

*A Hallowe'en Anthology: Literary and
Historical Writings Over the Centuries* (2008)

The Cinema of Tsui Hark (2001; paperback 2009)

The Halloween Encyclopedia

SECOND EDITION

Lisa Morton

McFarland & Company, Inc., Publishers

Jefferson, North Carolina, and London

LIBRARY OF CONGRESS CATALOGUING-IN-PUBLICATION DATA

Morton, Lisa, 1958–
The Halloween encyclopedia /
Lisa Morton.— 2nd ed.
p.   cm.
Includes bibliographical references and index.

ISBN 978-0-7864-6074-8
illustrated case binding : 50# alkaline paper ∞

1. Halloween — Encyclopedias.   I. Title.
GT4965.M673   2011   394.2646'03 — dc22   2011000088

BRITISH LIBRARY CATALOGUING DATA ARE AVAILABLE

Front cover © 2011 Shutterstock

Manufactured in the United States of America

McFarland & Company, Inc., Publishers
Box 611, Jefferson, North Carolina 28640
www.mcfarlandpub.com

Acknowledgments

Stumbling through the dark maze of Halloween fact and fallacy is no easy task, and I'm indebted to Rick Kleffel and Cheri Scotch for tips on Celtic references; to Chris Jarocha-Ernst for some haunted house lore; the staff of the Central Los Angeles Public Library (surely the most knowledgeable and helpful public servants in Los Angeles!); to Pamela Apkarian-Russell, Lesley Bannatyne, David Bertolino of Spooky World, Lori M. Garst (Curatorial Assistant, Biltmore Estate), Rich Hanf, Matthew Kirscht, Jack Santino, Al Sarrantonio, Stuart Schneider, Hank Schwaeble, and Tim of the late great Hallowed Haunting Grounds for providing some fabulous entries (and photos); Sue and Del (and the girls) at Dark Delicacies, for books, support and patience; Bob Johnson, for providing some great collectibles (and stress-relieving stories); Brett Thompson, for digging through endless boxes and putting up with my schedule; Dan and the Iliad Bookshop, for information, resources, time and sundry other things that authors need to live; Ricky Lee Grove, for — well, everything else; and Mom and Dad, for putting up with those endless weird Halloween costumes (see, they finally paid off).

Contents

Preface to the Second Edition

Just as it always has throughout its long history, Halloween has continued to evolve in the eight years since the first edition of this book was published. In 2003, for example, haunted houses were certainly nothing new, but there was hardly a massive haunted attractions industry that employed thousands and claimed to generate a billion dollars a year in revenue. Nor had "agri-tainment"— in which farmers convert part of their acreage into a seasonal attraction like a pumpkin patch or corn maze — yet become an important source of profit for many small farms and resulted in thousands of new Halloween adventures for city dwellers everywhere.

In the intervening eight years, Halloween has managed to weather unprecedented upheavals in the economy, politics, and even natural disasters. It's proven to be recession-proof, defying the gloomiest retailing predictions each year, and contrary to what the naysayers have often predicted, trick or treat for youngsters is still going strong. Halloween folk art has become widely available through various online sites (with some artists garnering significant followings), and the values of vintage collectibles from the holiday's past have risen sharply.

Sadly, not all of Halloween's recent transmogrifications have been happy ones: Halloween-related crime has also experienced an upsurge, especially hate crimes (students dressing up as Ku Klux Klan members, for example). Halloween's urban legends— which have moved from strictly oral tales to "netlore," transmitted via e-mail and social networking sites— have grown even uglier, with middle-class tensions reflected in paranoid tales of "gang initiations" that will kill masses of women on Halloween. These new fears (all baseless), with their potentially high body counts, make the old legends of razor blades hidden in apples seem positively nostalgic.

The study of Halloween's history has also taken a tremendous leap forward in the last few years, with the introduction of websites like Google Books. The world's libraries are now online, for the most part free to peruse and completely searchable. What formerly required special trips to a library, possibly consulting with a reference librarian, and hours poring over old books or squinting at shadowy microfiches can now be accomplished from home in minutes with a few search terms. Not only does this speed up and expand the practices of research, it also allows the writer or historian to more easily draw connections and formulate timelines. Hence you'll find in this edition not only entirely new entries (ranging from African Americans to the Mayan holiday of Xantolo), but also expanded and revised entries from the previous edition (the section on Samhain, for instance, is now far more precise in pinning down the origins of the mistaken notion that this was the name of a Celtic "Lord of Death"). New illustrations and of course a revised index have also been provided.

I'd like to say that this second edition of *The Halloween Encyclopedia* is now as complete as it could ever possibly be, but given Halloween's transforming (and transformative) nature, I know that won't be the case. I can only hope that the book will provide enlightenment and entertainment to its readers now ... and for at least a few years to come.

Preface to the First Edition

Halloween is arguably the most paradoxical of American holidays: Despite its ever-increasing popularity, it is also condemned by some and misunderstood by most. Those who celebrate the holiday have some vague idea of its antiquity, but they commonly believe that such modern rituals as trick or treat are ancient as well. Even historians, folklorists and other academics are often confused by the holiday, and the sources available until recently were riddled with error and fantasy. Throughout most of the twentieth century, for example, the Celtic year-end festival of Samhain was instead believed to be a celebration of the Celts' "Lord of Death," also supposedly named Samhain (modern archaeology and scholarship have now disproved this colorful if morbid notion). Likewise, Halloween's origins were partly attributed to the Roman harvest festival Pomona, when in fact Pomona was no more than a minor wood-nymph deity who was little honored outside of her sacred grove.

The concept of Halloween as a holiday and cultural phenomenon worthy of serious study is barely two decades old; only since the mid–1980s have we begun to accept that Halloween's unique place in modern society (especially American society) merits attention beyond horror fiction and children's books. Folklorists such as Jack Santino have led the way in understanding how Halloween's Celtic-Irish-Scottish roots as both harvest festival and commemoration of the dead have blossomed into the modern American rituals of "masked solicitation" and large-scale celebration. Now Halloween has exploded into a retailing bonanza, transforming a holiday which has been banned throughout the centuries into the second most popular day of the year in twenty-first-century America.

The first book devoted solely to Halloween was published just over a century ago; now this book is the first encyclopedic reference on the holiday. Like the earliest books on the subject, this book also covers history, folklore, fortune-telling and even party activities; however, unlike the earliest works on the holiday, this book draws on a century of sources.

Unfortunately, many of those source books are little more than collections of fairy tales. They often seem to have been poorly researched, and displayed prejudice or predilection on the part of their authors. For this volume, research included not just the standard Halloween references (including Ruth E. Kelley's 1919 *The Book of Hallowe'en* and Ralph and Adelin Linton's 1950 *Halloween Through Twenty Centuries*), but also references in the fields of Celtic, Roman and Irish history, chronicles of the Catholic Church, modern studies of paganism and witchcraft, folklore collections (including John Brand's standard *Observations on Popular Antiquities*, which includes its own set of errors), newspaper accounts, pamphlets and even booklets produced by American cities trying to curb destructive Halloween pranking. The present volume also, of course, includes entries on the more modern activities, including trick or treat, haunted houses, and retailing.

While it is not within the scope of this book to discuss every similar celebration (harvest festival or commemoration of the dead) throughout the world, there are entries on certain other celebrations which have influenced or been influenced by Halloween in some way (Thanksgiving, Martinmas), and entries on major festivals which are often compared to Halloween (Japan's Bon Festival, the Mexican Days of the Dead).

The entries are presented in alphabetical order, with cross-references in the entries in small capital letters throughout. References are also found in the index.

Two appendices have been included here: Appendix I shows a simple chronological timeline of the holiday's history, and Appendix II briefly discusses Halloween in literature and the arts. The main purpose of this second appendix is not to provide detailed analyses of the films, books and other works of art discussed, but rather to demonstrate how Halloween has been shown in — and changed by — popular media.

A

Acorn— Fruit of the oak; a tree is usually about twenty years old before acorns appear. Although oak trees were sacred to the CELTS and supposedly featured in many rites of the DRUIDS, acorns are infrequently mentioned in Halloween customs. This stanza from an 1898 poem by B. M. Teggart illustrates an Irish Halloween custom:

> And some have acorns— these once graced
> By fairy king and queen,
> Upon the low back hob are placed
> For luck, at Halloween.

Acorns are also mentioned in one German trickster story which is very similar to the legends behind JACK-O'-LANTERN: A farmer makes a deal with the DEVIL, and agrees to pay up when he harvests his first crop. The farmer then goes out and plants acorns.

Acrostics— A popular early twentieth-century American Halloween event, presented as either a party GAME or part of a school presentation (along with PLAYS, RECITATIONS, MONOLOGS and EXERCISES). In an acrostic, each letter of the word Halloween is used to spell out a Halloween activity (if presented onstage, each letter would be carried by a different child, entering one at a time until the name was spelled out across the stage). Here's a typical Halloween acrostic by Alice Crowell Hoffman:

> H appy children pranking,
> A pples bobbing, too,
> L ively little brownies
> L ooking straight at you.
> O wls with mournful hooting,
> W itches riding sticks,
> E lves and cats and goblins,
> E ach one up to tricks.
> N ow it can be plainly seen
>   That at last it's Halloween!

African Americans— The history of African Americans and Halloween mirrors the history of American racism. In his 1904 poem "Hallowe'en," black poet Charles Frederick White implies that African American children of the time participated in the same Halloween activities that their Caucasian counterparts did; however, Halloween party booklets and playlets from the 1920s and '30s paint a different picture, suggesting that stereotypes of African Americans developed and perpetuated in 19th century minstrel shows— mainly that blacks were superstitious and buffoonish— hadn't changed in decades. Here, for example, is a poem entitled "Superstitions" (which literally references the classic "mammy" stereotype), from a 1937 book for children:

> The old colored mammy who lives down the
>   road
> Says, "Don' you walk unner dat ladder!
> Go home if you sees a black cat cross yer paff
> And, chile, watch out for yer shadder."
> She says, "No luck ever come ter a house
> Where a dog he bay at the moon."
> She knows the meaning of spilling salt
> Or dropping a fork or spoon.
> She's superstitious— I know she is!
> But Hallowe'en— I remember them all—
> And believe them, too— don't you?

The Giant Hallowe'en Book from 1934 includes a playlet that uses a derogatory term as an eponymous character— "Rastus Goes Walking" (intended to be performed by white actors in blackface)— and the same book includes the suggested party theme "Hallowe'en in Harlem," in which the decorations are principally dolls made up as "darkies" with "black faces and big red mouths."

Visual depictions of African Americans at Halloween from this same period are similarly stereotyped, typically depicting young black children with exaggerated expressions fleeing in terror from various apparitions.

Halloween racism was hardly limited to offensive plays, POSTCARDS, and poems, however, as Halloween also became a special time for perpetrating racially-motivated acts of violence. The Ku Klux Klan, the notorious racist group, provided guidelines to members that included the suggestion that "harassing should always have a humorous twist and be in the nature of Halloween pranks to obscure the deadly seriousness behind the work"; summoned to appear before Congress in 1921, members of the Klan asked why their cowls should be questioned when Halloween celebrants routinely wore MASKS. In 1931, 7-year-old Truman Capote set off a scandal in Monroeville when he invited black children to his Halloween party; Klansmen appeared in full regalia, but were successfully rebuffed by the father of Capote's neighbor and friend, Harper Lee (future author of *To Kill a Mockingbird*). In 1959, eight white youths in the town of Corinth, Mississippi, killed a young African American on Halloween night, and set off months of interracial violence and tensions.

Racial stereotypes continue to appear at contemporary Halloween celebrations: In 2001, 185 students from Auburn University were suspended after they posted photos on the internet showing a Halloween party in which white students in Ku Klux Klan costumes acted out the lynching of other white students in blackface. In 2007, the Sigma Chi fraternity at Johns Hopkins University in Baltimore held a "Halloween in the Hood" party, and requested that those attending wear "ghetto" clothing, including "hoochie," "mack," and "hustla" costumes.

Occasionally Halloween worked in favor of African Americans: Famed singer Ethel Waters was persuaded to try her first attempt at a professional performance on Halloween, since she could attend the local nightclub safely protected by a mask. In a 1971 article, comic Dick Gregory commented on his childhood poverty and noted that Halloween was the only holiday he really enjoyed: "Halloween was the one day we could wear our regular clothes and people thought we were dressed for the occasion."

In the 1990s, one high school in Detroit, Michigan, attempted to combat racism on Halloween by renaming the day "Heritage Day," and suggesting that students dress as famous African American historical figures.

African Americans are not the only group to experience acts of Halloween prejudice: In Milford, Connecticut, for example, headstones in a Jewish cemetery were defaced on Halloween in 1999; and a 1989 incident in which a homeless man was beaten to death by a masked gang on Halloween in New York led other homeless to call the crime an example of "growing bigotry" towards the homeless.

Ahoppa Awan Tewa— Zuñi celebration held towards the end of October (the name means "the dead their day"). Food for the dead is thrown on the house-fire or carried to a "wide ditch" on the riverside. At nightfall, boys go about town in groups; at each doorstep they make the sign of the cross and say a Mexican prayer, or *polasenya*. In return, the boys are given presents of bread or meat. The Zuñi believe this day is completely a Zuñi tradition.

All Fools' Day (also April Fools' Day)— Traditionally held April 1. Although the origin of the day is uncertain, it's been celebrated as a day of practical jokes and PRANKING for the last few hundred years. Pranks perpetrated on this day traditionally have a designated victim, who is made aware of the situation when the prankster shouts out, "April Fool!" Some pranks— such as setting fire to a paper bag full of manure — are identical to Halloween pranks; others, such as persuading someone to go on a false errand, are specific to April Fools'.

In "Halloween in America: Contemporary Customs and Performances," JACK SAN-TINO notes that Halloween and April Fools' (the two days acknowledged for pranking) occur on almost opposite points of the calendar, and he suggests that April Fools' pranks represent a season moving from death to life (spring), while Halloween pranks reflect the time of moving from life to death (winter).

All-Hallowmas *see* **All Saints' Day**

All-Hallown Summer— The warm season which sets in about Halloween; sometimes called "the second summer," or (in America) "Indian summer." The French call it *L'Été de St. Martin*, or "St. Martin's Summer," and date it from about October 9 to November 11 (which is MARTINMAS). Also called "St. Luke's Summer" (October 18 is St. Luke's Day). In *Henry IV Part One*, Shakespeare uses the term: "Farewell, thou latter spring; farewell, All-hallown Summer!" *See also* WEATHER.

All Hallows' Day *see* **All Saints' Day**

All Hollands Day— Hampshire name for All Saints' Day. The day was celebrated with plum CAKES called "All Holland cakes" or "All Hallan cakes." A 1902 account notes the proper name for the round cakes is "Hallow buns," and adds that they are called "Holland cakes" at Petersfield.

All Saints' Day (also All Hallows' Day, All-hallowmas, Haliday)— Christian feast day observed on November 1, the eve of which is now celebrated as Halloween (from "All Hallows' Even"). The day celebrates all Christian saints (known and unknown); it's also the eve of ALL SOULS' DAY, so prayer for the dead figures in the days' rituals. A festival of the first rank, once with vigil and octave (an eight-day period celebrated after the festival, during which special prayers are said daily), All Saints' is also a holy day of obligation on which all Catholics are obliged to attend mass, and they must abstain from "work or business that would inhibit the

worship to be given to God, the joy proper to the Lord's Day, or the due relaxation of mind and body." The feast is held on the first of the octave, and is observed by Roman Catholics, Episcopalians, Lutherans, and some other Protestant denominations.

Reference to a feast like All Saints' first occurs in the writings of St. Ephrem Syrus (A.D. 306–373), while St. Chrysostom (A.D. 347–407) assigned to it a definite day, the first Sunday after Pentecost (when it is still observed in the East). The day was not fully established until the consecration of the Pantheon in Rome to Christian usage by Pope Boniface IV on May 13, 609 (the Pantheon was originally a pagan temple first built in 27 B.C., and was given to the Church by the Roman Emperor Phocas; it was consecrated to the Virgin Mary and all the martyrs under the name Santa Maria Rotunda). The day was celebrated on May 13 until Pope Gregory III (whose pontificate ran from 731 to 741) dedicated a chapel in the Basilica of St. Peter to "All the Saints" on November 1. Gregory IV (pope from 827 to 844) ordered its universal observance, and Sixtus IV (1471–1484) added the octave (which was suppressed in 1955) and liturgical vigil. At the Reformation the festival was retained in the calendars of the Church of England and many of the Lutheran churches; in the latter, however, it has fallen into complete disuse. In the calendar in the *Alternative Service Book* (1980), the Octave Day (November 8) is assigned to the "Saints and Martyrs of England."

The choice of date for All Saints' Day has spurred a considerable amount of debate among academics. Although many chroniclers of the Catholic Church believe the date was moved to November 1 (just after HARVEST) in order to more easily feed the many pilgrims who flocked to Rome for the celebration, most historians believe the date was shifted to assist Irish missionaries in turning the Celts away from observing their great festival of SAMHAIN, which began at sunset on October 31. A famous letter from Pope GREGORY I to a missionary on his way to England (dated 601) first discusses the doctrine of SYNCRETISM, or trying to co–opt pagan practices as opposed to aggressively stamping them out. Interestingly, one point in favor of this argument may be the original date for All Saints' Day: May 13 was once the final night of the three-day Roman festival of the dead LEMURIA.

All Saints' Day has been celebrated all over the world for hundreds of years, and nearly every country which celebrates it has developed unique customs. Some of these customs have obviously contributed to the contemporary rituals of Halloween, while others remain unique to All Saints' Day. In some areas there was little actual observance of All Saints' since it fell between Halloween (Samhain) and All Souls Day; a few British

Eleventh-century manuscript portrait of Pope Gregory I

areas, however, record specific All Saints' Day customs, such as a children's BONFIRE noted in eighteenth-century Leicestershire. In 19th century Derbyshire, it was a common All Saints' Day custom to decorate the graves of deceased loved ones with flowers. A medieval practice involved celebrating All Saints' Day with a procession around the church in which parishioners dressed as angels and saints (and even a few devils), and may have been a forerunner to the modern TRICK OR TREAT.

In Britain the day was once celebrated by the ringing of BELLS and by SOULING.

In France the day is known as TOUS-SAINT; graves there are decorated for the week prior to November 1. In one French custom, children ask their neighbors for flowers with which to decorate the churches on this date. In Brittany, macabre PRANKING is popular, with children putting up CANDLES in GRAVE-YARDS or rattling bones in pails on Halloween night.

In many European areas candles and lanterns are lit on All Saints' Eve and left burning through the night. In Germany, where the day is known as *Allerheiligen*, they call these "lights of the holy souls" *Seelenlichter*.

One of the loveliest All Saints' Day celebrations is found at the contemporary site of the notorious Nazi concentration camp Auschwitz in Poland. Each November 1st, visitors to the Auschwitz I site place thousands of lighted candles around the camp in commemoration of the camp's victims during World War II.

In Belgium, it's called *Aller-Heiligen Dag*; there the traditional observance includes cemetery visiting, grave decorating and candle lighting on the Eve.

In Spain at dark on Halloween CAKES and NUTS are laid on graves to bribe the spirits not to disturb the vigils of the saints.

In the Portuguese Cape Verde islands (off the west coast of Africa), the Day of the Faithful Dead (*dia di fiel difunt'*) was celebrated three days after All Saints' Day.

Families offered small amounts of money to priests to say a prayer for any departed relatives who had died at an age when they'd been "old enough to sin" (likely 12 years of age or older); GHOSTS were thought to be in attendance, and it was believed that lame ghosts had set out three days earlier to arrive in time. Children were warned to avoid a large plant called the *palh' fed'* on All Saints' Day; playing near the plant, which held white blossoms

1904 magazine illustration depicting All Saints' Day (by E. Friant)

large enough to hide under, might cause the unwary child to be caught by the *finad' pé quebrad'*, a ghost with a broken leg.

In certain areas of North America (e.g. New Mexico), All Saints' Day is celebrated by bringing FOOD for the parish priest. In Acoma, New Mexico, boys once went about in groups uttering an invocation which translated roughly to:

> Let's pray, let's pray,
> We are little angels,
> From heaven we come
> If you don't give to us
> Your doors and windows
> We will break.

(See DAYS OF THE DEAD for other references to angelic children on this day). The Acoma boys also rang a bell and uttered the prayer: "*Padre spirito santo amen.*" Food was placed in the cemetery for the dead.

In Mexico it's *El Día de los Santos*, or simply *Todos Santos*, and is celebrated as part of a larger festival (which incorporates both the Catholic tradition and pre–Columbian themes) known as Days of the Dead.

In Trinidad, FAMILIES visit graves on All Saints' Day, then return home, where they knock THREE times and then enter saying,

"Good night, good night. Who is here? I come, I come." Food prepared for the dead is unsalted, and families save the wax from candles burned on this day to cure colds, rheumatism, and other ills.

In the Philippines the day is called *Undas*, and families spend the day and night at graves, decorating, lighting candles, and even playing bingo or mah-jongg.

In Guatemala, the Santiago Atitlan Indians celebrate All Saints' Day and All Souls' Day with a kite festival, since they believe sending the kites up to the heavens helps them to communicate better with their deceased kin. The kites are very large and colorful.

In Bolivia it is *Kawsas Qanchis* ("Our Living with the Dead"), and the following day is *Kachaypari* ("send off"), when souls are sent on their way by the pounding feet of many dancers. Families feast, with a table set just for the returned souls' meals. Special foods include boiled beans, grain, and baked potatoes. Designated eaters called *Mihuq* even eat on behalf of the dead.

In New Orleans, All Saints' Day in the nineteenth and early twentieth centuries was a festive time, with visits to graveyards to clean and decorate tombs, mixed with feasting, partying, and gossiping; in fact, a 1904 guidebook to the city says that "New Orleans has two great festivals— the CARNIVAL, when she invites strangers from all parts of the world to come and make merry with her, and 'All Saints,' the great home festival, when, heart to heart, the entire city meets on common ground to pay its tribute to the loved and lost." Graves were decorated with huge bouquets of chrysanthemums, and boys often earned extra money by offering grave-cleaning services. New Orleans's state of Louisiana remains the only one in the U.S. which recognizes All Saints' Day as a legal holiday.

"All Saints' Day Weather"— In some parts of Europe it is common to call cold, foggy, misty conditions "All Saints' Day WEATHER."

All Souls' Day (also SOUL-MASS DAY, Saumas)— Christian celebration observed on November 2. All Souls' is a day of commemoration in the Roman Catholic Church on which special intercession is made for the souls of the dead in the belief that those not yet purified sufficiently will be aided by the prayers of the living. All Souls' Day (unlike ALL SAINTS' DAY) is not a holy day of obligation; it is celebrated with the recitation of the Office of the Dead, and the mass is a requiem. All Souls' Day is often celebrated with three special masses: one in honor of the departed souls, one in honor of a cause designated each year by the pope, and one in recognition of a cause selected by the parish priest.

The day was instituted as a memorial (called "day of all the departed ones" or *Omnium Defunctorum*) in 998 A.D. by Odilon, Abbot of Cluny (also known as ST. ODILO); according to one popular legend, he began the celebration after he was told by a pilgrim returning from the Holy Land about an island on which an opening to the infernal regions permitted travelers to hear the groans of the tormented. Pope Silvester II (who

served from 999–1003) approved and recommended it. By the end of the thirteenth century the day was almost universally observed; by the fourteenth century, Rome placed the day of the commemoration of all the faithful departed in the official books of the Western Church for November 2 (until 1970, the day was celebrated on November 3, if the second fell on a Sunday). However, the day was once deemed of such importance that if it fell on a Sunday it was celebrated on the previous Saturday, so that the souls in PURGATORY should not be forced to wait unnecessarily (thus All Saints' Day and All Souls' Day were occasionally celebrated together). Indeed, November 2 was chosen in order that the memory of all the "holy spirits" both of the saints in Heaven and of the souls in Purgatory should be celebrated on two successive days, to express the Christian belief in the "Communion of Saints." In the Greek Rite the day is held on the Saturday before Sexagesima Sunday and is called the "Saturday of the Souls" (*Psychosabbaton*). During the Reformation it was abolished in the Church of England, but its celebration survived among the Continental Protestants, especially in Saxony, where, though its ecclesiastical sanction has long since lapsed, its memory survives in popular custom. In 1915 Pope Benedict XV gave permission for priests to celebrate the afore–mentioned three masses on All Souls' Day (a privilege confined to this day and CHRISTMAS). The Mass contains the famous sequence "DIES IRAE" (since 1969 no longer obligatory). The liturgical color at all services on November 2 is black ("BLACK VESPERS"). In some areas priests lead a procession through the cemetery, blessing graves with holy water and reciting liturgical prayers for the dead.

Essentially, All Souls' is the adaptation of an almost worldwide custom of setting aside a part of the year for the dead. The EGYPTIAN FEAST OF THE DEAD commemorated the death of Osiris. The Greek commemorative feast of All Souls' was held on the last day of the ANTHESTERIA; the Romans celebrated theirs during the PARENTALIA, which occurred in February, and the LEMURIA, in mid–May. In Japan the BON FESTIVAL is celebrated at the same time that YUE LAAN is remembered in many Chinese-speaking areas of the world, in either July or August (the Chinese also celebrate CH'ING MING in April). The Zuni celebration of AHOPPA AWAN TEWA means "the dead their day," and the Odawa tribe in Michigan offer food to the dead during the annual ODAWA GHOST SUPPER.

Scholars have often suggested that All Souls' Day was inaugurated by the Church because All Saints' Day alone had not been successful in replacing the pagan CELTS' celebration of SAMHAIN, and All Saints' Day and All Souls' Day were often combined into a single long celebration. In fact, many of the traditions associated more strongly with All Souls' Day seem to be the real precursors of the modern celebration of Halloween.

In many Catholic countries the belief that the dead return on this day is so strong that FOOD is left on the tables, and FAMILIES decorate the graves of their dead. An eighteenth-century report notes children in Findern, Derbyshire (England) making special BONFIRES on November 2 called TINDLES, the purpose of which was to light the way out of Purgatory for dead souls. Prior to the Reformation, it was customary to distribute food and alms to the poor in return for their service of offering prayer for the dead on this day; the traditional food was usually reported as "SOUL CAKES," small CAKES sometimes described as hot-cross buns, current-topped buns or small round loaves. A traditional rhyme was sometimes spoken by the "soulers" on this day:

A Soule-cake, a Soule-cake,
Have mercy on all Christen soules for a
Soule-cake.

It is a custom in many Catholic areas of central Europe to ring church BELLS at the approach of dusk on All Saints' Day, to remind the people to pray for the souls in Purgatory. Families then extinguish all CANDLES except a blessed candle saved from Candlemas Day, say rosaries and offer prayers.

In eastern Wales, on the eve of All Souls' Day children beg house-to-house:

An apple or a pear, a plum or a cherry,
Or any good thing to make us merry.

In parts of Great Britain, "soulers" still circulate with a hobby horse (for the horse that bears away the souls of the dead on her back), and beg for "soul-cakes."

In France the *Jour des Morts* begins two or three weeks prior to the day, as shop-windows and kiosks are laden with wreaths and garlands of immortelles. On All Saints' Day or TOUSSAINT, cemeteries are visited and graves are cleaned and decorated; churches are draped in black on this day. In Brittany, the day was commonly acknowledged with prayer and visits to GRAVEYARDS, where milk might be poured over graves. One older Breton custom involved four men who alternated tolling the church bell for an hour on All Saints' Day after dark. Four other men went from farm to farm during the night ringing hand bells and chanting in each place, "Christians awake, pray to God for the souls of the dead, and say the *Pater* and *Ave* for them." Those inside their houses replied "Amen" and began to pray. In mid–nineteenth-century Brittany, a "procession of tombs" was held: All the celebrants formed a line and walked about the cemetery, calling the names of those who were dead, as they approached their resting places. On the Eve of All Souls' the religious service "BLACK VESPERS" was held. After church, the congregation proceeded to the ossuary, where bones from over-full graveyards were kept. The doors of the ossuary were opened on this night, and some knelt inside among the bones while others knelt on the grass outside, with the only light provided by candles burning on each grave. They sang the "Complaint of the Charnel-house," a Breton hymn. The ceremony of the *veille* continued after leaving the churchyard, with dinners of hot pancakes, curds and cider put out for the family spirits at home; fires were banked, chairs put around, and finally the families retired. A bell-ringer walked the streets to remind everyone of the wandering dead. Later, a band of singers—"the chanters of the dead"—went through the village and rapped on each door to wake all sleepers, whereupon they chanted another Breton hymn, "the Complaint of the Souls." On the Isle of Sein, four young men stayed in church during the night, tolling the bells hourly. Four other men went to every house on the island where someone had died during the previous year, and called on the residents to say the *De Profundis* with them. In Finistere (the western point of France) they say that on the Eve of All Souls "there are more dead in every house than sands on the shore." At Douarnenez, if any sailor or fisherman had drowned and the body had never been recovered, on All Souls' Day the women sailed far out with the men and said the *De Profundis* for their lost one at SEA.

In Provence, All Souls' Eve was the time for a solemn family reunion. An All Souls' folk song from Provence tells of a sexton who stole the shroud of a corpse, and the fate that befell him. The Bretons also tell a similar tale, that of YANN POSTICK and the doom that comes to him when he ignores the duties of All Souls' Day.

In Poland, and in Polish churches of the United States, the faithful bring to their parish priest on All Souls' Day paper sheets with black borders called *Wypominki* ("naming") on which are written the names of their beloved dead. During the evening devotions in November, and on Sundays, the names are read from the pulpit and prayers are offered. The Polish also once told the story of how, on MIDNIGHT on All Souls' Day, a great light was seen in the parish church; the souls of all the departed parishioners who were still in Purgatory would gather there to pray for their release before the very altar where they used to receive the Blessed Sacrament when still alive. Afterward the souls were said to visit the scenes of their earthly life and labors,

especially their homes. For this reason, doors and windows were kept open on All Souls' Day.

In Western Europe people still prepare special All Souls' Day meals of cooked beans or peas or lentils, called "soul food," which they afterward serve to the poor together with meat and other dishes. In Poland the farmers hold a solemn meal on the evening of All Souls' Day, with empty seats and plates ready for souls of the departed. Uneaten food is given to beggars or poor neighbors.

"All Souls' Bread" (*Seelenbrot* in German) is popular in many parts of Europe. In some sections of Europe boys might receive a cake in the shape of a hare, and girls would be given one in the shape of a hen. These cakes are made of braided strands of sweet dough (also used on All Saints') and are called "All Saints' cakes" (*Heiligenstriezel* in German, *Strucel Swiateczne* in Polish, *Mindszenti Kalacska* in Hungarian).

Although the Church does not have an established octave for All Souls, in some areas of central Europe the eight days following All Souls are devoted to prayers, penance and acts of charity. This time of the year is called "Soul Nights" (*Seelennächte* in German). Blessed candles are burned and the rosary is said every night. The Liturgical Prayer runs: "O God, Creator and Redeemer of all the faithful, grant to the souls of Thy servants departed the remission of all their sins, that through our devout prayers they may obtain the pardon which they have always desired."

In Germany the day is *Allerseelen*. At noon the church bells ring, freeing souls until the noon bell rings again the next day. KNIVES must not be left with blades upturned on this day, because the wandering souls could injure themselves; likewise, pans must not be left to stand over heat, although the stove should be kept lit to warm the otherworldly visitors. Bowls of butter and fat are left out to soothe their wounds, and cold milk to cool their souls. *Seelenwecken*, specially-shaped pastries, are given to children by their godparents. Children here once went house-to-house, RHYMING and receiving special BREADS.

Although FORTUNE-TELLING was most commonly practiced at this time in the British Isles, the Germans had several forms of All Souls' divinations; in one, a girl would go out on All Souls' Eve and ask the name of the first young man she met, since it would sound like her future husband's. Another belief was that to walk THREE times about a church while making a wish would guarantee that the wish would come true.

In Protestant areas of Germany, they celebrate *Totensonntag* or *Ewigkeitssonntag* in November on the Sunday prior to the first Advent Sunday.

At Utrecht, the day was originally called *Schuddekorfsdag*, or the day of "shaking a basket" over the fire: A basket of APPLES and CHESTNUTS was traditionally shaken over a fire until roasted, then given to children.

In Bohemia, chairs were grouped before the fire in a ring, one for each member of the family both living and dead.

In the Alpine provinces of Austria destitute children and beggars might go house-to-house reciting prayers and singing hymns and receiving small loaves of "soul bread" as reward. In northern Spain and in Madrid people distribute and eat a special pastry called "Bones of the Holy" (*Huesos de Santo*). In Catalonia a special All Souls' pastry is called *Panellets* ("little breads"). In Hungary on "Day of the Dead" (*Halottak Napja*), orphaned children might be invited into a family for All Saints' and All Souls' days, where they were served generous meals and given new clothes and toys. Hungarians also kept the custom of caring for forgotten and neglected graves as well as those of their own loved ones.

In one Catholic Alpine village, as soon as mass was heard on All Saint's Day, women began weaving wreathes of evergreen and FLOWERS, which were carried to the cemetery in the afternoon. Come evening, a lamp was placed on each grave as the family knelt nearby, often in snow.

In rural sections of Austria the holy souls are said to wander through the forests on All Souls,' sighing and praying for their release; children are told to pray aloud while going through open spaces to church and cemetery, so pitiful souls will have consolation. Another Austrian custom involved leaving food out overnight for ghostly visitors. Come morning, uneaten food was thrown into the fire.

There was an Austrian belief that on All Souls' Eve at midnight, a visitor to the cemetery would see a procession of the dead drawing after them those who were to die during the coming year. In the people's theatre at Vienna, a play called *The Miller and His Child* was acted out every All Souls' Eve that depicted this belief. In the play, a miller has a beautiful daughter, but opposes her marriage to a young man whom she loves; in despair, the young man goes to the cemetery on All Souls' Eve, and sees the ghostly procession — with both the miller and himself following, meaning the poor young girl will lose both father and lover in the coming year.

In Portugal, this is *Día de Finados* ("Day of the Dead"); *magusto*, or open-air feasts of wine and chestnuts, begin on the first, and children go about singing and begging "bread for God." Sometimes they receive *bolas de festa*, special Day of the Dead sugar cakes, flavored with cinnamon and herbs.

In Italy All Souls' is *Il Giorno dei Morti*. The day begins with solemn masses at five A.M., then the rest of the day is spent at graveyards, cleaning and decorating graves. A favorite food is *Fave dei Morti*, which translates literally to "beans of the dead" (and possibly relates back to a ghost exorcism ritual from the Roman day of the dead LEMURIA); these are actually small cakes which are bean-shaped, and made of ground almonds, sugar, eggs, butter and flour (these are also known as *Pane dei Morti*, or "bread of the dead"). During the middle ages it was also customary to prepare a fava bean soup to give to the poor on November 2, in memory of the dead. Engagements were sometimes announced on this day by placing the ring in a container with *Fave dei Morti*. Roads to cemeteries are still thronged with sellers of candles, plaster figures and food and drink. In Sicily, good children wake to presents left by dead relatives (likewise, in some Italian-American communities children put clean, polished SHOES outside their doors on All Souls' Eve, in the hopes of finding them filled with CANDY the next morning). In Palermo, candy dolls, or *pupi de cera*, are sold only from early September to November 2; these dolls, which range from two to 10 inches tall, are given as presents on All Souls' Day and often represent famous historical characters.

In Salerno and other areas of Southern Italy one medieval custom was to spread a table with food for wandering souls, then spend the day in church; upon the return to the house, if any food remained it was considered an ill omen. This custom was banned in the fifteenth century as being a pagan ritual, although it's also worth noting that the custom drew hordes of thieves to the city on this day.

In Naples All Souls' Day was celebrated with a somber trip to the cemetery, where graves were decorated with metal garlands and where visitors might pencil their names on the stones or even leave calling cards. There followed a riotous return home, with visits to roadside inns, which cleared more business on this day than on any other day of the year.

In the Italian village of Ravello, a curious All Souls' Day custom involved placing an effigy — which may possibly have been a real mummy — dressed in clothing from an earlier century, before the high altar.

In Belgium, All Souls' Eve on November 1 includes feasting on "All Souls'" cakes, in the belief that the more cakes eaten, the more souls are saved from Purgatory.

Armenians celebrate All Souls' on Easter Monday with an Office of the Dead; the Mass, however, is that of the Resurrection.

In the Syrian-Antiochene Rite they celebrate three separate days: The Friday before Septuagesima commemorates all departed priests; on the Friday before Sexagesima, all faithful departed are remembered; and on the Friday before Quinquagesima, "all those who died in strange places, away from their parents and friends" are commemorated.

In the Philippines, the day is *Undas*. Youngsters organize into singing groups called *nangangaluluwa* to collect funds (the singers represent the souls of the dead); children also engage in PRANKING. The people believe that failing to clean the tomb of deceased kin on All Souls' Day will result in a visit from the ghostly relatives. Illness has often been attributed to a failure to remember a relative's tomb.

In the Philippines a novena is held before November 2. Candles are burned at tombs and prayers are said every night. During these nine days people also prepare and clean their family tombs and graves for the great "Feast of the Souls." On All Souls' Eve young men go door to door asking for gifts of cookies, candy, and pastry, singing a traditional verse:

> If you will give us friendly alms,
> Please do not make us wait;
> We want to enter Heaven's door
> Before it is too late.

All Souls' Day is a public holiday throughout South America, with visiting and decorating graves found in nearly every country.

In Colombia, All Souls' Day is *Día de los Angelitos*, or "Day of the Little Angels." After noon on November 2, one of the members of a dance group goes house to house, carrying a wooden cross covered with flowers. A boy runs behind him ringing a bell, and children join them, stopping to sing at each house: "Angels are we, from heaven we come, asking alms, for ourselves." People throw fruit to the children, which in former times was taken to the church to share with souls in Purgatory, but in more recent times the food was shared with families.

In Peru, the roads between the *panteon* (cemetery) and towns are lined with vendors, selling food, drink, and OFRENDAS (small clay statues of animals, humans, household objects, etc., used as offerings). At the tombs, the oldest woman in the household directs the installation of a *posada*, or tent, under which family members and friends will gather during the nightlong vigil with the *animas*, or souls. Passersby who resemble deceased family members are asked to share the repast, since it is thought to go straight to the stomach of the deceased through the lookalike.

In Mexico a three-day observance from October 30 to November 2 is called DAYS OF THE DEAD; in some areas November 1 is also given to mourning dead children, while November 2 is reserved for the adult spirits.

On the Indian reservations of Pala and Rincon east of Oceanside, California, "Night of the Candle" is celebrated on November 2. During the day graves are decorated and candles placed about them, and celebrants sing hymns while a priest blesses each grave. At dusk the candles are lighted.

The Cochiti Pueblo Indians in New Mexico refer to this day as "Their Grandfathers Arrive from the West" (or "from the Dead"). Each family fasts and places a large quantity of food for the dead in the church; bowls of food are also set in the corners of houses. The material wealth of the household is put out for display, so visiting souls will know that their kin are prosperous. Candles are set out to light the way for the souls. Women stay at home, and men congregate in the ceremonial chamber, or kiva, where they sing and cut food into small pieces, which are thrown outside for the dead. The All Souls' Night Kachina Society moves from house to house, staying a few minutes at each to entertain ghosts with their dances.

At Santo Domingo, the "grandfathers" who are expected to come from the west are fed at noon on November 2. Every person digs a hole beyond the city limits, burying in it a bundle of food and feathers, after which they exclaim, "Here, eat, Grandfathers! After you eat, bring us crops!"

At the Zuñi Pueblo in west central New Mexico, "Grandmothers' Day" is the equivalent of All Souls' Day, and is celebrated around the end of October or early November, after the crops have been harvested. Men and boys go from home to home singing and receiving food, and all make food offerings to the dead.

An American folk belief is that for forty days after November 1 the souls of the dead all rise from their graves and roam freely.

Allantide — Cornish name for HALLOW-TIDE; derives from the nineteenth-century (and earlier) custom of giving each member of the family an Allan APPLE on Halloween. Eating the apple on Halloween night ensured good luck for the coming year.

Allison Gross — The title of a Scottish ballad in which the eponymous character, the ugliest WITCH "i' the north country" endeavored to seduce a fine young man. Because he rejected her, she turned him into an ugly worm "to toddle about the tree," but the queen of the FAIRIES, riding by on Hallow-even, broke the spell and changed him back to his "ain proper shape." This is the only known instance, in English or Scottish folklore, of a fairy undoing the spell of a witch.

Alphabet Game — A method of FORTUNE-TELLING at Halloween parties involving letters cut from a newspaper and then floated in a container of WATER; the letters might form the name of a future spouse.

An elaborate variant of this comes from Newfoundland: As the clock strikes MIDNIGHT on Halloween, a girl puts 26 letters of the alphabet, cut from paper, into a pure-white bowl which has been touched by the lips of a new-born babe only. She then recites:

> Kind fortune, tell me where is he
> Who my future lord shall be;
> From this bowl all that I claim
> Is to know my sweetheart's name.

Then she puts the bowl into a safe place until morning, when she is blindfolded and picks out the same number of letters as there are in her own name; from these letters she spells the name of her future husband.

In an American version, two complete alphabets are cut up and placed face down in water on Halloween night at midnight; those that have turned face up in the morning are the initials of the one you will marry.

Amusement Parks *see* **Haunted Houses; Spooky World**

Ancestor Night— Name for Halloween used by some practitioners of WICCA.

Animals *see* **Bats; Cats; Cows; Crows; Horses; Owls; Snowbirds; Sows; Spiders; White Hare**

Anoka, Minnesota— "The Halloween Capital of the World." Anoka claims to be the first U.S. city to put on Halloween celebrations to divert PRANKING. In 1920, George Green and Anoka civic leaders suggested the idea of a giant celebration; the Anoka Commercial Club and the Anoka Kiwanis Club both gave their full support to the idea, and a Halloween committee was organized to plan the event. That first year's festivities included a PARADE, a BONFIRE, and a giveaway of treats to local children. The CELEBRATIONS

Button from Anoka's 1996 celebration

have been held every year since (except 1942 and 1943, when they were cancelled because of World War II). Festivities now include a Miss Anoka Ambassador Scholarship Pageant, three parades (consisting of the "Light Up the Night" parade, in which all displays must be lit, the "Big Parade of the Little People," an entire parade dedicated to school children, and the Grande Day Parade, which is the second largest parade in the midwest and is always held the last Saturday of October), treat giveaways, and a children's PUMPKIN-carving contest. An estimated 45,000 spectators line up to view the Grande Day Parade.

Anthesteria— Sometimes called the Greek ALL SOULS' DAY, Anthesteria was a three-day festival in honor of Dionysus held annually at Athens from the 11th to the 13th of the month of Anthesterion (February-March). Its object was to celebrate the maturing of the wine stored at the previous vintage and the beginning of spring. The first two days, the *Pithoigia* (opening of the casks) and *Choes* (feast of beakers) were considered as ill-omened and required expiatory libations; on those days the souls of the dead walked abroad. On the third day, called *Chutroi* (feast of pots), a festival of the dead was held. Although the GHOSTS were welcomed to home feasts, where places were set for them, they were kept out of temples and sanctuaries, by crossing thorn branches over the entrances or daubing pitch on the lintels.

In later times the Anthesteria was largely replaced by Rousalia, held on Easter Tuesday, although there are also reports of Rousalia being held in conjunction with ALL SAINTS' DAY.

Anthropomancy— Divination using the entrails of human sacrifices, most often child or virgin, sometimes prisoners. Although anthropomancy is thankfully not included in any known Halloween FORTUNE-TELLING customs, it was supposedly practiced by the DRUIDS on SAMHAIN (although there is little evidence to support this).

Apkarian-Russell, Pamela— American Halloween collector and vintage COLLECTIBLES expert known as "the Halloween Queen." Apkarian-Russell has, more than any other individual, been responsible for creating an interest in collecting Halloween memorabilia and establishing it as a recognized hobby. In 1984 she began publishing *The Trick or Treat Trader*, devoted to both collecting vintage Halloween memorabilia and the holiday in general; what began as a joke among a half-dozen or so collectors is now the standard journal in the field and still publishing. Apkarian-Russell is the author of four books on Halloween collecting, and with a personal collection of over 35,000 items she probably holds the world's largest collection. In 2005 she opened the CASTLE HALLOWEEN MUSEUM, emphasizing all aspects of the holiday ("except blood and gore"), and including a research library. She is also a career deltiologist (expert in POSTCARDS), and runs an antiques business called "Chris Russell and the Halloween Queen."

Apple Parings— In this popular Halloween FORTUNE-TELLING custom, an APPLE is pared, then the peelings are waved over the head THREE times before being thrown over the left shoulder; supposedly the peelings will form the initials of one's future beloved. The fortune-seeker is advised to recite these lines while swinging the paring overhead:

> I pare this pippin round and
>   round again,
> My sweetheart's name to
>   flourish on the plain;
> I fling the unbroken paring
>   o'er my head,
> My sweetheart's letter on the
>   ground to read.

This divination was said to be popular with American Colonial maidens, who instead recited:

> By this paring let me discover
> The initial letter of my true
>   lover.

The poem to be recited is sometimes given as this:

> Paring, paring, long and green,
> Tell my Fate for Hallowe'en.

In a variant, the peelings are thrown into a bowl of WATER; another version (which is similar to one custom involving KALE) has it that the peel is hung from a nail by the front door, and the first man to enter will have the same initials as the future husband.

Apple Seeds— If APPLE PARING— or using the skin of an apple — is a popular Halloween FORTUNE-TELLING method, the use of the seeds within the apple is no less popular, and shows an even greater number of different customs.

In the simplest method, by cutting an apple in two, the seeds were read on Halloween to foretell the future: Two seeds showing predicted an early marriage, three predicted wealth (or sometimes a legacy), four foretold travel (or great wealth), five brought health (or a sea voyage), six showed wisdom (or great fame as an orator or singer), and seven a promise of fame (or the possession of a desired gift).

In another fortune-telling custom, two wet apple seeds were named for suitors and stuck to the forehead (or cheeks, or eyelids). The first seed to fall off indicated that the

This 1909 postcard shows a woman engaged in an apple paring divination.

love of him or her whose name it bore was not steadfast. In Nottinghamshire, this tradition was practiced with these lines spoken:

> "Pippin, pippin, I stick thee there,
> That that is true thou mayst declare."

Apple seeds applied in this matter might also be used to foretell poverty or wealth. In a variation, the seeds were named for "Home" or "Travel."

Apple seeds were also sometimes placed on the hearth instead of NUTS; a group were named for a girl's suitors and placed on the fire. The first pip to pop indicated her true love. In another version, THREE apple seeds were placed on a hot stove, and named for Toil, Ease and Travel; once the heat caused the seeds to jump, whichever was left closest to you foretold your future.

In one curious method, 10 to 12 apple seeds were placed in one palm, then the hands were clapped together; the number of apple seeds left would foretell the future, according to a spoken rhyme. In a variation, all the seeds from a single apple were placed on the back of the left hand, the palm of which was then struck by the right. The number of seeds remaining indicated the number of letters that would then be received over the next two weeks.

In another divination, 12 apple seeds were set aside while the names of 12 friends were written on twelve identical small slips of paper. The papers were then placed with the written side down, and mixed around. Then, while holding the apple seeds in the left hand, the following rhyme was recited, and at each line an apple seed was placed on a slip of paper, which was then turned over to reveal the friend matched to the line of the poem:

> One I love,
> Two I love,
> Three I love I say;
> Four I love with all my heart
> Five I cast away.
> Six he loves,
> Seven she loves,

> Eight they both love;
> Nine he comes,
> Ten he tarries,
> Eleven he courts and
> Twelve he marries.

Apples— Apples are probably the single most important food item associated with Halloween; they are featured in GAMES (primarily BOBBING FOR APPLES), FORTUNE-TELLING, FOODS ranging from candied apples to apple dumplings, and popular seasonal TOYS such as apple-head dolls. They have served as decoration and small JACK-O'-LANTERNS, and in the case of SNAP-APPLE NIGHT, apples are even a part of one name for Halloween.

Although the significance of apples in Halloween is often attributed to a Roman harvest deity called POMONA and her festival, the fruit's holiday importance more likely stems from both Celtic beliefs and its timing as a harvest food. Apples were held in nearly as much esteem by the CELTS and their DRUIDS as oak trees were. In Celtic mythology, the sacred tree Mugna was a yew that bore three kinds of fruit: the ACORN, the apple and the NUT. Apples were a sacred fruit in the Celtic otherworld (the Celtic otherworld was *Ynys Avallach*, the "isle of the apples," and was thought to exist off the west coast of Ireland); one of these fruits could provide immortality. In one hero story centering on FINN MACCUMAL, he encounters *Dercc Corra mac hUi Daighre* ("the Peaked Red One," also known as "the Man in the Tree,") a magical being who holds a bronze vessel in his left hand from which he produces nuts and apples. In another mythological tale, the hero Bran is lured to the otherworld when a goddess offers him an apple tree branch. Some Celtic mythology may have been transferred to the King Arthur legends— when Arthur dies he goes to the island of Avalon, a name that means "apple-island."

Games involving apples have been the central event at Halloween PARTIES for at least several centuries (a game of bobbing for apples is even depicted in a fourteenth-century manuscript, the *Luttrell Psalter*). In addition to bobbing for apples and snap-apple, apples were also used in a variation of the Easter egg hunt — apples and nuts were hidden around a house or grounds, and prizes were awarded to whoever could find the most. In another game, an apple was hung from a string overhead, then a chair or tall box was placed beneath it; contestants had to keep one hand on the chair or box, run around it as fast as possible seven times, then try to strike the apple with a stick. In an American combination of eating and gaming, two persons kneel, one on each side of a chair on which two apples are placed. With their hands tied behind their backs, the contestants must see who can eat the most in three minutes.

Apples figure prominently in Halloween fortune-telling. In addition to APPLE SEEDS and APPLE PARINGS, fortunes might be indicated by an apple game's first winner (i.e., the first to successfully bob for an apple). In one English custom, children put an apple under their pillow on Halloween to bring happy DREAMS; a variation of this suggests that an apple successfully secured by bobbing should be placed under the pillow to reveal one's future beloved in dreams on Halloween night. A variation of the midnight MIRROR fortune-telling custom has the girl eating an apple at MIDNIGHT on Halloween as she brushes her hair before the mirror. In another version, a girl stands before a mirror and slices an apple into NINE slices; she holds each slice on the tip of the knife before eating, and her future husband will finally appear to ask for the last slice (a slight variant to this custom states that she throws the ninth slice over her left shoulder, and at each slice says "In the name of the Father and the Son.") In a more complicated version, a girl should stand in front of a mirror, slice an apple, and hold each piece on the point of the knife over her left shoulder while looking into the mirror and combing her hair. The WRAITH of her future husband will appear in the mirror reaching for a slice of apple.

A custom from St. John, New Brunswick in Canada involved hanging an apple at chin height, rubbing the chin with saliva, and then banging the chin against the apple; if the apple stuck to the chin, it foretold a faithful marriage.

One custom that combines fortune-telling and a game involved twirling apples hung from strings near a fire; the order in which the apples dropped from the strings would foretell who would marry first, second, etc. (whoever possessed the last apple to fall would remain unmarried).

Apples have appeared in many forms as Halloween party food. Apple cider (usually served with DOUGHNUTS) is a tradition at American Halloween CELEBRATIONS. Candied and caramel apples are found at many outdoor Halloween celebrations. Apples are also popular in Irish homes on Halloween, found in pies, tarts, dumplings and apple pudding (the latter made of potatoes, flour and apples, with small fortune-telling tokens such as a ring, a coin and a thimble sometimes added).

Apples have also served as Halloween gifts: Until at least 1890, Cornish greengrocers always placed extra orders of fine Allan apples during the fall season, since they were a traditional gift for children on Halloween (although it was also recorded that Allan apples were sold on the Saturday nearest to Halloween, and given to every member of the family, to be eaten for luck, or — for older girls— placed under the pillow to induce dreams of future husbands.)

April Fools' Day *see* **All Fools' Day**

Ash (tree) *see* **Rowan**

Ashes— Ashes are a central element in a few Halloween FORTUNE-TELLING customs, mainly found in Ireland, the Isle of Man, and Lancashire. In one form of the custom, the fortune-seeker was told to blow on fine ashes; if they flew into the face, one's future marriage would be unhappy, but if they scattered in front of the seeker, a happy future was foretold.

Ashes from the fireplace that were flattened out around the open HEARTH would be carefully examined the morning after Halloween; any FOOTPRINTS found then would foretell the future. For example, if they turned toward the front door, it signified a death in the family within the year; if, however, they turned in the opposite direction, a marriage was indicated. One Irish story tells of a man who didn't believe in the return of the dead on Halloween, so he scattered ashes about the floor. In the morning he was found dead, and there were footprints in the ashes.

Ashes from Halloween BONFIRES (especially those that were sacred or kindled by "need-fire," or friction) were thought to have protective powers; they were sprinkled on fields, and even placed within SHOES.

One American Halloween GAME involved a "fate ring" created by sprinkling ashes (although FLOUR could be substituted) on the floor in a large circle. A participant would then be blindfolded and told to walk across the ring while the hostess recited:

> The ashes from the hearth we raked
>   And sifted in a ring;
> Step forth — your footprints will reveal
>   What luck the year will bring.

The blindfolded walker now responded:

> Go, unguided footsteps, go,
>   Fortune in your prints to show.

Footprints pointing toward an outside door foretold ill luck, while the opposite direction portended marriage or good fortune. The footprints might also point towards a future spouse.

Auld Lang Syne — Song with words set by ROBERT BURNS to an old Scottish folk melody, also known as "The Miller's Wedding" and "The Miller's Daughter." Although the song is most commonly associated with NEW YEAR'S Eve celebrations, in Scotland "Auld Lang Syne" was also traditionally sung at the end of Halloween PARTIES.

Autopsy — Popular Halloween presentation, performed in many variations. The version referred to as "Autopsy" involves setting up a back-lit sheet, behind which a "doctor" performs either an operation or an autopsy, removing various "body parts" which are handed around to the onlookers. In the variation often known as "Witch's Cauldron," a witch passes the parts down a line of partygoers; these parts would typically include an old glove filled with mush for a hand, a peeled grape for an eye, a soup bone, corn kernels for teeth, a wet sponge for the brain, a raw oyster for the heart, etc.

Other scenarios were also presented behind backlit sheets: For example, a 1938 book on the early art of home movie-making suggests staging a Halloween scene in which children glimpsed as silhouettes behind a sheet are chased by WITCHES and by their own toys.

Illustration of "autopsy," as seen through a back-lit sheet

Aztecs *see* Miccailhuitl and Miccailhuitontli

B

Backwards— Doing things in reverse order or backwards is a common theme in Halloween FORTUNE-TELLING customs and protective charms. For example, while on the road, wearing one's coat inside-out was protection against Halloween FAIRIES.

An American custom instructed a girl to walk into a room backwards at MIDNIGHT on Halloween while looking over her left shoulder, and she would see her future husband. A Pennsylvania divination suggested that one walk out the front door backwards on Halloween night and pick THREE blades of grass. The grass was then wrapped in orange paper and placed beneath the pillow to ensure that the evening's DREAMS would come true (in a variation of this, dust was used in place of grass).

Bannatyne, Lesley— Lesley Bannatyne is an American author of five books on Halloween, including *Halloween: An American Holiday, An American History* (1990), which inaugurated contemporary Halloween popular histories and paved the way for the numerous Halloween histories published since. Bannatyne's other books include *A Halloween How To: Costumes, Parties, Decorations, and Destinations* (2001), *A Halloween Reader: Stories, Poems, and Plays from Halloweens Past* (2004), and *Halloween Nation: Behind the Scenes of America's Fright Night* (2011), as well as the children's book *Witches' Night Before Halloween.* She has lectured extensively on Halloween, and provided the Halloween articles for the *World Book Encyclopedia*, *The Encyclopedia of Death and the Human Experience*, and *Be My Guest: An Encyclopedia of Entertaining.* She also held (for two years) an entry in the *Guinness Book of World Records* for "Largest Halloween Gathering" (which was actually a Halloween gathering of WITCHES reading poetry).

Banshee— Literally, fairy woman (from the Irish *bean* and *sidhe*); often described in Irish folklore as a messenger of death. Although the banshee doesn't figure prominently in Halloween lore, there are a few fairy tales that seem to mention the banshee in connection with Halloween: In "How Thomas Connolly Met the Banshee," the man of the title is walking home at dusk during "the first week in November" when he spots an old woman crouched by a bridge. Upon closer examination he sees not an old woman, but a creature wearing an otherworldly green gown, with unnaturally long hair and a corpse-like pallor. The thing screeches at him, then glides under the bridge and disappears. Thomas runs home, and the next day discovers that the banshee was heard wailing around the house of a neighbor who died early in the morning.

Banshees were also popular story subjects on Halloween, and were often described in stories as being accompanied by a headless coachman.

The male equivalent of a banshee was a *fershee*, although in all the banshee legends only female spirits are named.

Barley— In Shetland, a small stack of "bere," or barley, was set apart in an annual offering to "Broonie" (the origin or real meaning of this name is unknown). There was a divination involved with this, in which the fortune-seeker would go blindfolded into the yard and walk around the stack THREE times sunwise and three times "widdershins" (against the sun), with arms spread wide; at the last turn one would embrace the shade of the future spouse (this ritual was called "Fadomin' da Skroo"). If necessary, an undedicated stack would also suffice (or, in America, a haystack would do; at the end of running about it three times, a glimpse over the left shoulder would offer a peek at one's future spouse).

In "Hallowe'en" by ROBERT BURNS, a young man named Will attempts this FOR-TUNE-TELLING custom, but "the stack he fad-dom'd thrice" is actually timber, and he gets a fright when he mistakes a log for a terrible old woman.

Barm Brack— An Irish loaf or CAKE made with dried fruit, popular during the Halloween season. Quite often the barm brack serves as a FORTUNE CAKE. Barm brack is available commercially, and will often contain tokens including a ring (whoever gets this in a slice will be married in a year), a rag (spinsterhood), a pea (poverty) and a bean (wealth). The cake must be cut and buttered by a married person, out of sight of those who will be eating it.

Bats— Traditional Halloween symbol, mainly in the United States. The connection of bats to Halloween may be as simple as the fact that bats are nocturnal creatures (see also CATS and OWLS). However, the late-nineteenth-century popularity of bats is due largely to Bram Stoker's *Dracula*, in which the vampire count transforms several times into a gigantic bat; this gothic tale popularized the notion of the vampire bat (which is actually found in South America) throughout Western culture. Bats also have historical ties to WITCHES: Various parts of bats are used in witch spells and formulas, and there

Vintage bat wall decoration

has even been speculation that bats may have inadvertently been part of witch sabbats throughout the centuries, since they would feast on insects drawn to the warmth of fires lit by the witches as part of their outdoor revels. Depictions of bats, usually in the form of cut-out wall hangings, are popular Halloween decorations, and vintage pieces are sought-after COLLECTIBLES. Live bats also provide the decorations for the Halloween party in the book *Harry Potter and the Sorcerer's Stone.*

Bay-Leaves— Bay-leaves appear in one Halloween FORTUNE-TELLING custom: They were placed on or under the pillow on Halloween night to spur dreams of one's future sweetheart.

Bedposts— Even bedposts became objects of FORTUNE-TELLING on Halloween night: Before going to bed on the eve, different bedposts were designated to represent music, art, literature and business. The first bedpost seen upon awakening denoted one's future vocation.

In another custom, LEMONS were rubbed on the bedposts to provoke Halloween DREAMS of future spouses.

Beets— Beets were sometimes used in an American version of FORTUNE-TELLING customs centering on CABBAGES or KALE; they were pulled on Halloween night, and a round one indicated a happy life.

Beggar's Night— In some areas of the United States, Beggar's Night is October 30, the night before Halloween (and was sometimes used interchangeably with MISCHIEF NIGHT), but children would often TRICK OR TREAT on both nights. However, in some rural areas, Halloween is disliked because trick or treat is considered to be begging, so the night of October 31 is referred to instead as Beggar's Night.

There have always been those who have looked down on Halloween as a night for beggars: In Act II, Scene 1 of Shakespeare's *Two Gentlemen of Verona*, the character

Speed speaks of someone puling "like a beggar at Hallowmass." *See also* DEVIL'S NIGHT.

Begging *see* **Rhyming**

Bells— It was once common practice to ring church bells for all Christian souls on Halloween. King Henry VIII (who ruled from 1509 to 1547) once directed that "the Vigil and ringing of bells all the night long upon Allhallow Day at night" was to be abolished; and Queen Elizabeth (whose monarchy went from 1558 to 1603) likewise ruled "that the superfluous ringing of bells, and the superstitious ringing of bells on Allhallowntide and at All Souls' Day, with the two nights before and after, be prohibited." A 1517 Churchwardens' account of the parish of Heybridge, near Malden, in Essex, notes payments for repair of the bells "agenste Hallowmasse"; but a history of the parish of Hemingborough notes that a gentleman named Mr. Salvin was fined 40s for ringing the bells on the evening of All Hallow-Day in 1564. The custom was revived during Mary's reign, especially since the ringing of bells was thought (like SOULING or lighting a FIRE) to benefit souls in PURGATORY. Church bells were also rung on MIDSUMMER'S EVE, WALPURGISNACHT and at other times when evil spirits were thought to be abroad or powerful.

In Brittany, it was once the custom for a bellman to go about just before midnight ON ALL SOULS' DAY, warning of the coming of ghosts.

A Welsh belief was that on Halloween, as long as consecrated bells rang, WITCHES were hindered from causing harm.

Bells were also rung to celebrate GUY FAWKES DAY; in fact, in some British towns and villages November 5th came to be known as "Ringing-day" (the night of the 4th was sometimes called "Ringing-night"). In Middlesex in 1683, half-an-acre of land was given to the purpose of providing the local parish bell-ringers with a leg of pork on November 5th; the land, which was known as "Pork Acre," was rented out by the parish officers, and the proceeds given to the bell-ringers.

Some areas considered the November 5th ringing of the bells to be the start of the winter season bell-ringing.

Belsnickling— A CHRISTMAS mumming custom found in areas of German settlement throughout North America, its name derives from a German MUMMING tradition known as *Peltznickel*. Similar to numerous mumming and "masked solicitation" Halloween rituals (including SOULING and STRAWBOYS), belsnickling may have contributed an important element to the modern American Halloween celebration—TRICK OR TREAT. One description of belsnickling in West Virginia began on Christmas Eve, when a small group in costumes and masks led by "Old Belsnickle" visited homes in the community, guided by CANDLES placed in windows. A knock on the door would be followed by the announcement that "Old Belsnickle" was visiting, and the visitors would enter to line up before the residents. If anyone could be identified through the disguise, they had to perform a "trick," a small performance of song, dance, etc. If none in the group could be identified, they were treated to food and drink. As the group moved from one house

Vintage postcard showing a Halloween bell

to another, they were joined by family members from the last home, so the size of the group increased as the night wore on. It's possible that the phrase "trick or treat" derived from this custom, spreading out from West Virginia throughout the country. This custom is almost identical to a NEW YEAR'S mumming custom from the Yorkshire area in England (sans mention of Belsnickle).

Although the belsnickling custom omits the phrase "trick or treat" when practiced elsewhere, it takes on other interesting elements: In Nova Scotia, for example, the belsnickles served the purpose of both mummer and bogeyman — part of the performance involved querying terrified children as to whether they'd been good or not, and rewarding them with a piece of candy if they replied in the affirmative. Parents used belsnickles as a threat to bad behavior, and many children were actually afraid to venture outside after dark around Christmastime. At the end of each performance, the Nova Scotia belsnickles asked for "a bit of brouse," and were usually given a small CAKE or piece of fruit (which they carried with them throughout the night, and consumed at a party upon the conclusion of their rounds). In his 1972 article "Belsnickling in a Nova Scotia Island Community," Richard Bauman notes: "In recent years, belsnickling has died out on the Islands, though the Islanders see an echo of it in Halloween trick-or-treating…"

Beltane— The ancient Celtic festival held on May 1, or exactly six months from SAMHAIN (November 1). Beltane was one of the two great festivals celebrated by the CELTS, and was also an important QUARTER DAY; on this day fertility rituals were enacted, and the herds were driven out to pasture for the summer. Beltane was celebrated with many of the practices also found on Samhain, such as BONFIRES, feasting and sacrifices; and, like Halloween, it was a night when FAIRIES and WITCHES were abroad, making mischief (as at Halloween, ROWAN branches were placed above doorways on Beltane). In modern times Beltane is celebrated as MAY DAY; in some areas of Europe, the night of April 30th is celebrated as WALPURGISNACHT. Beltane is also one of the eight sabbats celebrated by practitioners of WICCA.

Ben-Weed— Scottish and Northern Irish name for the ragweed. Irish children who trod on this plant on Halloween night would be carried off to Fairyland. It was also thought that the FAIRIES rode the ben-weed on Halloween night while madly playing their fiddles.

Bible— Bibles were very popular in NEW YEAR'S and HOGMANAY FORTUNE-TELLING, with the most common custom being to open the book at random and read the first proverb one sees for intimations about the coming year. However, another form of divination using the Bible was sometimes reported in nineteenth-century American celebrations: A key is placed inside a Bible, which is then supported precariously, preferably on the little fingers of two children. A small rhyme is recited along with the letters of the alphabet; when the letter is reached which is the initial of the future spouse, supposedly the key will turn and the Bible will fall. A variant states that the key is placed on the sixteenth verse of the first Chapter of Ruth; a heavy band is then tied around the Bible and it is swung slowly while the alphabet is recited. The two letters at which the Bible stops are the two initials of the future spouse.

Black Cats *see* CATS.

Black Vespers— Refers to the custom (especially practiced in France) of draping churches in black on ALL SOULS' DAY for the evening mass; worshippers also usually wear black.

Blackberries— A particular Irish and Cornwall fairy tradition has it that blackberries and sloes can't be gathered and eaten on NOVEMBER EVE or after for as long as their season lasts, since the FAIRIES pass over them on

November Eve (Halloween) and render them inedible. A variant suggests that the DEVIL shakes his crutches over them on Halloween night, although in Sussex blackberries weren't eaten after October 10 —MICHAELMAS in the old calendar — when the devil was thought to have spit on them. In fact, there's some basis to this superstition, since it's about this time that night frosts set in, which render the berries bitter-tasting and shriveled. In some variations, the blackberries are not to be eaten after Michaelmas (now September 29), since it is said that the devil has trampled them, spat on them or even urinated on them after that point.

A gambling tradition holds that bad luck can be changed to good by hiding under a blackberry bush on Halloween night and invoking the aid of Satan.

Blackberries also figure in one FORTUNE-TELLING custom: A man who wished to learn the identity of his future wife could crawl under a blackberry bush on Halloween, where he would see her shadow. In a variation, a man could crawl into a briar bush that was rooted on both ends, and call on evil spirits to grant a request.

Bobbing for Apples (also "ducking for apples," "dookin' for apples," "Bob-apple") — The most popular of all Halloween GAMES. Although it's been claimed that bobbing for apples represents an old DRUID or pagan rite, there's virtually no evidence to support this (although we do know that the CELTS considered APPLES to be important, possibly even sacred). The *Luttrell Psalter*, a fourteenth century illuminated manuscript, contains probably the earliest reference to bobbing for apples, although the game had undoubtedly been played long before then.

In the classic version of the game, a large tub (either galvanized metal or wood) is placed on the floor or the ground and filled with WATER and apples, then contestants must kneel by the tub and attempt to retrieve an apple without using their hands (some versions even deny players the use of their

teeth!). It was also sometimes specified that that contestants could not move the apple to the side of the tub or pan, meaning they must plunge their faces completely into the cold water. Although the apple itself was usually the prize, a separate reward might also be given to whoever could bite the most apples. In one Scottish version, the apples are tum-

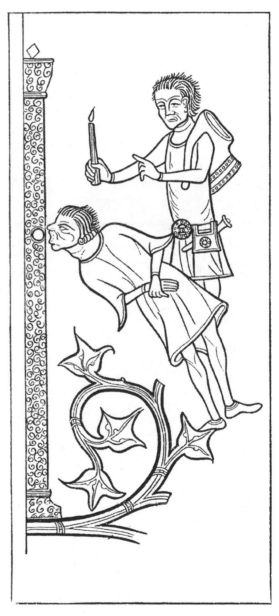

Illustration showing bobbing for apples from the *Luttrell Psalter*

bled into the tub and stirred with a wooden spoon or rod made of hazel or ash. Sometimes there was a custom regarding placing the apples into the tub: Each person at the party would choose an apple, and then all players marched around the tub in the direction of the sun (or *deas-iuil*) and threw their apples in. In situations where partygoers weren't interested in getting wet, the game might be played by standing over the tub and holding a fork in the teeth; the object was to spear an apple by releasing the fork at the right point (an American name for this variant was "mumble-ty-apple"). Sometimes coins of different denominations were inserted into the apples, so that a successful bobbing also guaranteed a small monetary prize (money might also be simply

Vintage postcard showing bobbing for apples

dropped into the tub with the apples—in fact, it might even replace the use of the apples entirely).

Sometimes bobbing for apples served as a FORTUNE-TELLING game. In the simplest versions of this, the first to successfully retrieve a stemless apple would be the first to be married, or a happy life was foretold for anyone who could successfully snatch an apple. In one version of the game, players marked their initials on an apple (or even inserted a small note), and marriage was foretold by whose apple one could successfully bite. Those who obtained an apple might take their prize to bed, place the apple under their pillow, and then have dreams in which their future spouses were shown to them.

A variation of bobbing for apples was to bite the apple while it was suspended from a string overhead (or sometimes scones covered in treacle or molasses might be used in place of apples). This variation of the game was called snap-apple or hanch-apple, and SNAP-APPLE NIGHT was sometimes used in place of Halloween (a variant of this suggests that doughnuts or candy can be used in place of apples, and that the objective is to eat the object off the string). Apples might also be attached to one end of a stick, while flour, a lighted CANDLE, a treacle bun, a potato or a bar of soap was attached to the other end; the stick was spun, and players had to try to bite the whirling apple (which might even have a small prize placed within it). In a variation of this custom, a barrel-hoop was suspended from the ceiling, with apples, candies, CAKES and candle-ends placed around its perimeter; the hoop was spun, and contestants had to try to bite an edible. In another version, peppers and bread might also be interspersed, and whatever could be bitten first would indicate the flavor of one's future married life.

Bogie Books— Beginning in 1909, Dennison (a company which specialized in the manufacture of paper goods, and which was among the earliest companies to feature a wide line of Halloween products) produced the "Bogie Books," detailed and heavily illustrated guides on how to use Dennison's Halloween products. These booklets typically ran 32 pages, and contained tips on decorating, COSTUMES, and PARTIES. They were produced until 1934, although a few years were skipped, and they were printed in both hardback and paperback. Because of their graphics (which were in color in later issues) and detailed descriptions of early Halloween CELEBRATIONS (and because, like many other early Halloween COLLECTIBLES, they were normally disposed of at the end of the holiday each year), they are now among the most sought-after Halloween collectibles; the 1909 edition is especially scarce, and may fetch over $2,000 on the collectors' market. Reproductions have been available since the early 2000s.

Cover of the 1919 edition of Dennison's Bogie Book

Bogies (also boggans, bogles, bogans, boggarts)—Malicious spirits found around British bogs (hence the name), which often take the form of either a demonic ram, a ghostly white cow or horse, or a monstrous hound with glowing eyes. Bogies probably led to the American idea of the "boogey man." In the Highlands of Scotland, Halloween bogies (who could be driven away by carrying torches around the homestead) were sometimes called "wirrey-cows." *See also* SAMHANACH.

Bon Festival (also *Bon Matsuri, Obon, Urabon*)—Bon Festival is one of the most important events for Japanese people (along with NEW YEAR'S Day); although descended from the Chinese festival of YUE LAAN, it is also sometimes thought of as the Japanese Halloween.

The purpose of Bon is to welcome the return of the ancestors in spirit form; it's typically a time when FAMILIES gather together (which also occurs at New Year's). In fact, in *The Daughter of the Samurai*, Etsu Inagaki Sugimoto describes it as "a happy time for all of Japan." Bon has been celebrated in Japan since at least A.D. 657 (it was supposedly inaugurated in China in A.D. 538, when it was called "festival of the spirits").

The period of Bon is at Moon 7, Days 13–15, or usually from August 13 to 15 (although the date is sometimes July 13 to 15, especially in America). Most government offices and companies are closed during this time, and many Japanese companies provide their employees with a week-long Obon holiday. In Buddhism the spirits of the dead are believed to return to their earthly homes on August 13, stay for three days and then depart for heaven again on the night of August 15. The preparations begin a day or so prior to the actual start of Bon, as houses are cleaned in anticipation of the spirits' return, and new clothes are purchased; *butsudan* (Buddhist family altars) are traditionally decorated with little animal figures made from vegetables, tea is poured and fresh food laid on the *butsudan* for the spirits. "Spirit altars" are set before the *butsudan*, and a priest may be asked to come and read a *sutra*. No life is taken on the first day, and gifts are given throughout the festival. Bon is sometimes referred to as the "Festival of Lanterns" (or "Feast of Lanterns"), because lanterns are lighted in cemeteries, and small FIRES are sometimes made at doorways to welcome ghostly visitors. On the last night of the festival lighted CANDLES are sent sailing off on floating lotus leaves (or *shoryobuni*, meaning "boats of the blessed ghosts"); as each little "boat" bursts into flames, the spirit contained in it is supposed to be released to return to the heavenly abode.

As with Halloween, Bon has many regional variations. For example, in Nagasaki, families that lost a relative during the past year make "spirit boats" with many lanterns to carry the soul to heaven. In the harbor front at Ohato, hundreds of elaborate boatlike floats pulled by families and friends make a parade through the city, with firecrackers lit along the way (a custom borrowed from the Chinese residents of Nagasaki). A BONFIRE is lit on the slopes of Mt. Nyogatake, in the shape of the Chinese character meaning "large." At Nachi Shrine in Katsura, twelve huge torches are lit by white-robed priests.

Possibly the most popular custom at Bon is the *bon odori*, or folk dancing; these rites are performed to welcome the returning ancestors' souls. The dances are usually performed by large groups of people wearing kimonos and straw hats; dancers often move in circles around the musicians or around a temporary platform set up in a broad, open space. The *bon odori* (which is supposedly joined by the dead as well) are first mentioned in Japanese literature about the late fifteenth century, and are based on the Buddhist legend of Moggallana, who wanted to help his mother's spirit escape from the realm of the *Preta* ("world of hungry devils"). He went to the Buddha, who advised him to make offerings to monks. He did, and

his mother was reborn into Buddha's beautiful land, where she lived peacefully and happily. Seeing this, Moggallana danced for joy and was joined by the monks.

Although Bon is typically celebrated with great joy, it is also a time (just as the Halloween season is in western culture) when horror films are typically released; features by Toei, Daiei and Shintoho featured spectral cats, vengeful female GHOSTS and haunted swamps.

Bones *see* Skeletons

Bonfire Night (also "Bon-a-fire Night" or "Bonnie-Fire Night")—In England, another name for GUY FAWKES DAY. In parts of Ireland, Bonfire Night also once referred to Halloween. Now, throughout Ireland the name generally refers to Eleventh Night, the eve of the Twelfth of July, a national holiday celebrating the victory of the Protestant William III over the Catholic James II at the battle of the Boyne. For Roman Catholics, Bonfire Night once meant the eve of the Assumption, August 15, and later referred to the eve of the anniversary of the imposition of internment police, August 8.

When Bonfire Night referred to Halloween, boys typically spent the season leading up to the night collecting material for their BONFIRES; while RHYMING took place in the evenings during the last few weeks prior to Halloween, the days were given to going house-to-house collecting material for bonfires—papers, magazines, garden cuttings, tires, wooden crates, and other items. As the material was collected, it had to be protected from marauding rival gangs who would try to steal it for their own bonfires; boys built small huts near their store of material, and would occasionally spend nights in them to oversee their hoards.

In parts of Canada (especially Newfoundland), Bonfire Night is still held on November 5, although the Guy Fawkes association has been largely forgotten. As in the Irish version, for weeks prior adolescent boys go house-to-house collecting flammable materials, although these Canadian cousins seldom include fireworks or effigy-burning. They do also hold smaller FAMILY bonfires, usually in yards or on beaches.

Bonfires— Once one of the most popular Halloween celebrations throughout the British Isles, bonfires are now confined largely to civil CELEBRATIONS or GUY FAWKES NIGHT.

There is considerable speculation over the meaning of the word "bonfire" itself. The earliest known instance of the derivation of the word occurred as *ban fyre ignis ossium* in the *Catholican Anglicum*, although some scholars believe it might be derived from *Bane-fire* (where *Bane* is a derivation of *Baal*, the name of a pagan deity); "boon-fire" (from the idea that neighbors all contribute a "boon"); or "bone-fire" (from the idea that pagans once threw bones into the fire). The likeliest suggestion is that the word probably comes from a Christian celebration, that of St. John the Baptist's birth; he was born in mid-summer, and it is believed that the saint's bones were burnt by the Roman Emperor Julian the Apostate in the mid-fourth century A.D. A mention from a 1493 accounting of royal expenses notes "the makyng of the bonefuyr on Middesomer Eve, 10s." The original spelling of the word was "bone-fire," with "bonfire" a relatively recent derivation.

Bonfires are often built with kindling collected or even begged specifically for that purpose, and collecting the materials may be an element of SOULING or begging. Bonfires lit in celebration of ALL SAINTS' DAY and ALL SOULS' DAY were usually lit on hillsides, but Guy Fawkes bonfires were often simply large piles of kindling assembled in the streets of a town.

Bonfires originated as a Halloween custom with the CELTS, who lit bonfires on their two greatest festival days, BELTANE (May 1) and SAMHAIN (November 1). Celtic lore records the kindling of FIRES at TLACHTGA each Samhain; all other fires were extinguished and re-lit with embers from the new fire. Celtic bonfires have also been explained as tributes to the sun, as protection against evil spirits, and as beacons to friendly spirits returning home on Samhain, but any such explanations are largely theories or suppositions. Bonfires may also have been used for animal and human sacrifice by the Celts and their priests the DRUIDS (sometimes involving construction of a huge "wicker man" into which the victims were placed). In a pageant presented at Sherbourne in 1905, two early (A.D. 705) British tribesmen who have recently been converted (not very successfully) to Christianity have this dialogue explaining bonfires:

THE CHIEFTAIN. Thou knowest, Gurth, the old gods are dead.
2ND ATTENDANT. I know we have ceased to worship them. But I fear them still. For dead they are not. Now they haunt the woods as evil spirits.
(*The others assent*)
1ST ATTENDANT. Wherefore, O Chieftain, turn away their anger.
THE CHIEFTAIN. Why, kindle a fire, then…

Tar barrels are lit on Guy Fawkes Day in this 1853 newspaper illustration

In fact, this passage probably contains more poetry than truth. More likely, Celt bonfires also had a practical side: Not only were taxes charged for the kindling of the Samhain fires on Tlachtga, but the ash was probably used as fertilizer in their fields.

One of the best explanations of the undying fascination with bonfires may be that given by Thomas Hardy in Chapter Three of his novel *The Return of the Native*, wherein he describes a Guy Fawkes Night celebration, with thirty bonfires blazing on hilltops all over one district. Although Hardy suggests that the custom comes from "Druidical rites and Saxon ceremonies," he goes on to suggest that "to light a fire is the instinctive and resistant act of man when, at the winter ingress, the curfew is sounded throughout Nature. It indicates a spontaneous, Promethean rebelliousness against the fiat that this recurrent season shall bring foul times, cold darkness, misery and death. Black chaos comes, and the fettered gods of the earth say, Let there be light."

The Christian third Council of Constantinople (A.D. 680) tried to abolish bonfires, and inadvertently provided a look at early bonfire customs: "Those fires that kindled ... over which also they use ridiculously and foolishly to leape, by a certaine antient custome, we command them from henceforth to cease." It is still a popular custom to leap over bonfires or dance around them, and may date back to a Druid ritual of driving livestock between two fires to ensure fertility or safety from evil forces. Another attempt to abolish bonfires was made in A.D. 742, when the practice of kindling by "needfire" (friction) was condemned as a pagan practice.

Another early look at bonfires is provided by traveler Thomas Pennant, who in 1772 wrote of the Scottish parish of Maylin, near Pitlochrie: "Hallow Eve is also kept sacred; as soon as it is dark, a person sets fire to a bush of broom fastened round a pole, and, attended with a crowd, runs about the village. He then flings it down, heaps great quantity of combustible matters on it, and makes a great bonfire."

If the Christian third Council was unsuccessful in abolishing bonfires, later church officials fared somewhat better when they complained that Halloween bonfires had become nothing but an excuse for drunkenness and recklessness— by 1860 Halloween bonfires in Scotland, which were once an adult activity, were set exclusively by boys, a custom which largely prevails to this day. Bonfires are not without specific dangers as well: Yarmouth in Great Britain, for example, suspended bonfires in 1893 after one toppled down on a spectator, killing him,

There are numerous different fire customs recorded throughout the British Isles. They may involve the belief that fire is a protective force: For example, in many areas of Scotland children carried blazing torches and, after sunset on Halloween, ran

Children prepare for a bonfire (photograph by Sir Benjamin Stone)

around the boundaries of their land to protect them from FAIRIES and other malicious supernatural forces, and to ensure fertility (it was crucial that the boys ran in the direction of the sun, or *deas-iuil*, not "widdershins" or *tuath-iuil*). Special attention was given to huts or houses wherein resided mothers and children young enough to be snatched by fairies.

One peculiar bonfire custom occurs in Hatherleigh, Devon, Great Britain, shortly after Halloween (actually on the night before the first Wednesday after Guy Fawkes Day). Two sledges carrying a total of six tar barrels are dragged to the highest point in town, and at dawn the first sledge is set afire and dragged around the streets. At 8:30 that evening the second sledge is set alight and also paraded through town before ending in a bonfire. Similar practices are recorded at the Scottish celebration of HOGMANAY: "Burning the clavie" involved carrying a torch (the "clavie" was the wood for the torch) and burning a tar barrel.

On the Isle of Wight, after the November 5th bonfires were lit, male spectators hurled fire-balls into them; the fire-balls were made of finely-packed oakum, and were held in wire casings with handles.

In the parish of Logierait in Scotland, faggots of heath and broom flax were carried aflame on poles by men who ran round the village. In the northeast of Scotland boys went house-to-house and begged a PEAT from each householder, saying "Ge's a peat t' burn the witches." When the fire was going, each boy in turn would lie down as near to the fire as possible, and others ran through the smoke and jumped over him. At the end of the fire, the boys scattered the ASHES ritually by kicking first with the right foot and then with the left; a GAME was to see who could scatter the most. In Aberdeenshire, as soon as the last spark died out the boys would cry "The devil take the hindmost!" and run. In Wales, when the last spark of a Halloween bonfire went out, everyone ran shouting, "The cropped black sow seize the hindmost!"

One peculiar bonfire-like custom was practiced in a Lancashire field near Poulton called (appropriately) PURGATORY FIELD. On Halloween, men assembled there in a circle and threw forkfuls of burning straw into the air, while onlookers fell to their knees and prayed for the souls of the departed in Purgatory. Farmers who participated also believed that the procedure was useful against the weed darnel.

The SAMHNAG was a bonfire built on Halloween by FAMILIES, usually on the highest point on or near their land. Part of the samhnag custom involved marking stones and throwing them into the fire; the next morning the ashes were examined carefully, since a missing stone indicated the death of its owner within the year.

In Lancashire Halloween fires were sometimes called either *Beltains* or *Teanlas* (or TINDLES), and were considered to be largely a Christian practice.

In Duffield, Derbyshire, a bonfire unrelated to Halloween or Guy Fawkes was held each year during the first week in November. Every night during the first week of the month, all the young men of the area yoked themselves to carts, and, proceeded by horns, collected trees and other wood along the lanes; on the first Monday of November, they built a great bonfire with the collected wood. The "wakes of Duffield" finished on that Monday night with the young men engaging in a "squirrel hunt," in which they all took pots, pans, and other NOISEMAKERS, went to Kedleston Park, and created a din with the intention of frightening squirrels into falling from the trees.

In America (mainly on the east coast), Halloween bonfires serve chiefly to entertain children, who often roast hot dogs or marshmallows over them. In France, Halloween bonfires were often used to roast CHESTNUTS. In a Welsh custom, NUTS thrown onto a bonfire predict the future: If the flames dance about when the nuts are thrown in, the coming year will be full of fun and excitement; but if the flames don't change, the coming year will be dull.

Bonfires are also recorded in some celebrations of the Japanese BON FESTIVAL.

Bonnach Samhuinn— Hallowe'en bannock or cake. A traditional Scottish Hallowe'en FOOD, made with the meal of the new CORN and washed over with a custard made with eggs, cream and honey, then toasted before the embers.

Boxty— Another traditional Irish Halloween FOOD, boxty is a BREAD made of potatoes and flour. It is also sometimes called Boxty-in-the-Pan, Boxty-on-the-griddle or simply boxty pancakes. Boxty was sometimes first served on Halloween and then eaten throughout the following three months, or it might have been served only on Halloween and Boxing Day. In this stanza from an 1898 poem, B. M. Teggart sets up boxty as a popular Halloween food with the Irish poor:

> Where there are neither sweets nor cakes
> Nor mutton, fat or lean,
> In a big pot the mother makes
> Boxty, at Halloween.

One amusing traditional folk rhyme about boxty runs:

> Boxty on the griddle,
> Boxty in the pan,
> If you don't eat Boxty,
> You'll never get a man.

Bradbury, Ray (1920–)— American author best known for the classic science fiction novels *Fahrenheit 451* (1953) and *The Martian Chronicles* (1950); Bradbury has also written more extensively about Halloween than any other major literary figure. His 1972 novel *The Halloween Tree* is a fictionalized account of the history of Halloween, as the mysterious Carapace Clavicle Moundshroud leads a group of small boys through the EGYPTIAN FEAST OF THE DEAD, SAMHAIN, and the Mexican DAYS OF THE DEAD. His renowned 1962 dark fantasy *Something Wicked This Way Comes*, about a mysterious carnival which preys on the dreams of the residents of a small town, makes ingenious use of the holiday by setting its story in the week before Halloween, suggesting that on this "strange wild dark long year, Halloween came early." In his novel *From the Dust Returned* (2001), Bradbury collects fifty years of short stories involving "the October People" (or the Elliott family) into one novel, about a magical clan of ghosts, winged men and mind-readers who reunite at Halloween (in the novel's afterword, Bradbury mentions the autobiographical nature of the family, which resides in his home state of Illinois). Bradbury's 1964 short story, "Heavy-Set," takes a non-supernatural look at the holiday, with a melancholy depiction of an obsessed bodybuilder who turns to his mother after a disappointing Halloween party. In the most frightening of his Halloween ventures, the 1948 short story, "The October

Ray Bradbury (left) and Jonathan Pryce as "Mr. Dark" on the set of the film version of Bradbury's *Something Wicked This Way Comes.*

Game," (from the collection *Long After Midnight*), Bradbury uses the fall season as a metaphor for a dying marriage, and depicts a particularly gruesome version of the classic Halloween game "Autopsy." That same year, Bradbury wrote "The Candy Skull," a short story set in Mexico during Days of the Dead. Bradbury has also written poetry about Halloween.

Both *Something Wicked This Way Comes* and *The Halloween Tree* have been adapted to film (both featuring screenplays by Bradbury), the former as a theatrical feature in 1983, directed by Jack Clayton and starring Jason Robards and Jonathan Pryce, and the latter as an animated television special in 1993. In November 2000, Bradbury was awarded the National Book Foundation Medal for Distinguished Contribution to American Letters.

Bread— The baking of special breads and CAKES is one of the oldest Halloween traditions, and may date back to the CELTS, who sometimes chose victims for sacrifices by marking one piece of bread or cake in charcoal. Special cakes and breads are involved in many different customs surrounding ALL SAINTS' DAY, ALL SOULS' DAY, and DAYS OF THE DEAD; however, in some areas of Europe it is supposedly bad luck to bake bread on Halloween, and will endanger all who eat it.

One of the earliest mentions of Halloween includes a reference to bread, as this line found in the *Festyvall* from 1511 indicates: "We rede in olde tyme good people wolde on All halowen daye bake brade and dele it for all crysten soules."

Bread (as compared to cake) figures in at least one FORTUNE-TELLING custom: Someone desiring to engage in WISHING would have a family member bring him a piece of dry bread at bedtime on Halloween. The bread was eaten slowly (and silently) while the person thought of a wish; if the dreams that night were pleasant, the wish would soon come true.

Bread also had some protective powers: A safeguard for travelers on Halloween was to carry a piece of bread crossed with SALT in a pocket. *See also* BOXTY.

Briar Thorn— The major component in a FORTUNE-TELLING custom: If a girl found a branch of briar thorn which had bent over and grown into the ground to form a loop, on Halloween she might creep through the loop THREE times late in the evening in the DEVIL's name, then cut the briar and put it under her pillow, all silently; she would then dream of her future husband.

Brighde— In a Scottish belief, Brighde was a goddess in the form of a youthful maiden who ruled over the warmer half of the year from BELTANE to SAMHAIN; the winter months were presided over by the CAILLEACH, or old woman.

Broom— Traditional instrument of WITCHES. Also, in parts of Europe it is considered bad luck to sweep on Halloween, because of the souls seeking sanctuary in the home. In Ireland, one particular FORTUNE-TELLING custom had a young girl with a mouthful of WATER riding a broomstick to her NEIGHBORS' door, where she would listen at the keyhole to hear the name of her husband-to-be. In

Early postcard showing a moon-face witch and her broom

another custom, girls rode wooden RAKES round the CORN stacks at MIDNIGHT on Halloween.

The association of witches and broomsticks seems to have been an invention on the part of the Christian witch-hunters, and may have represented a desire to persecute women (by associating witches with perhaps the most common household tool) in particular.

Brownies— Traditional brownies are house FAIRIES, who will serve an individual house by performing small household chores, and who are normally rewarded with small offerings of food (although in most cases it's also thought that a brownie will vanish if given a gift of clothing). Although some brownies could occasionally become mischievous and might even pinch or harass lazy human servants, they were on the whole useful and harmless. In Scotland, brownies supposedly lived in the hollows of trees, in caves, and in the recesses of ruined castles. The popular ballad "Aiken Drum" describes a brownie:

> I lived in a lan' where we saw nae sky,
> I dwalt in a spot where a burn rins na by;
> But I'se dwall now wi' you if ye like to try—
> Hae ye wark for Aiken Drum?

This 1936 RECITATION by Elizabeth F. Guptill is entitled, appropriately, "A Brownie," and was designed to be presented as part of a school PAGEANT (by a "tiny boy wearing a brownie suit, and carrying a JACK-O'-LANTERN"):

> A Halloween brownie am I,
> I like to play tricks on the sly.
> I'm happy and jolly,
> And brimful of folly.
> To play pranks on you I shall try.
>
> My old jack-o'-lantern and I
> Will come snooping around by-and-by.
> If you hear elfin laughter,
> See lights scurrying after,
> You'll know that the brownies are nigh.

"Building the House"— An Irish Halloween FORTUNE-TELLING custom in which 12 pairs of holly twigs are arranged in a circle, pushed into the ground and tied together at the top. A live turf representing the HEARTH is placed in the center of this "house," and the coupled twigs are named after the boys and girls present; whichever pair catches fire first indicates which boy and girl will first be wedded.

"Burning the Reekie Mehr"— A Scottish Halloween PRANKING custom in which a CABBAGE or KALE stalk is scooped out and filled with tow (the "mehr"). One end is lit and placed up against the keyhole on a door, then blowing on the other end will send plumes of smoke into the house. Pranksters occasionally followed this up with using turf to plug up the chimney, creating a house full of smoke.

"Burning the Witch"— A BONFIRE custom, in which a witch is burned in effigy on Halloween. Perhaps the most famous recorded example is a celebration held at Balmoral during the reign of Queen Victoria. A huge bonfire was kindled in front of the castle, and as the bonfire gained in intensity it was approached by clansmen in Highland dress. The clansmen marched around a cart that held the effigy of a horrid old witch called the Shandy Dann (actually a bastardized form of "Shan-dre-dan," the type of trolley or cart). At a dozen yards or so from the blaze, a pronouncement on the witch's guilt was made, and then both trolley and effigy were hurled into the fire. The entire performance was said to have been greatly enjoyed by the queen herself.

Burns, Robert (1759–1796)— Scottish poet most famed for his contribution to a song celebrating another holiday (the lyrics to "AULD LANG SYNE," the NEW YEAR'S Eve favorite), but also author of perhaps the best description of a rustic, pre-industrial Halloween celebration. His 28-stanza poem "Hallowe'en," written in 1785 documents the fortune-telling traditions and party customs of eighteenth-century Scottish villagers; it tells the sometimes amusing, sometimes bawdy, and sometimes frightening stories of a group of young people gathered together for the evening. Burns grew up on a farm himself (his father was a largely-unsuccessful farmer, and his brother, Gilbert, carried on the family tradition; Burns himself worked as a farmer and an excise-man), and so Burns had probably experienced such a Halloween gathering. His poem begins with a salute to the supernatural side of the holiday:

> Upon that night, when fairies light

Then Burns moves on to the heart of the poem in the second stanza:

> Some merry, friendly, countra folks,
> Together did convene,
> To *burn* their nits, an' *pou* their stocks,
> An' haud their *Hallowe'en*

Over the next two dozen stanzas, Burns describes such FORTUNE-TELLING customs as pulling the KALE, the three LUGGIE BOWLS, burning NUTS, winnowing CORN and sowing HEMP SEED. His fortune seekers usually arrive at rather down-to-earth answers; for example, "fechtin Jamie Fleck"— the skeptic who is dared to try the hemp seed test — is scared half out of his wits by a pig. When Uncle John gets the empty luggie bowl THREE times in a row, he hurls the bowls into the fire. And young Leezie heads out to dip her sleeve in WATER "where three lairds lands met at a burn," but is so frightened by the lowing of a renegade cow that she plunges right into the stream.

In the last stanza, Burns describes the rest of the evening:

> Wi' merry sangs, an' friendly cracks,
> I wat they dinna weary ;
> An' unco tales, an' funnie jokes,
> Their sports were cheap an cheery

Finally they finish with a dish of SOWENS and "a social glas o' strunt" (liquor), and the party — and poem — come to an end.

Burns also penned, in what he considered to be his best work, the supernatural tale

Robert Burns

of "Tam O'Shanter," an incorrigible drunk who sets off late from the tavern one night and stumbles on "warlocks and witches in a dance." In his drunken state, Tam O'Shanter nearly joins in the mad revelries, but is saved by his horse Maggie, who narrowly escapes the pursuing fiends, losing her tail to them as she leaps over a brook (demonic creatures and their servants can't cross running water).

Burns also mentions a classic Halloween divination involving WATER in the song "Tam Glen":

> The last Halloween I was waukin
> My droukit sark-sleeve, as ye kin;
> His likeness cam up the house staukin,
> And the very grey breeks o' Tam Glen!

The growing popularity of the work of Burns in the American West of the late 18th- and early 19th-century (many American cities actually celebrated Burns's birthday on January 25) may have been one of the factors that led to Halloween's increasing popularity in that area during that time.

Burton, Tim (1958–) American filmmaker whose films as a director included *Pee-Wee's Big Adventure* (1985), *Batman* (1989), and *Edward Scissorhands* (1990), before 1993's *The Nightmare Before Christmas* (which he co-wrote and produced). *The Nightmare Before Christmas* has become probably the most beloved Halloween film ever produced, with its unique mix of traditional Halloween iconography (PUMPKINS, GHOSTS, WITCHES, etc.) and CHRISTMAS; in 2006, it was re-released to theaters in 3D. Burton first created *Nightmare* as a poem while he was working as a Disney animator in the early 1980s. Disney initially passed on the idea (although it eventually produced the film in 1993), but Burton never gave up on the project, noting, "*Nightmare Before Christmas* is deeper in my heart than any other film." Eventually Disney

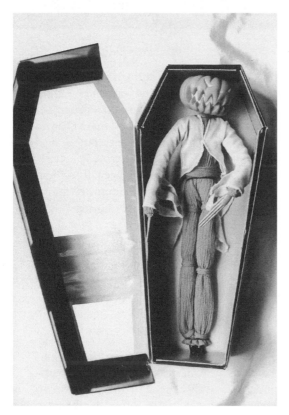

Glow-in-the-dark Jack Skellington toy from Tim Burton's *The Nightmare Before Christmas*

reconsidered and Burton, deciding he didn't have enough experience in stop-motion animation, passed the directorial reins to filmmaker Henry Selick. The film tells the story of Jack Skellington the Pumpkin King of Halloween Town, who stumbles on a magical doorway into the realm of Christmas and, bored with Halloween, kidnaps Santa Claus and inadvertently wreaks havoc by posing as the Jolly Old Elf on Christmas night. Although *Nightmare* was only moderately successful in the U.S. (where it became a cult favorite), the film became very popular in Japan. Its overseas success produced a whole line of COLLECTIBLES long after the movie's original American theatrical release (which produced surprisingly little merchandise), and re-energized Halloween as a collectible holiday. In 2001, the film also provided the basis for a seasonal makeover of the popular Disneyland attraction the Haunted Mansion; "Haunted Mansion Holiday," which features such popular *Nightmare* characters as Jack Skellington, Sally, and Zero, proved so popular that it has now become a regular feature, running each year from late September to early January.

Burton explored Halloween again in his 1999 version of the WASHINGTON IRVING classic *Sleepy Hollow*, which transformed Ichabod Crane from a gangly schoolteacher to a brilliant young inspector (Johnny Depp), investigating the mysteries of Sleepy Hollow. Christopher Walken appeared as the Hessian Horseman, who was depicted here with a head more often than not. The film's art direction emphasized its Halloween aspects, with rich vistas of pumpkin fields, gothic villages and haunted forests.

Buttons— In this FORTUNE-TELLING custom, by counting the buttons on the coat of the first person met on Halloween night (while reciting a counting charm), one could determine the true intentions of a suitor.

Bwyd Cennad Y Meirw (Welsh)—FOOD left outside on Halloween to feed the souls of the dead.

C

Cabbage Night— Name sometimes applied (mainly in eastern parts of the United States) to the night before Halloween, when PRANKING (such as pulling up and throwing CABBAGES) was practiced. In Halifax, Nova Scotia, and surrounding areas, the name was known as "Cabbage-Stump Night," after the habit of throwing cabbage stumps at doors.

Cabbages (see also KALE)— Cabbage is one of the most important FOOD items associated with Halloween, especially in Scotland. This folk rhyme even seems to make cabbage almost divine ("Haly" is an abbreviated form of "Hail Mary") in regards to Halloween:

> Haly on a cabbage stalk, and haly on a bean,
> Haly on a cabbage stalk, to-morrow's Hallowe'en.

In Scottish lore, pulling cabbages on Halloween is a method of FORTUNE-TELLING: If the cabbage head is white, a future mate will be older than the puller; if the head is green, the mate will be younger; if there's a great deal of dirt clinging to the head, your luck will be likewise great; if the cabbage heart tastes bitter, you'll have a difficult life. The cabbage is then hung over a doorway, and the first man to enter will bear the name of the girl's future husband (or, in an American version, the first man to enter and be hit on the head by the falling cabbage would bear the name). In a slight variation, men would pull a cabbage and examine the shape of the stalk to determine the shape of their future wife (long and thin or short and stout, for example). In another version, a clean, light cabbage promised heaven, while a cabbage darkened by frost foretold hell.

One method involved seven cabbages, which were chosen and named for seven members of the party. The cabbages were

Ellen Clapsaddle postcard showing cabbages used in Halloween fortune-telling

then pulled and their stalks examined. A traditional rhyme explains:

> One, two, three, and up to seven;
> If all are white, all go to heaven;
> If one is black as Murtagh's evil,
> He'll soon be screechin' wi' the devil.

This divination is captured in the story of "Red Mike," who was born on Halloween Eve. When the cabbage test was tried at a party where Mike was present, six stalks were found to be white, but Mike's was dark, wormy and foul-smelling. When Mike cursed at the company, a priest showed him a crucifix, and he fled, finally vanishing through a bog into the ground.

In Massachusetts, if a girl steals a cabbage she will see her future husband as she pulls it up, or meet him on her way home (if these steps fail she must put the cabbage up over her door and see whom it falls on); a variant of this belief stated that the young lady must pass through a graveyard to obtain the cabbage. Another Massachusetts custom instructed a girl to walk outside BACKWARDS on Halloween at MIDNIGHT, in her night-dress, and pull a cabbage from the garden; she would then see her future husband over her shoulder.

Cabbage was also popular in PRANKING. Boys might push the pith from the stalk, fill the cavity with tow which they set on fire, and then blow yard-long jets of flame through keyholes (a practice known as "BURNING THE REEKIE MEHR"). One of the more amusing and inventive Halloween pranks involved tying strings to the cabbages in a farmer's field, then making the cabbages apparently "walk" right out from under the astonished farmer's gaze. Unharvested cabbages also became missiles hurled against doors on Halloween night.

In Scotland, where it was believed by small children that new babies came from the roots of the cabbage-stalk, it was a popular custom to pile the stalks against doors and windows on Halloween night in hopes that visiting FAIRIES would set free one more baby soul from the stalks to bless the household during the coming year.

In Wales, LEEKS were often used in place of cabbage.

Cabbage broth was also a popular Scottish Halloween dish, and cabbage is a part of the popular Halloween food COLCANNON. In Armagh, Halloween cabbage was fed to a potential mate; it was said that "the ceremony was as good as arranged" if the desired person could be persuaded to take a meal with cabbage as part of it.

Cailleach— Means "old woman," and also refers to the last sheaf of CORN at the end of HARVEST; like the CORN DOLLY, this sheaf was sometimes hung in the house to provide good luck (although occasionally kisses were stolen beneath the cailleach, making it similar to the use of MISTLETOE at CHRISTMAS). In Scottish and Irish folklore, the cailleach was often an ancient woman or hag gifted with magic (similar to the WITCH or the BANSHEE), and whose assistance was sometimes sought in occult situations; the Cailleach was also sometimes referred to as a seasonal deity who provided over the winter months between SAMHAIN and BELTANE (while BRIGHDE ruled the summer half of the year). In some areas, the word is believed to have referred to a fairy woman dressed in red or green.

Cake— Cakes and bread were probably first associated with Halloween because of the holiday's proximity to HARVEST. The 1580 edition of *Five Hundred Points of Good Husbandry* notes the importance of baking cakes at the end of harvest:

> Wife, some time this weeke, if the wether hold cleere,
> An end of wheat-sowing we make for this yeare.
> Remember you, therefore, though I do it not,
> The seed-cake, the Pasties, and Furmentie-pot.

Not only was a Halloween cake once the centerpiece of Halloween PARTIES, but cakes were also used as a form of FORTUNE-TELLING. The most common cake custom involved baking small trinkets into a "FORTUNE CAKE" (each trinket was wrapped in oiled paper); one's future was foretold depending on whatever was found in one's slice of cake. For example, a ring indicated a happy marriage; a wheel foretold travel; a dime, wealth; a key, good luck in romance; a rag, poverty; a wishbone, a wish to come true; and a thimble indicated spinsterhood (or the ability of a woman to earn her own living). Less popular were the use of a chip of wood (for a COFFIN), indicating who would die first; and a sloe, foretelling who would live the longest (because the FAIRIES blight the sloes in the hedges come Halloween, so a sloe in the cake will be the last of the year). A small china doll would indicate who would have children; and a NUT would indicate marriage to a widow or widower (unless the kernel was shriveled, in which case the finder was destined for spinsterhood). Tokens are still baked into commercially available BARM BRACK cakes in Ireland (whereas in America ice cream — with tokens inserted — has replaced cake at some parties).

One of the most curious methods of cake divination was the "DUMB CAKE," which typically involved a number of unmarried young women (sometimes the number is specified as seven) who mixed a "dumb cake" together in silence (if any spoke, she would be last to wed). When the stiff, plain dough was placed in a pan, each girl took a new pin and pricked the initials of her sweetheart in the dough. Silence continued while the dough baked for 10 minutes, then those whose letters were still plain would supposedly marry before the year ended.

SALT cakes were also popular in divination. In an American custom, a girl would eat a salt cake and go to bed BACKWARDS without speaking. If she dreamt of her future husband bringing her a cup of WATER in a silver or gold goblet, it indicated wealth, while a tin goblet foretold poverty. Should she be foolish enough to help herself to a drink, she would never be married; and if the vessel out of which she drank was a gourd, she would be a pauper.

Cake has also been invested with the power to save souls on Halloween. SOUL CAKES were given to beggars in exchange for their prayers for the dead, and in Belgium, one custom involves eating cakes on All Souls' Eve in the belief that another soul is saved from suffering in PURGATORY for each cake eaten. The residents of Hirt (St. Kilda) celebrated the Festival of All Saints with a CAVALCADE and large cake in the form of a triangle that must be completely eaten in that one night. In Chichester, shops on All Saints were full of small iced cakes, the white frosting of which was thought to represent the white robes of the saints in heaven.

Cake Night— Another name for Halloween in parts of Britain (specifically Ripon, Yorkshire) where it was a popular custom to bake a CAKE for each member of the family on this night.

Calan-Gaeaf— Welsh term for Halloween night; it literally refers to the Calends of Winter, which begins on November 1.

Calcannon Night— Writing in his *Diary* from 1828, Humphrey O'Sullivan mentions that Halloween was sometimes called "Calcannon Night," after the eating of COLCANNON on the day.

Candles— Candles are one of the few constants in all versions of Halloween, at all times and all places; even in twenty-first century America, no house is complete at Halloween without the candle guttering inside the PUMPKIN or the luminaria near the front door. The importance of candles at Halloween certainly has something to do with the holiday's earliest incarnation as the onset of winter; nights were longer and colder, and evil forces were abroad. The glow of a candle provided warmth, light and protection.

In some parts of England Halloween was once celebrated with a Candle Parade (in Lancashire it was known as "LEET THE WITCHES," "lating the witches" or simply "lighting the witches"). It was believed that on Halloween night WITCHES gathered to do evil deeds and if lighted candles were carried about between the hours of 11 and MIDNIGHT the witches' power would be broken. Candles were kept burning in the stable all night to protect the livestock from evil forces. If one's candle went out (or was blown out by witches) during that time it augured evil for the carrier. One Halloween custom involved placing a lighted candle on the table during the evening's meal (typically CHAMP or COL-

CANNON), and if the candle fell it foretold the death of someone in the house.

Candles have also been used at Halloween in remembrance of the dead. Nearly every major commemoration of the dead, from the Japanese BON FESTIVAL to the Mexican DAYS OF THE DEAD to the French TOUSSAINT, involves burning candles for the dead, often at the graveside. In Britain, a popular All Souls' Eve custom was to light a candle for each deceased relative and place it in the windows of the rooms in which they had died. Candles were also placed in windows in Ireland (sometimes specified as THREE candles) to light the way for wandering souls on Halloween or on All Souls' Eve. A lighted candle should be placed on Halloween in any window that faces a GRAVEYARD. In Ireland,

This vintage postcard by Ellen Clapsaddle superbly illustrates the importance of candles on Halloween.

women made candles that were lighted only on Halloween, before which they prayed for departed souls.

Candles have been used in a variety of FORTUNE-TELLING customs. Some sound like miniature BONFIRE rituals: Twelve candles were placed in a row, and each was named for a month of the year. An unmarried woman would leap over the candles, and if her jump caused any to blow out, that would be the month in which she would be married; if none was extinguished, she was destined for a life of "single blessedness." In a variation, a jump over a single candle determined whether the jumper would have a trouble-free year (the flame was undisturbed) or one of woe (the candle was knocked over in the attempt).

Many divination customs centered on blowing out candle flames. The method might involve just one large tallow candle in the center of a table, from which unmarried women stood at a distance of three paces and tried three times to blow out the candle; the number of tries it took to extinguish the flame would reveal the qualities of the future husband (one indicated a rich man, two a man of rank, three a workman, and to not blow out the candle at all indicated no marriage). Or a candle divination might involve many candles: Seven candles were lit on a table, and the one seeking to know his future was blindfolded, then spun about three times and told to blow out the candles three times. The number of candles blown out foretold how many years would pass before the fortune-seeker was wed. If all seven were extinguished, it would be in the same year; if none was extinguished, the seeker would remain unmarried (although, curiously enough, there is a variant version of this custom in which the futures foretold are exactly reversed). If twelve candles were used, the candle with the extinguished flame would represent the month in which marriage would occur. A slightly different version of this custom specified that the blindfolded player was led in taking six steps away from three candles, then six steps in return; if the first candle was blown out, the player would marry within a year, if the second, two years, the third, three years, and if no candles were blown out they would remain unmarried. In another method, a candle flame is blown out through a funnel of paper; if the participant is successful on the first try, he or she will marry for love; if on the second attempt, for beauty; if on the third, for money; and if not by then, the marriage will be unhappy. One American custom involved different colors of candles, all ranged along a table. Those interested in knowing about their future spouses blew toward the candles three times. The candles they succeeded in blowing out would indicate the qualities of their future spouse (i.e., white denoted a mate with a "fine reputation," pink a handsome husband, etc.). A slight variation on this custom noted that the number of puffs taken to blow out a candle foretold the number of years before marriage; the colors suggested here included white (delight), red (well-fed), green (jealousy) and yellow (good marriage).

One of the oddest (and most macabre) forms of divination by candle combines candles and CHURCHES: First, a clod of earth was obtained from a churchyard, and set up in the home with 12 candles in it, named for 12 members of the Halloween party. Their fates were learned by how steadily the candles burned, and the first candle to be extinguished marked the first guest to die.

Candles were combined with other Halloween methods of divination, such as one involving WATER, explained by this anonymous 1937 poem called "The FIRE O' LOVE":

Take a tub of water, light a candle end,
On a flat cork place it, then it floating send.
Write your names on paper, twist the slips up tight,
Toss them to the water — many will ignite.
Those whose names float onward, never, never wed.
Thus an eighteenth century old tradition said.

In another custom, the Halloween fortune-seeker ate a spoonful of SALT, then car-

ried a candle in one hand and a MIRROR in the other while walking BACKWARD down the cellar stairs. Providing the seeker survived this, the mirror would reveal the seeker's future beloved. In a variation, a girl stood with a candle before a mirror on Halloween at midnight, and she would see the face of her husband; if no husband appeared by the stroke of 12, then she would see the DEVIL. Or, in lieu of melted LEAD, candle wax might be dropped into a goblet of water to read the signs formed there.

One fairly recent custom suggests placing a lighted candle in the sink on Halloween, then holding a THREAD over the flame while counting slowly. The number counted before the thread burns in two denotes the number of years before you will marry.

Candles have also been involved in some Halloween begging traditions. Not only are they traditionally used to light JACK-O'-LANTERNS, but they have even been the object of at least one begging custom: In Lancashire in the early nineteenth century, candles were begged house-to-house, rather than SOUL CAKES or other forms of FOOD and drink.

Although not exactly employing candles, a British storytelling game common at Halloween should be mentioned here: A bundle of glowing twigs from the fire was passed from hand to hand, and each person present selected one and then recited an installment of a tale until his stick burned to ashes. Sometimes CABBAGE stalks from divination games practiced earlier that evening were used in place of the twigs.

For about the last half-century figural candles have been popular Halloween decorating items, and vintage candles are now sought-after COLLECTIBLES, especially those made by Gurley, which usually show witches, pumpkins, GHOSTS or black CATS.

Candy— Candy first became popular at 19th century VICTORIAN PARTIES, when "taffy pulling" was a typical activity for youngsters. In fact, a 1908 *Good Housekeeping* article even suggests that taffy pulling took on a specific character at Halloween parties: "...taffy when cold was coiled and wound into all sorts and varieties of mysterious initials and symbols." Paper candy containers were among the most popular and earliest Halloween retail products, and were sometimes also crafted by hand, producing Halloween FOLK ARTS. Later on, candy containers were manufactured in plastic, sometimes doubled as TOYS, and are now among the most sought-after Halloween COLLECTIBLES.

With the introduction of TRICK OR TREAT, traditional Halloween foods such as APPLES, NUTS and homemade CAKES were largely replaced by manufactured and wrapped candies (which were easier for adults to dole out, since they required no preparations, and were also preferred by children). Probably the first major candy manufacturer was Brachs Candy Company, or E. J. Brachs Corp.; Emil J. Brach opened his first candy store in 1904, and by the 1920s he and his two sons were making CANDY CORN by hand. Prior to candy corn, the most popular candies were small B-B-sized pellets.

Halloween is the number three holiday for candy sales (behind Valentine's Day and Easter, but ahead of CHRISTMAS); in fact, it is estimated that one-quarter of all supermarket candy sales occur between September 15 and November 10. According to the American Express Retail Index on Halloween spending (in 2000), 77 percent favored some form of chocolate. The survey noted that the most popular candy for Halloween was Snickers (35%), followed by Hershey's (21%), Reese's Peanut Butter Cups (13%), Three Musketeers (10%), and Milky Way (9%).

Candy Corn— This popular Halloween confection was invented by the sons of two German emigrants to America. The Goelitz Confectionery Co. invented candy corn in the 1880s, and was producing it regularly by 1900. Today the firm's successor, Herman Goelitz, Inc., is best known as the maker of Jelly Belly jelly-bean candies.

Candy corn

Candy corn has become so popular that its distinctive shape (a cone) and colors (white, yellow and orange) have been recreated in Halloween CANDLES and other memorabilia, and has even had its own day declared: National Candy Corn Day is celebrated one day prior to Halloween, on October 30.

Carnival— Largely European name for the day preceding Lent, which is often filled with PARTIES, COSTUMES and CELEBRATIONS. In the United States Carnival is known as MARDI GRAS.

Carnivals— This popular form of Halloween entertainment may have originally developed as an institutionalized alternative to the destructive PRANKING of the 1920s and 1930s. Halloween carnivals are usually held on school grounds (where they help raise money for the school), and typically include amusement rides, games of chance, FORTUNE-TELLING, HAUNTED HOUSES, refreshments and live music. In the past, such activities as Halloween court (wherein "criminals" were tried and received five- or ten-minute sentences to "jail," a small wire-mesh enclosed space) and even homemade rides (similar to soapbox racers) were popular.

Carnivals are also popular in Britain on GUY FAWKES DAY, with some of the largest being celebrated at Lewes, Bridgwater and

Hatherleigh; these usually include PARADES and BONFIRES or FIREWORKS.

Carpenter, John (1948–) American filmmaker whose 1979 horror film *Halloween* became not only the most popular Halloween-themed horror movie ever made, but was also one of the most successful independent films ever made and the progenitor of an entire cycle of serial killer films (and a 2007 remake by writer/co-producer/director Rob Zombie).

Carpenter and producer/co-writer Debra Hill had been involved in talks with producer Irwin Yablans about making a thriller, when Yablans suggested it be set during Halloween. Hill and Carpenter agreed, and centered their script on Michael Myers, a murderer who escapes from a lunatic asylum to return to his hometown of Haddonfield, Illinois, where he murders teens and finally stalks the brainy and lonely Laurie Strode (Jamie Lee Curtis). Carpenter's extensive use of subjective camera angles (especially the astonishing four-minute-long opening shot) established a "killer's point-of-view" style that would be copied for years to come, in such films as *Friday the 13th* and the rest in the "slasher" cycle of the 1980s. Likewise, Carpenter and Hill's protagonist—a virginal and resourceful teenaged girl—would become a trope of horror films for the next two decades. However, the use of the holiday and its beloved symbols (JACK-O'-LANTERNS, HAUNTED HOUSES, COSTUMES) cannot be discounted as part of the film's success; indeed, the holidays were plundered for horror film titles (even *April Fools' Day* didn't escape), but none of

these follow-ups were able to achieve the financial or aesthetic success of *Halloween*.

The first film was followed by a string of sequels, beginning with *Halloween II* in 1981; however, Carpenter would never direct another film in the series, although he did co-write and co-produce (with Debra Hill) the first sequel. He was also involved as a producer on *Halloween III: Season of the Witch*, undoubtedly both the oddest film in this series and one of the strangest sequels ever produced, since it has absolutely nothing in

John Carpenter's *Halloween* (photo by Kim Gottlieb)

common with the first two films (although they are glimpsed playing on television sets in the background). Based on an uncredited script by legendary writer Nigel Kneale (best known for the British "Quatermass" series), *Halloween III: Season of the Witch* centers on a new antagonist, Conal Cochran (Dan O'Herlihy), whose "Silver Shamrock" company has a bestselling line of Halloween masks. When a mysterious death occurs involving the masks, a small-town doctor (Tom Atkins) and the daughter of a murdered store owner (Stacey Nelkin) investigate Silver Shamrock, and discover that the company is actually a front for a cult of ancient CELTS who plan on using a combination of magic and technology to murder America's children on Halloween night in a gigantic SAMHAIN sacrifice. The film is intriguing in its attempts to combine new Halloween icons (PUMPKINS, WITCHES) with ancient Celtic imagery (Stonehenge, even though the latter has been proven to pre-date Celtic history), but the movie lacks the pace, intensity, and visual style of Carpenter's first entry in the series.

Carpenter went on to direct many more films, including the horror films *The Thing*, *Christine*, *They Live*, *The Prince of Darkness*, *In the Mouth of Madness*, and *Vampires*, but none was as successful (or as important) as *Halloween*.

Cassilis Downans— Rocky green hills located in Scotland near the ancient seat of the Earls of Cassilis, famed (like the Cove of Colean) for being a haunt of FAIRIES, and singled out for mention in ROBERT BURNS's poem "Hallowe'en":

> Upon that night, when fairies light,
> On *Cassilis Downans* dance

A history of Cassilis Downans mentions a 17th-century earl, Alexander Kennedy, who frequently accompanied his young wife to the top of the Cassilis Downans "because she was anxious to see the fairies dancing there" (unfortunately, the story ended when the youthful wife attempted to run away with a gypsy boy, Faa; Faa and his gang were captured and executed by the earl, who locked his fickle wife away in a tower).

Castle Halloween Museum— Castle Halloween, located in Benwood, West Virginia, is the first museum dedicated to Halloween history and COLLECTIBLES. Housed in a former elementary school building and holding over 35,000 pieces, the museum was opened in 2005 by Pamela Apkarian-Russell and her husband Chris Russell. In addition to Halloween POSTCARDS, CANDY containers, COSTUMES, and FOLK ART, the museum also holds extensive collections of material based on *The Nightmare Before Christmas* and *Harry Potter*. Castle Halloween also houses a shop and a research library, and is open for viewing by appointment.

Cats— The association of cats (especially black cats) with Halloween is something of a mystery. Cats are usually shown with WITCHES (to whom legend assigned them the role of "familiar"), but the origins of this connection are equally uncertain. As with BATS and OWLS, cats may be popular at Halloween simply because they are nocturnal predators.

Unlike Halloween lore involving cats, which typically holds them to be evil, Egyptians believed cats to be sacred; killing a cat was punishable by death. In Norse mythology, cats were one of the sacred animals of the goddess Freya (a pagan association that may have led later on to the supposed relationship between cats and witches). According to romantic Celtic folktales, DRUIDS held cats in high regard and one who killed or injured a cat was sure to be punished by the animal's spirit. However, in truth there is little evidence that CELTS held cats in high veneration (there are some instances of cat-headed men and monster cats, most notably "Palug's cat," in later Welsh and Irish literature). In "Voyage of Maildun," Chapter XII tells of a palace guarded by a single small cat; when one of Maildun's men foolishly tries to steal a torque, he is slain by the cat, who leaves nothing of him but a pile of ashes. Another misconception holds that Druids feared cats as evil spirits and often burned the animals alive in SAMHAIN bonfires; again, we actually know very little about Druid rituals.

In later Irish mythology the eating of cats' flesh was one method of prognostication. In a Scottish Gaelic traditional rite called *taghairm*, a live cat is roasted slowly on a spit over a fire in the belief that its screams will call its feline companions, who will part with supernatural knowledge to save their companion. In addition, the throwing of cats into a BONFIRE was a folk custom of one or two towns in France, although this was performed on St. John's Eve (or MIDSUMMER'S EVE) in June and on the first Sunday in Lent, not on Halloween (as is sometimes mistakenly believed). The custom was abolished by King Louis XIV in 1648, though it continued in the provinces until as late as 1796.

While cats were usually believed to function as witches' familiars, one folklore belief was that witches turned tabby-cats into coal-black steeds to ride on Halloween (in Scotland, families often locked their cats away on Halloween in order to prevent them from being thusly used); however, a cat seen on Halloween might also be the witch herself transformed. The bone of a black cat could be prepared as an invisibility charm; the blood of a black cat could be used to heal a wound; or the liver of a black cat could be made into a powerful love potion. In American witch folklore, one can become a witch by boiling a live black cat, taking the bones to a spring and washing them there until the DEVIL appears; the bone being washed when the devil is first seen will be the witch's "lucky bone," to be carried with her always.

Cats could control WEATHER; ships often had cats onboard believing that no storm could wreck the ship as long as they had a cat. Conversely, a cat could be used to create a storm at sea, by fastening one to a human body part, then throwing the combination into the sea. The most famous case of this occurred during the reign of James VI of Scotland, later James I of England (and target of the Gunpowder Plot, which gave birth to the celebration of GUY FAWKES DAY). James had chosen Dano-Norwegian princess Anne to be his bride, and witches of both Norway and Scotland disapproved of the match. When the bride and fleet set sail from Norway for Scotland, witches caused a charmed cat with a human leg attached to it to be thrown into the sea. The resulting tempests were so severe that the fleet had to turn back, and in his impatience King James decided to set sail for Norway. This time witches tossed into the sea a cat with a dead man's knucklebone tied to all four paws. To make certain that the King did not reach his destination, the devil arranged a meeting with witches from both countries on the sea on Halloween night, when the King's fleet

Vintage black cat wall decoration

would be halfway across the North Sea. Sorceresses set out from both coasts in SIEVES and met the devil at the midpoint, where they also encountered a ship named *Grace of God*. They boarded her, feasted on her stores, then whipped up a storm that foundered the ship and drowned all aboard, so there would be no survivors to confirm the story. After sinking the *Grace of God*, more than a hundred witches sailed back to Scotland and held a great revel at the church in North Berwick where, after opening the lock with a witch candle, they danced around the pulpit, and rifled graves and vaults. However, James's piety overcame the devil's charms and he reached Norway safely; upon his return, the witches were caught and forced into confessions before being executed.

One traditional Scottish tale clearly sets up an association between cats and Halloween: "Twelve Great Black Cats and the Red One" tells the story of Murdo MacTaggart, who ignores warnings and tries to go fishing on All Hallowmass Eve. A great storm arises, and he takes shelter in a small hut on the shore. Twelve great black cats enter, led by a red one, and sing a dirge to Murdo, then demand payment. He spots a sheep belonging to the local laird nearby, and offers that. They take it, but return before Murdo can escape, and sing another dirge. This time he offers a cow, and once again they eat it and return. After the third dirge, Murdo spots the laird's dog, and sends the cats after it. They chase the dog, and Murdo escapes into a nearby forest, but when he hears the cats returning after failing to catch the dog he panics and climbs the highest tree he can find. The red cat spots him, and sends three of his black fellows up, but Murdo takes his knife and slays them. The red leader calls the remaining cats together, and they begin to chew at the roots of the tree in an effort to knock it over. Murdo panics and calls for help; fortunately there's a nearby church where the priest is gathered with the townspeople. They hear Murdo and run into the forest to help, arriving just as the tree is

knocked over. The priest confronts the cats, sprinkling them with holy water; the black cats disappear, and the red cat reveals himself to be "Auld Clootie" (the devil). When Murdo, the priest and the others investigate the black cats, they find nothing but empty cat skins, and Murdo resolves to never again go fishing on All Hallowmass Eve.

Cats are also the objects of SUPERSTITIONS—many of which are Halloween-specific—apart from witches: For example, if a cat sits quietly beside you on Halloween night, you will enjoy a peaceful life. If a cat rubs against you, it's good luck; it's even better if the cat jumps into your lap. If a cat yawns near you on Halloween, be alert and do not let opportunity slip away. If a cat runs from you, you have a secret that will be revealed in seven days.

Cats also starred in one Halloween GAME called "Meow, Meow": Players sat in a ring, and were asked to raise their hands when the ringleader called out something a cat could do. If they raised their hands at something a cat could not do, they left the ring.

A cat is the eponymous character in one of the most popular Halloween stories of all time: Edgar Allan Poe's "The Black Cat," which tells the gruesome tale of a murderer whose plan to hide his wife's body behind a false wall in the cellar is foiled by his feline.

In recent years there has been some concern over the safety of black cats on Halloween, when they're thought to be in danger of becoming sacrificial victims in some pagan or Satanic cult ritual. Many animal shelters and adoption agencies suspend black cat adoptions around Halloween.

Halloween COLLECTIBLES expert PAMELA APKARIAN-RUSSELL believes that black cats are the most sought-after items, even more so than JACK-O'-LANTERNS; for example, a 2006 auction of a candy container depicting a witch riding a large black cat fetched $8,250.

Cauldron—The word "cauldron" is derived from the Latin *caldarium*, meaning "hot-bath." Cauldrons are Halloween symbols usually displayed with WITCHES, who stand over them preparing their odious brews.

The special significance of cauldrons probably dates back to the CELTS, for whom cauldrons figured prominently in everyday life, mythology and artwork; the Celts also used cauldrons in ritual feasting and even in burial practices. Perhaps the single most famous Celtic artifact is the Gunderstrup cauldron, found in Denmark and probably made in the first or second century B.C. from panels of silver. The cauldron's beautifully-sculpted side panels show scenes of Celtic life and deities.

In the lore of the Celtic otherworld, magical cauldrons could not only protect warriors, but could even resurrect them, or provide endless food. In one tale, FINN MAC-CUMAL of the Fianna sends the Lad of the Skins to the King of the Floods, to take the great cauldron that is never without meat, and return with it. Through magic and wile

Ratchet noisemaker showing a jack-o'-lantern used as a witches' cauldron

the Lad succeeds, but Finn hears a magical voice telling him to return the cauldron. Finn and the Lad attempt to return the cauldron, but the King of the Floods raises his army on their approach. The Lad destroys the army, and they return home with the cauldron, but on the way the Lad is attacked by an old enemy. A shapeshifting battle ensues, and finally both the Lad and his foe die while in the form of birds. The Lad's wife raises him, then they take the Lad's final wages from Finn and leave.

In another Celtic legend, the hero Mac Cecht even uses a cauldron as a weapon, when he uses one to slay a band of outlaws.

Cauldrons also figure in later British tales: For example, in the old Welsh poem "The Spoils of Annwn," Arthur visits the Otherworld to try to obtain the magic cauldron of regeneration (which brings the dead back to life). It's possible that a panel on the Gunderstrup cauldron may depict this cauldron, since one scene shows a large god-like figuring lowering a smaller human figure into a pot or cauldron. The cauldron may even have been eventually transmuted into the Holy Grail.

Cauldrons also figure in modern-day WICCA rituals, in FORTUNE-TELLING games (a popular event at parties of the 1930s was to have a host dress as a witch, and pull the guests' fortunes from a cauldron), and in contemporary decorating (plastic cauldrons are used in displays or as candy holders for TRICK OR TREAT).

Cavalcade— From the Latin *caballicare* ("to ride on horseback"), "cavalcade" originally referred only to processions on horseback. In certain areas of Scotland, ALL SAINTS' DAY was celebrated with a cavalcade: The inhabitants of Hirt (St. Kilda) conducted an Anniversary Cavalcade of All Saints, which included a feast and a procession in which HORSES were ridden using only a straw rope for harness.

Ceiling— An American FORTUNE-TELLING belief states that if a girl looks upon her ceiling in the dark of her bedroom before falling asleep on Halloween, she will see the face of her future husband.

Celebrations— Despite its reputation in many parts of the world as a somber or placid day, ALL SAINTS' DAY and Halloween also have a history of large-scale celebrations as old as the holidays themselves.

SAMHAIN was celebrated with a great fair at Tara, which lasted for several days and included races, contests, markets and feasting. Fairs were once popular at Halloween time, just as CARNIVALS are today. For example, a great fair was recorded at Chateaurenard, near Avignon; the fair was used to open All Saints' Day, and was one of three special feasts celebrated there throughout the year. HALLOW-FAIR is still an entry in the *Oxford English Dictionary*, indicating the great popularity of fairs at Halloween; Hallowmas Fair in Edinburgh was an early celebration, recorded in the Edinburgh Charters in 1507 (it's still held today, and the traditional Hallowfair gingerbread is still sold there). ALL SOULS' DAY also had its own celebrations, often called SOUL-MASS hirings, since farmers hired their help for the next season there.

Halloween has been celebrated in America with large-scale celebrations since the beginning of the twentieth century; these events were often organized by townships or cities. Although these celebrations were often organized originally to provide an alternative to PRANKING, they now serve more to promote an area and to provide an outlet for local retailers, since they usually feature food and merchandise vendors.

Contemporary Halloween celebrations owe a large debt to GAY CULTURE, which has been mainly responsible for creating the three largest: The Greenwich Village PARADE (which boasts over two million participants and spectators, and is broadcast live internationally); the 10-day "Fantasy Fest" in Key West, Florida; and Halloween night in West Hollywood, California (which calls itself America's largest outdoor Halloween cele-

bration, and features live entertainment, COSTUME contests, and a highly-charged party atmosphere).

Many Halloween celebrations emphasize charity events. Halloween in New Orleans has become a large benefit celebration, with at least three nights of masquerades, balls, and parties (as well as the unorganized but large-scale Halloween night activities on the streets of the French Quarter). In the past, New Orleans Halloweens have raised over $2 million for charities in a single season.

ANOKA, Minnesota, calls itself "the Halloween capital of the World," a title officially sanctioned by Congress. It dates back to 1920, and features three parades, costume contests and more. However, the unofficial American Halloween capital must certainly be Salem, Massachusetts. In addition to being a destination point for practitioners of WICCA and other NEO-PAGANS, Salem also features 24 days of Haunted Happenings, including Costume Balls, walking tours and costume contests.

Anaheim, California, started a unique Halloween celebration in 1923: a window decorating contest among local businesses (window painting contests may have originally been instituted as an alternative to having the windows soaped or waxed on Halloween). The city also hosts a parade (because Anaheim is home to Disneyland, parades since the late 1950s have included Disney-themed floats) and a Halloween costume pancake breakfast.

Celebrations may also include or center on HALLOWEEN ATTRACTIONS such as PUMPKIN PATCHES, CORN MAZES, or HAUNTED HOUSES. Similar to haunted houses are TRAILS OF TERROR. Trails of terror have a history dating back 70 years, and a number of communities across the U.S. still host these popular outdoor activities. There are also PUMPKIN festivals held throughout both Canada and the United States.

The favored spots for children's Halloween celebrations over the last few years have been ZOOS; many zoos throughout

North America offer a "Boo at the Zoo" event, and the Louisville Zoo claims to host "The World's Largest Halloween Party," catering to costumed children and drawing around 90,000 guests.

The largest Canadian Halloween celebration formerly took place in Halifax, Nova Scotia, and was known as "Mardi Gras." Started in 1981, by 1984 the event attracted 15,000, with sections of streets blocked off; events include costume contests, dancing, and food and drink. By 1987, Halifax's "Mardi Gras" drew 40,000, but numbers diminished after police tried to clamp down on drunkenness. The Mardi Gras was ended in 1995, although some local merchants have tried to resurrect it.

Although Irish and Scottish BONFIRE and FIREWORKS celebrations have sometimes been sponsored by civic authorities as well, most European Halloween celebrations are considerably smaller than their American counterparts. In Ireland, Derry hosts what is known as "Ireland's first and number one Halloween Carnival"; in addition to "Ghost Tours of Haunted Derry," on October 31st the city hosts a gigantic free street party. The BBC wryly noted about Derry's street carnival that "people out of costume [are] considered abnormal."

There are only a few large-scale Halloween celebrations in continental Europe, and they're far smaller than their American brethren. The Frankenstein Festival in Germany purports to be the largest European celebration, and is held during the last three weekends at the site of Castle Frankenstein (an American group called "Tours of Terror" began hosting Halloween trips to "Dracula's castle" in Romania in 1998). The town of Retz, Austria, holds an annual Halloween festival (*Kürbisfest*), complete with pumpkins and a *Halloween-Umzug* ("Halloween PAGEANT"); in fact, the area around Retz is now known for its annual pumpkin harvest.

Celebrations can occasionally turn ugly: One of the earliest examples dates back to 1900, when University of Toronto students held their annual informal parade (a practice since 1884); after receiving complaints of mild vandalism and rowdy behavior, police restricted the students to campus. Boulder, Colorado's Halloween Mall Crawl was popular until 1989, when riots led to vandalism, drunkenness, fighting, and concerns over public safety. Some stores began to board up their doors and windows; by 1993 police succeeded in essentially ending the event that once drew nearly 40,000. San Francisco's annual Castro Street revel turned into a riot in 1994, when anti-gay protesters tried to interrupt the festivities; police detained nearly a hundred people and confiscated several loaded guns.

Celts— A number of barbarian tribes organized under the name *Celtae* (or the Greek form *Keltoi*), and spread across Europe and the British Isles; the Irish Celts gave history SAMHAIN, the forerunner of the modern version of Halloween. We know surprisingly little about the Celts, since most of their history and lore was transmitted orally, as opposed to being written down; and since it has only been within the last four decades or so that serious archaeological evidence of Celtic culture has been unearthed. Greek and Roman historians (including Caesar) recorded some observations of the Celts, but their observations are often colored by their perceptions of the Celts as both foes and pagans. Most of what we know of Celtic CELEBRATIONS and mythology comes from the Irish sagas, which were first set to paper by Christian monks, mainly from the ninth to the twelfth centuries.

Our understanding of Celtic history is further obfuscated by the unfortunate tendency of historians of the past to romanticize the Celts. When the DRUIDS were first rediscovered from classical sources, the philosophies then current in Britain had developed the ideal of the "noble savage" and the concept of "natural religion," both of which played a large role in the rise of the antiquarians' fascination with the Druids, megalithic monuments and the origins of the British people. The "Age of Enlightenment" had seen the rise of scientific thinking, but following it came the rise of Romanticism and many fringe areas of speculation. British and Anglo-Irish antiquarians such as William Stukeley, John Toland and Edward Davies, to name a few, started publishing a great deal of this sort of work. In their fervor, they even sometimes confused Celtic traditions with those of other pre–Christian peoples; for example, the popular misconception that Samhain was the name of a Celtic "lord of death" may have confused the name of the Celts' New Years' celebration with the name of an ancient Hindu deity, Samana.

The Greeks thought the Celts were one of the four great Barbarian peoples of the world (along with the Scythians, the Persians and the Libyans). Evidence of Celt warriors has been found as far south as Egypt; they can be traced clearly from about 450 B.C. on. The Romans frequently fought the *Galli*, or the Gauls, who were a Celtic people. After they suffered a devastating defeat at Delphi in 279 B.C., the Celts began to move north through Europe, leaving behind a few scattered tribes (including the Galatians in Northern Phrygia). By 58 B.C. the Romans had conquered Gaul, leaving Britain as the final outpost of Celtic power.

There may be traces of the Celts in northeastern Scotland as early as 600 B.C. (and mythology records the Celts in Ireland as early as 939 B.C.), but most historians agree that it wasn't until about 250 B.C. that Celtic settlers came from France to the east and south coasts of Britain, spreading west and south. The Celtic tribes brought with them their famed two-wheeled war chariots, their art style, and possibly the Druids. In 55 B.C. Caesar invaded Britain; in A.D. 43 Claudius began the conquest of Britain.

The history of Celtic tribes in Ireland is difficult to trace. They spoke a different dialect of the Celtish language, probably having first arrived around the sixth century B.C. Ireland remained unconquered by Rome, al-though the later Christian church modified and absorbed pagan beliefs and lore.

Celtic culture was divided into castes, mainly the warriors, the Druids, and the fili (who served as bards and seers). Celtic religion featured a pantheon of gods and created a rich and complex mythology. Two of the chief gods were the Dagda, a male deity whose name means "the good" or "the all-competent," and who served as protector of his tribe, controlling warfare and wisdom; and the Morrigan, sometimes known as "the Queen of Demons," who is both fertile and destructive. The coming together of the Dagda and the Morrigan on the night of the festival of Samhain ensured the continuing prosperity of the tribe and the fertility of the crops and animals in the coming year.

Cemeteries *see* **Graveyards**

Chalking—One old Halloween PRANKING practice was to chalk the backs of passersby, shout "Halloween!" and then run off. Chalking was popular in parts of England, especially at Diss, Norfolk. The custom may have derived from an earlier holiday called "Chalk-back Day," which was held on the Thursday before the fair day (the third Friday in September); at this event backs were chalked essentially in honor of the fall equinox. Sometimes a worn bag of flour was used in place of chalk.

Champ (also pandy)—Popular Irish Halloween FOOD similar to COLCANNON, made of mashed potatoes with milk, butter and LEEKS, sometimes prepared with FORTUNE-TELLING tokens (a thimble, a ring, and a coin). In the old days, the first two plates of champ were placed on top of the farm gate-pier.

In Scotland the dish was called "champit tatties," and was usually served at the end of a Halloween party, with tokens embedded.

Changelings—One Irish belief was that FAIRIES occasionally kidnapped human children and replaced them with a fairy child; this was often performed on Halloween. A

This 1917 postcard shows pranksters engaged in chalking

changeling could be forced to reveal itself by boiling eggshells in its presence (boiling eggshells would cause the imp to exclaim that in all his centuries of life he'd never seen the like, thus revealing himself).

Chestnuts— On Halloween, "chestnutting" was once a popular FORTUNE-TELLING and PARTY activity: Whoever found the first burr would be the first to marry; if the burr opened easily, the love would not last, but if it was difficult to open the love would last. *See also* NUTS.

Chickens— In some parts of Britain, WITCHES were supposedly unable to go near black chicken feathers, so on Halloween it was customary to kill a black chicken and hang it on the door to the chicken house; likewise, its feathers might be tied elsewhere (for example, to a dog's collar) for protection.

One MARTINMAS custom sounds suspiciously like a SAMHAIN or All Hallows Eve practice: Cockerel's blood was sprinkled on the interior and exterior corners of houses as protection against supernatural forces.

Chimney— A chimney figures in one Halloween FORTUNE-TELLING practice: The names of eligible or likely matches were written directly on the chimney-piece, and unmarried young men were led blindfolded to the list, where the name they touched would be that of their future wife.

China *see* **Ch'ing Ming; Yue Laan**

Ch'ing Ming (also Qing Ming)— Chinese festival of the dead with some similarities to ALL SAINTS' DAY and ALL SOULS' DAY.

Ch'ing Ming is the first of two Chinese festivals of the dead held each year (the other is YUE LAAN). Ch'ing Ming (which means "clear and bright") begins exactly 105 days after the winter solstice, which usually corresponds to April 5 or 6 in the Western calendar. Three days before Ch'ing Ming, all fires are allowed to go out, and no new fires are started for three days in honor of a heroic act from the Chou Dynasty (the day is sometimes called "Cold Food Day," since there were no fires with which to cook). Early on the day of the Festival, people visit their ancestors' graves, which are decorated with WILLOW sprigs, paper money and offerings of food. After feasts at the burial grounds, people return home and decorate their houses with willow branches. Ch'ing Ming is also a celebration of spring, and so it is customary to plant trees on this day.

In modern China (where anything remotely superstitious is held in disdain), the day has come to be one mainly for patriotic CELEBRATIONS, although in the more rural areas it's still celebrated with traditional visits to GRAVEYARDS and planting of trees.

Christmas— The most popular holiday in Western culture, celebrating the birth of Jesus Christ on December 25. Surprisingly, Christmas shares a number of factors in common with Halloween: Both were regarded in the past as favorable times for FORTUNE-TELLING; both have involved GUISING customs, RHYMING and MUMMING; both involve family gatherings and feasts; both have mixed pagan and Christian influence (Christmas was originally the pagan holiday of Yule, "the birthday of the Unconquered Sun"); and in the twentieth and twenty-first centuries both have been heavily marketed and generated billions of dollars in retail sales. Unlike Christmas, however, which emphasizes and reaffirms traditional values of family and gender, Halloween (in America especially) has become a night in which social norms are often inverted (children have power, cross-dressing is accepted, etc.) In fact, Halloween has even been referred to as "the Irish Christmas."

Like Halloween, Christmas Eve was also a night favorable to learning about one's future spouse. In fact certain practices, such as sowing HEMP SEED, could be performed on either Halloween or Christmas Eve.

Churches— Churches figure in Halloween history not only as places of worship on ALL SAINTS' DAY and ALL SOULS' DAY, but also as much-frequented sites in FORTUNE-TELLING customs.

In Wales, women used to congregate in parish churches on the night of Halloween and read their fates from the flames of the CANDLES they held; they also heard the names or saw the COFFINS of the parishioners who would die within the year. Another Welsh practice directed the curious to sit in the church porch at MIDNIGHT on Halloween in order to witness a procession of all those who would die in the parish during the coming year, all dressed in their finest clothes. Some versions of the custom state that the watcher must arrive promptly at 11 P.M., and be prepared to wait two hours; to fall asleep during this time means the watcher will die soon. If the watcher saw an apparition who turned back from the procession, that person would suffer a severe illness but would recover. In

Lincolnshire, all members of the parish would be expected to enter the church, but those who were destined to die wouldn't leave (and a couple who exited arm-in-arm would be married soon). Also in Lincolnshire, some participants reported feeling compelled to conduct a watch every year, while in other areas the watch must be conducted for three years before one would actually see the procession. In another variation of this custom, it was necessary to run around the parish church THREE times and then peep through the keyhole of the door to view the ghostly procession. In some of the Northern Counties of England, it was believed that the parish clerk would lead the spectral parade through the churchyard. These "church porch" customs were actually most common on St. Mark's Eve (April 24), and also on MIDSUMMER'S EVE.

A Welsh story concerns a man who was working in the church around the end of October; on the 31st, the workers received a bonus, and the worker in question promptly spent his on drink. When he returned to the job unfit to work, he fell asleep in a pew, and was forgotten; he awoke at midnight to the sound of a great commotion. Although he tried to crawl from the aisle, some unseen force impelled him back into his seat, and in the darkness he heard a great procession. He glimpsed the shadowy face and form of a neighbor, and exclaimed, "Lord, have mercy upon my soul," after which he felt the strength to move. Even though the doors had been locked by the sexton, they were now wide open, and the worker fled; the next morning the doors were once again locked. The neighbor the worker had glimpsed died within the year.

Sometimes the church porch watch was used as a marriage divination; in this case, the watcher must lay a flower on the porch at exactly 11 P.M., leave the church, and return at midnight. The watcher would see a bridal procession (the number of bridesmaids would indicate how many months would pass before the wedding took place), nothing at all (the watcher would not be married that year), or a funeral procession (the watcher would remain unmarried until death). A Welsh story tells of three young girls in Glamorganshire who went to the church on Halloween and peeped through the keyhole of the church door. One girl saw nothing; the second saw her grandfather; but the third saw herself as an aged bride, while the bridegroom fell at the foot of the altar steps. The third girl remained unmarried until she was 45, at which point she accepted a proposal of marriage. The marriage ceremony was conducted successfully, but as the bridal party turned to leave the bridegroom suddenly fell dead at the foot of the altar steps.

In Herefordshire, they tell of a particularly frightening version of the church-porch custom: On Allhallows Eve at midnight, one would look through the church windows and see an unearthly light inside, and the pulpit would be occupied by Satan in a monkhabit. His sermon will include the names of those to die in the coming year. One French story about this custom involves a man named Jack, who heard his own name and promptly died of fright.

Cinderella— Popular Grimm's fairy tale with a connection to Halloween because of the variant of the tale involving Cinderella's coach being fashioned from a PUMPKIN. References to Cinderella appear in children's RECITATIONS, POSTCARDS, etc.

Clairvoyance *see* **Second Sight**

Clothes— In an American SUPERSTITION, it was bad luck to leave clothes hanging on the line on Halloween night. In a custom from the neighborhood of Market Drayton in Shropshire, a group of young women would gather, and each would hang a shift over the back of a chair placed before the fire. At MIDNIGHT the girls recited a charm which lasted exactly ten minutes, and then waited to see whose shift would move first, since that predicted the first girl to marry.

There were also FORTUNE-TELLING methods involving SHIRTS and SHOES.

Clover— A FORTUNE-TELLING practice from Cambridgeshire, Norfolk, and Suffolk, practiced until the 19th century, involved finding a two-leafed clover on Halloween and placing it in your SHOES as per these lines:

> "Put it in your right shoe;
> The first young man you meet,
> In field, street, or lane,
> You'll have him or one of his name."

Clowns— Clowns have been popular Halloween figures ever since COSTUMING began to figure prominently in the holiday's celebrations. Clowns—principally the "whiteface" comic figures typically found in circuses—bear some resemblance to MUMMING performers, as well as the HOBO (also a promi-

A youthful clown celebrates in this 1920 postcard

nent Halloween figure). In the early part of the 20th century, clown costumes were home-made, featuring a jumpsuit with pom-poms, a comic hat, and colorful or oversized shoes; the hobo-style clown might, however, be garbed with ragged clothing and suspenders. A made-up face, with white grease-paint, red nose, and exaggerated features, may or may not have been part of the costume. By the 1950s, as Halloween costuming became commercialized, popular television clowns including Bozo and Clarabell (from the *Howdy Doody* children's show) became bestsellers for companies like Ben Cooper and Peter Puppet Playthings, Inc.

Clowns also provided the theme for Halloween PARTIES (especially those designed to resemble CARNIVALS) and performances, like the "Witch and Clown Drill" (with girls dressed as WITCHES and boys as clowns) listed in a 1927 Halloween booklet.

Coel Coeth (also Coel Certh)—Welsh name for the BONFIRE each family built in the most prominent place near the house on November Eve. Part of this tradition involved each member of the family throwing a marked white stone into the fire, after which prayers were said around the FIRE; in the morning any stones that could not be found indicated that person would die within the year.

An American version of this belief suggests simply that the stones be placed in an "outdoor fireplace."

Coffins—Coffins figure in many Halloween FORTUNE-TELLING customs. Usually, as in the popular custom of sowing HEMP SEED, to see a coffin means the viewer will die before marriage; in other customs, such as one involving IVY, to see a spot in the shape of a coffin means someone in the household will die within the year. To see a coffin dripping blood meant the viewer would die in a violent accident.

Coins—In parts of Scotland it was customary to throw a silver coin through the front door of the house on the morning of November 1st. The coin had to remain hidden where it had fallen to bring luck in money matters.

In Ireland, coins (rather than CANDY) are the preferred treat offered to children who engage in Halloween RHYMING. Coins are also the prize in many Halloween GAMES.

Colcannon (also callcannon, calcannon)—Traditional Irish and Scottish Halloween FOOD made of potatoes, onions and CABBAGE, often with a ring for FORTUNE-TELLING hidden inside. The first part of the name is taken from "cole," meaning cabbage; although the rest of the derivation is uncertain, legend has it that the ingredients were once pounded with a cannonball, hence the last part of the name. Colcannon was originally known as *coimhbleidhe*, and was so popular on Halloween that the holiday was sometimes referred to as CALCANNON NIGHT.

One sinister fortune-telling ritual involved a girl placing a bit of colcannon onto her stocking and placing it under her pillow on Halloween night; she then invoked the name of the DEVIL, and during sleep she would dream of her future husband.

Colean—House in Scotland; nearby sits the famed Cove of Colean, which (like CASSILIS DOWNANS) is supposedly a haunt for FAIRIES, and is named as such in ROBERT BURNS's poem "Hallowe'en":

> Or for Colean the route is ta'en,
> Beneath the moon's pale beams;
> There, up the *cove*, to stray an' rove
> Amang the rocks and streams
> To sport that night.

Collectibles—In America, Halloween is often considered the single most collectible holiday, although collecting Halloween memorabilia is still a fairly recent pastime. Collectors began to organize in 1984, when the first issue of PAMELA APKARIAN-RUSSELL's *Trick or Treat Trader* magazine appeared, and by the publication of the first book on the subject (STUART SCHNEIDER's *Halloween in America*) in 1995, Halloween collecting was well-established.

Unlike CHRISTMAS, Halloween decorations were often thrown away each year, making them scarce and sought by contemporary collectors. The earliest items are German glass CANDY holders, circa 1905, which can fetch over $500, especially for those which retain their original paint. Other German-made items are equally rare, including composition and pressed paperboard JACK-O'-LANTERNS, NOISEMAKERS, and die cut paper decorations; during World War I, imports from Germany ceased and American companies took over manufacture of Halloween items. COSTUMES are also popular, since they can represent not only nostalgia for the holiday, but also for a beloved character from movies, television, comics, music or even politics. Dennison, a stationery and party goods manufacturer, created yearly BOGIE BOOKS which gave suggestions for Halloween parties and costumes, and which are now among the most highly-prized Halloween collectibles.

Although Dennison's paper decorations were popular, the most collected paper goods come from the Beistle company, established by Martin Luther Beistle in 1900. Beistle produced cardboard lanterns, table decorations and wall hangings, often with superior graphics and embossing.

The 1950s also saw the introduction of plastics, and hard plastic toys became increasingly popular. E. Rosen/Rosbro Plastics produced plastic Halloween TOYS and candy containers from 1946 to the mid–1960s; today its wheeled toys (such as a CAT pushing a PUMPKIN) are very sought after and can easily fetch hundreds of dollars. In a curious example of holiday crossover, Rosbro occasionally took a toy produced for another holiday — such as a Christmas snowman — and transformed it into a Halloween toy simply by molding it in orange and black plastic COLORS. Union Products and Rosbro both produced plastic, battery-operated jack-o'-lanterns, designed for children to carry during TRICK OR TREAT. Pez candy dispensers, "nodders" and Hallmark items are also popular Halloween collectibles.

Collectible *Star Wars* Halloween costume

Mexican DAYS OF THE DEAD items are also collected, and often featured in galleries throughout the Southwest.

In 2005, Apkarian-Russell opened the CASTLE HALLOWEEN MUSEUM, which houses approximately 35,000 Halloween and related collectibles.

Colors—Orange and black are traditional Halloween colors in America (although not in other countries), and have been accepted as such since around the 1920s. In her 1919 *Book of Hallowe'en*, RUTH EDNA KELLEY states that "the prevailing colors are yellow and black"; however, the Dennison's BOGIE BOOK released that same year begins with a section titled "Hallowe'en Colors" and notes: "Orange is a bright and glowing color, well suited to decorating for Hallowe'en. Black and white give sharp contrast and gray has a softening influence." Orange suggests the colors of the HARVEST—PUMPKINS, CORN, squash and gourds—while black expresses the holiday's somber side, being the color (in Western culture) of mourning and death.

In some areas of Europe, RED clothing is likelier to be worn on Halloween, since red is thought to be a color which protects against malicious FAIRIES.

Colum Kill—Another name for St. Columba, an Irish priest who in the sixth century had been ordered to convert the Picts in Ireland. St. Columba successfully converted pagans throughout both Ireland and Scotland before he founded a monastery on Iona island off the coast of Scotland. His name was invoked in an Irish GUISING custom in the seventeenth century, when Irish peasants went begging house-to-house asking for money to buy luxuries for a feast and demanding in the name of Colum (or Columb) Kill, or St. Columba, that fatted calves and black sheep be prepared for the feasting. Although St. Columba's feast day is now officially given as June 9, there is some confusion as to the date in the past; not only was there another St. Columba (the patroness of two parishes in Cornwall, England, where she was put to death by heathens) whose feast day was November 13, but the feast day has also been given as October 24. The proximity of these dates may account for finding St. Columba's name connected to the Halloween ritual; there's also the possibility that the large Halloween celebrations in Derry, Ireland, may be connected to that city's veneration of St. Columba (several Derry parks are named after Columba).

In *Statistical Account of Iona*, St. Columba is also said to have been the first on record to possess the gift of SECOND SIGHT (he supposedly predicted the victory of Aidan over the Picts and Saxons).

In his paper "Trick or Treat: Pre-texts and Contexts," Tad Tuleja suggests that Halloween begging in the name of St. Columba may be one of the three traditions which led to the American TRICK OR TREAT (the other two are SOULING and GUY FAWKES DAY begging).

Columba, St. *see* **Colum Kill**

Commerce *see* **Retailing**

Corn—Associated with Halloween because corn (which usually refers to OATS outside of America) ripens in late October. Corn husking contests were popular at nineteenth-century American Halloween PARTIES (red ears of corn could be used in divination), and shocks of corn and corn stalks still are popular party and yard decorations.

Corn (or oats) has been employed in Halloween FORTUNE-TELLING for at least four centuries, although this use probably dates back to the first millennium. One of the most popular methods directed that the fortune-seeker go to the cornfield alone on Halloween night, and THREE times go through the motions of throwing (winnowing) corn against the WIND; on the third time, an apparition of the future spouse would pass by, and the keen observer might also be able to discern something about his or her station in life. A Scottish variation (as mentioned by ROBERT BURNS in his poem "Hallowe'en") involved going to the barn and taking both doors off their hinges, for there was the danger that mischievous spirits might shut the doors and cause harm; then the wecht, or instrument used for winnowing the corn, was taken and used to go through all the motions of letting down corn against the wind. This was repeated three times; and on the third time an apparition would pass through the barn, in at the windy door, and out at the other; its appearance would mark its employment or station in life. In another version of corn winnowing, the ritual had to be performed in the name of the DEVIL. In his novel of sixteenth-century Scotland, *The Monastery*, SIR WALTER SCOTT mentions Halloween divinations, and one character describes the results of corn winnowing: "'I had not winnowed the last weight clean out, and the moon was shining bright upon the floor, when in stalked the presence of my dear Simon Glendinning, that is now happy. I never saw him plainer in my life than I did that moment...'"

A simpler custom suggested hiding in the cornfield on Halloween night in order to hear what would transpire over the coming year.

In one divination, a spoonful of corn kernels (or sometimes beans or rice kernels) was emptied to a counting rhyme which would determine the profession of one's future spouse. In an American fortune-telling game, each guest tried to empty three tablespoons full of corn kernels into a quart milk bottle by watching in a MIRROR. The player with the highest score (number of kernels in the bottle) will be the one who at the age of 50 will have amassed the fortune in thousands of dollars as indicated by the number of kernels of corn.

One Irish custom was to take the last sheaf of corn at HARVEST time (usually just before Halloween) and hang it in the kitchen; then at CHRISTMAS it was taken down and spread out along a nearby hedge to feed the birds, a practice which brought good luck. The last sheaf was sometimes called "the corn maiden" (possibly derived from the old word "mod-dun," meaning an elevated spot, where the end of harvest was announced), the "CORN DOLLY," or "the kern baby," although in some areas it was the "CAILLEACH," or old woman. In his book on *Festivals, Ceremonies, and Customs*, Sir Benjamin Stone records a Northumberland tradition, in which the men "got the kern" at the close of reaping and dressed it in "a white frock with colored ribbons and crowned with corn ears." This "kern baby" was then carried to the barn on a pole, and was later placed in the church for harvest festivities.

In the Scottish custom known as "crying the kirn" (it has been suggested that "kirn" is actually derived not from corn but from "cairn," where Halloweens were supposedly once celebrated as SAMHAIN), on the last day of harvest, when the last handful of grain was secured, the reapers proceeded to the nearest high point and loudly proclaimed that harvest was done. Their scythes were collected, then thrown into the air; the direction of the falling hook was supposed to indicate the direction in which the reaper to whom it belonged was to go to seek work next harvest. If a hook broke in falling, an early death was predicted for its unfortunate owner; when the point sank into the soil, the owner would marry soon.

One harvest tradition involved winning the Cailleach, or last sheaf of corn. This was left standing but tied, and workers took turns throwing their sickles at it, to see who could cut it down (later, workers were blindfolded and swung their scythes to see who could "snig" the Cailleach). It was then taken in as a centerpiece at the harvest feast, and tied to the ceiling in the kitchen to bring good luck for the next year. It might also be hung up over the door, and used in divination: The

This 1909 postcard by Bernhardt Wall shows the importance of corn and harvest on Halloween.

first one through the door after the Cailleach was hung would be a future spouse.

Another corn harvest tradition involved biting off a piece of the cart that brought home the last load of corn, and then holding that piece in the mouth while going to listen at a NEIGHBOR's window; the first name heard would be that of the future spouse (the last load of grain communicated power to the cart).

It was once popular to weave various Halloween items from corn, straw and or rushes, such as hats, PARSHELLS, or rush ladders. The STRAWBOYS actually made costumes from straw.

In Scotland, it was noted that every animal in the barn received a whole "Hallow" (or sheaf of corn) for breakfast on Halloween, in addition to the usual amount of food; in the household the day was preserved as a "fanteen," or fast, until the evening.

CORN MAZES are now popular HALLOWEEN ATTRACTIONS throughout the United States and Great Britain.

Corn Dolly— A HARVEST custom with certain specific Halloween variants. Typically a corn dolly was a semi-human figure made

from the last sheaves of CORN (or OATS). In Scotland, when the last corn was cut after HALLOWMAS, the female figure made out of it was sometimes called the Carlin or Carline (the Old Woman), or the CAILLEACH. But if the corn was cut before Hallowmas, it was called the Maiden; if cut after sunset, it was called the Witch, and brought bad luck.

In his classic *The Golden Bough*, SIR JAMES FRAZER discusses corn dollies extensively, seeing them as evidence of ancient fertility rituals.

Corn Mazes— A corn maze is a type of HALLOWEEN ATTRACTION, although corn mazes aren't always exclusively tied to Halloween — they may simply be a form of "agri-tourism" or "agri-tainment," or a way of turning part or all of a farm into a tourist destination. Corn mazes are similar to the hedge mazes found in European gardens for centuries; however, the first modern corn maze, "The Amazing Maize Maze," was designed in the 1990s by maze designer Adrian Fisher (with Don Frantz). Corn mazes have become increasingly widespread in the U.S. over the last 20 years, as companies such as Fisher's firm in Britain, The MAiZE (in Utah) and Corn Mazes America have sprung up, offering farmers and corn field owners complete packages, which include design, cutting (using GPS technology), and operation of seasonal corn mazes. The crops used in corn mazes are usually a hybrid chosen specifically for this purpose, and they're planted later than corn grown for harvest, so they won't ripen until Halloween. Corn mazes can generate spectacular profits for farmers, returning nearly 200 times the amount of profit to be made from simply harvesting the corn, and many farmers attribute corn mazes to saving

The author checks a map in the corn maze at Forneris Farms in Mission Hills, California

their farms. There are now hundreds of corn mazes operating annually, with most being between 1 and 5 acres (the largest on record is Cool Patch Pumpkins in Dixon, California, with nearly 43 acres). Designs rarely feature Halloween imagery, but instead focus on either local happenings (a sports team, a state flag) or a depiction of the farm itself. Corn mazes are often combined with PUMPKIN PATCHES, Halloween face painting, HAYRIDES, and other Halloween attractions; occasionally a corn maze is also a haunted attraction, with actors and scares stationed throughout the maze. However, corn mazes are considered more "family-friendly" than haunted houses, and thus attract more children and elderly customers than haunted attractions.

Corn Meal— Figures in one American Halloween FORTUNE-TELLING practice: Corn meal is spread on the floor by the side of the bed on Halloween (or on top of a dresser) and ghosts come during the night to write the name of the future spouse in it.

Corpses— Corpses were featured in one macabre Welsh SUPERSTITION: WIND blowing over the feet of corpses on Halloween bore sighs to the houses of those who were to die within the year.

Costumes— Costuming on Halloween is an ancient tradition; although some popular historians like to say it started with the CELTS, there is virtually no proof of this. The earliest examples of Halloween costuming can be found in MUMMING, GUISING, and SOULING traditions. LORDS OF MISRULE might order masquerades, DAYS OF THE DEAD have long been celebrated in Mexico with costumed dancers, COLUM KILL beggars wore costumes, and children celebrating GUY FAWKES DAY dressed in rags. One traditional American Halloween game involved guessing the real identities of costumed partygoers. Modern Halloween CELEBRATIONS probably also owe something to the use of costumes at MARDI GRAS.

Halloween costuming in America

(where it is now most common) may have begun with a nineteenth century THANKS-GIVING practice, when children (mainly around New York) sometimes dressed in costumes and begged house-to-house. This practice (possibly along with the costumed CHRISTMAS custom of BELSNICKLING) may have led to the development of TRICK OR TREAT, the American Halloween ritual that defined Halloween for several decades in the twentieth century.

As with trick or treat, costuming for children was heavily promoted in many American cities as an alternative to destructive PRANKING. For example: Citizens and

The girl on the left wears a homemade, Disney-inspired costume (photograph circa 1930).

merchants of Danville, Illinois promoted a youngsters' costume contest beginning in 1912, complete with a parade and cash prizes. By 1916, the celebration had proven so successful that special trains were arranged on Halloween to bring thousands of young costumed celebrants to the city.

Costuming among adults caught on in the second half of the twentieth century, principally starting within GAY CULTURE, then spreading into the American mainstream. The influence of costumed comedy in the late 1970s (the Coneheads, Steve Martin's "King Tut," etc.), may have contributed to the popularity and certainly to the choice of many costumes for the next few years.

Whether for adults or for juveniles, Halloween costumes in the twentieth and twenty-first centuries have represented the pop culture of each decade: In the 1950s, television personalities, including Lucille Ball, Huckleberry Hound, Bugs Bunny, Kukla and Ollie were most popular. In the 1960s, more adult programming found its way into children's costumes, with the Addams Family, Barnabas Collins from *Dark Shadows*, and *Star Trek* all producing bestselling costumes. Rock and roll was also a part of the cultural landscape, and the Beatles and the Monkees were among the decade's most requested costumes. During the 1960s, Halloween costumes also reflected the country's political divides, with Green Berets stepping out toe-to-toe with hippies. In the 1970s and 1980s, slick character costumes prevailed, ranging from Scooby Doo to E.T. In the 1990s, one odd new trend emerged — the product as Halloween costume, with LifeSavers, Hershey Bars and McDonald's Big Macs all sharing sidewalks with Bart Simpson and the Power Puff Girls. In 2001, or, more specifically, in the wake of the devastating 9/11 terrorist attacks, far and away the most popular costumes were firemen and policemen. By the late 2000s, as schools sought to stem gang violence and protect diversity, students in some districts were prohibited from wearing anything that included a mask, a fake weapon, or that depicted a "horror character" or ethnic/gender stereotype; in one Illinois school, students were encouraged to wear costumes based on "animals and food."

Dennison started selling disposable paper costumes in 1916, and Sears, Roebuck sold its first costume in 1930. However, it wasn't until the boom in both trick or treating and the postwar economy that pre-made costumes really took off; collectors now consider the period from 1948 to the mid–1970s to represent the golden age of Halloween costumes. The prime costume manufacturers are Collegeville (now officially Collegeville-Imagineering, L.P.), which began in the early 1900s as a flag maker, but started producing costumes as early as 1920; Ben Cooper, who started in the early 1930s and licensed such popular characters as *Star Wars* and "Strawberry Shortcake"; and today's leader, Rubies Costume Company, founded in 1951 by Rubin and Tillie Beige. Early costumes were often made of flannel or cotton, but from about 1951 on costumes were made of silkscreened rayon or vinyl, and usually sold in a box which included a plastic MASK; "deluxe" costumes might also includes accessories such as wigs, mustaches, swords, etc.

By 1990, adult costuming began to overtake children's costuming. Western Costume Company in Hollywood (which usually supplies costumes to the film industry) rents approximately 4,000 costumes each Halloween, almost completely to adults. Adult costuming is not confined to Halloween PARTIES, however; studies have shown that Halloween costuming in the workplace can actually increase productivity and morale.

In the last few years it has also become popular to dress one's pet in a Halloween costume, with one in eight households costuming a pet.

Cows— In his comprehensive collection *Popular Beliefs and Superstitions: A Compendium of American Folklore*, Newbell Niles Puckett records several American beliefs regarding cows on Halloween. In one FORTUNE-TELLING ritual, a woman would sit up on Halloween night without speaking, and hang up a towel near her bedroom door, where she would also place a basin of WATER; at MIDNIGHT her future husband would come in to wash and dry his hands, and when he left the cows outside would begin "to bawl." Another (and even more whimsical) American belief is that cows talk to each other and to people on Halloween night.

In the Hebrides, a young man would dress in a cow-hide on Halloween night and carry a piece of burning hide to each household, bringing good luck to any who should inhale the fumes of the hide (at least one folklorist considered this practice to be a hold-over from ancient sacrificial customs).

Crack-Nut Eve — Variation of NUTCRACK NIGHT

The Craft *see* Wicca

Crossroads — Crossroads figure prominently in the mythology of the supernatural; for example, murderers and suicides were frequently buried at crossroads, in the hopes that their vengeful spirits would be so bewildered at their choice of paths that they wouldn't find their way home to wreak havoc. Lonely rural crossroads are particularly dangerous, and WITCHES' covens were believed to have chosen such locations for their gatherings.

A popular Scottish FORTUNE-TELLING belief involved sitting on a THREE-legged stool at the place where three crossroads met to hear at the hour of MIDNIGHT on Halloween the names of parishioners who would die during the coming year. If the listener brought gifts (or articles of clothing) and gave them to the fairy who called the names (one item for each name), the doomed would be saved.

A Welsh custom involved going to a crossroads on Halloween, where one could listen to the WIND and learn all the most important things that would happen for the next 12 months. A Welsh belief in former

times was that on All Hallows' Eve a dead soul was to be found at midnight at every crossroad and on every STILE.

In one Italian legend a man went to a crossroads at midnight on Halloween, and arrived in time to see a ghostly procession leave the cemetery and come down the road. The souls of the good tried to warn him to flee, but he didn't listen; when the horrible troop of the damned came near him, he fell dead.

Crowdie (also crowdy)–Lowland Scottish name for a dish of milk and meal, popular at Halloween, sometimes with a FORTUNE-TELLING token (a ring) hidden inside. See also FUARAG.

Crows — A Welsh SUPERSTITION is that if crows caw around the house in the afternoon of Halloween, a human or animal inhabitant of the house will soon be found dead.

Cruachan — A fairy cave of unusual size and significance, found in Connaught, known as "the hell-gate of Ireland." According to Celtic lore, the cave was unbarred on SAMHAIN Eve and a host of horrible FAIRIES, fiends and GOBLINS rushed forth, particularly a flock of copper-red birds led by a monstrous three-headed vulture, which blighted crops and killed animals by their poisonous breath.

Cuchulain — A Celtic hero of the Ulster cycle of epic tales. As with most of the CELTS' heroes, Cuchulain is involved in a number of SAMHAIN stories. On one Samhain night, Cuchulain's ship comes to the island of Rechrainn, where he finds a beautiful girl sobbing on the beach. She tells him that every year the Fomorians demand heavy tax (in an early story of the Tuatha de Danaan, the Fomorians are said to have demanded two-thirds of their milk, corn and children); this year her father the king couldn't pay, so they demanded he leave her on the beach as their tribute. When three Fomors appear, Cuchulain kills them.

Cyniver—In this Halloween FORTUNE-TELLING game, members of both sexes seek an even-leaved sprig of ash; the first of either sex to find one calls out "cyniver," and

is then answered by the first member of the opposite sex to find one. These two are thus joined in a wedlock prophecy.

Day Of Wrath *see* **Dies Irae**

Days of the Dead—In Latin American countries the first and second of November—ALL SAINTS' DAY and ALL SOULS' DAY—are known as the "Days of the Dead," or *Días de los Muertos*. In some areas these days are also known as known as *Todos Santos* ("All Saints"), *Día de los Difuntos* or *Fieles Difuntos* ("Day of the Departed" or "Faithful De-

Papier mâché Days of the Dead skeleton toy

parted"), or *Día de las Animas Benditas* ("Day of the Blessed Souls"). In some regions the evening of October 31 is the beginning of "Day of the Dead Children" (which is celebrated mainly around the family home); this is followed on November 1 by the "Day of the Dead Adults" (which is celebrated more at the graveyard), and continues to November 2. Only when November 2 happens to coincide with a Sunday is all All Souls' Day celebrated on November 3. The actual holidays are often preceded by a "week of the dead," although preparations can begin a month in advance of *Días de los Muertos*. In America, *Día de los Muertos* is usually celebrated only on November 2.

Days of the Dead combines Roman Catholicism with pre–Hispanic, mainly Aztec, celebrations. In pre-conquest Mexico, the Days of the Dead CELEBRATIONS took place as the Aztec feasts of the dead (MICCAILHUITL AND MICCAILHUITONTLI), held during the months of July and August. Conquering Spaniards tried to replace the Days with ALL SAINTS' and ALL SOULS' DAYS, but many of the surviving traditions, and the festive nature of *Días de los Muertos,* are probably pre–Columbian relics.

The contemporary celebration of Days of the Dead dates as far back as the 1740s, when a Capuchin friar, Francisco de Ajofrin, reported both the first known use in Mexico of the term "Day of the Dead," and the production and sale of figurines made from sugar paste (known as *alfeñique*). By 1766 the Royal Criminal Chamber prohibited attendance at cemeteries and also imposed a prohibition on the sale of alcoholic beverages after nine P.M., attesting to the fiesta's reputation for revelry. From the nineteenth and twentieth centuries come accounts of Mayan village celebrations of HANAL PIXAN, which is still recognized in the Yucatan and Quintana Roo areas of southeast Mexico. A nineteenth-century description by Fanny Calderón de la Barca mentions draping Catholic churches in black for Days of the Dead. A year later, in a letter from 1841, she makes the first recorded mention of sugar skulls (still one of the most popular aspects of Days of the Dead), and mentions old women manning stalls calling out "Skulls, *niñas*, skulls!" In 1858 the German-born Mexican farmer Carl Christian Sartorius published his *Mexico, Landscapes and Popular Sketches*, which included considerable description of Days of the Dead activities, especially the purchasing of new clothing and CANDLES. He also mentions young rogues who offered their services to pray for the dead, but usually did nothing but filch food and drink from the *ofrendas*, or offerings (these are usually elaborate altars to the dead). By 1971, the Days of the Dead had become so popular that the Ministry of Tourism of the State of Michoacán and the state agencies *Casa de la Cultura* and the *Casa de Artesanias* began a campaign to attract tourists to Michoacán with special emphasis on Days of the Dead celebrations. The small community of Tzintzuntzan, on the shores of Lake Pátzcuaro, received special attention because it was once the capital of the ancient Purepécha Empire. During the next two decades the influx of tourism actually began to define Tzintzuntzan's Days of the Dead celebration, with the Ministry of Tourism establishing a "Festival of Dances and *Pirekuas*" (*Pirekuas* are Purepécha songs), and outdoor dramas. By the 1990s the event had come to be known simply as *La Feria*, or "the Fair." Halloween has also made considerable inroads into Mexico's traditional Days of the Dead celebrations, often to the dismay of Mexican nationalists, who

have written against it and even painted elaborate murals (depicting a soccer player kicking a pumpkin-headed figure). In 1996, clerics in the Northern Mexican states prohibited the celebration of Halloween, declaring it to be secular and commercial, and representing a threat to the sanctity of the Days of the Dead. Nonetheless, working class Mexican boys can now be found wearing costumes and carrying plastic JACK-O'-LANTERNS, going through the streets and graveyards and begging for either their "*Jaloüín*" (a Mexican phonetic version of Halloween), or even for *mi calabaza*—"my pumpkin."

In some areas of Mexico, the Days of the Dead start on October 27, a day dedicated to the spirits of those who died without FAMILIES; they are received with bread and jugs of WATER placed outside houses. In certain villages, offerings are collected and placed in a corner of the parish church. On the next day, October 28, those who died by accident, murder or other violent means are offered food and drink, again placed outside the house (to keep away malignant spirits). On the night of October 31, dead children are received (although some areas break this down to the *los niños limbos*, or "infants in limbo"—children who died before baptism, and who return on October 30, while the souls of other children return on October 31). The child GHOSTS are gone by midday on November 1, at which time dead adults are received, beginning with whomever has passed away most recently. By the evening of November 2, the ghosts depart (sometimes led back to the family tomb by a trail of *zempasuchitl* (yellow marigold, the special flower of the dead) petals, the scent of which is thought to draw the dead spirits), and masked mummers may be needed to scare away stubborn ones. In a few areas the offerings and feasting occur on the *octava*, November 8 or 9.

The most exotic and beautiful of the Days of the Dead ceremonies (and the one most well-attended by tourists) is held in the Tarascan island village of Janitzio on Lake

Pátzcuaro, west of Mexico City. The ceremony begins on the day of November 1 with "The Vigil of the Little Angels," a ritual in which the island's children attend to the graves of deceased loved ones while their parents observe from the edges of the cemetery. On the eve of November 1, when women and children go to bed at sunset, since they will awaken at MIDNIGHT, men go about singing *alabanzas* (hymns to the dead). The young men also engage in a ritual called *Teruscan* ("reunion"), in which they pretend to "steal" various food items (with the blessing of all participants), and return to the *Guatapera* (a communal house), where the food is prepared and served to the participants. At midnight the women rise and dress themselves and their children in fiesta garments. They pack baskets of food for the OFRENDAS, or offerings. The special delicacy prepared for the ghosts here is roasted wild duck, killed several days earlier by hunting parties on the lake. At midnight on November 1, women and children climb steep paths to the hillside cemetery. Over each grave is placed an arch garlanded with *zempasuchitl* and hung with *panes de muertos* (bread of the dead); marigold petals are scattered on the family graves (Aztec tradition specified yellow for adults and white for children). Candles are lighted on each grave, and then the women and children sit all night by the graves while the men and grown boys linger on the outskirts of the cemetery, leaning against the wall singing *alabanzas* and taking sips from bottles of *pulque*. At dawn, the women open their baskets, offer the food to heaven, to the souls of the dead, and then to each other; they leave after eating.

Janitizio is also home to one of the most haunting Day of the Dead GHOST STORIES: When the Spanish conquered the Purepecha, the royal princess, Mitzita and her love Prince Itzihuapa tried to obtain a legendary treasure at the bottom of the lake with which to ransom Mitzita's father, but they were overcome by the ghostly warriors who guarded the treasure. Now, each Day of the Dead, Mitzita and Itzihuapa arise (along with the twenty spectral guards) and ascend to the island's hilltop to receive offerings.

In some villages masked *Comparsas* or mummers go house to house on the nights of October 31 and November 1, singing verses which might mock the foibles of each family they visit. It's also not uncommon to employ the services of *rezanderas*, professional prayer-makers. In Mixquic, immense cardboard skeletons guard the gates of the cemetery throughout the day, only to be joyfully burned at night. The Zapotecs in Yalalag dress in white shrouds and make their way to the graveyard wailing. The town of Huaquechula in the state of Puebla is famous for its large, beautiful shrines, decorated completely in white, and sometimes incorporating Christmas lights and garlands brought back from work trips to the United States. In the lush central states of Mexico, people of the Tenek tribe celebrate the time as XANTOLO, and celebrate with the construction of elaborate arches.

A Days of the Dead candy skull

In nearly all communities spun sugar skulls, often with children's' names written on the foreheads, are found, and are often given as gifts to friends. Rich *mole* sauce (flavored with chocolate) is cooked as a favorite food of the season, and copal incense is also popular in both homes and graveyards. *Dulce de calabaza*, or candied pumpkin, is a favorite treat, as is *atole*, an age-old drink made from corn meal, fruit and water. Poems called *calaveras* ("skulls") are sent to public figures, satirizing them; this tradition has also found its way north into some Mexican-American communities. *Calacas* (dancing wire and clay skeletons, often with heads and arms on wire springs) are common, as are cut paper banners called *paleles picados*. In some areas celebrants don wooden skull masks and dance in honor of their deceased relatives (a festivity which seems to be drawn completely from the Aztec *Miccailhuitl*). The wooden skulls are also placed on altars that are dedicated to the dead.

In Mexican-American communities (especially Texas), All Souls' and All Saints' Days mean trips to the *camposantos* (holy ground, or cemeteries), where graves are cleaned and decorated, and family picnics eaten graveside. As in ALL SAINTS' DAY customs reported from New Orleans, boys stand by the gates of graveyards with jugs of water, hoping to make money from helping to clean graves. One small community near San Antonio holds a candlelit procession from the parish to the graveyard, where the priest says mass and blesses the graves; citizens of another border town outside of Rio Grande City celebrate by saving up enough money in the weeks prior to *Día de los Muertos* to decorate the entire graveyard, not just their loved ones' plots. In addition, the day is often referred to as *el día de los difuntos* or *el día de los finados* ("day of the finished" or "departed"). In many poor border communities, graveyards don't have the luxury of perpetual care, so cleaning of graves is an important (and sometimes difficult) task. November 1 is also called *Día de los Angelitos* ("Day of the

Little Angels"), and the graves of children are given special attention on that day. Flowers are still popular, but modern decorations also include shells, plastic flowers and wreaths (or *coronas*, sometimes handmade), wrought iron or handmade flower-decorated crosses (*cruces*), and paper flowers. Once it was common to provide feasts at home for the visiting spirits, with sweet foods placed for the souls of children. The food was left untouched until midnight, at which time it was thought that the souls had eaten and drunk their fill, although it was believed that the "baby souls" had taken all the sweetness from the candies and cookies provided for them. Although these feasts are no longer common, *pan de muertos* is found in every bakery; it is good luck to be the one who bites into the plastic toy skeleton hidden by the baker in some rounded loaves. The loaves are eaten in memory of the dead, are sometimes shaped like bones or bodies, and are often topped with purple sugar.

By the late 1990s, Days of the Dead celebrations had begun to cross over into other parts of the United States, especially areas with large Mexican-American communities. It has gained particular popularity in the "Gothic" subculture, where it is viewed as a holiday that "hasn't been touched by Hallmark," notes "Goth King" Seth Lindberg. Tomas Benitez, an East Los Angeles resident who hosts large celebrations each year, said, "The Day of the Dead is not about ghouls and goblins, it's about life and death. In celebrating death, you are celebrating life as part of the same cycle...." Days of the Dead celebrations have also spread to non–Hispanic communities in the U.S.; parties usually consist of each person bringing photos or other remembrances of deceased love ones, and placing them on a communal altar for the evening, which is celebrated joyfully with music and food.

Altars (or *ofrendas*, even though the word technically means "offerings") remain one of the most common parts of Days of the Dead celebrations, and are now increasingly popular in the U.S. as well. Altars traditionally include photos and other remembrances of the deceased, a rod to drive away evil spirits, a mat to welcome the deceased, and something for them to eat.

Just as GUY FAWKES DAY and Halloween have become mixed in the minds of many Irish and British, so is Days of the Dead merging more with Halloween; for example, during the season one can find a "Día de los Muertos Halloween Fun House Party" in Los Angeles. In other areas of the U.S. where Mexican immigrants have settled, Days of the Dead may be celebrated with no more than a mass. Since their loved ones are often buried far away, visiting graveyards is impractical. See also FINADOS; MICCAILHUITL AND MICCAILHUITONTLI; NININ; XANDU YA; XANTOLO.

Death— In Ireland it was a common SUPERSTITION that the elderly and infirm were likelier to die at Halloween than at any other time of the year.

Debts— SAMHAIN, as the CELTS' New Year, was a time when obligations were settled — workers were paid off, and debts and rents were finished. Although some of this has shifted in modern times to MARTINMAS, there's still an Irish proverb that says, "Everyone has debts at Hallowe'en."

Decoration Day *see* **Memorial Day**

Detroit *see* **Devil's Night**

Devil— The devil is a popular Halloween symbol, featured in COSTUMES, decorations, POSTCARDS and other COLLECTIBLES. In theological terminology the devil is the chief of the fallen angels, and demons are sons of the fallen angels and human mothers. These angels were variously thought to have fallen because of envy (of man), or pride (because they would not submit to God). The devil is referred to by a panoply of names, including "Old Scratch," "Old Horny," "Auld Cloots" (*cloots* is a Scottish word referring to cloven hooves), "The Dickens," "The Evil One," "The Prince of Evil," Lucifer (from the Latin

for "light bringer"), Beelzebub (Hebrew for "Lord of the Flies"), Belial (Hebrew for "worthlessness"), Mephistopheles (from the legend of Faust), and Satan (Hebrew for "adversary"); the word "devil" comes from the Greek *diabolos*, meaning "accuser" or "slanderer." In Scotland, the devil is frequently referred to as "Auld Nick" (see, for example, ROBERT BURNS's poem "Tam O'Shanter"). There is some speculation among historians that the devil and other malicious creatures are actually ancient Celtic deities (or other horned gods, such as the Greek Pan), villainized by Christianity and transformed. Likewise, WITCHES (who, in contrast to actual WICCA practices, were thought to worship the devil, sell their souls to him and even engage in sexual relations with him) may be the followers of old Celtic pantheistic religions, forced into hiding by their dedication to their old religion.

In a few Halloween FORTUNE-TELLING customs, the devil's name is invoked. For example, in one custom a fortune-seeker must walk about a rick NINE times with a RAKE while saying, "I rake this rick in the devil's name." A vision of the future intended will then appear and take away the rake. Or, to

Wooden devil mask (decorated with porcupine quills) used in Mexican Days of the Dead festivities.

have prophetic dreams, a girl would search for a BRIAR THORN grown into a hoop, creep through it THREE times in the name of the devil, cut it in silence and go to bed with it under her pillow. In one Irish Halloween custom a girl sets a table with food in the name of the devil, and the FETCH of her future husband will come through the window to eat.

On Halloween (or any of the "three spirit nights") the devil, in the shape of a pig, a SOW, a horse, or a dog, prevented people from getting over STILES; or, in the guise of an old woman spinning or carding wool, he frequented lonely spots and scared people away.

The devil has also provided one of the most popular costumes throughout Halloween's history. A 1908 magazine article suggests this simple Halloween costume: "This [devil's] suit, by the way, was a pair of black riding tights, a black jersey, black gloves, and a fitted hood of black lining made for the occasion with protruding horns." In the 21st century, there are a literally dozens of variant devil costumes commercially produced for Halloween, including those tailored for men, women, and children, frightening creations with MASKS that feature "light-up eyes," and sexually suggestive representations (i.e., "Flirty Devil," "Sexy Devil," etc.).

The devil also provided the inspiration for several of the most popular American Halloween FOOD items, including deviled eggs (hard-boiled eggs in which the yolks are combined with mustard, vinegar, mayonnaise, and spices) and devil's food (or chocolate) CAKE.

Devil's Night — October 30, principally in the Midwestern American city of Detroit. Devil's Night is notorious for its arson; at its worst (1984), 297 fires were started in one night. The arson on Devil's Night began in earnest in 1983 (probably for a combination of reasons, including racial tensions and urban decay); fires burned throughout a three-day period, including the last two days of October and the first of November. Although most fires on this night have consisted of leaf piles or rubbish, the arson has also consumed both abandoned and inhabited buildings. After 1994 (when 182 fires were lit), Detroit mayor Dennis Archer launched a campaign to promote awareness and to enlist thousands of volunteers; as part of the campaign, October 30th was re-christened "Angels' Night." The city also razed vacant buildings, towed abandoned cars, and removed 190,000 discarded tires to keep them from serving as fuel. The efforts were successful, since Detroit reported only 41 fires in 1995, and arson levels have remained low since (despite fears in the late 2000s that the economic downturn and the increasing numbers of abandoned structures would lead to a return of Devil's Night). In 1996 Devil's Night made history, and it wasn't for the destruction that the night annually incurs: Representatives of six southwest Detroit gangs agreed to a three-day Halloween season truce and pledged to help stop Devil's Night arsonists.

Fires have not been a problem only in Detroit, however: In Camden, New Jersey, 133 fires were reported in 1991, and about 3,000 volunteers were enlisted to fight "MISCHIEF NIGHT" thereafter.

Devil's Night has also been known by a variety of other names, including Mischief Night, BEGGAR'S NIGHT, GOOSEY NIGHT, CABBAGE NIGHT, Mizzy (for "mischief") Night, Mat (for "mad") Night, and Damage Night.

Días de los Muertos *see* **Days of the Dead**

Dies Irae (Lat., "Day of wrath") — The opening words, and hence the name, of the sequence in the Mass for the Dead in the Western Church. It is now thought to go back to a rhymed prayer of late twelfth century Benedictine origin. The first printed Missal containing it as the sequence for Requiem Masses is that of Venice, 1485. Until 1969 its use was obligatory in Masses on ALL SOULS' DAY, on the day of decease or burial of the person for whom the Mass was offered, and on the anniversary of the death, though it could be omitted on other days. It may now also be omitted in all Masses of the Dead.

"Dies Irae" was adapted for use in Requiem Masses by the addition of the last six lines:

> That day is one of weeping,
> on which shall rise again from the ashes
> the guilty man, to be judged.
> Therefore spare this one, O God,
> merciful Lord Jesus:
> Give them rest. Amen.

Digging— In some areas of continental Europe, one SUPERSTITION held that it was bad luck to dig on Halloween, especially should one encounter human remains; the remedy was to immediately sow grain, which would bring saints to bless the field the following day.

Dinner— In an American FORTUNE-TELLING custom, a number of girls prepare a dinner, set a table, then stand behind the chairs, confident that their future husbands will come and sit in the chairs in front of them.

Disguises *see* **Costumes; Masks**

Divination *see* **Anthropomancy; Fortune-Telling**

Dough— In one FORTUNE-TELLING tradition, WATER and meal was first used to make a dough, then young men wrote the names of female friends on slips of paper, balled them up in the dough, and dropped them into a basin of water. As the balls melted apart, the names were revealed, with the first to become visible designating the young man's true love (this tradition could also be performed by young ladies to learn of their future husbands).

Doughnuts— A popular treat in American Halloween celebrations until recently (usually served with apple cider).

Dream of Angus (*Aislinge Oenguso*)— One of the loveliest of the CELTS' SAMHAIN legends. It tells of Angus, son of the Dagda (the Good God), who has fallen in love with a girl who has visited him in his sleep, and now his pining for her has made him ill. Angus discovers the girl is Caer Ibormeith; Angus goes with Bodb, another supernatural being, to Loch Bel Dracon, where he has heard she will be at Samhain. Upon arriving, Angus finds her chained with 150 other girls; he sends Ailell, king of Connacht, to Caer's father. Ailell returns to Angus and tells him that Caer must be chained because her magic is more powerful than her father's: She is in bird form one year and human form the next. Ailell tells Angus that Caer and the other girls will take on bird form at the coming of Samhain; sure enough, Angus sees 150 swans at the lake as Samhain starts. Angus changes himself into a swan and, together with Caer, they fly THREE times around the loch, then set out for his palace, chanting music that puts everyone to sleep for three days and three nights.

Dreaming Stones— A FORTUNE-TELLING method still popular with modern WICCA practitioners. On Halloween night, to seek a solution to a problem, go to a boundary stream and, with closed eyes, take from the WATER three stones between the middle finger and thumb, saying these words as each is gathered:

> I will lift the stone
> As Mary lifted it for her Son,
> For substance, virtue, and strength;
> May this stone be in my hand
> Till I reach my journey's end.

These THREE stones are carried home and placed under the pillow, and DREAMS that will give guidance are asked for; the stones will provide such dreams.

Dreams— Dreams on Halloween could be prophetic; an American belief is that to dream of someone on Halloween night means you will marry that person, but usually other items, such as NUTS or a sliver of WOOD in a glass of WATER, were employed to invoke dreaming. One simple FORTUNE-

TELLING custom consisted of writing the names of three sweethearts on slips of paper and placing these beneath the pillow. A dream of one of those named meant that person cared for you; if that name was also on the first slip drawn from beneath the pillow in the morning, that person would be the future spouse.

Some Halloween customs were designed to provoke dreams. In a Pennsylvanian tradition, prophetic dreams could be guaranteed by going out of the front door BACKWARDS on Halloween night, picking up some dust or grass, wrapping it in paper, and placing it under the pillow.

See also APPLES; COLCANNON; EGGS; ROSEMARY; SAGE; YEW

Druids— Members of the CELTS' priest caste. The name "Druid" has been erroneously thought to mean "knowledge of the oak" or possibly "deep knowledge"; many eighteenth and nineteenth century historians misinterpreted history to fit their idea of the "noble savage" or "natural religion." Druids belonged to the social elite and had control over festivals and all sacrifices (such as those probably performed at SAMHAIN), gave rulings on all religious questions, acted as judges in criminal cases, and arbitrators in disputes over land and legacies. Druids could enforce judgments by banning individuals from attending rituals and sacrifices, which was essentially a form of excommunication. Druid students were said to have spent 20 years studying, committing everything to memory. Caesar thought, "the doctrine of the Druids was invented in Britain," and then brought to Gaul on the continent; it is therefore possible that Druids originated in Ireland, and that their leaders were located there.

Druids figure prominently in a number of Celtic Samhain myths. In one story Dathi, king of Ireland in the fifth century, happened to be at the Druids' Hill (*Noc-nan-druad*) in the county of Sligo one Halloween; he ordered his Druid to forecast the future for the next year. The Druid passed the night on top of the hill, and the next morning made predictions that came true.

In the Scottish Highlands, the master of ceremonies at Halloween parties was nearly always in the COSTUME of a Druid.

Ducking for Apples *see* **Bobbing for Apples**

Ducks— In Buckhinghamshire, a popular rhyme once indicated that ducks at Halloween could be used to indicate the WEATHER for the rest of the year:

> "If ducks do slide at Hollantide,
> At Christmas they will swim.
> If ducks do swim at Hollantide,
> At Christmas they will slide."

Dumb Cake— Any CAKE made in complete silence, for purposes of FORTUNE-TELLING, and most effective on Halloween, St. John's Eve (MIDSUMMER EVE) and CHRISTMAS, but might also occur on ST. AGNES' EVE (January 21), St. Valentine (February 14) and St. Mark (April 25). The ritual usually calls for a number of women to participate, and must begin in the kitchen. The recipe for the Halloween dumb-cake was sometimes given as an eggshell-full of SALT, an eggshell-full of wheat and an eggshell-full of barley meal; the dough must be prepared without spring WATER. The dough is spread thin, and then each woman present marks her initials in the cake with a new pin. The cake is then set to bake, and each person in the room sits as far from the fire (or oven) as possible. Each person must turn the cake once, and all of this must be done between the hours of 11 and MIDNIGHT, in complete silence. As the clock strikes 12, the husband of the woman who is to be married first enters, and lays his hand on the piece of cake with her initials. The ritual varied when performed on other days, and quite often involved exactly THREE girls in the preparation of the dumb-cake.

A slightly different version of the ritual begins by stating that the women must meet between the hours of 10 and 11, in the kitchen, on Halloween night. Each places a handful of wheat flour onto a sheet of white paper and sprinkles it over with as much salt as she can hold between her finger and thumb; then one of the party must make it into a dough, being careful not to use spring water. Each young lady must then roll up a portion of the dough, spread it out thin and flat, and mark her initials with a new pin. Now the cakes were placed before the fire, and the women were seated as far from it as possible. This must all be done before 11 P.M., and between that time and midnight each must turn her cake once. When the clock struck 12 the future husband of the woman who was to be married first would enter and lay his hand upon the cake marked with her name. Throughout the whole proceeding, of course, not a word was to be spoken.

One variant suggested that the dough must be kneaded for 15 minutes with the left thumb only; to do so with the right thumb (or to speak) would bring misfortune. In another variation, a couple whose initials were plainly visible after the cakes had been baked was destined to marry within the year.

In some versions of the dumb cake ritual the cake must be eaten to know future partners, and in one case participants must walk BACKWARDS to their beds after eating the cake. In a particularly unsettling variation, after baking the cake girls removed all pins and unfastened their clothes before heading upstairs for their beds; en route, apparitions of their future husbands would try to snatch at them, and they could only escape by wriggling out of their clothing.

In an 1870 description of a party thrown by an English family in America, Helen Elliott (in "Hallowe'en," from *Godey's Lady's Book and Magazine*, November 1870) describes a variant called a "fate cake": One eggshell full of butter, one of sugar, and one of flour were mixed together and baked, with all the participants remaining absolutely silent. When the cake was done, each girl took a small piece and made a wish.

Dumb Suppers— American (Appalachian) Halloween FORTUNE-TELLING custom in which girls sat at a table in silence where a chair was left vacant for the FETCH of a lover to occupy. In Maryland, this game — which was there called a "silent supper"— required the young ladies to stand silently behind a chair and wait to see if it would be occupied by their future husband.

E

Each Uisg—*Each uisg* is a Scottish phrase meaning "water horse," and is also the title of a Scottish Halloween GHOST STORY. The *each uisg* was a demon that took the form of a huge black HORSE living within Loch Dorch; travelers who were caught by the water's edge at night were occasionally seized by the demon, dragged to the bottom of the lake, and devoured. One Halloween at the house of Duncan the weaver, Duncan's daughter Catriana decided to try the old FORTUNE-TELLING method of dipping her sleeve in WATER, and although her companions tried to dissuade her, she went to the loch. They soon heard her terrified shriek, and in the morning found only shreds of her clothing and the imprint of a hoof in the clay bank of the loch.

Earrings— An American SUPERSTITION is that earrings shouldn't be worn on Halloween (or on the Fourth of July); to do so will result in a loss of hearing.

Edin-Da-Hin-Veaul—*Edin-da-hin-Veaul* is a Gaelic proverb meaning "the jeopardy of Baal"; it refers to the ritual of passing between two fires (on SAMHAIN or BELTANE) as a method of purification or consecration (the proverb, however, has a similar meaning to "caught between the Scylla and Charybdis," meaning to find oneself in a difficult situation).

Eggs—A classic symbol of fertility, eggs figure prominently in several Halloween FORTUNE-TELLING methods. The most popular involve eggs and WATER. For example: THREE drops of egg white are allowed to fall into a glass of water, and the resulting shapes are read for initials or other signs, or the droplets suggest how many children a person will have. This method was often conducted for children who wanted to know how many siblings were still to come. A Scottish version specified that the first-laid egg of a pullet was preferred, and that clear spring water must be used. After a few drops of egg were allowed to fall into the glass, the questioner placed his or her hand over the top of the glass for about a minute, giving the egg in the water time to form into intriguing shapes. Another Scottish divination involved taking a mouthful of the egg and water, and going out for a walk; the first name heard would be that of one's future intended. In *Highland Superstitions*, Alexander Macgregor describes a Halloween party in which a young man's egg whites take on the appearance of a winding-sheet with a rent in it, indicating an early, violent death. Macgregor suggests that the young man became so disturbed over this prognostication that he drank heavily and eventually became a beggar who finally committed suicide by drinking a vial of laudanum.

An American method of divination from Maryland involved a FETCH: On Halloween, if a girl fried an egg on the stove, her future husband would appear to turn the egg. A custom from New Brunswick seemed to replace an APPLE with a hard-boiled egg: The egg was eaten without SALT before a MIRROR on Halloween to see the face of a future spouse (this divination was also sometimes performed as the young lady walked BACKWARDS up stairs).

In an Irish Halloween practice, women removed the yolk from hard-boiled eggs, filled the eggs with salt, and ate egg, shell and salt completely; if they avoided drinking water until morning, they would be rewarded with dreams of their future husbands.

In one American Halloween folk belief, if an egg placed in front of the fire by a young woman in love is seen to sweat blood, it is a sign that she will succeed in getting the man she loves. Another version of this story stated that a CAT would come in to turn the egg as it roasted by the fire, followed by the man who would become the girl's husband. If the unfortunate young lady was fated to die unwed, the shadow of a COFFIN would appear.

This 1911 postcard shows a woman performing a divination with eggs.

Egyptian Feast of the Dead— The Egyptian Feast of the Dead is one of the earliest known festivals commemorating the dead, and is sometimes thought to be the oldest ancestor of Halloween (in his fictionalized history of Halloween, *The Halloween Tree*, RAY BRADBURY begins with the Egyptians and calls their Feast of the Dead "TRICK OR TREAT old style").

The festival was held on the seventeenth of Athyr (about mid–November) and marked the day on which Set (sometimes known as Typhon), who envied the happiness of his brother Osiris and the goddess Isis, slew his brother, cut him into 14 pieces and scattered the pieces far and wide (although in another version Set or Typhon locked his brother in a sarcophagus which was placed in the sea). On this day, when the powers of good — like the yearly flood waters of the Nile — were in decline, no Egyptian would undertake a new enterprise; a venture down the Nile would surely lead to a crocodile attack. To begin a journey would mean never to return.

Osiris was said to be very popular with the common people, and so his festival was mournful (people lamented over a buried idol of Osiris, and priests beat their breasts out of grief), but these days were also celebrated with festive lighting. Oil-lamps were lit outside of houses and burned throughout the night. In Osiris's sacred city (Abydos), an eight-act drama was performed which portrayed Osiris's life, death, and his resurrection (similar PAGEANTS were presented at other major cities as well).

According to Plutarch, the festival lasted four days and was also a general commemoration of the dead (Osiris was the king and judge of the dead). The spirits of dead ancestors were guided home by the lights (also a feature of the Japanese BON FESTIVAL, the Chinese YUE LAAN, and, in some areas, ALL SAINTS' DAY and ALL SOULS' DAY celebrations), and were honored with feasting. The festival ended on a joyous note, as mummers and priests re-enacted the resurrection of the murdered god by Isis, who afterwards gave birth to their son Horus. The dead body of Osiris is sometimes depicted with CORN sprouting from it, suggesting that — like the CELTS' SAMHAIN — the Feast of the Dead also served as a celebration of the crops and a fertility rite for the next season.

Exercises— A form of RECITATION involving not just one child but many children, all performing in rhyme, often in a form of geometric progression where each new child adds a line to those already spoken. Exercises were popular in school PAGEANTS at Halloween in the 1930s.

F

Fairies (also faeries)— Also known as "the good people," "the people of peace," "the still folk," "the silently-moving people," "the wee people," "the little folk," "the gentle folk," *Daoine Coire* ("honest folk"), *Daoine Matha* ("good people"), PIXIES, piskies, *tylweth teg* (Welsh), POOKA, "fair family," corrigans (korrigans), *sidhe* or *sith* (pronounced "shee"), *daoine sidhe*, "the gentry," and "Tiddy People." Fairies are supernatural entities, generally small, who feature prominently in Irish mythology, often instigating mischief or malice on Halloween.

Usually fairies were believed to be a race of supernatural beings completely separate from humanity; some sociologists have suggested that fairies are actually the last remnants of the ancient Celtic gods and goddesses, literally and metaphorically reduced in stature by the rise of Christianity. Another theory once popular was that fairies were the mythologized remnants of an actual pygmy race which once inhabited parts of Britain and Ireland; this theory goes so far as to suggest that the pygmies were a Stone Age people who feared and envied IRON weapons, hence the use of iron as a protective element against fairies and evil forces. This theory, however, has been largely dismissed, since it lacks any real proof or evidence. Some believe that God made fairies on the third day of Creation, out of earth, air and water, but He did not give them souls. Another belief is that at the time of Lucifer's rebellion some angels sided with Lucifer and were cast into hell, where they became demons, others remained true to God, and stayed in heaven, and the indifferent ones, who failed to take sides, were cast out and condemned to dwell on earth as fairies until Judgment Day, when they will be annihilated (hence, their envy of human beings). In one tale, Finvarra, chief of the fairies, sought out St. Columkille (or COLUM KILL), the first Celtic missionary, to beg him to intercede for the fairies and give them hope of salvation, but the saint told them this was impossible and that the fairy people were doomed to extinction. Many of the fairy epithets such as "the good people" or "the still folk" come from a belief that to mention the fairies by name was to invoke them, whereas calling them by something derogatory might well provoke them.

A variation on a traditional Scottish rhyme seems to cross fairies with WITCHES:

> Heigh Ho for Hallowe'en,
> When the fairies a' are seen,
> Some black and some green,
> Heigh Ho for Hallowe'en!

In a few areas fairies were even thought to be the spirits of the dead. In a traditional tale usually called "November Eve," a young man who has foolishly stayed out late on Halloween is swept up in a band of fairies, where he meets Finvarra the Fairy King and Oonagh his queen. They give him fairy gold and wine, but when he looks steadily at any of them he sees neighbors who have died, sometimes many years before. When the fairies know that the young man has seen through them, they circle him and, shrieking with laughter, try to force him to dance. He resists until he falls senseless, and awakens the next morning in a stone circle, his arms badly bruised from the grasp of fairy hands.

Fairy rings (common throughout the British Isles, and actually caused by a fungus) were the subject of many SUPERSTITIONS; stepping into a fairy ring after sunset on Halloween was particularly dangerous. A Scottish poem warns:

> He wha tills the fairy green
> Nae luck again shall hae,
> An' he wha spills the fairy-ring
> Betide him want and wae;
> For weirdless days and weary nichts
> Are his till his deein' day.

On Halloween all the fairy hills (or *sidh-mounds*, or *raths*) were thrown wide open and the fairies would swarm forth. The spell of *fe-fiada* (invisibility) that was placed on the hills by the DRUIDS was lifted on this one day, and any man who was bold enough might then peep into the open green mounds and see treasures hidden within the *brugh*, or interior of the fairy dwelling. In a note to *Lady of the Lake*, SIR WALTER SCOTT mentions a method of gaining entrance to a fairy mound on Halloween: The seeker must go alone round the hill NINE times toward the left (*sinistrorsum*), and then a door will be opened into the subterranean realm; however, there can be no return to the mortal world.

One Irish belief is that you can't refuse what a fairy asks of you on Halloween. Another is that fairies make anything left unharvested after November Eve unfit to eat; anyone who dares to eat unharvested grains or berries will become seriously ill. Some early twentieth-century Irish suggested that the Potato Famine of the 1840s—which caused so many Irish to flee to America, bringing their Halloween traditions to the new country — was caused by fighting in the fairy world (likewise, a common Scottish belief was that fairies often battled on Halloween).

Bad fairies in Scotland were called "wicked wichts" and were always said to inflict *skaith* or damage; wichts might steal wives or babies, for example. In *Minstrelsy of the Scottish Border*, Sir Walter Scott records the tale of a Lothian farmer whose wife was snatched by fairies. A good fairy appeared to the husband and told him how to rescue his wife come next Hallow Eve, but when the time came the ringing of the fairy bridles so confused the hapless farmer that the procession passed before he could snatch his wife back, and she was lost to him forever. Fairies spiriting off mortals on Halloween is a common theme; often those so taken never return. One Irish man was luckier: He claimed to be taken by Halloween fairies to America, where he was shown both his daughter and his friend. Other fairy legends claimed that spouses who had been abducted and taken to fairyland might be recovered within a year and a day when the procession of the fairies was filing past on Halloween, provided the mortals had not partaken of elfin food while in elfinland. However, yet another folk belief is that to rescue a wife or baby stolen by fairies, a man first had to obtain from some fairy doctor or wise woman a special ointment that was rubbed on his eyes to enable the seeing of fairies. Then he must stand at a CROSSROADS on Halloween and wait for the fairy troop to pass by; their approach would be heralded by a gust of WIND. As the fairies passed, the watcher threw on them a handful of dust from the road or a splash of milk from a jug, and the fairies were then obliged to surrender any human being whom they had bewitched or stolen.

Fairies had three great festivals: May Eve, MIDSUMMER'S EVE and NOVEMBER EVE; one bit of folklore states that on November Eve they danced with GHOSTS. It was dangerous to see fairies at their revels on Halloween, as is clearly demonstrated in this tale from the Ferintosh district of the Highlands (or the Slope of Big Stones in Harris): Two young men were coming home after dark on Halloween, each with a jar of whisky on his back, when they saw a house all lit up by the roadside, with the sounds of MUSIC and dancing coming from within. Since there had never been a house there before, the house was actually a fairy mound, full of fairies, and visible only on Halloween. One of the young men entered and joined the dance, the other took the precaution of sticking a NEEDLE in the door; that disarmed the power of the fairies. He got out safely, but his friend did not. One year later, he came back and saw his friend still dancing. When they finished and took him out into open air, nothing was left but skin and bones.

Somewhat similar, but with a different set of morals, is the story of

An 1886 illustration from *Harper's Young People*, entitled "A Halloween Vision," showing an encounter with fairies.

Paddy More, a tall, rude fellow, and his hunchbacked-but-happy friend Paddy Beg. One Halloween they came upon a fairy mound full of light and music, and Paddy Beg was invited in. Paddy joined in the festivities, telling stories, dancing and singing, and the fairies rewarded him by removing his hump. The following Halloween Paddy More stumbled on the mound, and was also asked in. After he refused to take part in the merrymaking, the fairies stuck Paddy Beg's hump on his back and sent him home.

Sometimes valuable information may be obtained from fairies on Halloween, for those bold enough to attempt such a risky feat. One young man named GULEESH from the County of Mayo went to a rath or old fort near his house one Halloween, and stood on a gray old flag. He waited hours, and the fairies arrived. Guleesh listened, and heard one fairy saying to another that a magic herb grew by Guleesh's own door, and that if Guleesh plucked and boiled it and gave it to his sweetheart, the daughter of the King of France, she would recover from severe illness. He did, and they wed and lived happily after ever.

A variation of this tale is found in "Jamie Freel and the Young Lady," in which a diligent young man who works hard to support his widowed mother decides to investigate a nearby ruined castle which seems to be haunted every Halloween. He approaches the fairy revels, and is invited to join. He takes a fairy steed to a distant city, where a beautiful maiden is kidnapped (the fairies place a stick in her bed, and the stick takes on her likeness). Jamie tricks the fairies on the ride home, and manages to take the girl home with him (as in TAM LIN, the fairy people try to trick Jamie by changing the girl into a variety of strange forms). The fairies strike her dumb, and she lives for a year like that, helping out Jamie and his mother. At the next Halloween, Jamie returns to the castle, and overhears a fairy saying that the girl could be cured with THREE drops of the liquid in her glass. Jamie steals the glass, and restores the girl's voice. They head to Dublin to find her family, and finally Jamie is rewarded with her hand in marriage and great wealth.

Compare this to the humorous tale of "Peter Malone," who rides with the fairies on Halloween to Spain, where they follow a funeral to a church and the fairies persuade Malone to lift the church offerings. Upon return to his home, Malone is anticipating showing his wife his rich pocketful of money, but discovers instead a pocketful of horse dung.

Irish Halloween stories of chance meetings with fairies often involve storms; either a fairy has lost her way in a violent storm and stumbles into a human dwelling, or a wayward human encounters a fairy who offers assistance in reaching home. However, in Fermanagh no one took a short cut on the eve lest the fairies would lead him or her astray.

In a few stories fairies become the lovers of mortals. Every SAMHAIN a female fairy visited Fingin Mac Luchta, king of South Munster in the second century, and brought him to the *sidhs* to see their treasures and gather information; a fairy thus attached to a human was called a *lennan-shee*.

Sometimes stories about fairies also specify HARVEST day as a special time. In "Paddy Corcoran's Wife," Kitty Corcoran lies mysteriously ill for seven years until, on a harvest day, a fairy in a RED cloak appears to her and tells her that the fairies have made her ill because she threw out her dirty water every sunrise and sunset just as the fairies were passing by her door. Once she stops these practices, she becomes well and is healthy thereafter.

In some areas of Scotland it was believed that the last handful of corn reaped should be dressed up as a Harvest Maiden, or *Maighdean Bhuan* (see CORN DOLLY), and hung up in the farmer's house to keep the fairies out until the next harvest.

Sometimes plates of CHAMP or COLCANNON would be left out for the fairies on Halloween night; an American belief mentions leprechauns instead of fairies, and suggests that on Halloween night a bowl of boiled and peeled potatoes should be left out for the leprechauns. *See also* BANSHEES; CAILLEACH; BROWNIES; GOBLINS; LUNANTISHEES; POOKA.

Fairy Light *see* **Will o' the Wisp**

Falling Star— One American SUPERSTITION is that to see a falling star on Halloween night means your sweetheart is a witch.

Families— In many areas of Europe, Halloween is celebrated by family gatherings, while sociologists note that in America Halloween often inverts social ideas of family, by empowering children over parents. In *The Hallowed Eve: Dimensions of a Calendar Festival in Northern Ireland*, folklorist and Halloween expert JACK SANTINO says, "Halloween is a great family festival in Northern Ireland," and notes that "the more intensive, peer-oriented, outdoor activities [such as RHYMING and gathering material for BONFIRES] precede Halloween, while the family gatherings, meal, FIREWORKS, and bonfire all take place on Halloween itself." Similar celebrations such as the Japanese BON FESTIVAL and the Mexican DAYS OF THE DEAD also emphasize family gatherings.

Fawkes, Guy *see* **Guy Fawkes Day/Night**

Feanloe Night— Lancashire name for the eve of ALL SOULS' DAY, celebrated by lighting BONFIRES.

Feathers— In one Halloween FORTUNE-TELLING custom, three soft, fluffy feathers each have a small slip of paper glued to the bottom, one reading "blonde," one "brunette," and one "medium." Each feather is then held up by the top and blown into the air; the paper landing the closest denotes the hair color of your true love. To be sure, the test should be conducted THREE times.

Feralia— The first of the Roman festivals of the dead (the oldest, LEMURIA, is held in mid–May), and closely linked to the great festival of PARENTALIA (which Ovid refers to as the "Season of All Souls"). Most of what we know of Feralia comes from Book Two of Ovid's *Fasti*, which begins the listing for February 21 with these points:

> Tombs get tribute too. Appease your ancestral spirits
> And bring small gifts to the pyres you've built.
> The dead make small demands…

Ovid goes on to describe what happened when Aeneas neglected his duties during the season:

> …They say the resentful ancestors
> left their tombs, in the dead of night,
> and howled through the streets of city and countryside…

During Feralia Romans stayed inside their homes, all sanctuaries were closed, all ceremony in temples was suspended, and marriages were especially warned against. The only sacrifices made at this time were to the gods of the dead and to the dead themselves. Mourners went to family tombs outside the cities and performed *sacra privata*; offerings included (according to Ovid) "a tile wreathed with votive garlands, a sprinkling of CORN, a few grains of SALT, BREAD soaked in wine, and some loose violets." Ovid describes a spell which an old hag casts on Feralia — she performed a witchcraft ritual to bind "hostile tongues and unfriendly mouths." Concerning the origin of the name, Ovid tells us, "They called this day Feralia because they do what's fair." The next day (February 22) was called *Cara Cognatio*, or *Caristia* (Ovid mentions that "caring kin have named the next day *Caristia*"), and was a time of offering prayer to the gods, feasting and FAMILY gatherings. The feast celebrated on *Caristia* continued to be celebrated into Christian times, and was converted by the Catholic Church into the feast of St. Peter, held on February 22 until at least the twelfth century.

Festival of the Radunitsa— A Russian commemoration of the dead held on the tenth

day after Easter Sunday. Like certain ALL
SOULS' DAY CELEBRATIONS, drinks were
poured on graves, there was feasting and offering FOOD to the dead spirits, and *panikhida*
was sung in honor of the departed "Fathers."

Festival of the Unforgotten Dead *see* **Yue
Laan**

Fetch— The spectre of someone who is not
yet dead (as compared to WRAITH, which can
refer to the soul of one either living or dead);
fetches figure prominently in many Halloween FORTUNE-TELLING customs and stories, including those involving APPLES, BARLEY,
DUMB CAKE, EGGS, HEMP SEED, MIRRORS, RAKES,
WATER and YARN.

One traditional Scottish tale of a fetch
also involves the Scottish NEW YEAR'S celebration of HOGMANAY: "The Man Who
Missed the Tay Bridge Train" tells of two best
friends, Rab and Tam, who are born at exactly the same time and grow up together,
and are never apart until the day one must
return home from university to look after
the family business and the other goes back
to school. They agree to meet again when
Tam returns home for Hogmanay (which
was so beloved by the Scots that even Charles
II couldn't replace it with CHRISTMAS). As the
school-break arrives, Tam heads out for the
train, but there's a terrible storm brewing;
then, to his surprise, he encounters Rab, who
tells him not to take that evening's train. Tam
agrees, and returns to his school lodging; the
next morning he discovers that the Tay
Bridge was destroyed by the storm, and all
aboard the train had been killed. When Tam
finally makes his long way back home, he's
surprised to learn that Rab has been very sick
for the last two weeks, and hasn't left his bed,
although he does vaguely remember trying
to warn Tam about a disaster. They realize
then that Tam encountered Rab's fetch.

The word "fetch" seems to appear only in
Ireland, and in some areas it was believed that
the time of the fetch's arrival meant either
happy longevity (if seen in the morning) or
immediate death (if seen in the evening).

Fields— A number of Halloween FORTUNE-
TELLING customs (including those involving
HEMP SEED and CABBAGE) involve visiting a
field after dark on Halloween night. One of
the most unusual comes from Ross-shire:
The fortune seeker would steal out unseen
after dark to a field in which the furrows lay
due north and south, and enter from the west
side. He or she would then proceed slowly
over 11 ridges, and stand in the center of the
twelfth. There they would hear low sobs and
faint shrieks, signifying an early death, or
MUSIC and dancing, foretelling marriage.
This custom was thought to be more dangerous than most, since sometimes fortune-
seekers supposedly returned from the field
mad, or simply did not return at all.

Films *see* **Burton, Tim; Carpenter, John;
and *Appendix II***

Finados—DAY OF THE DEAD celebration
found in a number of South American countries, including Brazil and Ecuador. Although
the full name is *Dia de Finados* (or *Dia de Difuntos*), the holiday—celebrated on November 2nd—is typically referred to simply as
Finados. As with Mexican Day of the Dead
festivities, *Finados* is celebrated with special
foods and drinks, exchanges with neighbors,
and visits to cemeteries to clean and decorate the graves of loved ones.

Finn MacCumal (also Fionn, Finn Mac-
Cool)— Legendary hero of the CELTS who is
at the center of several SAMHAIN tales, most
notably one in which he slays the malicious
Aillen:

Every year at Samhain time, for many
years, a man of the *Tuatha de Danaan* came
out of *Sidhe Finnachaidh* in the north and
burned down Tara, the ancient seat of the
Irish kings. He was Aillen, son of Midhna;
he came playing MUSIC of the *Sidhe* (the Otherworld), and all the people who heard it fell
asleep. Aillen then opened his mouth and
breathed out ferocious flames that burned
Tara to the ground. Finn, who was told of
the approaching disaster upon a visit to Tara,

sought a weapon and was given a magical spear, which he used to kill Aillen; Finn was rewarded with the headship of the Fianna clan.

Fire— Fire (especially BONFIRES) is associated throughout Europe with many festival days, including all of the QUARTER DAYS, the solstices and the equinoxes; however, fire seems to have a particularly strong association with the history of Halloween. This association dates back to the Celtic SAMHAIN, when each family was required to relight the home hearth with embers from a fire kindled by the DRUIDS (and pay a tax in the process).

Folklorists and historians have put forth several theories on the importance of fires during holidays; Halloween authors often point to the holiday's bonfires as representing the dying of the sun that occurs each winter. In his classic study *The Golden Bough*, SIR JAMES FRAZER offers two possibilities: The "solar theory" (fire is a charm used to ensure the continued good benefits of the sun), and the "purification theory" (fire provides a magical means of purifying crops, cattle, etc.); Fraser leans toward the purification theory, but also suggests that the two theories need not be mutually exclusive. Halloween fires have taken the form of bonfires, fires lit to frighten away WITCHES, decorations (inside, for example, JACK-O'-LANTERNS), and flames used in FORTUNE-TELLING. In the Northern Counties of England, it was believed to be unlucky to let the fire die on Halloween night (the same held true for NEW YEAR'S Eve, MIDSUMMER'S EVE, and CHRISTMAS Eve).

An early custom recorded in Devon and other areas of the west of England involved begging fire from the wealthy on Halloween (the fire was usually offered with a small gift of money).

In ancient Lancashire, the head of each family would carry of bundle of burning straw around his fields, proclaiming:

> "Fire and red low
> Light on my teen low."

("Teen low" is undoubtedly a variant of *teanlas*, referring to a Halloween bonfire)

In the Northern Counties of England, a Halloween custom consisted of whirling a lighted brand before the face and singing this couplet:

> "Dingle, dingle, dowsie, the cat's in the well;
> The dog's awa' to Berwick, to buy a new bell."

The last sparks of the fire were observed; many indicated money, but a quick extinction meant loss of property.

Bonfires and FIREWORKS are also an important part of GUY FAWKES celebrations, and fire (in candles) is a key element of decoration in DAY OF THE DEAD.

See also CANDLES; COEL COETH; EDINDA-HIN-VEAUL; FIRE O' LOVE; HEARTH.

Fire O' Love— A popular eighteenth-century form of FORTUNE-TELLING often practiced at Halloween gatherings. Each person present writes her or his name on a piece of paper, twists it closed and then tosses it into a tub of WATER. A lit CANDLE end, attached to a flat cork, is placed in the water, where it comes into contact with the slips, burning them. When the candle end sputters and dies, the unburned slips are removed, revealing the names of those who will never marry.

Fireplace *see* **Hearth**

Fireworks— Although fireworks have virtually no association with the American Halloween, they are still a popular component of Irish Halloween CELEBRATIONS, despite the fact that all kinds of explosives were banned there in the 1970s. Fireworks may be either large community events or small "back-garden" displays; civic displays usually include additional entertainment such as PANTOMIMES put on by children, many with light horror themes. Large-scale fireworks displays are still very popular in GUY FAWKES NIGHT celebrations, and are even used in certain DAY OF THE DEAD festivals.

On Mischief Night in England (No-

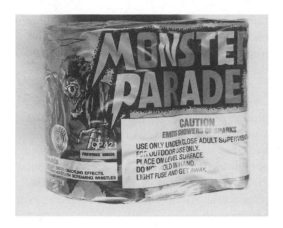

These Fourth of July fireworks would look more appropriate on Halloween.

vember 4), fireworks were also popular in PRANKING. A group of three or four "bangers" placed into a drainage pipe and lit was called a "lion's roar."

Flour— Several Halloween FORTUNE-TELLING customs involve alcuromancy, or divination from flour; for example, messages written on slips of paper were enclosed in balls of flour paste which were distributed at random. In another popular divination, a bowl was filled tightly with flour, then a wedding ring was inserted into some part of it. The bowl was then inverted upon a dish and withdrawn, leaving the mound of flour. Each guest cut off a thin slice, and whoever cut off the slice containing the ring would be married first.

One Halloween GAME consisted of putting small COINS in a large pan of flour, then asking guests to dig the coins out using only their mouths (this game, of course, resulted in many comically-whitened faces!).

Sometimes these two games were even combined, so that after the flour in the first divination had been cut, the seekers had to root through it with their mouths to find a token.

Flour also figured prominently in PRANKING, as one popular custom was to fill a sock with flour and swing it at unsuspecting Halloween passersby, leaving a large white imprint (a form of CHALKING). A 1908 description of a Halloween BONFIRE party for boys also mentions flour used against one young man who was dressed as the DEVIL: "The only revenge for this was now and then a thrust from one rebellious spirit who had come provided with an old stocking full of flour which when beaten against the black monster left undignified white streaks upon his sleek well fitting suit."

Flowers— In a French custom, children beg flowers from neighbors to decorate on ALL SAINTS' DAY. *See also* ROSES.

Folk Art— Although the definition of "folk art" itself is somewhat open (folk art has been described as everything from "non-academic" and "outsider" to "child art on an adult level"), folk art is undeniably an im-

"Freefall," contemporary folk art Halloween painting in ink and gouache by Matthew Kirscht (used with permission of Matthew Kirscht)

portant aspect of the Halloween celebration. Folklorist JACK SANTINO has noted that folk art "recognizes…the ephemeral but cyclical nature of the holidays," and suggests that Halloween folk art is rooted in history and tradition.

Halloween folk art can be as simple as a single carved JACK-O'-LANTERN, but it is often more complex, especially when various objects are combined in the form of yard display that Santino has called *assemblage*. Prior to the 19th century, there is little evidence of significant Halloween folk art; the CORN DOLLY, occasionally used in Halloween festivities, was typically more associated with HARVEST. However, as the VICTORIANS began to celebrate Halloween in their living rooms and yards, homemade party decorations that were essentially folk art began to increase in popularity. Although companies like Dennison and Beistle were producing commercial decorations that had become mainstays of Halloween RETAILING by the early 20th century, home-crafted decorations were also popular. A 1903 party booklet offers these tips on decorating (which mirror the modern folk art *assemblage*):

> …the lawn in front of the house should be decorated with hanging lighted jack-o'-lanterns. The eyes, nose, mouth in each one should be different and as grotesque as possible. If there is a fence around the grounds, put a jack-o'-lantern on each post. Drape black muslin above entrance to house; and, at center, over door, hang skull and crossbones.

Early 20th-century Halloween folk art pieces that have survived include hand-carved wooden NOISEMAKERS, candy containers, and hand-drawn invitations. The popular Dennison's BOGIE BOOKS of the 1920s and 1930s were — despite their main goal in selling commercially-made Halloween products — essentially guides to producing folk art (although some collectors of folk art draw a distinction between true folk art, produced entirely by self-taught artists, and crafts, which are produced from existing instruc-

tions). The Bogie Books include instructions on creating everything from nut cups and musical instruments to "Pumpkin Boy" table decorations and large-scale house decorations.

In the late 20th and 21st century, the explosion of the Internet has created new forms and interests in folk art (and, as one folklorist has noted, created new forms of "folk-speech"), and facilitated their distribution. Halloween folk art is now made and displayed year-round (the CASTLE HALLOWEEN MUSEUM includes a folk art section), and definitions of folk art have been further blurred by the fact that this art may now be purchased through online websites such as ebay.com and etsy.com. Groups such as "EHAG" (Eclectic Halloween Artists Guild) include artist members whose works include dolls, candy containers, furnishings, signs, and paintings that clearly mirror traditional folk art, and yet these artists refer to themselves as "professional," suggesting that their works may no longer be truly folk art. Most of these modern folk artists—for example, painter Matthew Kirscht — are clearly familiar with the history of the holiday and its folk art, and their works have become popular in part because of nostalgia (Kirscht sells limited edition reproduction postcards and books of his works, while his original paintings frequently command high prices); but these artists also possess more skill and self-awareness than the classic folk artist, again suggesting that modern lines between true folk art and popular commercial art are blurring. However, contemporary Halloween folk art is still based on the same icons found in Halloween folk art over the last century (jack-o'-lanterns, black CATS, WITCHES), and embodies the "charm" and "whimsy" often cited as being key elements of folk art, as well as the vivid COLORS and traditional themes.

Food— As with virtually all holidays, Halloween has its own special foods, which serve the holiday in different ways. However, since Halloween is one-part HARVEST celebration, food has particular importance at this time and serves in an unusual variety of ways: As offering for the dead, as feast for the living, as PARTY fixings, as decoration, in FORTUNE-TELLING customs, in GAMES, and, most recently, as the CANDY provided to children during TRICK OR TREAT.

Late October marks the end of the harvest, and in Europe this meant an abundance of APPLES, NUTS, CABBAGES, PUMPKINS (in America) and potatoes (in Ireland). In the lore of the ancient CELTS, their celebration of SAMHAIN was marked with feasting and offerings to the gods (possibly also to the dead, although there is no archaeological evidence to support this). The EGYPTIAN FEAST OF THE DEAD and the Roman FERALIA were also marked with feasting and offerings, and it is possible that part of the reason November 1 was set as the date for ALL SAINTS' DAY was that it was easier to feed the pilgrims pouring into Rome after the harvest.

The earliest mentions of Halloween nearly all refer to food, usually BREAD or CAKE; throughout Europe and the British Isles special SOUL CAKES were prepared and given to the poor or to beggars, usually on All Souls' Eve (and usually as a form of payment in return for prayers offered for souls in PURGATORY). In Scotland and Ireland, Halloween mumming was rewarded with food; a 19th century Scottish mummer described receiving, at the conclusion of a performance, "suet dumplings in a cloot (cloth)…and if you were lucky your slice obtained a surprise, either a miniature doll or a tiny silver threepenny piece." Meals were set out for the visiting dead; in Mexico special sweets were prepared for spirit children during DAY OF THE DEAD, and during the French TOUSSAINT milk was poured on graves.

Special foods were also prepared purely for the living, especially in Ireland and Scotland: Apple tarts or dumplings, "sonsie kebbuck" (a lucky cheese), "banbrishd" (whipped cream), "brandered bannocks" (grilled barley- or pease-meal cakes), BARM BRACK, BOXTY, BWYD CENNAD Y MEIRW, CHAMP,

COLCANNON, CROWDIE, FUARAG, LAMBSWOOL, MRASTYR, SOWENS, and STAMPY all came to be associated almost exclusively with Halloween. There were, however, virtually no Halloween dishes that featured meat; this may be due to Irish churches having originally designated October 31 as a fast day. In America, favorite foods included apple cider, DOUGHNUTS, POPCORN, and PUMPKIN PIE.

Cakes (and sometimes other food items such as MASHED POTATOES or ice cream) were presented as fortune-telling games, with small tokens hidden inside; to receive a portion of food with a token foretold one's future. A ring indicated marriage; a coin, wealth; a small china doll, children; a thimble, "single blessedness"; and a sloe, long life.

Other foods became the agents of other forms of prognostication: Apples, BARLEY, BAY LEAVES, BEETS, cabbages, CORN MEAL, EGGS, FLOUR, HERRINGS, KALE, LEEKS, LEMONS, NUTMEG, NUTS, OATS, and PEAS have all helped young people to learn about future mates or fate. Sometimes divinations require a complete meal: In one such practice, a girl would prepare an especially good meal and lay it out to tempt an appearance of her future husband, who would then be bound to her.

Halloween involves a number of food games: Aside from the classic BOBBING FOR APPLES, there is also "the RAISIN race," SCADDING THE PEAS and SNAPDRAGON.

Some foods are known by their relation to FAIRIES: CHICKENS, SALT and oatmeal all had special protective properties, while BLACK-BERRIES were blighted by the fairies (or sometimes the DEVIL) on or about October 31.

CORN, pumpkins, oranges, apples, potatoes, and (in Great Britain) TURNIPS have all made fine Halloween decorations.

Halloween parties sometimes centered around food themes, with guests invited to attend in costumes based on harvest fruits and vegetables. Menus for early 20th-century Halloween parties frequently featured heavy foods, and this suggestion from a 1917 article might explain why: "To insure the dreams of goblins and the frightful glimpses of futurity which one's Hallowe'en slumbers should not fail to bring it is well to have one's menu decidedly indigestible" (the menu in this article includes Lobster Newburg, cheese soufflé, roast quail, and waffles with syrup).

Finally, probably no other holiday has as many alternate names which are food-based as Halloween does: The holiday has gone by ALLANTIDE, CABBAGE NIGHT, CAKE NIGHT, CALCANNON NIGHT, CRACK-NUT EVE, NUTCRACK NIGHT, and SNAP-APPLE NIGHT.

Footprints— In Ireland, footprints found on the morning after Halloween indicated the presence of ghostly visitors during the night. If the footprints were coming in, it foretold a birth in the household; going out was an omen of a death.

In North Lincolnshire, a FORTUNE-TELLING custom (used on both St. Mark's Eve and Halloween) had the opposite meaning: ASHES were placed on the hearthstone, or beans on the floor of the barn. If a girl found footsteps there the next morning, they belonged to her future husband.

Fortune Cake— Once the centerpiece of Halloween parties (especially in the late nineteenth century), a fortune cake was an ordinary cake except that a ring, a thimble and a dime were baked into it (sometimes other symbols as well). A ring denoted marriage, the thimble spinsterhood, and the dime wealth. In later years, fortune cake pieces were even marketed and sold as sets. In Ireland, BARM BRACK was a specific type of cake used exclusively as a fortune cake at Halloween.

Fortune-Telling— Fortune-telling or divination was, up until the mid-twentieth century, one of the most popular aspects of Halloween. The popularity of fortune-telling on Halloween is often ascribed to its beginnings as SAMHAIN, the CELTS' New Years' celebration, when it was thought that the borders between this world and the Otherworld were down, and as such divination was possible on this night. Although fortune-telling (es-

pecially those customs involving love and romance) was practiced on other days as well (including ST. AGNES' EVE, MIDSUMMER'S EVE and even CHRISTMAS), there were more and a wider variety of customs practiced on Halloweens past than any other day of the year. In his introduction to *Halloween and Other Festivals of Death and Life*, JACK SANTINO also describes divination as "oriented toward life-enforcing events such as love, courtship, and marriage at a time when seasonal activities include harvesting in preparation for the dead of winter."

By far the largest percentage of Halloween fortune-telling rituals was focused on determining the identity of one's future mate. Common themes in these rituals include performing certain actions BACKWARDS, using the number THREE (or three times three, NINE), DREAMS, WATER, APPLES, and out-

This Ellen Clapsaddle postcard shows two children engaged in a classic form of fortune-telling on Halloween.

door activities, such as those involving KALE or HEMP SEED. In a few the DEVIL was invoked, while in a few others the Lord or Mary are called upon. Some involve dire circumstances and were considered dangerous (see CHURCHES and FIELDS), but most were considered harmless and in time transformed into mere party games (see BOBBING FOR APPLES). Quite a few involved finding tokens in food (BARM BRACK, FORTUNE CAKE, or MASHED POTATOES).

A great many of the divinations involved seeing a future spouse in some ghostly form, known as a FETCH or wraith. However, these rituals also offered an opportunity for an earthly suitor to make his intentions known. As author MARTHA ORNE notes in the 1898 *Hallowe'en: How to Celebrate It* (in regards to the tradition of WALKING around the block with a mouthful of water): "A clever hostess will send two unsuspecting lovers by different doors; they are sure to meet, and not unfrequently settle matters then and there."

In one verse, SIR WALTER SCOTT suggests a particularly frightening method of divination:

For on Hallowmas Eve the Nighthag shall
 ride,
And all her nine-fold sweeping on by her
 side,
Whether the wind sing lowly or loud,
Stealing through moonshine or swathed in
 a cloud.
He that dare sit in St. Swithin's Chair
When the Nighthag wings the troubled air,
Questions three, when he speaks the spell,
He may ask and she must tell.

In Scotland a fortune-teller was called a spaewife, and was very busy indeed on Halloween.

Scrying, performed mainly with crystal balls, is practiced by some, especially WICCA adherents, on Halloween. Pendulums may also be used, in a method somewhat similar to the famous Ouija board, still a popular fortune telling game at Halloween.

For more fortune-telling customs, see also: ALPHABET GAME, ANTHROPOMANCY, APPLE PARINGS, APPLE SEEDS, ASHES, BARLEY, BAY LEAVES, BEDPOSTS, BEETS, BIBLE, BRIAR THORN, BUILDING THE HOUSE, ROBERT BURNS, BUTTONS, CABBAGES, CAILLEACH, CAKE, CANDLES, CEILING, CHESTNUTS, CHIMNEY, CLOTHES, CLOVER, COINS, CORN, CORN MEAL, CORPSES, CROSSROADS, CYNIVER, DINNER, DOUGH, DUMB CAKE, DUMB SUPPERS, EGGS, FEATHERS, FIRE O'LOVE, FIRES, FLOUR, FOOTPRINTS, GRAVEYARDS, HAIR, HARROW, HERRING, IVY, KNOTS, LAUNDRY, LEAD, LEEKS, LEMONS, LIME-KILN, LIVELONG, LUGGIE BOWLS, MATCHES, MATRIMONY (SAINT), MIDNIGHT, MILFOIL, MIRRORS, NEIGHBORS, NUTMEG, NUTS, OATS, PEAS, PEAT, POPCORN, PUMPKINS, RABBIT'S FOOT, RAKE, ROSES, SAGE, ST. ANDREW'S DAY, SALT, SCADDING THE PEAS, SHIRTS, SHOES, SHRUBBERY, SIEVE, SNAILS, SNAPDRAGON, SPIDERS, STRAW, TEA-LEAVES, THREAD, WALNUTS, WEDDING RING, WILLOWS, WIND, WISHING, WOOD, YARN, AND YEW.

Frazer, Sir James George— Born in Glasgow in 1854, Frazer was a social anthropologist whose classic work *The Golden Bough* (first published in a two-volume edition in 1890, followed by the twelve-volume 3rd edition in 1915) brought together a wealth of Halloween folklore and tales in what was the first serious historical overview of the holiday. As detailed in *Balder the Beautiful Volume I* (part VII of *The Golden Bough*), the lengthy chapter on "The Halloween Fires" pulls together FIRE and FORTUNE TELLING customs, history, GHOST STORIES, and tales of FAIRIES and WITCHES from all over the British Isles (Frazer relied on both existing sources such as *Brand's Popular Antiquities* and his own interviews and correspondence). Frazer, who was knighted in 1914 and who produced a number of other important works, passed away in 1941. Although many of Frazer's theories were later discredited (for example, his beliefs in Social Darwinism), *The Golden Bough* remains both the first work to seriously examine Halloween customs from a social and anthropological viewpoint, and an invaluable collection of Halloween myth and lore.

Fuarag— Gaelic name (derived from the Gaelic word for "cold") for a dish of milk and meal, popular at Halloween, often with a ring hidden inside. When prepared specifically for Halloween, it's referred to as *Fuarag na Samhna*, and is referred to in the lowland areas as CROWDIE.

G

Gallotians— In early twentieth-century Scotland, the "Gallotians" were a form of MUMMERS who went house-to-house in old COSTUMES and blackened faces, while carrying wooden swords; they put on a crude play with fighting at each house. At either the beginning or end of the presentation, an old patchwork-clad man with a MASK passed a hat around while saying:

> Here comes I, old Keek-um funny,
> I'm the man that lifts the money.

The name "Gallotians" bears a strong resemblance to "Galatians," the name of a tribe of CELTS, so it is possible this custom may have pagan origins.

Games— As a favorite activity of PARTIES, games have a long association with Halloween; however, Halloween games have special meaning, since they're often combined with FORTUNE-TELLING practices. For example, in one variation of a treasure or scavenger hunt game, a ring, a thimble and a penny were hidden around a room; whoever found the ring would soon be wed, the thimble's finder would remain unmarried, and the penny's collector would become wealthy. BOBBING FOR APPLES was sometimes turned into a form of divination, although usually the goal was simply to manage the difficult feat of obtaining an apple. Ouija boards provided any home with a way to obtain messages from the spirit world, and were popular in the twentieth century.

Guests might be blindfolded or dis-guised as ghosts (with pillowcases placed over their heads), and asked to play a game such as one in which they were given an apple stem, shown a PUMPKIN across the room resting on a chair, then spun around THREE times and told to place the stem in the pumpkin (in fact there are numerous varia-

1954 Whitman "Pin on the Hat" Halloween game

tions of "Pin the Tail on the Donkey," including professionally-produced "Pin the Tail on the Black Cat" games). Other games involved guessing (such as "Meow Meow," a game centered on the abilities of CATS) or storytelling (as in one which involved passing a bundle of glowing twigs from hand to hand—*see* CANDLES).

Games also extended to larger sporting functions in some areas: For example, the community of Cullen in Banffshire, Scotland, once celebrated both Halloween and CHRISTMAS by heading to the local shores for games of football and running. The games commenced after a procession to the sands led by pipers and music, and the winners—who were crowned with bonnets adorned with feathers and ribbons—led the procession to return to the town. The evening saw a special ball, during which the day's champions still wore their triumphant bonnets.

Whist and bridge were both popular Halloween games, and special Halloween tally cards for these games are now fine COLLECTIBLES.

Gate— Although gates figured most prominently in Halloween PRANKING (which even earned the holiday the name of GATE NIGHT), they also figured in one FORTUNE-TELLING custom involving CHURCHES: On Halloween night the fortune-seeker stood by a churchyard gate at MIDNIGHT to see souls of the dead in the coming year. However, the watcher ran the danger of being the first to die and becoming "the churchyard walker" until another foolish soul took his or her place.

Gate Night— This alternative name for Halloween derived from the fact that, during the nineteenth and twentieth centuries, gates were so often stolen in PRANKING.

Gay Culture— Like the NEO-PAGANS, the gays in the United States are a sub-culture who have claimed Halloween for themselves, and in the process boosted its popularity across all ethnic and sexual lines. It has been said that "Halloween is to gays what St. Patrick's is to the Irish," and there has been speculation that Halloween may have become popular with gays partly as a night to celebrate and to "let off steam" in the wake of the AIDS epidemic (and possibly eight years of the Reagan Administration, which saw more attempts to oppress gays and gay rights). Halloween's COSTUMING traditions have long offered a haven to transvestites and transsexuals; for example, beginning in 1938, Finnie's Club in Chicago held a yearly Halloween Masquerade Ball for "Female Impersonators" which ran through the late '50s. The Greenwich Village PARADE gained in popularity largely due to the influence of the local gay residents, and likewise Halloween festivities in Key West, West Hollywood, and San Francisco have also thrived, due to gay participation.

Ghost Stories— The association of ghost stories with Halloween probably dates back to the very beginnings of the holiday, as a day when the sun died, the night ruled, and the souls of the dead walked. Certainly there is a considerable body of ghost stories (or tales about malicious FAIRIES) surrounding

This vintage postcard catches young pranksters in the act on Gate Night.

SAMHAIN, and there is even a Catholic legend that ODILO initiated ALL SOULS' DAY because of a story he heard about the wailing of suffering souls. Several of the classic American stories told at Halloween, including "The Legend of Sleepy Hollow" by WASHINGTON IRVING, feature ghosts prominently, while such ghost-story films as *The Haunting*, *The Innocents* and, more recently, *The Sixth Sense*, have become favorite holiday viewing. There are also several ghost stories told during DAY OF THE DEAD festivities. Strangely, prior to the 20th-century ghost stories were more commonly told on CHRISTMAS Eve than during Halloween (see, for example, the Charles Dickens classic *A Christmas Carol*). *See* EACH UISG.

Ghost Table— A Maryland Halloween FORTUNE-TELLING custom, in which a table was set by the hearth with EGGS placed for each person who wanted to know his or her future spouse. At MIDNIGHT, the spirit of a CAT was believed to float through the door, followed by the ghostly image of a COFFIN. The spirit (or FETCH) of a person then drifted through the door and turned the egg of the person it would marry.

Ghosts— A Brittany proverb states that "on Halloween there are more souls in each house than there are grains of sand on the shores of the sea," and certainly Halloween has always been a time when ghosts were believed to walk more freely. In most parts of the world where the Catholic church has influence, the ghosts of departed family members are thought to return on ALL SOULS' DAY, and are welcomed; however, malicious spirits are also abroad at this time. In the region of the Vosges they believe that on Halloween night it is literally impossible to walk without treading on the souls of the dead; in this same region, windows are left open and beds uncovered on this night so that ghosts can return to enjoy some mortal comforts. One tradition in this area was to leave a basket of HAZELNUTS near the HEARTH for the dead to enjoy; it was also considered bad luck

to hunt on this night, since the woods were full of these wandering souls. In Brittany leftovers— typically pancakes, cider and curdled milk— are set out for the hungry ghosts on fresh white linen; musicians— who claim to sometimes feel the cold breath of their invisible guests— supply entertainment. In parts of Italy, one superstition involves not sleeping in one's bed on Halloween night, since the wandering dead seek rest. It is also bad luck in certain areas to leave livestock out on Halloween, since the wandering ghosts might seek to mount the horses or milk the cows dry. In Aurillac (Cantal) it was believed that on the evening of November 2 the souls of all those who would die in the coming year assembled at MIDNIGHT in the cemetery, where the Grim Reaper led them to their future graves. In fact, practicing cer-

An eerie 1909 postcard showing a Halloween witch and a ghost.

tain rituals in CHURCHES or at CROSSROADS might enable one to see ghosts on Halloween (although the watcher often ran the danger of becoming one himself).

Ghosts and their favorite haunts are very popular on Halloween; for example, Room 3312 (formerly Room 302) at the Hotel Del Coronado in San Diego, California — which is said to be haunted by the ghost of a VICTORIAN woman named Kate Morgan — is booked on Halloween for years in advance (even though the Hotel insists that one's chances of seeing a spectral guest are just as good on any other night).

At Newton Castle, Perthshire, the apparition of the Green Lady of Newton Castle is said to be most likely to appear at Halloween, and her gravestone is also supposed to turn around three times.

Armboth House in Cumbria was reportedly haunted following the drowning of the householder's daughter on Halloween, the night before her wedding day. The house now lies submerged beneath Thirlmere reservoir, but supposedly the sound of BELLS can still be heard, and a ghostly dog swims in Thirlmere Lake (where the young woman was murdered).

The violent events of GUY FAWKES DAY have given rise to a number of alleged hauntings, and the Halloween death of HARRY HOUDINI prompts a yearly séance to contact his ghost.

Ghosts must certainly be one of the most popular Halloween icons, along with JACK-O'-LANTERNS, CATS and WITCHES. There are dozen of ghost COLLECTIBLES produced every year, including CANDLES, yard decorations, windsocks, etc., and perhaps the classic Halloween COSTUME still consists of cutting eye-holes in a white sheet.

Gobble-Uns— See GOBLINS. In James Whitcomb Riley's poem "Little Orphant Annie," a young girl offers various brief descriptions of misbehaving children, and finishes each with the warning that "the Gobble-uns 'll git you ef you don't watch out!"

Goblins— Malicious FAIRIES, goblins are sometimes said to be the French equivalent of the English, Irish or Scottish fairy (the word comes from the French *gobelin*, a malicious spirit which troubled a Normandy town). A hobgoblin was a goblin more interested in harmless pranks than causing real injury.

One American folk belief is that goblins leave swamps on Halloween to haunt wrongdoers.

Goosey Night— Regional American name that refers to the night before Halloween, found in areas of the east coast, mainly New Jersey, and is synonomous with MISCHIEF NIGHT; in parts of Texas. In New Jersey, where Goosey Night PRANKING the night before Halloween has remained a problem into the 21st century, police in 2009 began issuing warnings and enforcing curfews (8 or 9 P.M., depending on the town) on this night.

Graveyards— As the final resting place of the dead, graveyards are an integral part of ALL

Goblins ride owls in this fanciful vintage postcard.

SAINTS' and ALL SOULS' DAY (and DAY OF THE DEAD) rituals. In many Catholic traditions, families visit graveyards at this time to clean and decorate the tombs and graves of their departed loved ones. In some areas the parish priest may actually conduct mass in the cemetery, lead parishioners in a procession through the graveyard, and bless individual graves.

In New Orleans, for several weeks before Halloween clear up to the afternoon of the 31st, it was a tradition (up until the mid-twentieth century) to clean the city's cemeteries. In Cajun areas, a nocturnal Mass was said in cemeteries on Halloween night. Candles that had been blessed were placed on graves, and FAMILIES sometimes spent the entire night at the graveside. Boys picked up extra money by waiting outside cemetery entrances and offering to clean graves for pay. FLOWERS— usually chrysanthemums— were placed at graves; in fact, this tradition was held in such esteem that families would go hungry in order to afford the largest or best flowers. On Halloween day street vendors gathered around graveyards and a party-type sense prevailed; nowadays, however, Halloween in New Orleans is associated with the French Quarter, which boasts one of the largest costumed CELEBRATIONS in the country. In earlier times, nuns begged money outside the graveyards and statues of saints were sold by vendors.

One New Orleans URBAN LEGEND tells of the African-American woman who for more than 40 years left a single blossom at the tomb of a white soldier killed in the Civil War; when the flower stopped appearing on All Saints Day, graveyard observers knew the woman had died.

There was at least one Creole WISHING custom in New Orleans: Before Halloween, a handkerchief must be purchased, then kept unused and clean. On November 1, the wish-seeker would leave home as early as possible, silently, and go to a cemetery, where he or she must enter by the main gate. The next step was to walk from there to the opposite wall, along the graveyard's main avenue, and somewhere on its length pick up a piece of dirt; this was tied in one corner of the new handkerchief, while the wish-seeker silently expressed the most heartfelt wish. Now the wish-seeker must leave the cemetery by the same gate used to enter, and go to a second cemetery; these same steps are repeated there, with the bit of dirt from the main walk tied into a second corner of the handkerchief with a second wish. A third cemetery was visited, with a third clod of dirt tied into a third corner, while the wish-seeker made a final wish. The last step was to return home, ball the handkerchief up and throw it up to the top of an armoire, or the cornice of a high window, anywhere high up where it would remain undisturbed. If the wish-seeker has successfully performed this ritual in complete silence, all three wishes will come true within the next year.

Graveyards weren't always treated with reverence, however, since they also figure in Halloween PRANKING: In both Ireland and America it was common for mischievous boys to dress as GHOSTS and hide out in cemeteries, frightening passersby with sudden appearances or their ghostly lanterns (made from PUMPKINS or TURNIPS).

One old belief was that lost friends could be met at graveyard GATES on Halloween night (although one also risked meeting those whom one had wronged or injured).

A European SUPERSTITION is that the dead emerge from their graves on Halloween to pray in churches. An American superstition stresses avoiding cemeteries on Halloween, since to meet the spirits of the dead who walk on that night would result in one's own death. The Irish version of this is that the dead will return on All Hallows to take revenge for any hurt done to them while alive, so graveyards should be avoided on this night; one should never turn to look if footsteps sound behind, since to meet the glance of a dead man is to die oneself.

Greece, Ancient *see* **Anthesteria**

Gregory I (Pope) (aka Gregory the Great, aka St. Gregory) (A.D. 540–604)— Gregory I figures in the history of Halloween as the main architect behind the Catholic Church doctrine of SYNCRETISM, or co-opting existing pagan practices, rather than trying to aggressively stamp them out. Halloween probably owes some of its history as a combination of pagan and Christian rituals to Gregory.

In A.D. 601 Pope Gregory wrote a letter to Abbot Mellitus, who was on his way to England, discussing the survival of pagan places and customs, and Christianity's response. In the letter, Gregory suggests:

> …the temples of the idols in those nations ought not to be destroyed; but let the idols that are in them be destroyed…. For if those temples are well built, it is requisite that they be converted from the worship of devils to the service of the true God…. And because they have been used to slaughter many oxen in the sacrifices to devils, some solemnity must be exchanged for them on this account … [they may] celebrate the solemnity with religious feasting, and no more offer beasts to the Devil, but kill cattle to the praise of God….

Although Gregory's letter nowhere specifies co-opting existing festivals or holidays, there is nonetheless a considerable amount of speculation that this letter established a policy of setting church celebrations (i.e., ALL SAINTS' DAY) on traditional pagan festival days (i.e., SAMHAIN). The mission to England is usually considered to be one of the greatest successes of Gregory's pontificate, although he also fostered the development of liturgical music (the term "Gregorian Chant" is from his name). He was canonized immediately after his death, and his feast day is celebrated in the Western Church on September 3 (although March 12, the anniversary of his death, is still observed in the East).

Greysteel— This Irish town experienced a horrific Halloween terrorist event on October 31, 1993, when gun-bearing terrorists burst into a pub frequented by both Catholics and Protestants, and shouted the American phrase "trick or treat!" as they opened fire, killing 13.

Grülacks— Young men of Shetland dressed in fantastic COSTUMES on Halloween, with tall, hand-woven straw hats and multi-colored ribbons, and with faces concealed by veils, who went GUISING house-to-house. Their leader was called the Skuddler; another carried a fiddle and was nicknamed the Reel-Spinner; in some reports, there was also one dressed in black known as the Judas. One carried a "buggie," a bag formed from the intact skin of a sheep, which they used to collect money and FOOD (such as traditional CAKES called *burstin brunies*, as well as mutton, sausages, and cheese) as they went house to house, offering song and dance. They all carried long sticks, which they thumped on the floor of the home as they grunted like pigs, and they would only enter a home after being invited in by shots fired by the home-owner. One mid-19th-century description of them by travelers unfamiliar with the custom suggests that they presented a frightening image, and were occasionally mistaken for FAIRIES. The next evening they assembled at a house or barn, where they were joined by sisters and sweethearts in a great feast and night of GAMES, singing and dancing. Uneaten food was given to the needy. Grulacks also occasionally visited weddings; it was thought to be a sign of great respect to see them appear at a wedding.

Guising— A possible forerunner of the American TRICK OR TREAT, guising was most popular in Scotland, where it was practiced on two holidays, HOGMANAY and Halloween. Hogmanay guising seems to be related to CHRISTMAS, since the guisers were often called Yule Boys and usually represented religious characters (specifically, the Twelve Apostles). Halloween guising is often believed to be a remnant of pagan Celtic practices, but there is virtually no evidence that the CELTS or their DRUIDS donned COSTUMES for Halloween; the blackened faces sported by some guisers are believed to echo an ancient Druid custom of rubbing BONFIRE ASHES on the face as a means of magical protection. It is also believed that guising was performed to fool wandering Halloween spirits, although contemporary guising has lost any meaning but the pleasures of dressing up and collecting rewards.

Guising is reported as far back as 1585, when it was an adult practice, but now it is confined almost solely to young children. The Scottish children don "fausse faces" (grotesque masks), and emerge after nightfall carrying TURNIP lanterns or KALE-runt torches. They join in small groups and sing a traditional rhyme:

> Hallowe'en! A nicht o' tine!
> A can'le in a custock!

Or one enjoyed more by mischief-makers of the past ran:

> The nicht is Hallowe'en and the morn's
>   Hallowday,
> Gin ye want a true love, it's time ye were
>   away!
> Tally on the window-brod,
> Tally on the green,
> Tally on the window-brod,
> The nicht's Hallowe'en!

At each door they asked "Please to help the guisers!," and were rewarded with APPLES, NUTS and small COINS. The practice is a variation of "thigging," which is the practice of soliciting gifts on special occasions, and should not be confused with begging. After guising they held BONFIRES, then it was home for indoor festivities.

Guleesh Na Guss Dhu (Guleesh Blackfoot)—Well-known Irish Halloween tale centering on Guleesh, a boy who never washes his feet. On Halloween night—when he turns 21—his father beats him and he runs from the house, only to encounter a fairy host, who he follows into their rath. When the fairy folk call up magic horses to ride, Guleesh follows suit and rides with them to Rome. When they realize Guleesh has joined them, they tell him that the beautiful daughter of the King of France will be married tonight, and they want to kidnap her before the wedding, but they need Guleesh's help, since she can't cling to a fairy. While in Rome, Guleesh wants to see the pope about getting his parish priest reinstated; he threatens to burn down the pope's house, so the pope gives him a bull for the priest. Then Guleesh and the FAIRIES ride to France, where they enter the wedding invisible to mortal eyes. They take the princess (who turned 18 that day, and was to be married against her will), make her invisible, and Guleesh rides with her back to Erin. When they land, Guleesh decides he can't turn her over to the fairies, so he utters a charm that turns their horses to BROOMS and sticks; in return, they strike the princess dumb. Guleesh takes the bull and the princess to his priest, and the priest agrees to keep the girl and pass her off as a niece. A year passes, during which Guleesh and the princess fall in love. Halloween night comes again, and Guleesh waits for the fairies, hoping to persuade them to restore her speech. The fairies happen by and Guleesh hears them mention that an herb growing right by his front door would, when boiled, cure her. Guleesh finds the herb and boils it, and the Princess regains her power of speech. She returns to France, Guleesh follows her, and finally they are wed.

Gunpowder Plot *see* **Guy Fawkes Day/Night**

Guy Fawkes Day/Night (also November the Fifth, Bonfire Night, Firework Night, Squib Night, Plot Night, Pope Day)—This British holiday, held on November 5, commemorates the failed attempt of a group of conspirators (including Guy Fawkes) to blow up Parliament in 1605. It was declared a holiday in 1606, and because of its proximity in the calendar to Halloween, there was naturally a considerable amount of crossover between the two observances. In fact, when Halloween was banned in Britain in the mid-seventeenth century, Guy Fawkes Day absorbed many of the Halloween rituals and kept them alive. Guy Fawkes Day may also have contributed to Halloween's most popular contemporary practice, TRICK OR TREAT.

Guy Fawkes Day commemorates the discovery (on November 5, 1605) of a plot to blow up the British Parliament on opening day (in 1605 the date for the opening was moved several times, mainly because of fear of plague outbreaks; prior to November 5, it had been set for October 3). Although the leader of the conspiracy was actually Robert "Robin" Catesby, Fawkes (who had taken the name "Guido Fawkes" since an ill-fated mission in 1603 to secure the aid of Spanish Catholics) was the man discovered with 36 barrels of gunpowder beneath the House of Lords in the early hours of November 5, and so was the first conspirator to be arrested (Catesby was slain by a posse at Holbeach on November 8). The conspiracy was originally triggered by the oppression of the English Catholics; after having suffered under the long reign of Queen Elizabeth, their hopes for some reprieve were swiftly dashed when the new monarch King James I ascended the throne in 1603, and soon made it clear that his tolerance for Catholicism (he had allowed his wife, Queen Anne, to convert to the religion sometime in either 1600 or 1601) was extremely limited. Catholic oppression extended from heavy fines to death (for harboring priests). Even though most Catholics (or "papists") were opposed to violent treason (especially after Spain signed a treaty with England in 1604), there were those who believed that fiery insurrection was the only means left to them; thus, Catesby's circle of conspirators eventually included 13.

Their plan — which not only included destroying the royal family and the House of Lords on November 5, the (revised) opening day of Parliament, but also kidnapping James's nine-year-old daughter Princess Elizabeth, with the idea of setting her up as a puppet ruler — was discovered prior to the actual unfolding, probably by hints leaked by the conspirators to mentors. A famed piece of evidence called "the Monteagle Letter" — an anonymous missive received on October 26 by Lord Monteagle which forewarned of the conspiracy — may have been a forgery by one of the very lords who had been privately warned. On November 1, Father Henry Garnet, later falsely implicated as the plot's Jesuit mastermind and finally executed on May 3, 1606, led several of the conspirators' kin in a solemn ALL SAINTS' DAY mass, followed on November 2 by the even more sober rituals of ALL SOULS' DAY. Fawkes (who had been tortured so severely that he was too weak to ascend the gallows without assistance) was hanged, drawn and quartered on January 31, 1606.

Response to the Plot, the trials, and the executions was almost immediate and plentiful — there were newspaper cartoons, speeches, and a book entitled *A Discourse of the manner of the Discoverie of the Gunpowder Plot*, ascribed to the king himself but

Children at work on their "guy" (1853 newspaper illustration)

probably ghost-written by Francis Bacon. Upon the same day that the conspiracy was discovered and averted, BONFIRES were lighted to celebrate, thus beginning a tradition that has now continued for over four hundred years. In January of 1606 the Parliament appointed November 5 "a holiday forever in thankfulness to God for our deliverance and detestation of the Papists." A special service for the holiday existed in the English *Book of Common Prayer* until it was excised in 1859. In 1647, it was the only festival not abolished by Parliament.

The day's tradition was well established by 1677, when *Poor Robin's Almanack* tells us:

> Now boys with
> Squibs and crackers play,
> And bonfires' blaze
> Turns night to day.

The classic celebration of the day included bonfires and MUMMING. An effigy

GUY FAWKER.
(From the English Prayer Book of 1607.)

Guy Fawkes enters the House of Lords in this seventeenth-century illustration.

called "the guy" was often created, and served as the centerpiece of begging by children before being carried through the streets and tossed onto a bonfire. The rhymes recited by the juvenile beggars are one of the most famous aspects of Guy Fawkes Day. The following song was found in some parts of the north of England:

> Hollo, boys, hollo, boys,
> Let the bells ring :
> Hollo, boys, hollo boys,
> God save the queen.

> Pray to remember
> The fifth of November,
> Gunpowder treason and plot,
> When the king and his train
> Had nearly been slain,
> Therefore it shall not be forgot.

> Guy Fawkes, Guy Fawkes,
> And his companions,
> Strove to blow all England up;
> But God's mercy did prevent,
> And saved our king and his Parliament.

> Happy was the man,
> And happy was the day,
> That caught Guy,
> Going to his play,
> With a dark lanthorn,
> And a brimstone match,
> Ready for the prime to touch.

> As I was going through the dark entry,
> I spied the devil.
> Stand back! Stand back!
> Queen Mary's daughter,
> Put your hand in your pocket
> And give us some money,
> To kindle our bonfire.
>   Huzza! Huzza!

In some areas, the classic rhyme was altered to fit some aspect of the local history, as in these lines that appear in a Nottinghamshire version:

> Gunpowder Plot shall never be forgot
> While Nottingham Castle stands upon a
>   rock.

An amusing local variant from Cleasby in Yorkshire included a reference to an old woman named Bella Brown, who was well-known for her "Tom Trot," a toffee made of treacle and butter. Yorkshire boys in the 19th century recited these lines around their Guy Fawkes Eve bonfires:

Gunpowder Plot shall never be forgot
As long as Bella Brown sells Tom Trot.

Another popular rhyme:

Guy Fawkes Guy, never come a' nigh,
Hang him on a lamp post and there let him die.
Here comes old Ragged Jack, with all his ragged clothes.
Tie him to the lamp post and burn him to his nose.

A variation of this "lamp post" rhyme ran:

Guy! Guy! Guy!
Stick him up high.
Stick him on a lamp post
And there let him die.

At Pembroke College in Oxford, November 5th rhyming was even institutionalized, as undergraduates prior to the mid-18th century were asked to make two copies of celebratory verses, one of which was presented to the master, and the other placed in the Hall for all to see.

As Guy Fawkes Day CELEBRATIONS became increasingly more riotous, they were suppressed, and the celebrations were enjoyed more by children (beginning in the eighteenth century). Children would gather around their hand-made effigies and beg "a penny for the Guy" from passersby; the money was often used to buy FIREWORKS for the evening of November 5. In some areas of Britain, children went house-to-house begging coal for bonfires; in others they went GUISING. "Chubbing" was the act of collecting wood for bonfires (although in Oxfordshire this practice was known as "going

a-progging"). "Guy faces" were masks that could be bought for the holiday; these were usually sold in the same shops selling fireworks for the day.

The holiday was celebrated in virtually every English village except Scotton, near Knaresborough, Yorks, which is close to the hall where Fawkes lived as a boy and where his ghost is supposedly still active.

At Slaugham in the 1890s, the fire was always built up round a tall, stout green post, especially chosen so that it would char but not burn. It was called "the scrag"; when the flames had died down, the scrag was uprooted and carried away on men's shoulders, and taken to each of the two local pubs where it was "sold" for drinks. In Hertfordshire, "Guy Fawkes Fireballs" were old rags covered in pitch and rolled into a ball; these were slung between two poles, set alight and carried flaming through town and village streets. The butchers of Clare Market had their own method of celebrating Guy Fawkes Day: One of them dressed as Guy Fawkes, and was seated in a cart accompanied by priest and executioner. The cart was drawn through the streets as if to the place of execution while money was solicited from onlookers, and later spent in carousing. At Hartley Wintney in Hampshire, villagers as-

Bates.   R. Winter.   C. Wright.   J. Wright.   Percy.   Fawkes.   Catesby.   T. Winter.
THE GUNPOWDER CONSPIRATORS—FROM A PRINT PUBLISHED IMMEDIATELY AFTER THE DISCOVERY.

An early engraving showing "The Gunpowder Conspirators."

sembled on Guy Fawkes Day at four points around the village, and at a signal they tossed 200 brands onto a great bonfire. Even three days later the ashes were still hot enough to roast CHESTNUTS. In Sussex, boys begging for material for their bonfires sang:

> A stick and a stake,
> For King George's sake!

Those who wouldn't give might find their BROOMS or fenceposts missing. At Rye in the 1860s and 1870s, there were even reports of people being tarred and feathered on Guy Fawkes Night.

At Marlborough in Wiltshire was found one of the more peculiar celebrations: On November 5th a dozen or more men assembled around the bonfire and followed each other round it, holding thick club sticks over their shoulders, while a few others standing at distances outside this moving ring with the same sort of sticks beat those which the men held over their shoulders as they passed; meanwhile, they all shouted and screamed loudly. This lasted about half an hour at a time and would continue at intervals until the fire died out.

Another unusual custom was found in Yorkshire at Doncaster: On the 5th of November, the town musicians stood on top of the church steeple and waited for the congregation to leave the morning service, at which point they played "God Save the King." This custom ran for nearly a century, although originally the tune played had been "Britons Strike Home."

In commemoration of the Gunpowder Treason, the vaults beneath the Palace of Westminster are still searched each year prior to the opening of Parliament by a detachment of 10 of the Queen's Body Guard of the Yeomen of the Guard. In 1760 a new piece of ritual was added, after a wine-seller named Old Bellamy rented some of the vault space as storage; now each search is concluded with a drink of port.

Although contemporary Guy Fawkes Day celebrations are sometimes confused or combined with Halloween festivities, the holiday is still celebrated with its own distinctive rituals throughout England. Lewes now hosts the last of the grand, old-fashioned Guy Fawkes Night celebrations (the festivities also commemorate the days of the Marian persecution, when 17 Protestant martyrs were burned at the stake from 1555 to 1557). The first record of Bonfire Night in Lewes dates to 1679; by 1929, 100,000 torches were burned in Lewes on Guy Fawkes Night. In the current celebration, five or six separate bonfire societies each hold their own processions, fireworks and bonfires, but they combine forces for the Grand United Procession, which features over a mile of effigies (often of current unpopular public figures, which are exploded to great applause), bands, banners, flaming torches, and over 2,000 participants. Each of the societies also throws a flaming tar barrel into the river Ouse, and visits the town's war memorial. The most historic society is the Cliffe Society, whose members dress up as Vikings in horned helmets (others include the Commercial Square Pioneers, who dress up as American Indians; the South Street Juveniles, whose costuming is Siamese; the Waterloo, who appear as Genghis Khan and the Huns, and Borough, who array themselves as Zulus). The Cliffe Society uses antique banners and Bonfire Prayers, and burns both the pope and Guy Fawkes in effigy. The Lewes procession starts every year about 8 P.M., and winds on for nearly two miles; the COSTUMES worn by the society members are intricate, and sometimes old, passed down from father to son. Cliffe (named after the chalk cliff that towers over the town) doesn't take part in the procession but mocks it with pantomime, and remains the most seriously anti-papist of the Bonfire Societies. The societies also carry effigies of leaders who have protested bonfires and effigy burning, although sometimes the effigies are just huge heads on stakes. The effigies can be as tall as 30 feet, and have even included such American figures as Ronald Reagan.

The Lewes celebration is not without its own history of controversy. In 1779, after an attempt to ban the bonfires, a notice was pasted up on the Horsham Town Hall which read in part:

> Man, if you will believe us in advising you for your own good, all of you that have the least hand in trying to prevent the fire and fireworks in the town would best come off, for it is determined between us to have a fire of some sort, so if you will not agree to let us have it in peace and quietness, with wood and faggots, we must certainly make a fire of some of your houses, for we don't think it a bit more sin to set your houses a fire, and burn you in your beds, than it is to drink when one is thirsty.

During the nineteenth century, authorities again attempted to clamp down on dangerous celebrations, and the conflict came to a head in 1847 with rioting; a compromise was finally reached in which the "Bonfire Boys" agreed to be responsible for the conduct of the crowds.

In 19th-century Exeter, Guy Fawkes celebrations began at 4 A.M. on the morning of the 5th, as cannons were fired off around the city. Youngsters spent the day parading their "guys," and fireworks were fired off throughout the day. A bonfire was held in the Cathedral yard, and the festivities continued until around two A.M. the following morning.

A 1904 account from Guildford notes that all the High Street merchants closed their shops on the Fifth and "provided means for extinguishing fires." Early evening saw a procession of young men disguised in "grotesque costumes" and carrying fire-making supplies, which they used to construct a bonfire opposite Holy Trinity Church. Damage was often serious, including broken windows, and stolen fencing and gates; after 1868, these practices were banned.

The Hatherleigh Guy Fawkes Carnival has been held since 1907; it includes a hunt, a children's costume parade and contest, PARADES, floats, a disco, and (unofficially) the burning of tar barrels, a custom which has declined in recent years due to the increasing difficulty of obtaining barrels. The Bridgwater Guy Fawkes Carnival was organized in 1882, and usually includes 100,000 spectators, and 125 floats featuring electric light bulbs. The festivities traditionally end with a fireworks display called "the squibbing."

On the island of Guernsey off the coast of Britain, Guy Fawkes Day festivities once included a house-to-house MUMMING ritual, with participants in costumes and painted faces, and accompanied by as many as 17 HORSES. They wheeled an effigy of Guy Fawkes to each house, and collected money from about 2 P.M. in the afternoon until 10 P.M. that night. Afterwards, they hung the effigy from a gibbet, and set fire to it while riding the horses around the pyre. The next night was called "share-out," as the money collected was shared out among all the participants.

Not all 5th of November festivities centered on bonfires or guys: Around parts of Lincolnshire, up until 1860, guns could be fired anywhere in a parish on that day. A 1641 account from Elmswell, East Yorkshire notes that wagons were put away for the winter on "Powder treason day." In parts of Norfolk, a hollowed-out turnip jack-o'-lantern was carried on Guy Fawkes' Night. One of the most curious practices was found in Holderness, where on the eve of the 5th of November, the bells were rung, the church lit, and each boy in the parish was provided with a strip of leather attached to a cord with which the boys then beat the church pews. In one town the beating was called "babbling." In Lincolnshire, on Guy Fawkes' Night they practiced certain bonfire divinations (including throwing a stone into the bonfire and searching for it the next morning) that had formerly belonged to Halloween.

One community in Britain, Tower Hamlets, has in recent years attempted to use the November 5th celebrations to acknowledge some of their diverse ethnic populations—in various years, the day has focused on celebrating a Bengali fairy tale, the Olympics, and Mexican parties.

When the Guy Fawkes Day celebration crossed the Atlantic — where New England colonists were less likely to celebrate the savior of a British monarch — it became Pope Day, a celebration of anti-papist sentiments. As Pope Day/Bonfire Night became increasingly anarchic, it was frequently condemned; even George Washington called it "ridiculous and childish." Likewise, an American almanack of 1746 notes of the day:

> Powder-plot is not forgot
> Twill be observed by many a sot.

Nevertheless, the day was celebrated in East Coast U.S. towns up through the late nineteenth century (or about the time that Halloween finally arrived in America). American Guy Fawkes Day revelers sometimes carried PUMPKIN lanterns and NOISEMAKERS, and indulged in PRANKING and bonfires (with dancing). American celebrations from the eighteenth century were often supplemented with revolutionary political demonstrations; for example, in 1774 effigies of Lord North (the British prime minister), Thomas Hutchinson (the Tory Governor of Massachusetts), the pope, and the DEVIL (holding a lantern in the shape of a tea canister) were all burnt. Another patriotic Guy Fawkes celebration of eighteenth-century America involved a man riding an ass, wearing huge jack boots and a horrifying mask, called Joyce, Jr. He assembled a mob of men and boys (who whistled a particular tune), and they rode to terrify adherents to the Royal Government (prior to the Revolution).

The American celebrations also often involved only children, as groups of young boys carrying pope effigies about on boards or small carriages were common. At night they assembled tableaux featuring effigies of the pope, the devil and other religious figures on larger wagons; these were then wheeled about, sometimes with dancers performing atop them as well. The entire procession would go house-to-house, reciting a poem that began:

> The fifth of November,

> As you well remember,
> Was gunpowder treason and plot;
> I know of no reason
> Why the gunpowder treason
> Should ever be forgot.

The rhyme concluded with:

> Here is the pope that we have got,
> The whole promoter of the plot.
> We'll stick a pitchfork in his back
> And throw him in the fire.

The boys collected money, and concluded the evening with a feast and a bonfire of the effigies. In some areas the boys carried large sticks which they thumped on the ground in time with the rhyme.

In some American areas Guy Fawkes Day celebrations were halted after 1775 in deference to the French, who were deemed an advantageous ally; George Washington also feared offending Canadians, who had likewise become valuable allies. The November 5th celebrations were finally abolished for good in America in 1833. Toward the end of the nineteenth century, as Pope's Night lost its meaning in the U.S. areas where it was still celebrated, it was actually called "Pork Night."

Guy Fawkes Day was also celebrated in other areas of the British Empire. In New Zealand, they recited this rhyme:

> Please to remember the fifth of November,
> The gunpowder treason and plot.
> I see no reason why the gunpowder treason
> Should ever be forgot.
> Four and twenty barrels lain down below,
> Blow old England overflow.
> Happy was the night, happy was the day,
> See old Guy Fawkes going to his den
> With a dark lantern and a candle in his hand.
> Get out! Get out! You dirty ole man!
> Holla, Holla, boys, make the bells ring.
> Holla, Holla, boys, God Save the King.
> A pound of cheese to choke him,
> A bottle of beer to wash it down,
> A jolly good fire to roast him.
> Christmas is coming, the pigs are getting fat,
> Please put a penny in the old man's hat.
> If you haven't got a penny, a hapenny will do.
> If you haven't got a hapenny, God Bless You.

Money was often given to the child able to say this rhyme the best (or the loudest). Sometimes mischievous adults were known to heat COINS on shovels before throwing them out to the children. By 1949, the rhyme had been replaced by the far simpler "A penny for the guy, Mister?"

In modern Ireland Guy Fawkes Day is not commonly celebrated, although it is sometimes confused with Halloween.

Just as with Halloween, Guy Fawkes Day has both its own SUPERSTITIONS and its own foods associated with it. Given the violent and tragic nature of the Gunpowder Plot, it is not surprising that a number of GHOST legends would be connected to the event, including Fawkes's at Scotton; conspirator Robert Wintour's wife Gertrude at Huddington (she haunts "Lady Wintour's Walk" in the woods); and sympathizer Stephen Littleton's groom Gideon Grove, who escaped the havoc at Holbeach only to be caught and killed in some fenland near Wombourne, where his ghost now appears as a "phantom rider." A whimsical superstition that prevails among the fishermen of Hastings and Brighton is that shoals of HERRINGS make their appearances off the coast during this season because they come close to shore to see the bonfires (fishermen claimed that herrings were first caught each year around the 5th or 6th of November).

Foods distinctive to the holiday include "Bonfire Parkin," a special heavy cake made of oatmeal (or flour), molasses (or treacle) and ginger (in Leeds and other areas this cake was so popular that the holiday came to be known as "Parkin day"); "Thar" or "Tharf cake," found in South Yorkshire, Lancashire, and Derbyshire, and possibly named after an old Scandinavian celebration of the god Thor; and there was even a candy known as "Plot Toffee" or "Bonfire Toffee" (the principal ingredients are butter and black treacle), although as referenced above this candy was also known as "Tom Trot" in some areas. In Derbyshire, money was saved throughout the year to make the tharf cakes, which were eaten at a different house each year in a custom called "tharf-cake joinings." At Hathersage, it was customary to keep a bit of the cake until the following year's celebration. In Bradwell, the "thar-cake joining" took place within the family, as each family member shared the thar cake. Methodists in Bradwell held a "thar-cake supper" on the Saturday nearest to the fifth of November. In a newspaper article from 1898, a gentleman commented on the practice of giving a case of sponge cakes to some civil servants on November 5th and speculated that "if the custom could be traced back to its origin, the cakes would be found to be the old 'soul-cakes.'"

BELL-ringing was also popular at Guy Fawkes Day/Night, with instances dating back to at least 1627 (when a Northumberland record book shows a payment made to ringers for "Gowayes Day" on November 5th).In some areas of Britain (especially Lancashire and Yorkshire), November 5th bell ringing was so popular that the day was called "Ringing day." In Beverley, an annual hiring fair held each November 5th was called "Ringing-day Fair."

Guy Fawkes experienced a surge in popularity when graphic novel writer Alan Moore turned him into the anti-fascist protagonist of his 1988 series *V for Vendetta*. After the 2006 film of the series was released, Guy Fawkes masks and other memorabilia became popular COLLECTIBLES.

Gypsies—Gypsies are a nomadic ethnic group who have become stereotyped as romantic fortune-tellers, and so their image has frequently been incorporated into Halloween CELEBRATIONS since the early 20th century. Correctly identified as the Roma or Romani people, the name "gypsy" derived from the fact that gypsies were mistakenly believed to have originally come from Egypt; they actually originated in India approximately 1,000 years ago, and spread to Europe by A.D.1300 Many Romani immigrated to North America in the 19th century, until

1885, when Roma were officially excluded from U.S. immigration policy.

The stereotype of the gypsy was a carefree, exotic fortune-teller; the 1891 book *Gypsy Sorcery and Fortune-Telling* states that "Gypsies…have done more than any class on the face of the earth to disseminate among the multitude a belief in fortune-telling…" As Halloween celebrations spread throughout the U.S. in the late 19th-century, Scottish and Irish FORTUNE-TELLING rituals associated with the holiday were adapted as well, and the gypsy image became popular at holiday PARTIES. A 1908 article from *Good Housekeeping* places the gypsy squarely at the center of Halloween festivities: "While the games of dipping into saucers with mysterious mixtures and chewing thread in pursuit of RAISINS went on one by one, the little WITCHES were carried off to a dark corner to hear wonderful fortunes read from their palms by a dark gypsy lady whom no one recognized as an older sister." Gypsy COSTUMES were easy to make at home, and the gypsy was frequently interchangeable with the witch. In addition to gypsy costumes and gypsy fortune telling paraphernalia (including various "Gypsy Fortune Teller" or "Romany Fortune Teller"

card decks), gypsies were also a popular source for Halloween parties: A 1932 booklet suggests, for example, a gypsy themed party, with scarves draped over lamps and drawings of gypsy wagons on the walls.

A 1934 Halloween RECITATION clearly connects gypsies, fortune-telling, and Halloween:

> To read the shadowed future
> A gypsy is quite good,
> And crystal gazing, too,
> Will tell you what you would.
> But for mysterious signs
> That nowhere else are seen,
> You must invite your future
> The night of Hallowe'en.

Gypsy costumes, usually consisting of colorful scarves, peasant blouses, and costume jewelry, were popular with all age groups at least until the 1950s, when commercially available costumes based on popular television series characters dominated the market. Still, companies like Ben Cooper continued to produce gypsy costumes (some with plastic masks of exotic female faces), and gypsies remain popular choices for Halloween costumes to the present time.

Hair— An old English FORTUNE-TELLING custom involves stealing out at MIDNIGHT on Halloween, plucking a small lock of hair from one's head, and hurling it to the night breeze; whichever direction it blows in indicates which direction one's future intended will come from. Poet John Gay refers to this custom in "Thursday, or the Spell" from his 1714 *The Shepherd's Week*:

> I pluck this lock of hair from off my head
> To tell whence comes the one that I shall
>   wed.

> Fly, silken hair, fly all the world around
> Until you reach the spot where my true love
>   is found.

In another hair divination, at midnight on Halloween a girl would brush her hair THREE times before a MIRROR; if the man who was to be her husband appeared in the mirror over her shoulder, she would be married within the year.

Several divinations center on finding a hair in a PEAT (the color will indicate the hair color of one's future spouse). Another in-

Go out alone at midnight,
Pluck out a lock of hair.
Send it on the evening breeze
To find your loved one fair.
The way it takes to flying
Is where your love is sighing

This 1923 postcard creates its own Halloween divination using hair.

volves writing different hair colors on pieces of paper attached to three FEATHERS, and blowing the feathers into the air; the one that lands closest indicates the hair color of one's future spouse.

It was thought to be good luck to find a hair from the "fro'ing stick" in the CROWDIE on Halloween.

Hallow-Fair— A fair or market held at Halloween. See CELEBRATIONS.

Hallow-Fire— A BONFIRE lit in celebration of Halloween. In 1799 the *Statistical Account of Scotland* noted that "the hallow fire, when kindled, is attended by children only."

Hallow-Tide (also ALLANTIDE, HOLLANDTIDE, all hallowentyde, hallen-tide)— The season of ALL SAINTS' or the first week of November.

Halloween Attractions— Not to be confused with HAUNTED HOUSES, Halloween attractions are seasonal outdoor attractions such as CORN MAZES, PUMPKIN PATCHES, or haunted HAYRIDES; they are considered a form of "agri-tourism" or "agri-tainment." Like haunted houses, Halloween attractions charge admission and appear for only a short time around Halloween. There are estimated to be over 1,500 Halloween attractions annually, and they have become an important source of revenue for many small farms.

Halloween Bleeze— A Scottish name for Halloween BONFIRES. In some descriptions, Scottish Halloween bonfires are described as being surrounded by a circular trench symbolic of the sun. In Perthshire, the Halloween bleeze is made when heath, broom and dressings of flax are tied to a pole, which is then set afire and carried about by local young men (several were carried throughout the village at the same time, making an impressive sight on a dark evening).

Halloween Crab (*Gecarcinus quadrates*)— Also known as moon crabs, mouthless crabs, and harlequin land crabs. A common nocturnal land crab found in many areas along the Pacific coast of Central and South America (principally Costa Rica). These crabs derive their name from their black carapace and bright orange legs (they also have purple claws), and from the coloring on the front of the carapace that gives them the appearance of a JACK-O'-LANTERN face. Because of their vivid coloring, they're also sold as exotic home terrarium pets. Not to be confused with the Halloween hermit crab, a Hawaiian crustacean named for its vivid orange and red banded legs, and also sold as an aquarium pet.

Halloween Ladybug (*Harmonia axyridis*)— These harmless insects earn their name from their black and orange coloring (rather than the usual ladybug colors of black and red), and from making an annual appearance in October. Originally from Asia, these tiny beetles created a Halloween scare in October of 1995 when they began to swarm in areas of the American Northeast in alarming numbers. They typically seek shelter during October and November until the following spring, and they began appearing in large numbers inside homes and other buildings. Although deadly to harmful aphids, humans need fear only one aspect of Halloween ladybugs: Their orange blood is extremely foul-smelling, a usual defense tactic against larger predators (including human housewives).

Halloween Origins and Development— There are many names for Halloween, including Halloweve, Halleve, Hallowtide, Hollandtide, Hallowmas, November Eve, Holy Eve, Whistle Wassail Night, and Hallowe'en. The modern name "Halloween" (for the festival celebrated on October 31) derives from "All Hallows' Even," or the night before ALL SAINTS' or "All Hallows' Day." The word "hallow" is from an early English word for "holy," and until about A.D. 1500 "hallow" was a noun commonly applied to a holy personage or saint. "All Hallows' Even" was first abbreviated to "Hallowe'en," and sometime in the mid-twentieth century the use of the apostrophe was dropped, leading to the contemporary name for the holiday.

Halloween is largely a combination of two celebrations: As a HARVEST festival, it is similar to the American THANKSGIVING and the European MARTINMAS (which is celebrated on the day once belonging to Halloween, November 11); and as a commemoration of the dead, it may have roots in the EGYPTIAN FEAST OF THE DEAD (which mourned the passing of the sun god Osiris), the Greek ANTHESTERIA, and the Roman festivals of both FERALIA and LEMURIA. Most cultures celebrate a day in commemoration of their dead, and contemporary festivals include Japan's BON, China's YUE LAAN and CH'ING MING, and the American MEMORIAL DAY. However, for the last century it has been commonly accepted that Halloween's closest ancestors were two pre–Christian celebrations, the Celtic SAMHAIN and the Roman POMONA (both believed to have been held on or about November 1). With recent advances in archaeology and folklore studies, we now know that many of the previous assertions were in error. For example, Samhain was often described as being the name of the Celtic "Lord of Death," when in fact the CELTS had no such deity and the name means "summer's end"; and there is no festival for Pomona (a minor wood-nymph or hamadryad) in the old Roman calendar. Samhain was traditionally a time when animals were slaughtered at the approach of winter, and the 1848 *Five Hundred Points of Good Husbandry* by Thomas Tusser notes:

> At Hallowtide, slaughter time entereth in,
> And then doth the husbandman's feasting begin.

Likewise, the *Statistical Account of Scotland* from 1793 says of one parish (Forfar): "…between Hallowmass and

A nineteenth-century engraving entitled "All-Hallow Eve in Kilkenny, Ireland" by Edmund Fitzgerald.

Christmass, when the people laid in their winter provisions, about twenty-four beeves were killed in a week…"

Recent scholarship on Halloween has waged a heavy debate concentrating on whether the holiday owes its character to the pagan Samhain or to the Christian All Saints' Day (and the subsequent November 2 celebration of ALL SOULS' DAY). However, it seems difficult to ignore the large differences between the way the holiday is still celebrated in Celtic areas such as Ireland (with BONFIRES, PRANKING and GUISING), and the way it is celebrated throughout the rest of Europe (with sober church services and grave decorating). Furthermore in some parts of Ireland the day is still referred to as Samhain, ample testimony to that pagan festival's endurance.

In Ireland, Halloween is often connected to FAIRIES, who may also represent relics of Samhain. Alexander Montgomerie's sixteenth-century poem "Flyting against Polwait" shows the connection between fairies (or "gude ncybouris," according to Montgomerie) and Halloween:

> In the hinderend of harvest, on allhallow
>   evin,
>   Quhen our gude ncyhbouris rydis, if I reid
>   rycht,
> Sum buklit on ane bwnwyd and sum on ane
>   bene,
>   Ay trippand in troupes fra the twilycht;
> Sum saidlit on a scho-aip all graithit in grene,
>   Sum hobland on hempstalkis hovand on
>   hicht,
> The King of Phairie and his court with the
>   elph-quene,
>   With many elrich incubus was rydand that
>   nycht.

("Buklit" = mounted; "bwnwyd" = ragweed; "scho-aip" = she-ape; "graithit" = arrayed)

And George Macdonald's poem "Hallowe'en" demonstrates that GHOSTS (or possibly fairies again) prevailed in Scotland on Halloween:

> It's the nicht atween the Sancts and Souls
>   When the bodiless gang aboot,
> An' it's open hoose we keep the nicht
>   For ony that may be oot.

Modern Halloween also owes a considerable debt to the English GUY FAWKES DAY (November 5), which may have given Halloween some of its rowdier aspects. Prior to the establishment of Guy Fawkes Day on 1606, the few references to Halloween that appear mention SOUL CAKES, BELLS and even BOBBING FOR APPLES; PRANKING doesn't seem to appear until after the introduction of Guy Fawkes Day, which was celebrated during Protestant times when Halloween itself was banned as too Catholic or "popish." Folklorist JACK SANTINO has conducted interviews with contemporary Irish natives who literally don't know whether they celebrate Halloween or Guy Fawkes Day.

Until 1582, Europe operated under the Julian calendar, instituted by Julius Caesar; however, the Julian Calendar actually made each year 11 minutes too long, amounting to an entire day in 128 years. By 1582, the calendar was 10 days off, making it difficult to reconcile religious days (which were often calculated by phases of the moon — for example, Easter is celebrated on the first Sunday after the full moon next following the vernal equinox) with civil days and seasonal changes. On October 5, 1582, Pope Gregory XIII instituted a new calendar, and ordered that the day should be changed to the 15th (Gregory's system gives the average year 26 extra seconds). However, because the Gregorian calendar was considered Catholic, some areas of Europe were longer in adopting it than others; in England, for example, it was not accepted until 1751, a decision which caused many Protestants to demand the return of their 11 days.

One of the earliest records of a Halloween party appears in 1629, and was recorded in the journals of eminent lawyer, writer, and parliamentarian Bulstrode Whitelocke. Even though the Protestant king Charles I was in power, Whitelocke's records and biography describe an evening of dancing in St. Dunstan's Tavern: "…on All-hallows day, which the Templars considered the beginning of Christmas, the master, as soon as the evening was come, entered the hall, followed by sixteen revelers. They were proper, handsome young gentlemen, habited in rich suits, shoes and stockings, hats and great feathers. The master led them in a bar-gown, with a white staff in his hand, the music playing before them. They began with the old masques; after that they danced...till it grew very late." This was nearly twenty years before Parliament — in 1647 — abolished all festivals but Guy Fawkes Day.

The importance of Halloween in modern Irish society is shown by the fact that schools have a Halloween break; and the Monday nearest to Halloween is recognized as a bank holiday in the Republic of Ireland. Up until the early twentieth century, Halloween was held in greater significance than CHRISTMAS in Ireland. In parts of Ireland the term "Old Halleve" refers to November 12.

In Scotland, the famed ROBERT BURNS poem "Hallowe'en" (1785) suggests that Halloween was still popularly celebrated there through the close of the 18th century. But by 1833, Scots seem to have consigned the holiday to children, as this description from Scottish explorer Captain J. E. Alexander suggests (this was written as Alexander made his way through Canada): "We spent the evening of Halloween among drowned woods and swamps and a deluge of rain whilst we recounted the legends and ghost stories with which the Scottish crones are wont to affright their juvenile audience on that dreaded night and then had a round of music."

Although Guy Fawkes Day was celebrated in America up until the end of the nineteenth century (and despite the emigration of over a quarter of a million Ulster-Scots to America in the eighteenth century), Halloween was almost completely forgotten until the influx of Irish and Scottish immigrants in the mid-nineteenth century, driven here largely by the Potato Famine from 1846 to 1852. (Another current debate stems over which of these ethnic groups was likelier to have brought Halloween to America.) Even after the famine had ended, another six

million Irish left the country (joining over a million who had left during the actual famine years); 80 percent of these emigrants came to America. Over the next half-century, Halloween gained in popularity and was celebrated largely as a harvest festival, with hay rides, corn-husking, and BOBBING FOR APPLES, and it was enjoyed almost completely by adults. Strangely enough, as Halloween was on the ascendant in America, it was declining in Great Britain and Ireland, where the practice of bonfires was dying out, partly because they had inspired considerable drunken violence and partly because many locales had simply stripped the areas of burnable brush. A small piece from the November 1, 1876 edition of the *New York Times* suggests that "the glory of this once popular festival has departed." Nevertheless, Halloween had started to spread out from American Scots-Irish enclaves into the VICTORIAN middle class, who found its divination customs quaint; middle-class periodicals such as *Godey's Lady's Book and Magazine* and *Harper's Monthly Magazine* began to describe Halloween festivities and offered tips on hosting seasonal PARTIES. What was probably the first Halloween book, MARTHA RUSSELL ORNE's 48-page *Hallowe'en: How to Celebrate It*, was published in 1898, indicating that the holiday had firmly settled into the middle class of America.

By the end of the nineteenth century, the Irish love of Halloween pranking had spread to American youngsters, who roamed the countryside on this night, removing GATES, tipping outhouses and frightening farmhouse inhabitants. As the country became more industrialized, pranking moved into the cities; at first it retained an innocent nature, with egg-throwing, CHALKING and NOISEMAKERS the favored pastimes, but it quickly became more destructive, with lights broken, fires set and pedestrians tripped. This "rowdyism" reached a peak during the Great Depression, forcing many Eastern American cities to take action.

When curfews and increased police

presence proved ineffective, the cities began to institute instead alternative forms of entertainment for children. Costuming and parties had become popular adult Halloween activities during the first decades of the twentieth-century, and so these ideas were now transferred to children. Youth groups such as the Boy Scouts and the YMCA organized parties and carnivals, and parents were also encouraged to join forces (since this was the Depression and money was spare) to provide private entertainments. Combine this with the GUISING and MUMMING traditions of Halloween (and Guy Fawkes Day), and the popular American TRICK OR TREAT was born, effectively replacing destructive pranking. Meanwhile, adult celebrations of Halloween were on the decline, possibly due to Prohibition (1920 to 1933).

This 1928 postcard shows a young prankster getting the upper hand over an authority figure.

Trick or treat also gave rise to the commercialization and marketing of Halloween in America (although the custom spread slightly to European countries as well). Masks, COSTUMES, candies, decorations, lanterns and more all brought millions of dollars to RETAILING; by the end of the twentieth century, Halloween was second only to Christmas in the amount of holiday dollars (six billion) spent on it.

By the 1960s, the first URBAN LEGENDS of dangers to trick or treaters began to surface, and by the 1980s children were being encouraged to avoid trick or treating, because of poisoned candy or razor blades hidden in apples by anonymous malefactors (ironically, this craze may have been fueled by the public's fascination with the decade's "slasher" horror films, a cycle begun by JOHN CARPENTER's *Halloween*). Even though there was not a single documented incident of an anonymous psychotic killing a child, the public bought into the scare and Halloween as a day for children began to decline. However, at the same time its popularity with two subcultures was gaining: The GAYS claimed the day for themselves with PARADES such as the one in Greenwich Village; and the NEO-PAGANS (who were energized by the 1979 release of Margot Adler's *Drawing Down the Moon*) tried to transform the day into a deeply-felt celebration of the ancestors.

By the 1990s, trick or treat seemed to be on the rise again, only to be dealt another blow, this time by fundamentalist Christian groups who believed the holiday celebrated the DEVIL. In literally hundreds of web sites and books, these groups spread their belief that costuming and even carrying JACK-O'-LANTERNS constituted sins; however, their "proof" was drawn almost entirely from inaccurate and obsolete sources, such as Ralph and Adelin Linton's 1950 *Halloween through Twenty Centuries*. Halloween survives, however, probably in large part because, as Jack Santino suggests in his introduction to *Halloween and Other Festivals of Death and Life*, it serves a purpose in the calendrical cycle: Images of birth (at Christmas) are followed by images of growth and fertility (spring and Easter), and then by images of death (at Halloween). The holiday also has a special meaning for twentieth- and twenty-first-century children: Sociologists and folklorists have suggested that trick or treating is an inversion of the usual power structure, the one day a year when children are "officially licensed" to have power over adults. It is also the first real holiday in the American school year, and even though there is no school break for the holiday in the U.S. (save for in the state of Louisiana), it nevertheless represents the first occasion for merrymaking after the beginning of the school year.

In 2001, many journalists predicted a disastrous Halloween in the wake of the September 11 terrorist attacks on the United States, but instead the holiday enjoyed its biggest year ever, with record numbers in retailing, parties, parades and trick or treating. These amazing statistics attested to the holiday's adaptability and unshakable entrenchment in America. The American conception of Halloween — especially trick or treating — has also spread to other countries; for example PUMPKIN and jack-o'-lantern decorations have become popular in Germany and Austria. Trick-or-treating is still uncommon in Europe, but parties are popular. Not all of Europe is welcoming the arrival of this largely American holiday, however; for example, Polish and Austrian church leaders attacked the newly-imported customs in 2001, saying they were "humiliating" and "alien to our traditions." Similarly, church leaders in Mexico denounced the holiday there in favor of their own DAYS OF THE DEAD.

In his essay "Carnival, Control, and Corporate Culture in Contemporary Halloween Celebrations," Russell W. Belk suggests that "Halloween may be becoming co-opted in subtle ways by being transformed into a vehicle for nurturing corporate and consumer cultures," but he also believes that the holiday's "…participative humor … invigorates it and contributes to its longevity."

One of the most fanciful explanations for the origins of Halloween is found in the work of philosopher and theosophist Alvin Boyd Kuhn, who suggested that the date of October 31st was chosen as a festival day because of its position exactly forty days after the fall equinox, with forty days being symbolic of rebirth and new life.

Halloween Room (Biltmore Estate) — The Biltmore estate in Asheville, NC (often referred to as "America's largest home") was built on 125,000 acres of land by George Vanderbilt in 1895. The downstairs area contains the Halloween Room (named after a holiday party once held there), a former storage area that was transformed into a party room by John Cecil and Cornelia Vanderbilt Cecil in 1924. The history of the Halloween room remains somewhat shrouded in mystery; one story has it that the room once housed a 26-day party, celebrating Cornelia's 26th birthday in 1926. At one party, guests were encouraged to paint on the walls, and the room is still decorated with these images, many of which depict Russian fairy tales (which were popular in the 1920s).

Halloween Sadism — Term applied by some folklorists and sociologists to contemporary events such as supposed poisoning of TRICK OR TREAT candy or placement of razor blades in APPLES. See URBAN LEGENDS.

Hallowmas (also allhallowmass, hallomese, halumes, hollomass, hallamas, Hallowmasday) — Specifically, the feast of ALL SAINTS'. Shakespeare uses this term in *Richard II*:

She came adored hither like sweet May;
Sent back like Hallowmas, or short'st of day.

SIR WALTER SCOTT uses "Hallow-Mass Eve" in his poem "ST. SWITHIN'S CHAIR."

Hallowmass Rades — A Scottish phrase referring to a Halloween gathering of WITCHES. A powerful kin of Satan called "the Gyre Carline" was said to preside over these "trysts"; she carried a wand so powerful that it was claimed that on one Halloween, when angered over a high tide that had interrupted a "rade," she'd actually turned part of a bay into dry land. The Scots put enough credence into this belief that they occasionally dated important events from their relation to these "rades" — i.e., "I was christened o' the Sunday after Tibbie Fleucher's Hallowmass rade." A traditional story set on LOCHERBRIGG HILL describes a Hallowmass rade and a young man who escapes from one.

Hanal Pixan— Traditional Mayan celebration of the dead that was combined with Catholic practices to form the contemporary DAY OF THE DEAD celebration, which occurs in the southeast areas of Mexico (principally Yucatan) from October 31st to November 8th. "Hanal Pixan" translates roughly as "the soul's path through the essence of food," and the celebration features a number of specific FOODS; it also incorporates certain aspects of Mayan burial practice (which occurred in the home), and the Mayan belief that the universe was square (represented in *hanal pixan* altars). The first day, October 31st, is devoted to the souls of children, who are offered chicken stew, pumpkin sweets, chocolate, and other sugary treats (spicier foods are avoided). On November 1st, the celebrations switch to adult spirits, who are offered *el balche*, a drink made from tree bark, and *mucbil* chicken, a sort of tamale pie which requires days of preparation and is cooked buried in the earth. Rosaries are said (depending on the location, the rosary may be spoken in both Mayan and Spanish), and visits are made to the cemetery. After eight days, the souls are feted a final time before they depart, this time with a special tamale called *chachak-wah*. Presentation of the food is also important, and usually incorporates a deceased loved one's favorite drink and even cigarettes; usually soap and a bowl of water are provided, for the visiting dead to wash their hands. The tablecloth is typically white, with a green crucifix in the center, which also ties into the Mayan belief of the *ceiba* tree as the pillars of the sky.

In the past, *hanal pixan* also incorporated unique burial practices: From November 2 through November 9, the bones of any who had been interred within the last two or three years were removed (to make room for new burials); the bones were cleaned, blessed and placed in small boxes. The boxes were taken home for one night, where offerings of FOOD were made; the family feasted, and finally the box with the bones was returned to a special "house" (or ossuary) in the GRAVEYARD. In the mestizo-populated city of Hoctun, some of the inhabitants still open tombs and sarcophagi each year during *Hanal Pixan* to clean the bones of their ancestors.

The Yucatan state capital of Merida has made a profitable industry out of the yearly *Hanal Pixan* celebration, holding altar contests and presenting performances by the local *ballet folklorico*. Recently, Halloween features have begun to appear in October 31st celebrations, with some merchants now selling COSTUMES and plastic JACK-O'-LANTERNS. *See also* MICCAILHUITL AND MICCAILHUITONTLI.

Harrows—"Passin' the Harrow" was a Halloween FORTUNE-TELLING practice in Shetland, one which supposedly foretold not just a future spouse's identity but far more of the future. The practice consisted of placing THREE harrows spaced some distance apart outside the open door of a barn; at MIDNIGHT on Halloween, the one who wished to know his fortune was blindfolded, and then walked into the yard BACKWARDS, where he stepped over the three harrows and finally through a barn window. At the end of this ritual, the individual would supposedly fall into a trance state and receive visions, which were never revealed to anyone else.

Harvest— At its most basic level, Halloween is one-part commemoration of the dead and one-part harvest celebration. In the Celtic calendar SAMHAIN was the day that livestock were brought in from the fields, marking the end of an old year. Typically, harvest had been completed about a month earlier, but modern-day Halloween celebrants in Ireland often associate harvest with Halloween, which is when crops of CABBAGE, potatoes and CORN have completed harvest. In America, the association of corn, PUMPKINS, gourds and APPLES with the holiday bring up definite harvest associations. Early twentieth-century Halloween artwork also often shows anthropomorphized vegetable people, in addition to depictions of cornstalks and harvested fields. In late nineteenth-century Ireland, Halloween was sometimes called "the Feast of the autumn."

Harvest figures are a traditional Halloween decoration; SCARECROWS are especially popular in America, even though they serve no practical purpose (since there are no crops left to protect). The most popular harvest figure was once the CORN DOLLY, made from the last sheaves of corn; contemporary scarecrows are still made of corn stalks, but usually also include old clothing with a pumpkin head. These modern figures are typically surrounded by other Halloween symbols, such as JACK-O'-LANTERNS, WITCHES and gourds (in "The Folk Assemblage of Autumn: Tradition and Creativity in Halloween Folk Art," JACK SANTINO calls these collections Halloween assemblages and suggests that, even though they may include store-bought items such as paper SKELETONS or plastic jack-o'-lanterns, the overall assemblage represents an authentic FOLK ART).

Harvest Thanksgiving—A day celebrated in CHURCHES of different denominations (except Roman Catholic) throughout Ireland from mid– to late–October. The celebration was instituted in 1843 as a means of bringing drunken harvest celebrations into the church, where harvest thanksgiving services are behind only Christmas and Easter in popularity. This unofficial religious festival is usually observed on a Sunday in September or October after the harvest is gathered. Customs include decorating the churches with fruit, FLOWERS and vegetables, which are later donated to charity. Special hymns are sung, and there is frequently a visiting preacher. In medieval England, LAMMAS DAY (August 1) was probably recognized as a thanksgiving for the first fruits and wheat; this custom was revived by R. S. Hawker at Morwenstow, Cornwall in 1843. The *American Prayer Book* of 1789 already contained a form of thanksgiving for the fruits of the earth that was used on THANKSGIVING Day (which is officially observed on the fourth Thursday in November).

Haunted Houses—Haunted houses (which are distinguished from HALLOWEEN ATTRACTIONS such as CORN MAZES and PUMPKIN PATCHES) have become one of the most popular Halloween activities in North America, ranging from small yard displays all the way up to SPOOKY WORLD, which calls itself "America's Halloween amusement park." Why the popularity of these attractions exploded in the 1970s is uncertain, but the boom was probably fueled by a decrease in TRICK OR TREATING, an increase in adult (and teen) celebration of the holiday, and the increased gore in horror films. Recent estimates put the number of haunted attractions charging admission at some-

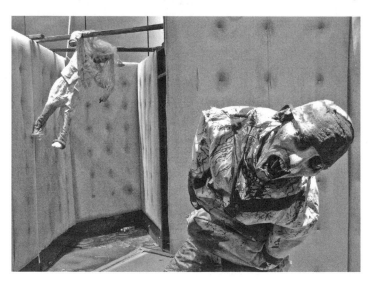

Padded room from Rich Hanf's 2004 "House of the Living Dead" haunted attraction (photograph courtesy of Rich Hanf)

where over 2,000 (with an additional 1,000 charity attractions, usually open on Halloween or a few days around the holiday). The entire Halloween attraction industry (which includes Halloween attractions and haunted attractions) is estimated to gross over one billion dollars annually.

Haunted houses generally feature a number of different rooms or exhibits, with mazes that visitors must pass through in between. They tend to center on three themes—

"Knott's Scary Farm" (photograph courtesy of Knott's)

the classic monster (vampires, werewolves, ghosts, zombies, etc.), the completely unique horror (an evil dentist, demented clowns), or the recreation of a very particular movie monster or scene. They also range in size from simple front-yard exhibits to amusement parks made over for Halloween. In the latter category, the best known are probably Knott's Berry Farm in Southern California, whose "Knott's Scary Farm" started in 1973 and also features stage shows and rides; and Universal Studios, which has presented some unique exhibits in the past, including one designed by famed horror writer Clive Barker (however, in 2001 Universal dropped its Halloween plans in the aftermath of the 9/11 terrorist attacks). Some haunted houses, such as Akron, Ohio's Haunted Schoolhouse and Haunted Laboratory, have emphasized a mix of these themes; others, such as the Mucklebones' Monster Museum in Marian, Ohio, focus on film recreations (included here are *Psycho*, *The Shining* and *Nosferatu*).

Haunted houses are now a cottage industry unto themselves, with professional attractions, full-time professional "haunters," and "home haunters" (or those who merely dress up their yards extensively) to cater to. They have their own journals (*Haunted Attraction* magazine), their own trade organization (the International Association of Haunted Attractions, or IAHA for short, formed in 1999), their own books, videos, employee handbooks, and safety manual (the latter put out by IAHA), and hundreds of companies that cater to the industry. They also have their own trade shows, dominated by TransWorld's annual Halloween, Costume and Party Show, with more than 15,000 attendees, TransWorld features more than 700 suppliers, and dozens of free seminars. TransWorld also hosts a National Haunt and Attractions Show, which is usually held in conjunction with the "HCP" convention.

Haunted houses evolved during the 1990s and 2000s from amateur productions in which the main scare was provided by actors, to complex and expensive events featuring "movie quality special effects." Many attractions boast hydraulic creatures, motion sensors, foot-pedal triggers which activate animatronic creatures or motorized props, special makeup effects and sets created by Hollywood artists (many of whom have found profitable employment in the haunted industry as computer effects have phased out their film work), animation and CGI effects, and 3D effects requiring glasses.

Professional haunters like Rich Hanf— author of the "Haunted Attraction Employee Handbook" and creator of how-to videos— work year-round designing attractions, marketing, and attending haunters' conventions and industry shows. In 2010, there were an estimated 2,500 full-time professional haunters in the U.S.

In the 1990s, the pinnacle of haunted houses was probably Utah's Rocky Point, which was voted number one by both *Fright Times* and *Fangoria* magazines in 1999. Supervised by Cydney Neil, Rocky Point was begun by her brother Neil Crabtree in 1979, then eventually moved from its original location (in an old restaurant built by Neil and Cydney's father) and became two very large shows, with locations in both Ogden and Salt Lake City. In 2000 Rocky Point added over 50 new sets, covering over 50,000 square feet. Exhibits included the "Slasher Wax Museum," "Psycho Circus in 3-D," and the "Bat Caves." Open for about six weeks before Halloween, Rocky Point entertained over 70,000 each season, and was a major fundraiser for local charities. Rocky Point ended its run in 2006.

In 2009, the Guinness Book of World Records awarded the Cutting Edge haunted house in Fort Worth, Texas, the title of "Largest Walk-Through Horror House." With 235,000 square feet, the Cutting Edge employs 150 actors and crew members, and takes over an hour to traverse.

According to *Hauntworld* Magazine, the best haunted house for 2008 and 2009 was Baton Rouge's 13th Gate. The attraction is noted for its elaborate sets, which occupy 40,000 square feet of both indoor and outdoor space, and focus on 13 different themed areas. Owner and designer Dwayne Sanburn also emphasizes his 80 actors, many of whom are professional actors or theater majors from local universities.

Probably the most elaborate and longest-running of the haunted houses offering film recreations is the Witch's Dungeon in Bristol, Connecticut. It was started over 40 years ago by Cortlandt Hull, a film buff whose great uncle Henry Hull had starred in the 1935 film *Werewolf of London*. Hull began by creating full-sized models of his favorite monsters, with help from his parents, and opened in October 1966. Over the years he has honed his skills with the help of make-up icons John Chambers and Dick Smith, and such film stars as Vincent Price, June Foray, Mark Hamill and John Agar have recorded voice tracks for the Dungeon. Now his exhibit includes very authentic and detailed renderings of the eponymous stars of *The Creature from the Black Lagoon, The Fly, Dracula, The Mummy*, and many more. Hull estimates that he receives around 1,500 visitors a year.

On the West Coast, the king of Halloween movie recreations was undoubtedly Bob Burns. Sometimes referred to as "the Godfather of Halloween," Burns is a lifelong monster fan and mask collector who started his Halloween presentations in 1967, with a recreation of Frankenstein's laboratory in his living room. Being located in Burbank, California, allowed Burns to enlist the help of many special movie effects wizards over the years, including Academy Award winners Dennis Muran and Rick Baker. Growing bigger every year, Burns's yard and house displays have included tributes to *Forbidden Planet, This Island Earth, The Creature from the Black Lagoon, The Time Machine* and *The Exorcist*.

In the category of unique haunted house displays, certainly one of the most unusual — and most beautiful — was the Hallowed Haunting Grounds in Studio City, California. Begun in 1973 and inspired in large part by Disneyland's "Haunted Mansion," the Hallowed Haunting Grounds emphasized quietly spooky ghost effects (or what is known in the haunted house trades as a "soft yard haunt"). A peek into the windows of the house revealed the transparent shade of a little girl, a ghostly organist, and the disembodied head of a medium; the front yard held bulging crypts, statuary that seemed to watch you, and a hooded monk releasing sparkling spirits from a well. Hallowed Haunting Grounds (which was free) closed in 2005. In 2007, a yard haunt known as The House at Haunted Hill opened just a few minutes from the former site of the Hallowed Haunting Ground, and featured even more elaborate effects, with animated projections, an original score, and a complete story involving a 1930s starlet whose marriage has gone horribly wrong.

Some haunted houses even become works of art unto themselves: For example, a haunted farm in Pennsylvania once invited local artists to design different rooms, an idea which resulted in such unique creations as a bathroom featuring a maze of pipes and "the Plunger Man." Airbrush artist Stuart Smith has provided spectacular art for Rocky Point's "Psycho Circus in 3-D," as well as other haunted attractions.

Haunted houses have also recently been transmogrified into "morality plays" by some Christian organizations; these "HELL HOUSES" feature the same extreme scares and gore found in other haunted houses, but present them with the goal of literally scaring their patrons into religion.

The haunted house is also a popular motif in Halloween COLLECTIBLES, offered as cardboard wall decorations, porcelain pieces, signed and limited art prints, and GAMES. *See also* TRAILS OF TERROR.

Hawthorn— It was once thought dangerous to sit beneath a hawthorn tree on MAY DAY or Halloween because FAIRIES were attracted to them.

Hayrides— Hayrides— which typically involve loading paying customers into a wagon or truck full of hay for a short ride around a farm or rural area — may be seasonal or specifically HALLOWEEN ATTRACTIONS, and have become commonplace "agri-tourism" or "agri-tainment" for farmers across the United States. Hayrides may be part of a

A ghostly organist and harpist perform in the music room of the Hallowed Haunting Grounds (photograph courtesy of Hallowed Haunting Grounds).

larger destination point which also includes PUMPKIN PATCHES and CORN MAZES, in addition to such activities as face-painting, games, and JACK-O'-LANTERN carving. Hayrides were popular activities in rural Halloween celebrations of the nineteenth century, when a hayride to a party was commonplace. Now "haunted hayrides" are included in many large-scale Halloween CELEBRATIONS such as SPOOKY WORLD.

Hazelnuts— Although virtually all NUTS can be used in Halloween FORTUNE-TELLING, hazelnuts had special significance to the CELTS: FINN MACCUMAL ate the salmon of knowledge and gained knowledge that came from the nuts of the nine hazels of wisdom that grow beside the well that is below the sea.

Hazelnuts are also the specified charm in John Gay's oft-quoted lines from his mock-pastoral *The Shepherd's Week* ("Thursday, or the Spell"):

Two hazel nuts I threw into the flame,
And to each nut I gave a sweetheart's name:
This with the loudest bounce me sore
    amaz'd,
That in a flame of brightest colour blaz'd...

Hearth— In some areas of Ireland, one Halloween custom was to leave chairs near the hearth (which was laid with coals) on Halloween, for returning souls to warm themselves. The hearth is also involved in some FORTUNE-TELLING practices, including those involving NUTS and writing names on the CHIMNEY.

"Hell Houses" — Perhaps the most bizarre manifestation of church opposition to Halloween is to be found in the Christian "Hell Houses." Created by the Pentecostal Abundant Life Christian Center in Colorado, "Hell Houses" are presented as Halloween HAUNTED HOUSES, but in place of the usual monsters and tableaux they feature depictions of acts believed to be anti-religious or sinful: Gruesome abortions, drug addiction, AIDS victims, etc. They typically end with the appearance of the DEVIL, and offer guests a chance to be "saved" instead. In 1996 there were approximately 300 variations of these lurid presentations across the country, drawing an estimated 700,000 visitors. One such attraction, located in Cedar Hill, Texas, is the subject of George Ratliff's critically-acclaimed 2002 documentary *Hell House* (this particular haunted house generated a great deal of controversy in 1999 by including a scene depicting the Columbine high school shootings).

Hemp Seed — Hemp was traditionally grown in Scotland for its fiber, and the sowing of the seed was a favorite FORTUNE-TELLING custom there. To perform this divination, it was necessary to first steal out of the house unnoticed on Halloween night, go to a FIELD and there sow a handful of hemp seed, harrowing it with anything that could be easily drawn. While performing the harrowing, the following words must be repeated: "Hemp seed I saw thee, hemp seed I saw thee; and him (or her) that is to be my true love, come after me and pou thee." At some point a glance over the left shoulder would reveal the FETCH of the future spouse, in the act of pulling hemp. In some versions of the custom, the rhyme ends instead with, "come after me and shaw thee"; other variations

completely omit the harrowing, and here the rhyme ends with, "come after me, and harrow thee." Another version states that the hemp seed must be sowed by a young woman over NINE ridges of ploughed land, saying "I sow hemp seed, and he who is to be my husband, let him come and harrow it"; over her left shoulder she would see the figure of her future husband. In northeast Scotland lint seed was used instead.

In his poem "Hallowe'en," ROBERT BURNS describes the custom:

> Then up gat fechtin Jamie Fleck,
> An' he swoor by his conscience,
> That he could saw hemp-seed a peck;
> For it was a' but nonsense;
> The auld guidman raught down the pock,
> An' out a handful gied him;
> Syne bad him slip fra 'mang the folk
> Sometimes when nae ane see'd him:
>   An' try't that night.

As Jamie sows the hemp seed, he calls out:

> Hemp-seed I saw thee,
> An' her that is to be my lass,
> Come after me, and draw thee,
>   As fast this night.

The skeptical Jamie gets his come-uppance, however, when he is startled by an apparition that turns out to be "Grumphie," or a SOW.

Another version of this divination dictates that a girl must go at MIDNIGHT on Halloween to a churchyard, and while tossing hemp seed over the left shoulder recite:

> Hempseed I sow, hempseed, grow.
> He that is to marry me,
> Come after me and mow.

The spirit of her future husband will then appear carrying a scythe. If no spirit appears, the girl will not marry soon; if a COFFIN appears, the girl will die before she can marry.

William Black's 1890 story "A Halloween Wraith" refers to hemp-seed sowing as "one form of incantation which is known to be extremely, nay, terribly potent, when all others have failed" (and the young lady performing the ritual expects to be "terribly frightened").

Herne. The Hunter *see* **Spectre Huntsman**

Herring— One Halloween FORTUNE-TELLING custom involved eating a whole SALT herring (bones and all) in THREE mouthfuls, then silently retiring to bed; the future spouse will appear in a DREAM to offer WATER to quench the resulting thirst.

Hindu *see* **Holi**

Hoboes— Like the Halloween images of the GYPSY and the CLOWN, the American hobo is an anarchic, outsider figure who has been important to American Halloween CELEBRA-TIONS since the beginning of the 20th century, inspiring both COSTUMES and PARTY activities.

The hobo is an impoverished laborer who wanders from town to town in search of food and employment. The American hobo originated after the Civil War, and the number and visibility of hoboes increased tremendously with the expansion of the American railroad (which grew from 30,000 miles in 1860 to 230,000 miles in 1890). It was during roughly this same time that Halloween celebrations moved from rural locations (mainly those occupied by Scottish and Irish immigrants) to the American middle class. During the first two decades of the 20th century, hoboes were popular figures in American culture (especially comic strips), and they were frequently depicted as happy, clown-like figures in ragged clothing. This image quickly found its way into Halloween celebrations, especially since it offered the appeal of a costume that was simple to make at home—charcoal might be used to smudge the face, and tattered castoff clothing completed the outfit.

Although the number of hoboes and their popularity greatly declined after the Great Depression of the 1930s, the image continued to be a popular one at Halloween. During the 1950s, as Halloween costuming became commercialized, manufacturers like Collegeville offered hobo outfits (complete with plastic masks, derby hat, and oversized bow tie), and party guides continued to suggest hobo-themed Halloween parties, which usually came with menus of beans, hot dogs, and POPCORN, and activities which included guests making their own NOISEMAKERS. Commercially made hobo costumes are still popular, and are now made for both male and female hoboes.

Hogmanay— Scottish NEW YEAR'S celebration which involved house-to-house begging and may have been a forerunner of Halloween TRICK-OR-TREAT customs.

Hogmanay was sometimes described as the most important day in the Scottish calendar and was celebrated with a number of rituals, including the common New Year's Day custom of "first-footing" (meaning that the household's luck for the coming year would be determined by the first visitor to enter that day), and GUISING or MUMMING practices. Some describe groups of young men who went house-to-house on New Year's Eve, blowing horns to announce their coming, demanding gifts of food or money, and offering a good luck charm or a blessing on the house in return. Other areas record children in COSTUMES who went house-to-house, begging treats of oatcake or bannock (in fact the day was sometimes known as "Cake-day"), while reciting a rhyme:

> Hogmanay!
> Trollolay!
> Give us your white bread
> And none of your grey.
> Get up, gude wife, and shake your feathers,
> And do not think that we are beggars.
> For we are bairns come out to play
> Get up and gie's our Hogmanay.

The "Carmina Gaedelica" shows that curses were invoked on homes that didn't treat their Hogmanay holiday visitors.

The term Hogmanay has been recorded since the seventeenth century, and probably derives from the old French *aguillanneuf*, "to the mistletoe to new year." It has been suggested that this may be a descendant of DRUID New Year's or SAMHAIN rituals involving MISTLETOE, but there is unfortunately no proof to support this intriguing idea.

Holi— Hindu festival held in India on the fifteenth day of the light half of the moon, in the Hindu month of Phalguna (usually March). Although this is a spring festival, it is sometimes called the Hindu Halloween. For a week before Holi, boys go door-to-door collecting fuel for BONFIRES, which are lighted on Holi night with horns, drums and dancing. At sunrise water is poured on the embers, and people dip their fingers into the warm ASHES and mark their foreheads for luck. The day is sometimes called the "Festival of Colors" because it is celebrated by throwing colored water and colored powders at everyone. The day is also celebrated with a feast, and boys indulge in PRANKING and use of NOISEMAKERS.

One legend to explain the day comes from a female demon called Holika who devoured children every spring; one year, people prepared for the demon's coming with fires and horns to mock and confuse her, then they burned her up. Other legends suggest that Holika was the sister of *Samvat*, or the Hindu year. The first year he died, Holika burned herself on her brother's pyre, but was restored to life by her act of sacrifice.

Holidays *see* **Christmas; New Year's; Thanksgiving**

Holland Fair— At Cirencester in England, Halloween was sometimes called Holland Fair, after a hiring fair traditionally held on that day. The name was still in use as late as the early 20th century, although the hiring fair itself hadn't existed for some time. This is one of the few instances of a hiring fair occurring during Halloween, since they typically took place on MARTINMAS.

Hollantide (also All-Hallowtide, All-hollantide Hallow-tide, Hollandtide, Hollentide)— Now obsolete name for Halloween, found throughout the British Isles, but especially used in the Isle of Man. Although

some records noted that the Manx celebrated Halloween with references to HOGMANAY, another account records a form of MUMMING that involved specific Hollantide references and RHYMING:

> This is old Hollantide night;
> The moon shines fair and bright;
> I went to the well
> And drank my fill;
> On the way coming back
> I met a pole-cat;
> The cat began to grin
> And I began to run;
> Where did you run to?
> I ran to Scotland;
> What were they doing there?
> Baking bannocks and roasting collops.

This rhyme was shouted by young men who went house-to-house, and were rewarded with food and drink.

Hollantide typically applied to the eve of October 31st, but the annual Manx "Great Hollantide Hiring Fair of the Island" was held on November 12th.

Holly *see* **"Building the House."**

Holy Water— In parts of Ireland, animals and livestock might be sprinkled with holy water on Halloween to protect them from WITCHES and FAIRIES. Holy water might also be sprinkled on doors for protective purposes.

Homosexual *see* **Gay Culture**

Horses— In parts of Ireland, SUPERSTITION held that horses would not pass through certain areas on Halloween night because of the presence of FAIRIES. In Scotland, witches were supposedly able to transform men into horses that they would ride to occult gatherings; the story LOCHERBRIGG HILL tells of one such transformation that occurred on Halloween night.

Horse races were a part of the traditional Celtic celebration of SAMHAIN.

Horseshoe and Hobnail Service— The Horseshoe and Hobnail Service was an ancient ritual (more than 700 years old) regarding rent payment that was held in London each October 31st, and continued into the 20th century. Each Halloween, the City Solicitor would appear at the Office of the Queen's Remembrancer at two P.M. The Queen Remembrancer's clerk would then issue this proclamation: "Tenants and occupiers of a piece of waste land called The Moors, in the County of Salop, come forth and do your service." The Solicitor then performed the service by cutting through one bundle of twigs with a hatchet and another with a bill-hook. A second proclamation was then made: "Tenants and occupiers of a certain tenement called 'The Forge,' in the parish of St. Clement Danes, Middlesex, come forth and do your service." The Solicitor then counted six horseshoes and sixty-one hobnails and, upon announcing the numbers, was answered by the Queen's Remembrancer, "Good numbers." The service apparently originated as a result of the large Flemish horses that were ridden by the Knights Templars and that were shod at "The Forge"; this practice is also similar to those involving repayment of DEBTS at SAMHAIN and, later, MARTINMAS.

Horseshoes—Horseshoes occasionally appear in depictions of Halloween scenes, usually as symbols of good luck. In earlier times, however, horseshoes would have served a different purpose at Halloween: They were nailed up over entrances (and sometimes under, as on the steps leading up to a doorway) as protection against WITCHES.

Houdini, Harry (1874–1926)—Hungarian-American magician and escape artist. Born Ehrich Weiss, Houdini, who came to fame performing such stage illusions as the infamous "Chinese Water Torture" before packed houses, developed an interest in spiritualism and mediumship during the last few years of his life. His book *A Magician Among the Spirits* documents his experiences with mediums, all of whom he denounced as fakes and frauds; and yet Houdini retained a belief that he himself could return. He passed a code phrase—"Rosabelle believe"—to his

wife Bess shortly before he died on Halloween, 1926, of peritonitis. Bess began holding séances, and in 1929 a young medium named Arthur Ford apparently delivered the correct message, but it was later revealed that Bess had inadvertently given the message out prior to Ford's delivery. When Bess tried to end the séance tradition in 1936, it was picked up by other magicians, including Houdini's ghostwriter Walter Gibson. The séance continues to be held every Halloween, and regularly draws some of the biggest names in the field of magic. With the advent of the Internet, a second yearly séance was opened to anyone with Internet access; participants in the "cyber-séance" are asked to log online at a particular time on Halloween night, open themselves to spiritual contact, and report back any contact with Houdini.

House-to-House Parties—Also known as "progressive" parties, these were instituted in the wake of the severe PRANKING of the early 1930s; they also offered an opportunity to parents who were just scraping by in the Depression to combine their assets. A typical plan for a "house-to-house party" might include six houses, with children led from house to house by adult "ghosts." Each house would host a different activity: The first house would give each child a hat and MASK, and play a GAME; the next house would host a decoration-making contest; the third house would provide another game, such as BOBBING FOR APPLES; the fourth house would provide a backyard game, then serve dinner; the fifth house would provide dessert and a FORTUNE-TELLING game; and the last house would end the night with GHOST STORIES and prizes awarded for all previous games. A variation might give each house a different decorating and entertainment theme, such as the Haunted House, the Witch's Cavern, or the Pumpkin Inn. The success of these parties may have led to the development of the classic TRICK OR TREAT custom.

Hungry Ghost Festival *see* **Yue Laan**

India *see* Holi

Ink *see* Witches' Ink

Iron—Iron was usually thought to provide protection against FAIRIES on Halloween; a piece of iron, for example (or sometimes a dead ember) might be placed in an infant's cradle as protection on this dangerous night. In the region of the Vosges, however, iron had a less pleasant association: An iron ball rolling down a slope on Halloween was thought to be a soul in torment, and any passersby who encountered it would find great difficulty in returning home; they would also be assaulted by a horrible burning odor.

Irving, Washington (1783–1859)— American author sometimes referred to as the "The Father of American Literature." Irving is now chiefly remembered for the two short stories "The Legend of Sleepy Hollow" and "Rip Van Winkle," both of which he adapted from existing German legends, and both of which

are set among Dutch communities on the Hudson River. Both stories first appeared in 1820's *The Sketch Book of Geoffrey Crayon, Gent.*, and established Irving as an international literary celebrity. Both stories were supposedly found among the papers of "Diedrich Knickerbocker," a (fictitious) historian, and although neither of them mentions Halloween specifically, both include numerous elements now associated with the holiday, and in fact they may even have influenced our modern concept of Halloween.

"The Legend of Sleepy Hollow" may be the most oft-told Halloween tale of all. Set in the rich autumn of the American Northeast, it centers on Ichabod Crane, a gangly school teacher who falls for Katrina Van Tassel, the beautiful daughter of the wealthy Baltus Van Tassel; Ichabod's rival for her affections is Brom Bones, a brawny and burly practical joker. After a party involving late-night GHOST STORIES, Ichabod heads home only to encounter the terrifying Headless Horseman. A long chase ensues, and Ichabod seemingly vanishes, although a smashed PUMPKIN is found in the road the next day. Brom and Katrina are happily wed, and Brom is "observed to look exceedingly knowing whenever the story of Ichabod was related."

"Rip Van Winkle" offers the story of a harmless layabout who wanders into an enchanted mountain glen one day, where he finds a strange party in progress. He makes the mistake of sipping some liquor he's been ordered to serve, and he falls asleep. He awakens to find his gun rusted,

An 1849 illustration from Washington Irving's "The Legend of Sleepy Hollow" by Felix O.C. Darley.

his beard grown long, his home abandoned, his children matured — in short, he has slept 20 years. The story's conclusion suggests that Rip encountered the GHOSTS of Hendrick Hudson and his crew.

Both stories have been adapted to other media many times. "The Legend of Sleepy Hollow" has been the basis of both an animated Disney short (released theatrically as the second half of the 1949 feature *The Adventures of Ichabod and Mr. Toad*) and TIM BURTON's 1999 *Sleepy Hollow*, which transformed Ichabod Crane into a brilliant young inspector trying to solve the mystery of the Hollow's Hessian Horseman.

Ivy — In one early-twentieth-century British FORTUNE-TELLING practice, ivy leaves were left in water overnight at Halloween, and if in the morning black spots or COFFIN-shaped marks had developed it meant someone in the household would die within a year.

Boys could invoke prophetic DREAMS on Halloween by cutting 10 ivy leaves without speaking, then throwing one away and placing the rest under the head to sleep on.

In Cardiganshire people practiced a variation on a classic custom which usually involves NUTS: Two ivy leaves were placed on the fire, representing an unmarried couple (a pointed leaf for the man, and a rounded leaf for the woman); if the leaves jumped toward each other in the heat, the couple would marry, but if they flew apart the couple would soon quarrel and separate.

J

Jack Frost — Although more often associated with winter and CHRISTMAS, Jack Frost also figures in some early-twentieth-century Halloween PLAYS, RECITATIONS, etc., usually as a symbol of autumn and the coming of winter that are part of late October. For example, *The Topaz Story Book: Stories and Legends of Autumn, Halloween and Thanksgiving* (edited by Ada M. and Eleanor L. Skinner, 1928) contains the poem "Jack Frost" by Gabriel Setoun, with these lines that definitely seem to set Mr. Frost as a spooky Halloween figure:

> The door was shut as doors should be
>   Before you went to bed last night;
> Yet Jack Frost has got in, you see,
>   And left your windows silver white.

Jack-o'-Lantern — Possibly the single most popular Halloween symbol, the contemporary jack-o'-lantern usually refers to a PUMPKIN carved into a grinning or malicious face, used for decoration in American homes. In Europe (especially Ireland and Scotland), a jack-o'-lantern is usually a carved TURNIP, and, unlike its American counterpart, is actually carried as a lantern (hung from a stick or string) on Halloween night. Jack-o'-lanterns are used not just extensively for decoration at Halloween, but are also featured in Halloween GAMES, while pumpkin seeds

A classic Halloween jack-o'-lantern

figure in some FORTUNE-TELLING rituals, and of course pumpkin-flavored FOODS are popular as well. Jack-o'-lanterns might also be carved from other fruits and vegetables, including APPLES and squash.

Folklorist Jack Santino notes that the jack-o'-lantern embodies both harvest and the character of the trickster. In its trickster aspect, jack-o'-lantern comes from a long line of European trickster mythology. Some of the stories of Jack O'Lantern resemble those of Jack O'Kent, a legendary hero and trickster. In Britain jack-o'-lantern is another name for WILL-O'-THE-WISP, and his name is also sometimes spelled Jack-a-Lantern and Jacky Lantern. Although both jack-o'-lantern and will-o'-the-wisp usually refer to the mysterious lights encountered around swamps and bogs, Jack is sometimes considered to be a PIXIE, and is the subject of this rhyme:

Early postcard showing boys with jack-o'-lanterns mounted on sticks

Jack-o'-the-lantern! Joan the Wad,
Who tickled the maid and made her mad!
Light me home, the weather's bad.

Jack-o'-lanterns frequently haunted swamps and bog areas in Britain. These lights are properly called *ignis fatuus* (meaning "foolish" or "false fire") or marsh gas, and are given off by rotting vegetation and animals; ghostly lights that appeared specifically around graveyards were called Corpse Candles. In folklore, these lights are sometimes believed to be the souls of sinners condemned to walk the earth eternally; in coastal areas, they're believed to be the souls of men who have drowned and never received proper burial.

Jack-o'-lanterns encountered in the wild were mischievous, malevolent entities; they might cause a horse to throw a cart, or even give chase. The bobbing lights must never be followed, for they'll attempt to lead any foolish human to death in a deep, watery swamp or over a cliff. In Britain (where jack-o'-lanterns were sometimes called BO-GIES), there was only one sure protection against a jack-o'-lantern: First any lanterns must be extinguished (before they were dashed to the ground by the Jack), then the unlucky souls must throw themselves to the ground and hold their breath. In America (where it was often believed that mysterious lights were the products of malicious WITCHES), if one encountered a "jack-ma-lantern," the protective ritual was to turn one's pockets inside-out, draw a circle in the dirt and make a cross on the ground, then recite, "In the name of the Father and the Son and the Holy Spirit, drive these witches away with their evil jack-ma-lanterns." Other means of protection included stabbing a KNIFE into the ground, and throwing oneself to the ground, with eyes shut, ears plugged and breath held.

British variants of the name included Peg-a-lantern, Hob-with-a-lantern, Hobardy's lantern, Lantern Men, Kit-with-a-canstik, Kitty-candlestick, Joan-in-the-wad, Jacket-a-wad, and Gillion-a-burnt-tail; the

Scottish also call them "Uist Lights." One Scottish story was that a girl from Benbecula misbehaved, was cursed for her wrongdoings and disappeared, only to have her spirit become a "great fire." In Switzerland, the lights are thought to be the soul of a miller deceased 20 years before.

Certain jack-o'-lanterns have their own characteristics: Gill-of-the-burnt-tail draws a streak behind itself. If a will-o-the-wisp is seized, only a bone is left in one's grasp. A Hessian legend explains the *irrwisch* as the body of a dead usurer, whom the devil has flayed, stuffed with straw and made fly as a burning wisp.

The help of a jack-o'lantern can be implored with a rhyme:

Jack of the lantern, Joan of the lub
Light me home, and I'll give you a crub
[crumb].

After the service had been rendered, one must say, "Thank 'ee, Jack." In Germany they instead would say "Gelts Gott," since by doing this the soul was released.

The mythology behind Jack-o'-lanterns is rich, and many of the stories are set on Halloween; they are also often associated with the evils of drink (in fact, Will-o'-the-wisp is sometimes described as having a "face like a brandy bottle"). Perhaps the most common one begins one Halloween night when Jack, a notorious drunk, has one too many drinks at the local pub and his soul begins to slip from his body. The DEVIL appears to claim it, but Jack suggests they have one drink together before going. The devil tells Jack he has no money, and Jack suggests that he change himself into a sixpence, then change back after paying. The devil transforms into the coin, and Jack snatches the sixpence and puts it in his wallet, which has a silver catch in the shape of a cross, so the devil is trapped. Jack makes him promise to leave for a year, then frees him. Next Halloween, Jack runs into the devil on a lonely country road. Nearby is an apple-tree, and Jack suggests they each have an apple, but the

1911 postcard by artist Ellen Clapsaddle

devil says the fruit is too high up to reach. Jack suggests the devil stand on his shoulders, and when the devil does Jack whips out his pocketknife and cuts the sign of the cross on the trunk of the tree, and the devil can't come down. This time Jack makes the devil promise to leave him alone for good, and the desperate devil agrees. Before next Halloween, Jack dies and is turned away from heaven, but the devil turns him away from the gates of Hell. Jack asks for a light to find his way back, and the devil throws him a chunk of live coal from the hell furnace. Jack puts it inside the turnip he's been gnawing, and with this jack-o'-lantern he has been wandering the earth ever since.

An early African-American version of the story omits both the mention of Halloween and the use of a turnip or pumpkin for a lantern at the end; it also suggests that "when he come to a ma'sh, he done got los', an' he ain' nuver fine he way out sence," placing the mysterious light firmly in a swamp setting. The jack-o'-lantern or will-o'-the-wisp was greatly feared in the South, where it was believed that they would lure their victims to drown in bogs or rivers, or be torn apart in thorn bushes, all while exclaiming, "Aie, aie, mo gagnin toi" ("aie, aie, I have you"). The early African-Americans based their stories on European tales, and often called it "Jack-muh-lantern," "Jacky-m-Lantuhns," or "wuller-wups." One legend of the jack-o'-lantern, describes it as being a hideous creature about five feet in height, with goggle eyes and a huge mouth, long hair on its body and hopping about like a gigantic grasshopper. Some African-Americans also believed that jack-o'-lanterns could come in either sex, as a "man-jacky" or a "woman-jacky."

The Irish have a story of Billy Dawson, a rogue and drunk, who drinks so much that his nose becomes highly flammable and bursts into flames when an enemy catches it with red hot tongs. Billy's bushy beard helps fuel the fire, and now he roams the countryside, plunging into icy bogs and pools in a desperate attempt to quench the fire of his nose.

In a North Carolina version, Jack is a sharecropper working his parcel of land with the devil. He gets the devil to agree to a 50-50 split of each individual plant — "…I'll take the top of the CORN and you take the bottom…." When the devil realizes that Jack has conned him, he hurls a blinding light at Jack, and warns him never to let go of that light.

In a Welsh version, Sion Dafydd of the Arvon hills sells his soul for wealth and the power to adhere to anything. When the devil finally comes for him, he climbs into an apple-tree and the Devil is unable to take him.

In stories centering on Will-o'-the-wisp, Will is usually a blacksmith (although his name is also given as Jack). In the most common Will tale, an impoverished but wicked smith makes a deal with the devil to have money for a year. During the year, one night the smith offers an act of kindness to a traveler, and his hospitality earns him three wishes. Instead of wishing for his own salvation, he wishes that anyone who takes the bellows on his forge will be unable to let go; that anyone who sits in his chair will be unable to rise; and that anything placed in his purse will never come out unless he removes it. At the end of the year, Satan appears, and the smith tricks him into taking the bellows. Finally the smith releases Satan, only if he promises him another year. At the end of that year, Satan returns, but this time the smith tricks him into sitting in his chair, and releases him only upon promise of another year of freedom and money. Finally Satan returns, and the smith dares him to change into a sixpence; the devil does, and the smith snatches him up and places him in his purse. The smith then hammers the purse until the devil agrees to free him. Finally, when the smith dies, he's barred from both heaven and hell, and given only a lump of brimstone to light his way as he roams the earth. The Smith's name is sometimes given as Sionnach, and from this name derives the term *teine Sionnachain*, or "great fire."

In a Shropshire version of the legend, Will is a blacksmith who fixes a traveler's horse's shoe. The traveler is St. Peter, and he grants Will a wish; Will chooses to live his life over. He does, and spends it drinking and gambling once again. Finally he dies and arrives at hell, but the devil tells him he has learned so much wickedness in two lifetimes that he is more than the devil's match, and he denies him entrance. St. Peter denies him entry into heaven, and finally Will returns to the devil, who reluctantly offers him only a coal from the hell-fires to warm him. Now Will wanders the moors, still practicing malice and deceit by luring innocent travelers to their doom.

Joel Chandler Harris records an African-American variation of this tale,

"Jacky-Ma-Lantern" from *Uncle Remus: His Songs and His Sayings*. In this version the devil (or "the Bad Man") comes for the drunken "blacksmif," who makes a deal instead for the chair, the forge and money. When the devil returns in a year, the blacksmith traps him in the chair; a year later, he traps the devil at the forge. A year later, the devil returns and puts Jack in a bag for the trip to Hell, but on the way the devil stops to join in a Fourth of July barbecue (in a curious switch of holidays!). While the devil eats, the blacksmith escapes from the bag and puts a bull-dog in his place. When the devil arrives in Hell, his hungry imps are shocked to find the dog, which attacks them until the devil throws it out of Hell. Finally the blacksmith dies, and is denied entry into both Heaven and Hell, leaving him to hover between the two planes forever.

Zora Neale Hurston includes a version of the tale in her collection *Of Mules and Men* which ends with the devil tossing Jack a coal so he can start a Hell of his own.

In an American version, Jack sells his soul to the devil at a CROSSROADS in exchange for seven years of power. At the end of seven years, the devil comes for Jack; Jack asks him to get down an old shoe he has placed above his door, and when the devil complies, Jack nails his hand to the wall. After obtaining the devil's agreement to leave him alone, Jack releases the devil, but on the day he dies he is denied entrance to both Heaven and Hell (at Hell the devil throws a chunk of burning coal at him). Now Jack relieves the boredom of his eternal wandering by luring unwary souls to their doom.

One other American version begins with Wicked Jack the blacksmith making the deal for the chair and the hammer, but his third wish is that the large thorny bush outside his shop will pull in headfirst anyone who touches it (also in this version, the devil sends two of his sons first before coming, and he himself ends up in the bush, all within the space of a few minutes).

There are numerous other examples of trickster stories throughout Western history; earlier variants usually center on Death, rather than the devil; usually Jesus or St. Peter grants wishes to the protagonist, and typically the story notes their disappointment when the hero chooses some form of trickery over salvation. In some German variants Jack-o'-lantern becomes the Wandering Jew.

In his article "Halloween Imagery in Two Southern Settings," Grey Gundaker suggests that the image of the jack-o'-lantern has come to have special significance among Southern African-Americans, "...because of [the] rich fund of oral tradition." Gundaker cites uses of the jack-o'-lantern in non-seasonal African-American yard assemblages, and mentions that the phrase may have even once been transmuted into the name "Jack Mulatta."

The practice of transforming a pumpkin into a jack-o'-lantern predates the popularity of Halloween in America: In his 1850 poem "The Pumpkin," John Greenleaf Whittier recalls his own boyhood and pumpkins:

> When wild ugly faces we carved in its skin,
> Glaring out through the dark with a candle within!

And of course WASHINGTON IRVING's famous 1820 story "The Legend of Sleepy Hollow" includes a pumpkin that has been mistaken for a goblin's head, suggesting it may have been a jack-o'-lantern (as indeed it is usually depicted in illustrations and adaptations). An article from 1867 refers to the jack-o'-lantern as "the pumpkin effigy," and notes that its use (mainly in provoking scares) may have stemmed from Guy Fawkes Night practices in England. An 1885 magazine article suggests that carving Halloween jack-o'-lanterns is the American boy's version of lighting bonfires, and by 1898 — when the first Halloween book, MARTHA RUSSELL ORNE's *Hallowe'en: How to Celebrate It* appeared, jack-o'-lanterns as key elements of Halloween were firmly established.

Jack-o'-lanterns— which are sometimes accompanied by bodies made of straw, other vegetables, and rags (like a SCARECROW)— are usually placed in windows or on porches of homes; prior to the use of electricity in American homes, jack-o'-lanterns were often placed over gas jets in place of the usual glass globes. On Halloween night they serve an important purpose in the practice of TRICK OR TREAT, since a lit jack-o'-lantern normally signifies a home that is participating and dispensing treats. Although jack-o'-lanterns are traditionally made by carving away sections of the pumpkin to produce a grinning or fearsome face, a jack-o'-lantern may also be made by cutting or scraping away only the outer sections of the pumpkin's rind, leaving a thin layer of skin that glows when lit from within. Although the traditional jack-o'-lantern is otherwise undecorated, they may also be painted or accessorized with added, three-dimensional details.

In more recent times, jack-o'-lanterns have been featured in a number of Halloween-themed movies and television shows. The 1966 *It's the Great Pumpkin, Charlie Brown* played on the jack-o'-lantern's prominence as the most important icon of the holiday. TIM BURTON and Henry Selick's popular *The Nightmare Before* Christmas (1993) gave its protagonist Jack Skellington a jack-o'-lantern head, and the impish "Sam Hain" from Michael Dougherty's 2008 film release *Trick 'R Treat* is revealed to have a head similar to a jack-o'-lantern. See *also* Neep Lanterns.

Jack Pumpkinhead— Jack Pumpkinhead was originally a character in L. Frank Baum's 1904 fantasy *The Marvelous Land of Oz* (the first sequel to Baum's classic *The Wonderful Wizard of Oz*). In the book, Jack is a pumpkin-headed SCARECROW manufactured by a boy named Tip to scare his guardian, the sorceress Mombi; however, Mombi decides to reverse the trick by bringing Jack to life. Jack went on to appear in numerous other Oz volumes, with the 23rd book in the series (by

Ruth Plumly Thompson) named *Jack Pumpkinhead of Oz*. In later books, Jack had to continually replace his rotting pumpkin heads with new ones.

There are no direct references to Halloween surrounding Jack, although the first book clearly paints him as an autumnal figure (Tip decides to make Jack "…one day, after the corn had all been cut and stacked") and refers to his head as a "Jack Lantern" (although Tip, being unfamiliar with other children, is unaware of the notion of placing a candle inside the carved-out pumpkin). However, Jack Pumpkinhead went on to become a figure commonly associated with Halloween: Some early 20th-century paper goods catalogs featured decorations depicting a pumpkin-headed figure named "John Pumpkin Head," and the amusement park Santa's Village in Southern California (which closed in 1998) featured a costumed Halloween figure named "Jack Pumpkinhead." Jack Pumpkinhead may also have served in part to inspire the pumpkin-headed Jack Skellington in TIM BURTON's *The Nightmare Before Christmas*.

Japan *see* **Bon Festival**

Jewelry *see* **Earrings; Wedding Ring**

John R. Neill's illustration of Jack Pumpkinhead and Jellia from *The Marvelous Land of Oz*

Kale (also *kail*)—Curly-leafed vegetable which may be the oldest form of CABBAGE, kale is interchangeable with cabbage in a number of well-known means of Halloween FORTUNE-TELLING. In the Scottish "Pulling of the Kale," couples walked hand-in-hand through a FIELD (preferably belonging to either a spinster or bachelor) and, with eyes closed, pulled a bunch of kale. The size and shape of the stalks and the amount of soil clinging to them foretold the future; for example, a straight stalk foretold a tall, straight, handsome mate, and dirt clinging to the kale promised money. The state of the heart of the stem (sweet, sour, brittle, hard, etc.) foretold the disposition of a future mate. Finally the kale would be nailed over a doorway, and whoever entered beneath the kale first would be one's future mate (or, if the first to enter was already married, the first letter in his or her name would also be the first letter in the name of the kale-puller's future spouse). Often kale stalks were numbered, so that the third man through the door would match the girl who had the third stalk. ROBERT BURNS's "Hallowe'en" refers to the custom:

> Then first and foremost, thro' the kail,
> Their *stocks* maun a' be sought ance;
> They steek their een' an' graip an' wale,
> For muckle anes an' straight anes.

In the next stanza, Burns goes on to describe what happens to the kale after it has been pulled:

> An' gif the custoc's sweet or sour,
> Wi' joctelegs they taste them;
> Syne coziely, aboon the door,
> Wi' cannie care they place them
> To lie that night.

(The "custoc" is the heart of the stem; "joctelegs" are a type of knife.)

In Scotland the importance of the "cus-toc" can be further measured by this traditional Halloween night children's rhyme:

> Halloween a nicht—a teen
> A can'al an' a custoc.

In some areas the kale had to be pulled from a neighbor's yard without the neighbor's consent or knowledge; ideally the neighbor should be unmarried. In some parts of Scotland, this divination was practiced exclusively by young girls who walked into the kale patch BACKWARDS, and picked the first

The curly-leafed greenery shown in this vintage postcard is probably kale.

kales their heels caught on. In Fife, however, the kale-runts were carried home backwards.

Also in Scotland knots on the kale stock under any clinging earth indicated no children.

In another Scottish custom, the kale-runt is thrown on the ground, and whatever direction the head points indicates the direction of one's next journey. A kale-runt could also be placed under the pillow on Halloween night to induce DREAMS of the future spouse.

In *Witchcraft and Second Sight in the Scottish Highlands*, John Gregorson Campbell tells this eerie tale of a kale-pulling: A girl who lived in Skye was in love with a sailor who had shipped off to the East Indies. On Halloween night she went to a kale patch, and as she grasped the kale she felt something hurtle by her and strike the kale. The kale was straight and tall with rich dirt clinging to the root, but embedded in the stalk was a knife. All the other young people present denied having thrown it or knowing to whom it belonged. When her lover returned a few months later, he told her that on Halloween night he was leaning over the side of the ship, thinking of her and of the festivities that were going on in Skye and feeling homesick. He had his knife in his hand, since he had just been mending rope. In his reverie he let the knife slip from his fingers and fall into sea. The girl then produced the knife she had found in the kale stalk, and he identified it as the one he had lost.

In Scotland, a kale-runt torch might be carried in lieu of a TURNIP lantern; this was simply a stem stripped of leaves and hollowed out to carry a CANDLE.

Later, when Halloween celebrations had moved to cities where kale patches were not easily found, one *Dennison's* BOGIE BOOK suggested that a sandbox planted with sticks could be imagined to be kale (for use in the "Pulling of the Kale" divination).

Kef Ann Anaon— A special log reserved for the dead, used in Halloween HEARTHS in some parts of Brittany.

Kelley, Ruth Edna— Kelley (1893-1982) was an American author and librarian who is now known chiefly as the author of *The Book of Hallowe'en* (1919), the first serious study of Halloween. Running 195 pages, Kelley's book features information on the holiday's CELEBRATIONS as practiced throughout history and around the world, and it includes illustrations and an index. Originally published in an attractive hardback with decorative binding, the book has since been reprinted numerous times and can also be found in its entirety at a number of internet sites; the first edition has now become a highly-sought after Halloween COLLECTIBLE and brings high prices on the resale market.

Cover for Ruth Edna Kelley's *The Book of Hallowe'en*

Knives— Carrying a black-handled knife was thought to be protection against malicious Halloween FAIRIES. Also, stabbing a knife into the ground was one counter-charm to malevolent JACK-O'-LANTERNS.

A knife also figures in one FORTUNE-TELLING custom involving LEEKS, wherein a girl would place a knife in the leek field on Halloween night, and the FETCH of her future husband would appear, pick up the knife and throw it.

Knots—In an Irish FORTUNE-TELLING practice, a girl took a length of rope to a well, placed her feet on either side of the well, and tied NINE knots in the rope, reciting with each knot tied:

> I tie this Knot that it should knit
> To see the lad I ne'er saw yet,
> To see the lad in his array,
> The clothing he wears every day.

The girl then returned silently to her home and went to bed, where she had DREAMS in which her future husband was revealed to her.

A variant notes that the girl must use her left-hand garter (although she can also use a string), and tie THREE knots; as each knot is tied, she repeats this colorful rhyme:

> I knit this knot, this knot I knit,
> To see the thing I ne'ever saw yet —
> To see my love in his array,
> And what he walks in every day;
> And what his occupation be
> This night in sleep be shown to me;
> And if my love be clad in green,
> His love for me it is well seen;
> And if my love be clad in grey,
> His love for me is far away;
> But if my love be clad in blue,
> His love for me is deep and true.

The garter was laid under the pillow to invoke dreams of the future husband.

L

Laa Houney—Manx name for Halloween (they also sometimes call it *Sauin*, after SAMHAIN). In Manx it was celebrated on November 12, according to the old Julian calendar.

Ladders—A ladder of plaited rushes hung at the foot of the bed ensured DREAMS of a future mate on Halloween.

Lambswool—Traditional Irish Halloween drink made of bruised and roasted apples combined with milk or ale, and spices and sugar. The name may derive from the words "La Mas Ubhal," meaning the day of the apple or fruit; or it may come from the drink's distinctive froth, which suggests fleecy lamb's wool.

Lammas Day—A festival of the first HARVEST celebrated August 1; in the Celtic calendar the day was *Lughnasad*, and was a QUARTER-DAY. The name derives from "loaf" and "mass," since it was customary in the early English Church to bless BREAD made from the first-ripe CORN at Mass on this day. A later explanation suggested that it derived from "lamb" and "Mass," denoting that it was a time at which a feudal tribute of lambs was paid (at York). Like Halloween or SAMHAIN, Lammas Day was a time to practice certain protective rites against FAIRIES and WITCHES.

Lanternes des Morts—In twelfth- to four-teenth-century France, stone buildings like lighthouses were erected in cemeteries; on Halloween lanterns were kept burning in these structures to safeguard people from the wandering dead, hence their name ("lanterns of the dead").

Latin America *see* **Days of the Dead**

Laundry— In parts of Europe one SUPERSTI-TION considers it bad luck to do laundry on Halloween, since it means the death of a family member in the coming year; it is especially ill fortune to wash a sheet, because of its resemblance to a funeral shroud.

Lead— Pouring melted lead from an iron spoon into cold WATER (preferably through a WEDDING RING or a key) is one method of Halloween FORTUNE-TELLING; when the lead hits the water it solidifies into odd shapes in which the future can supposedly be read. This 1937 poem entitled "The Magic Lead" suggests the use of the custom as a Halloween "stunt":

> Melted lead poured out in water
>   Strange shapes will assume,
> So if you'll these forms decipher
>   You may well presume
> That they represent your future,
>   Plain as plain can be.
> For example, ships will tell you
>   That you'll go to sea.
> Books will point you out a scholar,
>   Guns, a soldier, brave and bold.
> Everyone shows something different,
>   Waiting to be read and told.

Sometimes lead-pouring seemed to be combined with LUGGIE BOWLS, so melted lead was poured into THREE bowls of water. The use of EGGS was similar, since the egg whites dropped into water also formed unusual shapes; a variant of this ritual used sand instead of lead.

Leeks— In Wales, leeks served in FORTUNE-TELLING customs similar to Scottish ones involving CABBAGE or KALE. Specifically, a girl walks BACKWARDS into the leeks on Halloween night and sticks a KNIFE among them, then conceals herself nearby and waits; she will eventually see her future husband pick up the knife and throw it into the center of the leek-bed.

"Leet the Witches"— Fire custom in which a CANDLE or torch is carried about on Halloween night, to burn or "leet" (light) invisible WITCHES supposedly flying about on their broomsticks.

A Lancashire tale tells of a farmer near Pendle who began to suffer misfortunes, including the death of cattle, crops and two of his children. The farmer told his wife they would have no rest until November, since on Halloween he would "leet the witches,"or carry a candle to their meeting-place on the local hilltop; if he could succeed without the candle being blown out, he and his family would be protected from witchcraft for a year. On Halloween the farmer and his servant Isaac set out after 10 o'clock, each carrying a branch of ash with sprigs of bay tied to it as protection against thunder and lightning, and with their candles in their other hands. Just as they were turning toward home, a Satanic face appeared in the window of a tower, and both their candles went out. Both men cried out "God bless us!" and the noise and light from around the tower disappeared instantly. In the dark the two men were separated; old Isaac made it to the farm, and the farmer was found the next day at the bottom of a gorge with a broken leg. The following year the farm celebrated unaccustomed prosperity, leaving the farmer's wife to conclude that the candle flames must have been blown out after MIDNIGHT.

See also BURNING THE WITCH (a custom involving burning witches in effigy).

Lemons— A Halloween FORTUNE-TELLING custom suggests that a young woman carry lemon peels with her all day, then rub them on the four posts of her bed at bedtime. If the man she loves also loves her, he will appear in a DREAM that night and present her with two lemons.

Lemuria— With FERALIA, Lemuria is the other (and older) Roman commemoration of the dead. It was held from May 9 to May 13, on the odd days (even days were considered unlucky). During this time the dead walked and had to be propitiated. *Lemures* were wandering spirits of the dead returned, and were defined by Porphyrion as "wandering and terrifying shades of men who died untimely deaths," and by Nonius Marcellinus as "nocturnal apparitions and terrors of ghosts and beasts."

In Book Five of Ovid's *Fasti*, he describes the main ritual performed at Lemuria: It was held on the final night, when the head of the family arose at MIDNIGHT (or when the "night is half over"), made the sign of the fig, washed his hands in pure WATER, and then walked barefoot through the house, spitting out black beans from his mouth and saying, "With these beans I redeem me and mine." This was repeated NINE times, while ghosts supposedly came behind him and picked up the beans. At the conclusion of this sequence, he washed and banged bronze pots and pans, asking the ghosts to leave:

> When he's said, "Be gone, ancestral
>   spirits," nine times,
> he looks back and regards the ritual as
>   rightly done.

According to Ovid, the holiday's name derived from the death of Remus, one of the twin founders of Rome; his "bloodstained ghost" appeared to his brother Romulus and asked him to mark a festival day in his honor. Romulus called it the Remuria, but over time the name altered slightly into Lemuria.

As with Feralia, this was a time especially unlucky for marriages.

The day of Lemuria's final night, May 13, was the original date set by Pope Boniface IV for the celebration of ALL SAINTS' DAY (A.D. 609), suggesting that Boniface may have been heeding POPE GREGORY I's advice to co-opt pagan celebrations rather than try to destroy them.

Lesbian *see* **Gay Culture**

Lime-Kiln— Halloween FORTUNE-TELLING method in which an unmarried young person approached a lime-kiln

(a kiln in which limestone is burned to prepare calcium oxide, or lime) on Halloween, and threw a ball of blue YARN into it while holding one end. If a pull was felt on the other end, the question "Who holds?" was asked, whereupon the future intended would pronounce his or her full name.

In his poem "Hallowe'en," ROBERT BURNS describes the custom as enacted by one young lady:

> …She thro' the yard the nearest taks,
> An' to the kiln she goes then,
> An' darklins grapit for the bauks,
> And in the blue-clue throws then,
>   Right fear't that night.
> An' 'ay she win't, an' 'ay she swat,
> I wat she made nae jaukin;
> Till something held within the pat,
> Guid L — d! But she was quakin;
> But whether t'was the Deil himsel,
> Or whether 'twas a bauken,
> Or whether it was Andrew Bell,
> She did na wait on talkin
>   To spier that night.

("Blue-clue" refers to a clue of blue yarn; "swat" is sweat; "jaukin" is joking; "pat" is pot; "bauken" is a bogie; and "spier" is ask)

In a variant, a girl takes two balls of yarn, throws them into the lime-kiln, then, when she feels a tug on the yarn, recites, "In the name of the DEVIL who is holding my

A vintage Halloween postcard illustrating the lime-kiln divination.

yarn?" A voice from the kiln offers her future husband's name, and a very uncomplimentary name for the girl herself.

In *Witchcraft and Second Sight in the Scottish Highlands*, John Gregorson Campbell tells of an incident at a Halloween gathering when the village tailor hid in the kiln, and in answer to a girl's query called out, "The devil!" The girl fled with a shriek and was so terrified that she would not walk with any of the lads during the following year for fear that he would prove to be the devil.

Livelong (also orpine, American cudweed)—A type of herb harvested in Ireland on MIDSUMMER'S EVE; if it was found to be still green by Halloween, the one who harvested it would prosper, but if it had turned yellow or had died, it foretold death for the one who had picked it.

Locherbrigg Hill—Located in Scotland four miles from Dumfries, Locherbrigg hill (or "knowe") is the location of one of the strangest traditional Halloween stories: Derived from an old ballad, "WITCHES' Gathering Hymn," the story tells of a witch who created a diabolical bridle (made from the skin of an unbaptized infant) and used it to transform a young man into a horse. When one of his friends inquired about his ill health and manner, he advised his friend to lie in a certain place on Halloween night. His friend did so, and found himself magically transformed into a gray steed when the witch shook the bridle over his head. She rode the enchanted horse to Locherbrigg hill, where she took place in a hellish "tryste" with other witches and warlocks. The terrified young man managed to fling the bridle off, and returned to his human form. When the witch came for him at daylight, he shook the bridle over her head, turned her into a horse, and rode her back to his own stable. Once there, he released the witch from the spell, and after promising to never reveal his Halloween adventure, was allowed to keep the bridle.

Lord of Misrule—Once a figure of English royalty from Halloween to Candlemas, the Lord of Misrule was typically a serving man in a lord's household who was selected to rule the household and preside over CHRISTMAS festivities (the custom later applied only to the Twelve Days of Christmas). Lords of misrule were appointed in both the king's court and by the lord mayor of London. They often had from 20 to 60 officers under them, and were provided with musicians and MUMMERS. The Lord of Misrule gave orders which had to be obeyed, and supplied punishments when he was not obeyed (he might, for example, assign a punishment for not drinking enough!). An A.D. 1401 description notes that during this time "there were fine and subtle disguisinges, Maskes, and Mummeries." In Scotland (where an ordinance suppressing the practice was passed in 1555), the title was the Abbot of Unreason.

Luggie Bowls—A FORTUNE-TELLING custom in which THREE bowls (luggies are small bowls with handles, or "lugs") are placed side by side, one holding clear WATER, one hold-

Scottish-themed postcard showing the three luggie bowls

ing dirty water and one empty. The fortune-seeker is blindfolded, then the future is predicted by which bowl is touched first (by the left forefinger): If the clear water, the seeker will wed and live happily; if the dirty water, the seeker will wed but lead an unhappy life; and if the empty bowl, the seeker will remain unmarried. In a variation, soapy (dirty) water indicated marriage to a widow or widower.

In "Hallowe'en," ROBERT BURNS describes a Scottish variant:

> In order, on the clean hearth-stane,
> The luggies three are ranged,
> And ev'ry time great care is ta'en,
> To see them duly changed:
> Auld uncle John, wha wedlock's joys
> Sin Mar's year did desire,
> Because he gat the toom-dish thrice,
> He heav'd them on the fire
>   In wrath that night.

("Mar's year" was 1715; "toom-dish" is the empty dish.)

In a Scottish variation, the bowls were placed by the HEARTH, with clean water indicating that the future spouse would be a virgin; dirty water foretold that the spouse would be a widow or widower; and empty augured no marriage. The ritual was repeated THREE times, and every time the arrangement of the bowls was altered. In a less-common variation, the bowls are filled not with water but objects— specifically, gold (a rich marriage), a ring (an early marriage) and a thimble (no marriage). On the Isle of Man, the objects indicated the profession of the future husband — a bit of net, a fisherman; meal, a miller; and earth, a farmer. In an American custom, the bowls were filled with earth (a death coming soon), water (no marriage) and a ring (a marriage will occur soon). An Irish version uses three bowls with clean water (will live to see another Halloween), earth (will die within the year), or meal (will live a long and prosperous life). The three bowls might hold moss (luxury), dust (an auto trip) and thorns (an unhappy marriage). Another one used one bowl of clean water (marriage), one with water mixed with clay (marriage to a widower), and one with clay (no marriage). In a colorful American variation, the bowls with filled with colored water: Red meant great fortune; blue, a trip across water; and clear, a great honor bestowed.

Sometimes the number of bowls (or plates) varied. An Irish custom uses four plates on a table, one with clay (death), one with water (marriage), one with rosary beads (life as a nun) and one with nothing (an old maid). One version used different liquids in four bowls: water (a peaceful, happy life); wine (a rich, noble career); vinegar (widowhood); and an empty bowl (will never marry). An American variant used four bowls or dishes, one with dirt (divorce), one with water (a trip across the ocean), one with a ring (marriage) and one with a rag (no marriage at all). Another American version suggests thirteen dishes, with the contents indicating the disposition of one's future spouse, as follows: Sugar (sweet), pepper (hot-tempered), vinegar (sour), water (weak), cocoa (bitter), cornstarch (smooth-tongued), butter (unctuous), peanuts (nutty), washing powder (caustic), soap flakes (slippery), angel's food (angelic), sponge cake (sponging), and devil's cake (wicked).

In a Scottish version, six plates were placed on the floor, each with different contents. Another variant had a number of objects simply placed directly on the floor of an otherwise empty room. Objects might include dough (a life of ease), a rubber band (a lively or snappy life), a sharp thorn (a troublesome path), clear water (an unruffled life), and a key (good luck or travel). Sometimes seven plates were used instead of six.

During World War II, one American variant saw different bowls representing different branches of the armed forces: If a bowl with red cloth was chosen, for example, it indicated that the chooser would marry an army man, while blue cloth indicated a sailor.

Lughnasad *see* **Lammas Day**

Lunantishees— A tribe of FAIRIES said to guard the blackthorn trees or sloes; they will not allow a stick to be cut on November 11 (the original date of SAMHAIN, now MARTINMAS); anyone who dares cut a blackthorn at that time will suffer some misfortune.

Lundy— In Northern Ireland "the Lundy" is occasionally burnt in effigy in place of "the Guy" in both GUY FAWKES NIGHT and Halloween CELEBRATIONS. Robert Lundy was a seventeenth-century governor of Derry City thought to be a traitor, and although he is more commonly burnt in effigy in December, his effigy may also appear on the earlier holidays.

Luther, Martin (1483–1546)— Founder of the German Reformation. On October 31, 1517 (Luther chose the day since he knew the church, which was the Church of All Saints, would be heavily attended on that day), Luther's 95 theses on indulgences were posted on the door of the castle church at Wittenberg. The theses came to be viewed as a manifesto of reform, which eventually led to the formation of various Protestant denominations, and so October 31 was also known as PROTESTANT REFORMATION DAY.

M

Maes-Y-Felin Field— Field in Wales where "Druidical stones" (supposedly resurrected by the DRUIDS) were said to grant wishes to anyone who whispered to them on Halloween (it was also believed that on MIDSUMMER'S EVE these stones whirled around THREE times, and made curtsies).

Magic *see* **Houdini, Harry; National Magic Day**

Mardi Gras— Also known as Shrove Tuesday, since it immediately precedes Ash Wednesday (and is the last day before Lent and the 40-day period of fasting and abstinence), which means it occurs in February or March each year. The name derives from the French for "Fat Tuesday," and the day is commonly celebrated in New Orleans (although it actually started in Mobile, Alabama), Trinidad, France and Italy. Like Halloween, it is celebrated with COSTUMES, PARTIES and feasting; also, like Halloween, it precedes a solemn period. Unlike Halloween, New Orleans Mardi Gras is largely organized by "krewes," the first of which was the Mystick Krewe of Comus (formed in 1857); these krewes build floats, stage PARADES, organize costume balls and masquerades, and choose a king and queen for the next year. "Carnival" refers to the entire period between Twelfth Night and Lent, when many balls and parades are presented, and includes the actual day of Mardi Gras.

Mardi Gras is the American version of CARNIVAL. In the history of Europe, Carnival has typically included banqueting, entertainments and chaotic processions. In Rome especially, Carnival (from the Latin *carne vale*, or "farewell meat") was a grand celebration, ending with each reveler lighting his *moccoletto*, or wax taper, on the final night. As with Mardi Gras (and, later, Halloween), many revelers dressed in costume. In many areas, "King Carnival" is an effigy burned at the conclusion of Carnival (although in Mardi Gras "King Carnival" is a human being, who carries the title for a year).

Martinmas— Held November 11, this largely European holiday may have earlier marked a

Germanic pagan NEW YEAR'S feast similar to the Irish Celts' SAMHAIN. St. Martin (A.D. 317–397) was the Bishop of Tours and the patron saint of the HARVEST, and Martinmas is celebrated throughout Europe with an emphasis on the harvest. In many respects, Martinmas is the European Halloween, especially considering that, prior to the use of the Gregorian calendar, November 11 was November 1, or the current date of ALL SAINTS' DAY. Martinmas shares many customs with Halloween: In addition to HARVEST festivities, both are a time for feasting on special foods, and for religious observances. It has been recorded that in Germany children carry JACK-O'-LANTERNS (*Martinslaternen*) on this day and sing:

> Let's be happy, let's be gay,
> Let's be children all today.

In Germany, Martinmas was celebrated throughout the Middle Ages with comic plays and songs; in some British locales, there are records of fifteenth-century GUISING and MUMMING on the day (in Yorkshire, mumming practices that began on Martinmas and continued through Christmas were recorded into the 19th century). In the Netherlands, house-to-house begging, BONFIRES and jack-o'-lanterns are all part of the Martinmas festivities. An old British ballad, "Martilmasse Day," describes the holiday's merriment:

> It is the day of Martilmasse,
> Cuppes of ale should freelie passé;
> What though Wynter has begunne
> To push down the Summer sunne,
> To oure fire we can betake
> And enjoye the crackling brake,
> Never heedinge Wynter's face
> On the day of Martilmasse.

Other stanzas describe journeys to the city to see "costlie shows" and dancing until late in the evening.

In Yorkshire, the Sunday closest to Martinmas was often the day of celebration and was referred to as "Rive-kite Sunday" or "Tear-stomach Sunday."

Like the Celtic festivals of BELTANE and Samhain, Martinmas marked (with Whitsun in May) one of the two major divisions of the year until the sixteenth century, when these days were largely replaced by Easter and MICHAELMAS (see QUARTER DAYS).

Some Martinmas celebrations employed FIREWORKS as well as bonfires. In Fenny Stratford, near Bletchley, the traditional celebration (which continued into the 20th century) included firing small, strangely-shaped cannons known as the "Fenny Poppers." This same town had a house called "St. Martin's house," which bore this inscription on a stone set into the wall: "This house was settled on the parish officers of this town for the annual observance of St Martin's Day-Anno Domini 1752." Rent collected from the house was used annually to provide entertainment for the town's residents on Martinmas.

Also like Halloween, on Martinmas financial affairs were settled—church-scot (tax) was paid, as were wages and leases. One British St. Martin's Day tradition is the Payment of Wroth Silver at Knightlow Cross, Stretton on Dunsmore, near Rugby, Warwickshire; this ritual dates back over a thousand years. At the northern end of the village is a stone that is the last remaining piece of ancient Knightlow Cross. Participants must arrive at the stone before the sun rises on Martinmas, and at seven A.M., the steward of the Lord of the Manor reads a notice requiring payment and the names of those responsible; anyone who is derelict pays a fee which consists partly of "a white bull with red ears and a red nose." Those making payments are required to go around the cross THREE times, declaring the Wroth Money, which is then thrown into a cavity of the stone and taken out by the steward. Afterwards, the participants (usually about 40 in number) are treated to breakfast by the Duke at the village inn, the "Dun Cow," where they toast the Duke of Buccleuch and the Earl of Dalkeith. The custom probably was once the collecting of toll fees for use of the Lord's roads by cattle.

Martinmas was also the traditional day for the holding of Hiring Fairs in Britain, and was often called Pack-rag Day (because servants packed and set off in search of new employment). Young people who sought farm work journeyed to these fairs, and stood in lines while a farmer or lord selected from among them their help for the next year. The hiring was completed when the master gave a "fessen-penny" (usually a shilling) to his new help, and after the hiring the last night of the fair was celebrated with dancing and merrymaking.

The period between Halloween and Martinmas was a vacation time for many servants, who might celebrate on Halloween in Scotland with this song:

> This is Hallaeven,
> The morn is Halladay;
> Nine free nichts till Martinmas,
> As soon they'll wear away.

Martinmas was the time when preparations were made for the coming winter. In *Letters from a Gentleman in the North of Scotland* (1754), Edward Burt observed that the Scots "salt up a quantity of beef on or about Martinmas" (a similar practice was observed at Samhain). In some areas it was thought that the WEATHER on this day foretold the weather of the coming winter—the wind's direction for the following three months would be determined by its direction on "Martlemas Eve." In Leicestershire, a saying ran: "When the ice before Martlemas bears a duck, then look for a winter of mire and muck"; on the other hand, in Staffordshire the saying was, "If a duck can walk a pond at Martinmas, there will be a mild winter." In other areas it was a custom to foretell the weather by eating a goose on Martinmas Eve, and reading the marks on the breast-bone (white meant snow, dark meant hard frost). In fact, Martinmas was often celebrated with a special feast centered on roast goose (called in Germany *die Martinsgans*).

In Cumberland, Martinmas was the day on which stray sheep, which had been collected throughout the season, were exchanged and returned to their owners. Cumberland was also home to a charitable practice established by Thomas Williamson in 1674, who included conditions in his will to provide the local poor with mutton or veal at Martinmas.

Certain protective rituals were practiced at Martinmas. An Irish Martinmas custom was to sprinkle the blood of a farm animal or CHICKEN in the corners of the house, on doorposts and windows, and in stables as protection against evil forces during the coming year.

Unlike Halloween, Martinmas was also a celebration of wine. According to the Ancient Calendar of the Church of Rome, "Wines are tasted and drawn from the lees. The Vinalia, a feast of the ancients, removed to this day. Bacchus in the figure of Martin" (some scholars have suggested that Martinmas may even represent the ancient Greek day of ANTHESTERIA). One proverb about the holiday promises:

Collection of "wroth money" on Martinmas (photograph by Sir Benjamin Stone)

If you raise your glass
At Martinmas,
Wine will be yours
Throughout the year.

In fact in an area known as Martinsal Hill, the holiday was even referred to as "Martinalia."

Between World Wars I and II, there was a brief attempt made to establish a second BONFIRE night on the date of Martinmas to mark the armistice which ended the First World War, but the idea lasted only a few years.

In former times Martinmas or Martini was the official start of winter and the 40-day Christmas fast; today, however, *Martinstag* marks the unofficial start of the Christmas shopping season in much of Europe.

Mashed Potatoes—A variation of the FORTUNE CAKE, especially popular in Ireland. A ring, a thimble and a dime are placed into a dish of mashed potatoes; whoever finds the ring in his or her portion will be happily married (or, if already married, will have good fortune); the thimble foretells spinsterhood; and the dime, money. If a girl got the ring and managed to hide it under her tongue until the dish was emptied, she was thought to have the enviable ability of being able to hold her tongue, without losing her cunning.

In Scotland mashed potatoes are called "champit tatties." In the Highland, cream-CROWDIE— essentially whipped cream — is more popular.

Masks—It is unknown how long masks have been a part of Halloween; although there is considerable speculation that the CELTS wore COSTUMES and masks on SAMHAIN, there is no evidence to support this. The custom may have been acquired from Scottish HOGMANAY mumming customs (masks are also worn in other MUMMING customs), or may have been the earliest form of PRANKING.

What is known is that masking became one of the most popular aspects of Halloween in the twentieth century. Masks and costumes have become an integral part of TRICK OR TREAT and Halloween PARTIES. However,

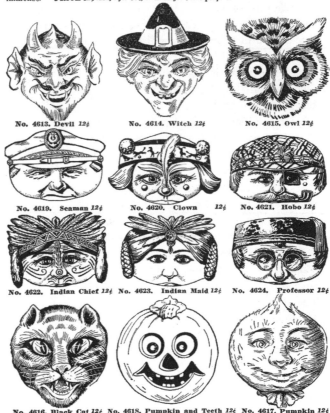

This 1929 ad for masks includes not just a pumpkin-head, but also a turnip-face (**lower right**).

the use of Halloween masking hasn't always been enthusiastically endorsed — a 1951 Halloween party book suggests that "masks may easily encourage rowdyism at a large party, and should not be allowed."

Masks were at first simple, made of cardboard or paper and sold by paper manufacturers like Dennison's. Buckram — the same stiffened cloth used in bookbinding — was probably the most popular material for Halloween masks through the middle of the 20th century; buckram masks might be manufactured by companies like A. S. Fishbach (in which case they might be waxed or have a layer of painted rayon), but they were also frequently homemade. In the 1950s, plastic manufacturing boomed, and plastic masks began to dominate the Halloween market. Plastic masks typically covered only the face (and were held on by elastic strings), whereas buckram and the later rubber masks incorporated full over-the-head designs. Buckram and rubber masks also often had hair attached (although the hair might be made of a material like straw or cotton), whereas hair on plastic masks was simply sculpted into the design.

In the 1960s, the leading manufacturer of masks was Don Post Studios in North Hollywood. Post had acquired an exclusive license to recreate the Universal movie monsters (the first one was produced in 1948, when Post released a Frankenstein mask based on the monster as portrayed by actor Glenn Strange). In 1966 Post released the Deluxe Universal line, or "the Calendar Masks," so called because they were featured in a monster calendar released that year. These masks, which were sculpted by Pat Newman, are among the most COLLECTIBLE of masks now. Don Post Studios, which produces about a million masks a year, says its all-time bestseller is the Tor Johnson mask (Johnson was the Swedish wrestler who starred in Edward D. Wood Jr.'s *Plan Nine From Outer Space*, and whose hulking, bald visage has become common at sporting events as well as at Halloween).

Matches— Several Halloween FORTUNE-TELLING customs involve matches. In one, a match is lit over a sink full of WATER; when the match tip falls, its direction will indicate where one's true love can be found. If the match burns up without breaking, the true love is already present, and you may have one wish instead.

Another practice involves trying to blow out a match flame through a funnel of paper, and suggests that:

> If you blow it the first time you'll marry for love.
> If the second, because you rate beauty above.
> If the third, you will marry for money in sight,
> And if not then, your marriage will just be for spite.

In another divination, a lighted match held in the right hand was used to trace a circle in the air; if the match was still burning when the motion was completed, marriage within the year was certain.

Matrimony, St.—Because Halloween was the key holiday in the year for practicing love spells and romantic FORTUNE-TELLING customs, there are a few nineteenth and early twentieth century references (especially on postcards) to a non-existent "Saint Matrimony" as the holiday's patron saint.

May Day— The first of May was BELTANE in the old Celtic calendar, and marked one of the two turning points of the year (SAMHAIN, or November 1, was the other). Like SAMHAIN and Halloween, May Day (the eve of which was also known as WALPURGISNACHT) had customs involving BONFIRES, WITCHES and FORTUNE-TELLING. One British belief held that witches took the form of hares on that day, and hares found among cattle were killed.

In a magazine article from 1895, M. E. Leicester Addis tries to argue in favor of a greater American celebration of May Day by noting that "We have adopted Halloween as our own; why not its companion and sister feast…?"

Memorial Day (also Decoration Day)— Sometimes called a "lay ALL SOULS' DAY," this American holiday is celebrated on May 30 in honor of those who have died in military service. Although the exact origin of the day is uncertain, it probably came about in the wake of the Civil War, when it may first have been instituted by General John A. Logan, commander-in-chief of the Grand Army of the Republic. In 1868, he called on all soldiers to visit the resting places of their fallen comrades-in-arms. By 1897 it was a legal holiday in most states, celebrated with cemetery visits, PARADES and patriotic speeches. Unlike Halloween, however, Memorial Day has no iconography or symbolism of its own, but seems to share the patriotic red, white and blue motif of the Fourth of July (albeit without that holiday's gleeful spirit).

Romanians celebrate a Memorial Day on May 31; food, drink, money and *dari* (presents) are given away (especially to children), in the belief that "Whatever one gives away in this world one gets back tenfold in the next."

Mexico *see* **Days of the Dead**

Miccailhuitl and Miccailhuitontli— The two most widely recorded Aztec festivals of the dead, which probably served (at least in part) as the basis for contemporary Mexican and Mexican-American celebrations of DAYS OF THE DEAD. *Miccailhuitontli* means the "Little Feast of the Dead" (sometimes known as "Feast of the Little Dead Ones"), and honored the spirits of deceased children (just as October 31 does in many contemporary Mexican celebrations), while *Miccailhuitl* means "Great Feast of the Dead" (occasionally called "Feast of the Adult Dead"), and honored the adult spirits. These two feasts were also known as the *Tlaxochimaco*, "The Offering of Flowers," and the *Xocotl uetzi*, "The Xocotl Falls" (*xocotl* is a fruit). The feasts were held in the ninth and tenth months of the Aztec year (which included 18 months). Festivities included offerings of FOOD and FLOWERS, feasting and dancing, and

the creation of the *xocotl*, a huge tree which was felled, stripped, and brought into town, where it was greeted with singing, dancing and food offerings. On the twentieth day of the tenth month, captives were led first to the *tzompantli*, or rack holding the skulls of previous victims; then they were led to the top of the temple, where they were thrown into a fire and their hearts were removed. The sixteenth-century Dominican friar Fray Diego Durán recorded that after the sacrifice, dances were performed around the *xocotl* by nobles "covered with feathers and jewels," and with painted bodies.

Another description of *Miccailhuitl* mentions that the feast began on the third of August, and that food and drink were placed on the tombs of the dead for four years after their death, since the Aztecs believed the souls had to endure a difficult four-year jour-

Dancer costumed in Aztec garb in Days of the Dead celebration

ney to the afterlife. It is also recorded that the larger feast began on August 23, and included a verbal invitation to the dead to join their families.

The Aztecs had several other days dedicated to remembrance of the dead, including one held in the eighteenth month which included a family gathering, a feast of *tamales* (still a traditional Days of the Dead food), and offerings to the dead.

Although debate continues over how much influence these pre–Columbian rituals had on the contemporary Days of the Dead, Durán noted that "…the feast has been passed to the Feast of Allhallows, in order to cover up the ancient ceremony."

Michaelmas— The feast day of the archangel Michael (in the *Book of Common Prayer* the day is dedicated to Michael and All Angels), kept on September 29, and one of the four QUARTER DAYS of the English business year. In the Roman Catholic Church the day now commemorates Gabriel and Raphael as well. Michael is usually depicted wielding a sword and fighting a dragon, which probably derives from a passage in Rev. (12: 7–9), in which Michael leads the angels in a fight against a dragon, who is actually the DEVIL.

Michaelmas, like Halloween, was celebrated in the past with BONFIRES, special "St. Michael's cakes," a feast of roast goose (like MARTINMAS), and certain forms of FORTUNE-TELLING: For example a ring (foretelling early marriage for whoever found it) might be hidden in the "Michaelmas pie." In *The Vicar of Wakefield*, Oliver Goldsmith refers to "religiously cracked nuts on Michaelmas," suggesting that Michaelmas also shared some of Halloween's uses of NUTS.

Midnight— The traditional hour of most magic or evil, especially on Halloween; the boundary between one day and the next (or, on SAMHAIN, one year and the next). Most FORTUNE-TELLING customs specify midnight as the hour at which the ritual must be conducted, and midnight was also a time to protect crops and livestock from the forces of

evil. In certain areas of Britain, for example, farmers would patrol their fields one hour before midnight on Halloween, keeping an eye out for WITCHES or FAIRIES.

In Ireland, an old SUPERSTITION was that one must be inside by midnight on Halloween, because at that time the doors of PURGATORY were opened and the dead souls were released to wander the earth.

Midsummer's Eve— Although the summer solstice technically falls on June 21, midsummer is usually celebrated (in Europe) on June 24, the Feast of St. John the Baptist. The festivities include BONFIRES, processions and FORTUNE-TELLING customs (especially those involving HEMP SEED). Some customs are seasonal, such as those that pertain to freshly-bloomed ROSES, but others are shared with Halloween (and, like Halloween or ALL SAINTS' DAY, are celebrated on the night before the holiday). One Midsummer's Eve custom was "the Church Porch Watch," which involved a night-long vigil from the church porch in order to see apparitions of those who were to die that year (sometimes the apparitions were even said to come and knock at the door). This custom (which is further described under CHURCHES) was widespread in parts of Great Britain into the nineteenth century (and was also celebrated at St. Mark's Church on St. Mark's Eve, April 25).

In *The Sketch Book*, WASHINGTON IRVING notes that "on Midsummer eve … it is well known all kinds of ghosts, goblins, and fairies become visible and walk abroad."

Milfoil (also yarrow)— An herb gathered on Halloween and placed beneath the pillow to provoke DREAMS of future husbands.

Milk— In parts of Brittany, it was once the custom on TOUSSAINT to pour milk over or near the tombs of one's ancestors.

Mirrors— There are numerous variations on the well-known Halloween FORTUNE-TELLING legend of seeing the face of one's future beloved in a mirror. In perhaps the most popular version, the seeker holds a CANDLE in one hand and a mirror in the other, and walks BACKWARDS down steps; at the bottom of the stairs, the beloved's face will appear in the mirror. A variation suggests that the seeker must walk backwards outside beneath the MOON to the middle of a cornfield while these words are spoken:

> Round and round, o stars so fair!
> Ye travel and search out everywhere;
> I pray you, sweet stars, now show to me
> This night who my future husband (wife)
>   shall be!

An American variation notes that while walking downstairs backwards (and carrying a mirror), each step must be counted; at the thirteenth one will see a reflection of one's future husband. A late nineteenth-century version from Atlanta, Georgia, mentions that the woman's hair must be unfastened, her feet bare, and she must recite a short verse. A version for men recommends standing before a mirror in a dark room, and after reciting a small chant the man would see numbers form on the mirror, indicating the letters of the alphabet that made up his future spouse's name.

One classic divination suggests that a girl stand before a mirror on Halloween at MIDNIGHT and slice an APPLE into NINE slices, holding each on the tip of a knife before she eats it. As she holds up the ninth slice, the image of her future husband will appear over her left shoulder, asking for the final slice. It is sometimes indicated that this ritual must be performed by moonlight, and may be practiced on any moonlit night during October or November.

Another method of mirror fortune-telling says that if a young unmarried woman stands before a mirror on Halloween and combs her HAIR, then the face of her future intended will appear in the mirror, glancing over her shoulder.

An American custom involves standing so that through a window a woman may see the moon in a glass she holds; if she counts the number of reflections she will know how many pleasant things will happen to her over the next 12 months. Another American divination suggests that at the stroke of midnight on Halloween, a woman stand with her back to a mirror while holding another mirror, and she will see her future husband's face in the reflection.

A Scottish custom also involved COINS: At midnight on Halloween, the one seeking one's fortune went to one's room alone, with a SIEVE and three silver coins, and stood between the mirror and the window, with one's back to the latter, and while gazing steadfastly into the mirror sifted the coins continuously. Presently one would behold in the glass the panorama of their future life.

Vintage Halloween postcard showing a woman moving backwards at midnight while enacting a mirror divination.

In an interesting variation of the party fortune-telling game involving WITCHES' INK, a message was written on a mirror in chalk and then erased. The guest would breathe gently onto the mirror, which would then reveal the written message.

Mischief Night— A night of PRANKING variously reported as April 30 (May Eve), October 30 (also known as DEVIL'S NIGHT), October 31 (Halloween) or November 4 (the night before GUY FAWKES DAY). In the 1950s the date was reported across many English counties as November 4, but in the nineteenth century it was widely recorded as April 30. Regarding the November 4 date, much of the pilfering on this night was to gather material for Guy Fawkes Day BONFIRES. In other areas of Britain (especially Scotland), the name has almost always been known to refer to Halloween. A 1914 account of Mischief Night records it as occurring on All Hallows E'en, and describes activities very similar to American Halloween prankplaying of the same period: "...I have known doors taken off hinges, gates opened, doors whitewashed, and door latches tied." In a few parts of Britain and mainly the U.S. (East Coast), it is the night of October 30. Acts range from simple pranking (tying doorknobs together, moving GATES, etc.) to outright vandalism (smashing bus shelters, hurling bricks through windows and lighting fixtures, etc.).

Mischief Night has been in the news several times for unfortunate reasons: In 2001, the November 4 prankplaying in Halifax (Great Britain) got out of hand, when smashed windows led to the destruction by arson of the Actors Workshop theatre school (several cars were also burned out); the night's actions further enflamed tensions between Muslims and whites in this post 9/11 community. A year later, in 2002, Michael Skakel, nephew to Robert F. Kennedy, was convicted of beating 15-year-old Martha Moxley to death on Mischief Night (October 30) in 1975. *See also* BEGGAR'S NIGHT; GOOSEY NIGHT.

Mistletoe— Supposedly revered by the Celtic DRUIDS (especially when found growing on an oak), mistletoe is usually associated with CHRISTMAS, when it is hung above doorways where anyone found standing beneath it may be kissed; but there are a few reports of it being used for similar purposes at Halloween celebrations, especially in late nineteenth-century America.

Mistletoe also had protective powers: If a sprig was cut with a new knife on Halloween after the cutter had walked THREE times around the oak tree sunwise, it was a sure guard against harm in battle or evil charms perpetrated by WITCHES.

Money *see* **Coins; Debts**

Mongfind (also Mongfinn, Moingfhionn, Moingfhinne)— A Celtic character who is somewhat enigmatic. In some accounts she is a mythological sorceress; in others she was the daughter of Fidach of Munster, wife of King Eochu Muigmedon and stepmother of Niall; in yet another account she is a snow or frost goddess; and she is also sometimes confused with the goddess Morrigan. In virtually all of her different aspects she presents the characteristics of a warrior queen, and in some stories she was said to be the one who trained or tested future kings. She supposedly died one SAMHAIN Eve when she took poison prepared for her brother; thereafter some of the peasantry called Samhain *Feile Moingfhinne* or "the Festival of Mongfind," because on that night women addressed petitions to her and celebrated her prowess as a witch.

Monologs— Another popular form of Halloween entertainment in America during the 1920s and 1930s. Unlike RECITATIONS (also designed as solo performances), monologs are not rhyming performances, and the performer usually portrays another character, often in costume.

Moon— Since the moon will be in a different phase at each Halloween, it figures in very few divinations (FORTUNE-TELLING customs involving MIRRORS must sometimes be performed beneath the moon). However, the moon is a prominent feature in Halloween decorations, often shown with WITCHES, OWLS, or black CATS.

The moon is part of at least one odd American custom, but it is a paper moon: A cardboard moon is hung on a wall at the Halloween party. Each guest is blindfolded, then turned about THREE times; if, after the blindfold is removed, the moon can be seen over the right shoulder, good luck is to follow.

The moon also features in several American SUPERSTITIONS: One says that if the moon is half full on the night before Halloween, it will rain for three days. Another holds that the half-full moon on that night actually portends bad luck for the coming month.

Full moons on Halloween are rare; 2001 saw the first in over 30 years.

This Halloween clicker noisemaker (note toad shape to clicker) shows the moon along with other Halloween symbols.

Some astronomers have suggested that JACK-O'-LANTERN carving was inspired by the "harvest moon" seen in October.

Mother Goose— Traditional collection of nursery rhymes dating back over 300 years which has provided a theme for the Halloween celebrations of very young children since at least the early 20th century (when both Halloween CELEBRATIONS and illustrated editions of *Mother Goose* became popular). Mother Goose characters including Little Bo Peep, Miss Muffet, Jack Horner, Old Mother Hubbard, and The Pumpkin Eater were early popular choices for children's Halloween COSTUMES, and the nursery rhymes have also provided themes for children's PARTIES and performances. An 1889 description of a Mother Goose-themed Halloween party at Vassar College describes games and costumes, and RUTH EDNA KELLEY's 1919 *The Book of Hallowe'en* suggests a Mother Goose recital for Halloween entertainments; the Dennison's BOGIE BOOKS recommend "Jack Horner Pies" for table centerpieces at children's Halloween parties, and a 1915 Halloween party guide suggests a "Mother Hallowe'en" theme for a party presentation. By 1937, city planners looking to entertain children at Halloween (rather than allow them to engage in malicious PRANKING) commonly suggested Mother Goose parties (along with PIRATE and HOBO themed celebrations). Characters like Miss Muffet and Bo Peep remain popular for both children's and adults' costumes.

One URBAN LEGEND, which has been around in various forms since 1968, suggests that a homicidal maniac dressed as Bo Peep will be stalking a college campus or dormitory on Halloween night.

Mountain Ash *see* **Rowan**

Mrastyr— Traditional Manx Halloween supper, made of potatoes, parsnips and fish pounded and mixed with butter.

Muck Olla— An Irish tradition that continued as long as the early twentieth century, and may have been a precursor of TRICK OR TREAT. In this ritual, a group of young men were led on All Hallows' Eve from house-to-house by a white-robed man in a horsehead MASK, called *Lair Bhan* (White Horse). At each house the young men blew horns (also a feature of Scottish HOGMANAY mumming), and demanded tribute to "Muck Olla," a legendary boar spirit, who would ensure the farmer's continuing prosperity. Tribute was typically paid in the form of butter, eggs and farm produce. Muck Olla is occasionally referred to as a Celtic deity, but there is no evidence in Celtic literature to support this.

Mummering; Mummers *see* **Mumming**

Mumming (also mummering)—From the Danish word *mumme*, meaning to parade in MASKS. Mumming occurs at holidays all over the world, and is one of the most popular British calendar customs. Although it takes on many different forms, mumming typically involves a masked or disguised performance (often of a traditional "mumming play") offered at each house in a neighborhood in return for some reward, usually of food or drink. Mumming is performed at different seasons throughout Great Britain, but in Cheshire it is specifically a Halloween activity, where the mummers are known as soulcakers or soulers. The typical mumming play begins with an introduction of the mumming team, then follows a rough plot in which a hero takes on a rival champion, and is badly wounded in combat. A doctor is called for (in Halloween plays the doctor typically arrives on a "wild horse"), and, usually after some playful banter about the doctor's fees, the hero is brought back to life. The play closes with a short speech asking for food or money, although the players may follow the play with in-dividual performances of song or dance. Women or girls did not typically participate in mumming.

On the Isle of Man, mummers used to go around on Halloween singing in the Manx language "Tonight is New Year's Night, Hogmanay!" (the Manx associated Halloween with the Celtic NEW YEAR'S celebration of SAMHAIN).

Music—Although Halloween is not generally associated with any music, the holiday nevertheless has some musical connections. Throughout the British Isles, SOULING and MUMMING have involved some form of singing, and the Irish and Scots have several Halloween legends involving either pipers or fiddlers. One such is the story of Ned Pugh (or Iolo ap Huw in Welsh), who entered the cave of Tal y Clegyr (which was regarded as a place of wonder) on Halloween (in one version of the story Iolo was drawn into the cave by mysterious hands). He disappeared there while playing "Ffarwel Ned Puw," or "Ned Pugh's Farewell," which has been retained in memory of him. In a Welsh version of the story, a shepherd, hurrying past the mouth of the cave on Halloween, heard a burst of wild fiddling, and saw Iolo, but his head was loose, as if it was about to fall off, and he bore an expression of horrible agony. A lighted

1909 postcard showing a musical Halloween celebration

lantern suspended by a rope hung between his shoulders, and the head and horns of a goat were fastened upon his breast. The shepherd watched until Iolo was drawn back into the cave; then, two years later the shepherd was in church early on CHRISTMAS morning when he heard the same music coming from beneath his feet. The shepherd whistled the tune to the vicar, who transposed it into music, thus creating "Ffarwel Ned Puw." In the other world, Ned or Iolo exchanged his fiddle for a bugle, and so became hunstman-in-chief to Gwyn ab Wud; now, every Halloween he may be found cheering Cwn Annwn, "the Hounds of the Other World," over Cader Idris (see also SPECTRE HUNTSMAN).

Like Christmas carols, Halloween once boasted its own songs, although they often took their music from existing tunes ("When Johnny Comes Marching Home" became "When Hallowe'en Comes Round Again," for example), and were frequently performed as part of Halloween PAGEANTS by school children, rather than sung by families or carolers. Nineteenth-century PARTIES often included a singalong, with current songs (i.e. "My Sweetheart's the Man in the Moon") that had a Halloween flavor.

In Ireland the folk song "*Is Fada O Bhaile A D'Aithneoinn*" tells the story of a girl who has lost her love, and who believes she will die before the next Halloween.

Halloween in America has acquired something of a theme song: The immensely popular "Monster Mash" by Bobby "Boris" Pickett. Additionally, Halloween-themed CDs and compilations continue to sell well every year. By the 21st century, there were a number of Halloween-themed internet radio stations, most of which play throughout the year, and may feature anything from old radio plays and horror movie soundtracks to contemporary rock songs with a horror theme.

National Magic Day— October 31 is also National Magic Day in the United States. The day was instituted in 1938 by a magician named Les Sholty who originally suggested that October 31st be "Houdini Day," in honor HARRY HOUDINI, who died on October 31, 1926; Mrs. Houdini gave her blessing to calling the day National Magic Day in honor of Houdini. Not long thereafter, the week prior became National Magic Week, and is still celebrated with magic displays in libraries and free performances by magicians all over the country. The Society of American Magicians (for which Houdini had served as president for the nine years prior to his death) encourages its local assemblies to celebrate the week, and at the conclusion of the week the assemblies receive recognition on the Society's website.

Needles— Needles figure in both Halloween protective charms and Halloween FORTUNE-TELLING. In one divination, 25 new needles are lined up on a plate; WATER is poured over them, and the ways in which the needles move are then read (i.e., crossed needles indicate enemies who are sharp-tongued). In a variation of this custom, each person at a party placed a greased needle on the surface of water in a basin; movement to or away from other needles was prophetic (or, specifically, two needles would foretell whether lovers would come together or move apart). In another custom, new pins or needles were used to prick sweethearts' initials in dough as part of a DUMB CAKE ritual.

Another fortune-telling GAME involved participants trying to thread a needle while seated on a round bottle placed lengthwise on the floor; the first to succeed would of course be the first to be wed.

One particularly unwholesome American game suggested that a fortune-seeker run around the square with a mouthful of pins and needles, then return home and look in a MIRROR, to see either the face of a future husband or a COFFIN.

In one other divination method, a boy and girl were paired off, and one held a thread while the other held a needle. If they could successfully thread the needle, they were destined for each other. Onlookers might chant:

> Needly, thready,
> Steady! Steady!
> Where's the thread? The needle's ready.
> Now you have it, and now you don't!
> Now she will, and now she won't!
> Aim it true, and aim it straight,
> And behold your future Fate!

Needles were also a means of protection from evil forces on Halloween: A steel needle placed in a collar or sleeve was defense against malicious FAIRIES for late-night Halloween travelers, or a needle stuck in the doorway of a fairy mound would allow one to enter and leave safely.

Neep Lanterns—JACK-O'-LANTERN made by scooping out a TURNIP and placing a CANDLE inside. "Neep" (which is derived from the Latin *napus*) is actually closer to the root word than the more commonly known "turnip" is.

Neighbors—A number of FORTUNE-TELLING customs depend on hearing a neighbor utter a name which would be that of the future husband or wife. Although these customs usually involve an agent such as WATER, a BROOM or a part of a cart loaded with the CORN harvest, at least one Irish custom specifies simply that a girl go to a neighbor's door on Halloween and listen, and the first name she would hear spoken would be that of her future husband.

Neo-Pagans—Neo-Pagans are typically those who have polytheistic and animistic beliefs; they include WICCANS, Reformed DRUIDS, Odinists, Feraferia and others. Most Neo-Pagans hold Halloween or SAMHAIN as a major festival day or QUARTER DAY; among Wiccans, for example, it is one of their eight "sabbats." Some Neo-Pagans also refer to the day as Shadowfest or ANCESTOR NIGHT.

Nera—The hero at the center of possibly the most famous Celtic SAMHAIN myth: One Samhain in CRUACHAN, clan leaders Ailell and Maeve say they'll reward any man who can put a gad (a coil of twisted twigs) about the foot of either of two men hanged on the gallows the day before. Some warriors try, but because it is Samhain they all return. Nera volunteers (to win the gold-hilted sword Ailell has offered), and he succeeds. When he puts the coil about the corpse's foot, the corpse speaks to him; the dead man says he died thirsty and would like a drink. Nera hauls the dead man on his back to a nearby house, to get a drink, but the dead man spits the drink into the faces of the house's inhabitants, who all die. Nera returns the corpse to the gallows, and upon his return Nera sees all of Cruachan in flames. He sees a *sidhe* army and follows it into a hill, where he spends three days. He takes a wife who tells him the secret location of the crown of the king of Brium (one of the three great wonders of Ireland), and tells him to return to Cruachan and ready the men for the next Samhain, since the *sidhe* army can only attack then. Nera's wife also tells him that the sight of the devastated Cruachan was an illusion, and that he must return to Cruachan; to prove his story, he's given summer flowers. Nera goes back to Ailell and Maeve, who are convinced when he produces summer flowers (in autumn) and he spends the year with them. On the next Samhain they invade the hill and steal the crown, but Nera stays behind forever inside the hill.

New Year's—New Year's Day includes many customs and celebrations which are strangely similar to Halloween (which was, after all, the CELTS' New Year's Day, or SAMHAIN). For example, in the British Isles rituals were performed to protect houses from malevolent forces (one such ritual involved striking a dried cow-hide with a stick and beating on the walls of each house while special rhymes were pronounced). In Allendale, Northumberland (in England), the new year is welcomed by costumed men who make a BONFIRE partly out of tar barrels. On the Isle of Man, many of the FORTUNE-TELLING rituals observed on Halloween (or the old New Year's Eve) are also observed on the modern New Year's Eve. In the Scottish New Year's celebration of HOGMANAY, costumed MUMMING was observed.

Nine—The number nine figures prominently in many Halloween FORTUNE-TELLING customs; for example, an APPLE is sliced into nine pieces, or HEMP SEED is sowed over nine ridges. The importance of nine is undoubtedly due to the fact that THREE is an important number in both Celtic and Christian traditions, and three is also the square root of nine.

Ninin—DAYS OF THE DEAD celebration found among the Totonac Indians in the Mexican state of Veracruz, *Ninín* or Days of the Dead actually begins on October 18 (San Lucas), although preparations (gathering of food and wood for altar-building, etc.) usually start two months or so previously. On the eighteenth, food offerings are made to the deceased and to the saints. On October 31, the altars are finished, and sweet, mild foods are put out in anticipation of the returning spirits of dead children. On the following day the children depart and the adult souls arrive; the food is accordingly changed, to

spicier entrees and alcoholic drink. On November 2, rockets are fired off, food is taken and placed on the tombs in the cemetery, and special altars are left outside houses for orphaned spirits. On *Xa aktumajat,* or the octave days of November 8 and 9, families bid farewell to first the spirit children, then, on the following day, the departing ghosts. Finally on San Andres (November 30), a final farewell is said to the ghosts, who will not return until next season.

Totonac storytellers have their own Day of the Dead ghost story about a young man who did not prepare for *Ninin*, but instead went out with his friends. Upon returning home, he encountered a group of the dead, including his own parents; all the dead happily carried offerings except his relatives, who sobbed. The young man hurried home and set out offerings, but he took ill and died soon thereafter, and the offerings instead served as food during his funeral.

Noisemakers—Halloween noisemakers were once an essential part of Halloween, first in the early twentieth century when PRANKING was popular, then in the latter half

Vintage Halloween noisemakers, including a tambourine, a horn, a rattle, a clicker, a whistle, a "frying-pan," a "mallet," and two ratchet styles.

when TRICK OR TREATING had largely replaced pranking. During the pranking period, noisemakers were often homemade and designed to startle unsuspecting neighbors; probably the most popular noisemakers at this time were the TICKTACK and the RATTLE-TRAP or horse fiddle (now commonly known as a "ratchet"). When trick or treating became popular, noisemakers, like COSTUMES, largely ceased being homemade and were mass-produced in a variety of styles, nearly all featuring colorful graphics. Carl B. Holmberg, in his article "Things That Go *Snap-Rattle-Clang-Toot-Crank* in the Night: Halloween Noisemakers," suggests that noisemakers were replaced by Halloween-themed movies and soundtracks, by adults playing atmospheric MUSIC or sound effects to greet trick-or-treaters, and even by heavy metal music.

As with many other COLLECTIBLES, the earliest noisemakers were produced in Germany, and were usually rattletraps of wood, often featuring a small composition Halloween character (a black CAT or a PUMPKIN) perched atop the noisemaker. Later the toys were manufactured in the U.S., usually made of tin and wood (later tin and plastic), and produced almost entirely by four companies: J. Chein, T. Cohn, U.S. Metal Toy and, especially, Kirchhof (which eventually dropped one "h" from its name). Noisemakers included rattletraps or ratchets (in square, round and oval shapes), bells, whistles, "frying pan" clangers, rattles (in both round and "mallet" styles), tambourines, clickers or "crickets" (which often used a traditional toad shape, with Halloween graphics applied to the existing form), squeakers and horns (including "blow-outs").

Nos Calan Gaeaf (also *Nos-Galan-Gaeof* or *Nos Cyn Calan gauaf*)—"The Night of the Winter Calends"; a Welsh name for SAMHAIN.

November Eve—Another name for Halloween, especially used in Western Ireland. Originally November 1 fell on what is now November 11 (before the Julian calendar was replaced by the Gregorian calendar); in some areas, November Eve was still celebrated on the day before November 11 even after the calendar change.

"November Eve" is also the title of one of the most well-known stories about FAIRIES on Halloween.

November the 5th *see* Guy Fawkes Day/Night

Numbers *see* Nine; Three

Nutcrack Night—A British name for Halloween, because of the custom of placing NUTS on the fire to crack (a form of divination). Should not be confused with "Cracknut Sunday," a tradition celebrated in the area of Kingston-upon-Thames on the Sunday before MICHAELMAS; parishioners filled their pockets with nuts, which they cracked so loudly during the service that it had to be suspended at times. This practice was abolished about the end of the eighteenth century.

Nutmeg *see* Nuts

Nuts—As with APPLES the significance of nuts at Halloween is often linked to the Roman harvest goddess POMONA, but probably stems more from Celtic beliefs. The CELTS especially venerated HAZELNUTS, and nuts and apples are often linked in Celtic lore.

A Scottish FORTUNE-TELLING belief centered on the burning of nuts on Halloween: A pair of nuts are named for each member of a couple, then placed on a fire. If they burn to ashes together, the couple will enjoy a long, happy life together; but if they sputter and roll apart, they will separate soon. Sometimes this rhyme was recited as the nuts were placed:

> If you hate me spit and fly;
> If you love me burn away.

A less pleasant variant of this rhyme from Sussex was recorded:

An Ellen Clapsaddle postcard showing nuts used in Halloween fortune-telling.

If he loves me, pop and fly,
If he hates me, lie and die.

The ASHES from the nuts might be collected and placed under the pillow to promote prophetic DREAMS.

In a version from Hertfordshire, a girl threw one nut on the fire, which represented her true love. If the nut burst quickly, it was a good omen, but if it never burst at all, the unfortunate girl was destined for spinsterhood. A variation of this custom is more specific: CHESTNUTS are used; if one hisses and steams, it indicates a bad temper in the human counterpart, but if both perform in this manner, it augurs strife. Charles Graydon lays out the custom in these lines from "On Nuts Burning, Allhallows Eve":

These glowing nuts are emblems true
Of what in human life we view:

The ill-matched couple fret and fume,
And thus in strife themselves consume;
Or from each other wildly start,
And with a noise forever part.
But see the happy, happy pair,
Of genuine love and truth sincere;
With mutual fondness while they burn,
Still to each other kindly turn;
And as the vital sparks decay,
Together gently sink away;
Till life's fierce trials being past,
Their mingled ashes rest at last.

A variation is suggested in this anonymous 1937 poem, "The Test of the Nuts":

I've named three nuts and placed them
    Side by side on the grate,
The one which cracks is unfaithful,
    The lover I know I should hate.
The one which blazes with brilliant fire,
    Tells of high regard, 'tis said,
But the one which burns with a steady
    flame
Names the man whom I shall wed.

Sometimes this method involved only two hazelnuts, with the choice involving nuts which cracked (unfaithful) against nuts which burned steadily to ashes (true). A variation of the three-nut custom involves THREE chestnuts named and placed on a HEARTH. If they separate, so will those for whom they are named; those jumping toward the fire are going to a warmer climate; those jumping from the fire, to a colder climate; if two gentlemen jump toward one another, it means rivalry. In a Welsh custom, nuts thrown onto a BONFIRE predict the future: If the flames dance about when the nuts are thrown in, the coming year will be full of fun and excitement; but if the flames don't change, the coming year will be dull.

In another roasting custom, a nut was named for each person present, and placed on the fire. If a nut burned quietly, life would be even and uneventful; if it popped right out of the grate, it might mean that that person would travel; if it stayed in the grate but popped and exploded the owner would have an exciting time without traveling; and if the nut burnt up, the owner would not get his or her wish.

One fortune-telling method involved three different nuts—a walnut, a hazelnut, and a nutmeg—which were grated together and mixed with butter and sugar into pills. A young woman seeking to know the occupation of her future husband took the pills just before bedtime on Halloween, and her dreams supposedly foretold her future: Golden dreams indicated a gentleman; odd noises and tumults, a tradesman; and thunder and lightning, a traveler.

In Wales, on Halloween people would cast WALNUTS or hazelnuts (or sometimes stones or pebbles) into the fire. When these were shot out by the heat, or if the nuts burst, the younger folk ran away, fearing the "goblin black-tailed sow" would come and drive them into the flue.

One British party GAME involved chestnutting on Halloween; the one finding the first burr would be the first to marry. If the burr opened easily, love would not last long; if it was hard to open, then the romance would be lasting. *See also* ACORNS.

Oats— Oats (which are often referred to as CORN) figured in a number of FORTUNE-TELLING customs. In a Scottish divination, girls went to the barnyard on Halloween and pulled THREE different stalks of oats; if the third stalk lacked the "top-pickle," or grain at the top of the stalk, the puller would enter into marriage no longer a virgin. This custom is gently mocked by ROBERT BURNS in his poem "Hallowe'en," when Rob helps Nelly lose her "tap-pickle … when kiuttlin in the fause-house/wi' him that night."

A more modest variant is suggested by this 1920 poem:

> A maiden pulls three stalks of oats,
> And if, upon the third,
> That maiden finds no head of grain,
> Her marriage is assured.

In a variant of this custom, the number of top-grains counted in a handful of oats indicated the number of children the grain-counter would have. In another version, three ears of "corn" (oats) were drawn from the stack after dark on Halloween, and placed under the pillow by an unmarried girl. In her dreams that night she would see her future

husband reaping the oats (sometimes these ears must be drawn from the maiden-sheaf, or CORN DOLLY). In one American custom, a young man put NINE grains of oats in his mouth and took a walk; the first name he heard would be the name of his future wife. In Ireland, this same ritual was practiced with the sexes reversed. A 1927 Halloween party pamphlet suggests that the savvy hostess will send a man out one door of the house and his ideal partner out of another.

Oats were also used in an Irish HARVEST divination: For a good harvest, an oat CAKE was placed under the pillow the night before harvest; in the morning one had to eat the oat cake before opening one's eyes.

Oats had protective powers on Halloween as well. In Ireland, oaten meal and SALT were mixed and sprinkled with holy water; during the Halloween meal a pinch of this mixture was taken by the mother or any older member of the FAMILY, and the sign of the Cross was applied to the forehead of each member of the family. This would protect them from evil spirits and FAIRIES during the coming year.

Oatmeal and salt (a dry mixture) might

also be applied to children's' heads on Halloween night to keep fairies from stealing them away.

Obon *see* **Bon Festival**

Ocean *see* **Sea**

Odawa Ghost Supper— A celebration of the dead held on or around November 2nd by the Odawa Indians of Michigan. The celebration is similar to Mexican DAYS OF THE DEAD festivities, with a feast given and gifts offered to deceased loved ones, and special wreaths made for decoration of graves and tombs. Prior to the arrival of missionaries, the Ghost Supper was celebrated in the spring and involved making the offerings directly to the uncovered remains of the deceased. The festival is still celebrated, and includes a ceremonial fire which the first plate of food is offered to; the festivities are open to the public, and usually draw hundreds of guests.

Odilo, St. (961 or 962–1049)— The fifth Abbot of Cluny, Odilo (or sometimes Odilon) left a permanent mark on the Liturgy by introducing ALL SOULS' DAY. He was canonized in 1063, and has his own feast days on January 1 or 2, or on April 29 in the order.

Ofrendas— Although the word "ofrenda" means "offering," this Mexican DAYS OF THE DEAD custom more commonly refers to the elaborate collages put together in memory of deceased family members. Ofrendas typically include religious icons, photos of the dead, their favorite food and drink, and sweets (for deceased children). However, some ofrendas are more elaborate: The town of Huaquechula is famous for its spectacular ofrendas, which often include brightly-colored pottery made specifically for the occasion, electric lights, and yards and yards of white satin, meticulously draped and pleated around these large displays.

Another area, Iguala, prepares *tumbas vivientes*, or "living tombs." These displays

Days of the Dead *ofrenda*

typically include a painted backdrop, a coffin with a photo of the deceased atop it, and live actors dressed as angels, death or other figures. Families are welcome to view these "living tombs," and FIREWORKS lit near the doorway announce a household with a living tomb display.

A very popular ofrenda is dedicated each year by Dolores Olmedo to Diego Rivera. Set up inside the Anahuacalli Museum in Mexico City, this very large display includes elaborate papercuts, papier mâché skeletons, painted ceramic figures, flowers, and sugar skulls.

Ofrendas have recently been recreated in the collage art of Mexican-American artists, and are frequently on view in galleries throughout the Southwest around October.

O'Hanlon, Shaun— An Irish GHOST STORY tells of a man who sat down under a "haunted tree" on Halloween, and was greeted by a spectre in black who told him that he had been a member of the Molly Maguires and had sold out NINE of his comrades to the government for money; however, like Judas, he had never spent the money. He told his listener where the hidden money could be found, and asked that it be turned over to a priest, to say nine prayers. The listener did as told; a year later he returned to the haunted tree, and this time the spectre, now dressed in white, revealed that his name was Shaun O'Hanlon and that, because of the listener's generosity, his spirit was finally released after 60 years of wandering.

Oiche Feil Na Marg—Irish name for All Souls' Eve, or the evening of November 1. In some areas (especially Northern Ireland), this is actually the night (rather than the 31st) on which it is believed that souls return to their homes from PURGATORY. A typical celebration would be to leave chairs near a stoked HEARTH, after the FAMILY had recited a rosary and retired early. However, the family would rise at MIDNIGHT, say a longer rosary (15 decades—hence the night's occasionally being referred to as "the night of the long Rosary"), put more fuel on the fire and return to bed. Some believed the dead returned for exactly one hour; to accommodate them, doors were left unlatched on this night.

Oiche Na Spirdeanna—"Spirit Night"; another old Irish name for Halloween.

Oiche Shamhna—Irish name which translates roughly to "the night of SAMHAIN."

Oiche Shean Shamhain—Irish for "Old Halloween Eve," referring to the night of November 11 (which was the night of November 1 prior to the change from the Julian to the Gregorian calendar). This name was still familiar to some areas of Ireland by the mid-nineteenth century. Old Halloween Day was known as *Lá Shean Shamhain*.

Oidhche Na H-Aimléise—In Waterford, Halloween is called *oídhche na h-aimléise*, "the night of mischief or con."

Orne, Martha Russell—American author of non-fiction books (mainly grammar guides) and plays who is now chiefly known as the author of *Hallowe'en: How to Celebrate It* (1898), the first book to focus solely on Halloween. The 48-page booklet includes some history of Halloween and party tips; it also includes many fortune-telling practices, which seem to be drawn mainly from the ROBERT BURNS poem "Hallowe'en." Many of the later Halloween party booklets—which became very popular in the 1920s and 1930s—owed a considerable debt to Orne's book.

Osier—Species of WILLOW, the branches of which are often used in basket-work. In some parts of Britain peeled osier twigs were placed over doors and all entrances on Halloween as a protection against WITCHES (see also ROWAN).

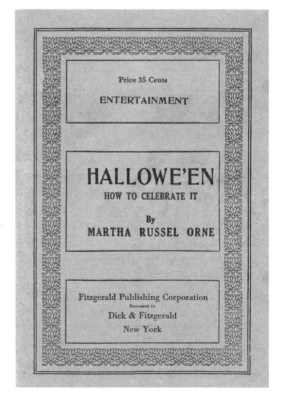

Price 35 Cents

ENTERTAINMENT

HALLOWE'EN
HOW TO CELEBRATE IT
By
MARTHA RUSSEL ORNE

Fitzgerald Publishing Corporation
Successor to
Dick & Fitzgerald
New York

Cover of Martha Russell Orne's *Hallowe'en: How to Celebrate It*

Owls— Like BATS and CATS, owls are hunters whose nocturnal habits may be directly responsible for their association with Halloween. Owls had some minor role in Celtic mythology, appearing on artifacts and in the tale "Math Son of Mathonwy," in which the hero Lleu takes revenge on his adulterous wife by transforming her into an owl. In modern Scottish Gaelic the owl is *cailleach oidhche*, or "night hag," while in Welsh it is *aderyn y corff*, "corpse-bird." Although ravens figured far more prominently in Celtic lore, they are rarely seen in Halloween symbolism.

It was once believed that WITCHES could transform into owls, and owls seen around farms on Halloween night were killed.

In both literature and folklore the owl's cry (especially the barn owl's screech) means death or disaster. To see or hear an owl in daylight is especially ominous, as is having one knock against a window.

In Wales, if owls were heard hooting on the evening of MARTINMAS, it was regarded as a very bad omen for the entire district or village.

Vintage Halloween ratchet noisemaker showing an owl with a jack-o'-lantern.

Pageants— Popular form of school and church entertainment in the early twentieth century. Pageants involved many costumed children, often portraying historical characters; "Hallowe'ens of Long Ago" was a popular theme, involving children portraying DRUIDS, ancient Scots, Romans celebrating POMONA, etc.; sometimes children also dressed as famous characters from fiction, fairy tales and nursery rhymes, such as "Humpty Dumpty," "Jack Be Nimble," etc. The first major American Halloween pageant was held in Fort Worth, Texas in 1916, with the World War I theme "Preparedness for Peace" (with 4,000 costumed schoolchildren).

Pantomimes— A form of entertainment like a ritualized, highly stylized one-act play, often performed in costume. Pantomimes were popular Halloween entertainments for early twentieth-century schoolchildren. These PLAYS were often performed with no performers speaking but a narrator or reader.

Parades— Although parades have been part of GUY FAWKES DAY celebrations for centuries, they have been a significant part of Halloween for not quite a century. Halloween parades first became popular in the 1920s and 1930s as a way to provide children with an alternative to destructive PRANKING. Probably the most famous Halloween parade in the world is the Greenwich Village parade in New York. This parade essentially started when Ralph Lee, a puppeteer and theatre director, gathered 150 friends in 1973 to celebrate Halloween with a procession of giant puppets (the giant articulated snake was to become a perennial favorite). Within 10 years the parade had gained worldwide renown and was attracting a half-million spectators and participants. The parade was transformed over those 10 years from a small, intimate piece of street theater to a huge event; also participating in the transformation was the GAY community, since the parade provided an opportunity for drag queens and gay designers to display their wares in an open, festive atmosphere (although many of the gay activities took place not in the parade itself but in the parallel Christopher Street promenade). In 1987 Ralph Lee resigned as the parade's organizer, but the parade continued under new leadership. It was broadcast live for the first time in 2000, and still draws over two million; it also pumps an estimated $60 million into the local economy. The parade spans approximately a full mile, includes nearly 60,000 costumed participants, and is credited as being America's only major night parade. The Greenwich Village festivities also include PARTIES for charity, theater events, food stands, etc.

Key West in Florida has hosted the Halloween parade "Fantasy Fest" since 1978. The festival starts 10 days prior to Halloween, and includes toga parties, celebrity lookalike contests, and even a contest for costumed pets.

Justin Rudd's "Haute Dog Howl'oween Parade" in Long Beach, California, bills itself as "the world's largest Halloween pet event." Drawing around 700 costumed dogs and thousands of spectators, the parade launched in 2000, includes a costume contest, a bulldog kissing booth, and a "pumpkin drop," and contributes thousands of dollars to pet shelters and charities each year.

Allentown, Pennsylvania held its Halloween parade on the Tuesday evening nearest to October 31, a tradition which began in the late 1920s. ANOKA in Minnesota, which calls itself "the Halloween Capital of the World," hosts no less than three parades each Halloween season. See also CELEBRATIONS.

Parentalia — Roman holiday involving ancestor worship, held between February 13 and 20. Parentalia was a period for appeasing the dead (*Placundis Manibus*), and lasted until February 21, when FERALIA was celebrated. During the days of Parentalia, all temples were closed, no fires were burned on altars, and no marriages were performed.

Parshell (also parshal) — Irish cross made from twisting CORN husks or STRAW into a cross (in some instances the cross is begun with two sticks, around which the straw is woven). The parshell is placed over a doorway on Halloween (on the inside), and will protect the household from evil influences and illness for one year. It must be replaced each Halloween; the removal of the old parshell must be accompanied by a shout of "Fonstarenheehy!" Parshells are similar to Bridget's crosses, woven for St. Brigid's Day.

Parties — Halloween parties are probably as old as the holiday itself. Accounts of SAMHAIN in Celtic mythology describe THREE days of feasting, drinking and sporting events. One of the earliest written mentions of Halloween, from the 1493 *Festivall*, contains this description of what sounds like a contemporary Halloween party: "Good frendes suche a daye ye shall haue all halowen daye." ROBERT BURNS's famed 1785 poem "Hallowe'en" describes a Scottish party, including drinking, eating, FORTUNE-TELLING, gossiping, GAMES and carousing. A description of an Irish Halloween party from 1834 mentions that the front door was taken from its hinges and set down on the bare earthen floor of the farmer's house to serve as a dance floor, that divination with NUTS was practiced at the peat fire on the HEARTH, APPLES were eaten, KALE stalks pulled, the LUGGIE BOWLS brought out, and GHOST STORIES told until sunrise. Possibly the earliest description of an American Halloween party may be found in the November 1870 issue of *Godey's Lady's Book and Magazine*: The article "Hallowe'en," by Helen Elliott, describes a party thrown by the Barlowes, a British family transplanted to the banks of the Ohio River. The party is for children (specifically girls), and begins by asking the children to enter the house by stepping over a BROOM that is placed across the doorway to keep WITCHES out. Activities include pulling molasses candy, playing SNAPDRAGON, burning nuts, pouring hot LEAD into water, and a fortune-telling game which sounds like a variation of the luggie bowls: Each girl was led across the floor blind-folded to choose either a basin of water (she'll marry for love), a goose wing (she'll marry an old man), or a pile of ASHES (she'll die an old maid).

A typical boys' party from 1916 is described in the children's book *Hallowe'en at Merryvale*, by Alice Hale Burns: As the boys enter the house, they are each given a ghost costume (a pillowcase for the head and sheets). The house is lit only by JACK-O'-LANTERNS, possibly decorated with cornstalks or even some store-bought decorations. APPLES have been hung to swing from an overhead post, and each boy must try to take a bite. There's a game of taffy pulling (with greased fingers). A "witch" (a parent in costume) appears, and gives each boy a fortune written in "WITCHES' INK"; after the witch leaves, the boys hold their fortunes over candle flames to read. Next, 10 CANDLES are lined up, and the boys vie to see who can blow out the most with one breath. A pan of FLOUR is brought out, and contestants must try to find a buried dime using only their mouths. Then they're seated around a table where the centerpiece is a "paper pie" — when the pie is opened, it is revealed to be full of bug, frog and mouse toys. Crackers are snapped for

A 1916 illustration of a boys' Halloween party.

paper hats, and a CAKE with tokens baked into it is sliced and passed out. Finally, prizes are given to the winners of the various games.

By 1932, Boy Scout troops and civil authorities hosted large parties to lure boys away from PRANKING; these events included treasure hunts, HAUNTED HOUSES, and "TRAILS OF TERROR." HOUSE-TO-HOUSE PARTIES — in which NEIGHBORS joined to provide five or six differently-themed party environments in each of their houses — were precursors to the modern TRICK OR TREAT.

Within the last three decades, Halloween parties have begun to cater more to adults than to children. Large-scale events at ZOOS, malls, and other civic centers usually provide entertainment for kids, while adults attend private parties, nightclubs, or CELEBRATIONS held later in the evening.

Parting of the White Bread *see* **Pierce's Charity.**

Patrick, St.—Ireland's most famous saint (who gave his name to a holiday celebrating Irish tradition) plays a small role in a few SAMHAIN tales. In one, Cailte, St. Patrick and others came to a pillar stone named *Cloch-nan-arm*, or "the Stone of the Arms or Weapons." When St. Patrick asked how it had acquired that name, Cailte informed him that the Fena of Erm (Celtic knights commanded by FINN MACCUMAL) used to come to the stone every Samhaintide to sharpen their weapons. In another tale, when a minstrel appeared to St. Patrick on the day before Samhain, the saint was put to sleep by the minstrel's powerful fairy MUSIC.

Peas—Several FORTUNE-TELLING customs involve peas: In one, a handful of peas were tossed in with green beans for the Halloween meal; finding a pea in a spoonful of beans foretold either good luck or marriage during the coming year. A reversal of this custom from Northern England is called "SCADDING THE PEAS": A peapod is slit, a bean pushed in, and the opening closed again. The full pods are boiled, then shelled and distributed to guests with butter and salt. The one finding the bean on his plate would be married first.

In another custom (similar to a famous one involving NUTS), two peas were named for lovers and placed on a hot shovel. If a pea jumped, that person would be unfaithful; if a pea burned or ignited, that person was truly well loved.

John Gay describes another test in his "Thursday, or the Spell," from *The Shepherd's Week*:

> As peascods once I plucked I chanced to see
> One that was closely filled with three times three;
> Which when I crop'd, I safely home convey'd,
> And o'er the door the spell in secret laid; —
> The latch moved up, when who should first come in,
> But in his proper person — Lubberkin.

("Peascods" are peapods.)

The 1580 edition of *Five Hundred Points of Good Husbandry* suggests planting peas at Halloween:

> "Green peason or hastings at Hallowtide sow,
> In hearty good soil he requireth to grow."

Peat—In parts of Britain it was once thought to be unwise to build a Halloween fire with peat, since WITCHES could smell peat burning from great distances (oak logs were used instead).

Peat also figured in several FORTUNE-TELLING customs: On Halloween night, a young man or woman would go to a peat-stack and turn NINE divots; on turning the ninth, a vision of the future spouse would appear briefly; a variant of this recommends that the fortune seeker take the kitchen BROOM and ride it "in the manner of a witch three times round the peat stack" to cause the apparition to appear. In another divination, if a mouthful of the top sod of the house wall or a mouthful of the clod above the gate lintel is taken into the house between one's teeth on Halloween, any HAIR that may be found in it indicates the hair color of one's future partner. A similar result may be achieved by placing burning peat into WATER in which one's feet have been washed overnight, then the peat is examined for any hairs.

In one unusual Irish custom, on Halloween night THREE sods of peat were cut, and in the morning if there was any living thing to be found on them it was a sign (a flying insect was a bad man, a crawling insect a quiet man).

Peltznickel *see* **Belsnickling**

Pierce's Charity—A Shropshire tradition practiced on ALL SAINTS DAY, also known as "the parting of the white bread." A Mr. Pierce had, in his will, set aside 20s yearly for the widows and widowers in Sweeney; 10s was used to make the bread, which was distributed equally, and the remaining amount was given out as money. The ritual was conducted in a lane near the village, under the open air.

Pirates— The classic image of the pirate —frequently shown with tri-cornered hat or bandana, eye-patch, and earrings— has been one of the most popular Halloween COSTUMES from nearly the beginning of the 20th century. The pirate as Halloween icon is stressed, for example, in a 1937 catalog of Halloween paper decorations, which sells a set of four face cutouts: A WITCH, a JACK-O'-LANTERN, a black CAT, and a pirate; and a 1965 children's book says that Halloween "is for funny masks and pirate hats…" Not only were pirate costumes and MASKS popular, but so were pirate-themed holiday PARTIES. In one example, a mid-century Halloween party booklet suggests that the house be dressed for a "ghost ship" on Halloween and that each guest be named for a famous buccaneer. "Treasure hunt" GAMES— in which small prizes or objects were hidden around the house — were popular Halloween party entertainments, and naturally leant themselves to pirate themes. And the skull and crossbones— which had been the symbol of pirates since the 18th-century — naturally intersected with Halloween.

The popular cultural image of pirates was first firmly established with the publication of Robert Louis Stevenson's classic *Treasure Island* and its pirate villain Long John Silver. *Treasure Island* was first published in a children's magazine in 1881 (and in book form two years later), about the same time that the celebration of Halloween in America was moving into the middle class. The iconic pirate provided the template for a simple homemade Halloween costume, and the popularity of the pirate was continually fed by film and literature, ranging from the first theatrical performance of J. M. Barrie's *Peter Pan* in 1904 (introducing Captain Hook), to the Douglas Fairbanks and Errol Flynn pirate films of the 1920s and '30s (i.e., *The Black Pirate* and *Captain Blood*), to the runaway success of Disney's 2003 *Pirates of the Caribbean* movie (based on the long-running

ASSORTED HALLOWEEN DECORATIONS

Halloween character heads of Witch, Cat, Pumpkin and Pirate. Six designs, die cut, printed in Orange, Black and Green, hole on top for hanging. Size 12x12 inches.

No. 15/55H.   Per Dozen **$0.50**
                 Per Gross **5.00**

1937 catalog illustration showing pirate and witch decorations

Disneyland theme park ride). *Caribbean*'s pirate hero Captain Jack Sparrow (played by Johnny Depp in the movie) became one of the most popular Halloween costumes of the 2000s.

Pixies (also piskeys)— Variation of FAIRIES; also known as "the little people" in Irish lore. Pixies are thought to live underground, and become disturbed if the land above them is changed in any way. They're active on Halloween, along with leprechauns and WITCHES, and are known for causing people to lose their way; the victim can escape by turning some item of clothing inside out. They are shapeshifters, who may appear as animals or balls of light, and they may operate in groups (dancing in circles). They tangle horses' manes at night, cause strange noises and operate like poltergeists. If given clothes, pixies may happily disappear, crying:

> Pixy fine, pixy gay,
> Pixy now will run away.

In some beliefs, pixies are thought to be the souls of unhappy infants who died before receiving baptism.

Plays— Popular custom for schoolchildren throughout the twentieth century. Halloween plays often feature WITCHES, PARTIES, and mildly spooky situations. See also RECITATIONS, PAGEANTS, MONOLOGS, PANTOMIMES and EXERCISES.

Plough Day (sometimes Plough Monday)— The first Monday after Twelfth Day (January 6); the day on which farm workers traditionally returned to work after the Christmas break. A Plough Monday supper was often given by the farmer for his men, who would race to be the first back to work the following day.

Workers also sometimes performed MUMMING—"plough plays"—on this day. In one custom observed on the English Plough Day, ploughmen begged gifts house-to-house, and threatened to damage the grounds with their ploughs should they be denied (thus, they offered a "trick" if a "treat" was not forthcoming, causing some scholars to see Plough Day as a possible forerunner of modern TRICK OR TREAT).

Poisoning *see* **Halloween Sadism; X-Rays**

Pomona (from the Latin *pomum*, meaning fruit)—One of the biggest mysteries surrounding the pre–Christian history of Halloween may be the influence of Roman festivals. Many references cite a Roman festival dedicated to the goddess of the fruits, Pomona; this festival was usually said to have been held on November 1, and celebrated with feasting on NUTS and APPLES. Yet in the actual Roman calendar there is no festival dedicated to Pomona, and little is known of any rites surrounding this minor mythological figure. The standard guide to Roman festivals, Ovid's *Fasti*, only covers the first half of the year; the volumes covering July through December were probably left unwritten after Ovid's exile by the emperor in A.D. 8. In *Phases in the Religion of Ancient Rome*, Cyril Bailey states that Pomona "never had a festival in the old calendar," while W. Warde Fowler notes in *The Roman Festivals of the Period of the Republic*, "Of all the months in the Roman year November is the least important from a religious point of view. It was the month of ploughing and sowing—not of holiday-time; then, as now, it was a quiet month, and in the calendars, with the exception of *ludi plebeii*, not a festival appears of any importance." Fowler also notes that the last major Harvest festival of the year (the Romans had four) was *Equus Ad Nixas Fit* in early October. In addition, the Romans never conquered Ireland, so any

combining of the Irish and Celtic SAMHAIN and pagan Roman customs is unlikely (although the Roman festivals of FERALIA and LEMURIA—both of which commemorated the dead—may have had some influence on the Catholic observations of ALL SAINTS' DAY and ALL SOULS' DAY). The mistaken notion of a festival dedicated to Pomona probably began in the early 19th century: For example, a magazine article from 1813 states: "The 1st day of November seems to retain the celebration of a festival to Pomona, when it is supposed the summer stores are opened on the approach of winter." Later that century, the connection between Pomona and Halloween is firmly entrenched, as an 1883 article "Some Roman Remains" from the Charles Dickens-edited weekly magazine *All the Year Round* states that "it would be perhaps going too far to say that the nut-burning charms believed in by the peasantry of the North of England and Scotland upon Hallowe'en, are of Roman origin, yet we

"Pomona and Vertumnus" by Francesco Melzi (1517–20)

know that the festival of Pomona was held about the end of November…"

What is known of Pomona is that she was the subject of one fairly well-known mythological tale, told by Ovid as "Vertumnus and Pomona." According to Ovid (and later, Bulfinch, in his classic mythology collection), Pomona was a wood-nymph or "hama-dryad" (a dryad dedicated to some particular tree), who carried a pruning knife in her right hand, and was sought by many gods and deities (including Pan), but she turned them all down. Vertumnus was the god of the changing year, and sought to woo Pomona by changing into the forms of a ploughman, a fisherman, a reaper, and finally an old woman. In the last form he first tried to convince Pomona of the virtues of Vertumnus; but when she remained unmoved, he told her the story of Anaxarete, who was so cold to her lover Iphis that he hanged himself, and while she watched his funeral train pass by she changed into a marble statue. Finally Vertumnus changed into his proper form, and Pomona, moved by his story and his beauty, agreed to become his wife.

Pomona is referred to as a "fruit-spirit" by some historians; she had a flamen (a dedicated priest, the Pomonalis) and a sacred precinct, a Pomonal, 12 miles from Rome. Sometimes she is said to have been feted during the *Vertumnalias*, a festival held August 13 in honor of Vertumnas.

In post-Roman Empire times, Pomona has been celebrated by artists since Leonardo da Vinci painted her sometime prior to 1519 (when he died). She has since been painted either singly or with Vertumnus or other deities by Titian, Peter Paul Rubens, Nicolas Poussin, Luca Giordano, Antoine Watteau, Anthony van Dyck, and Francesco Melzi. Also, Pomona is mentioned in Milton's *Paradise Lost* (1667), further testimony to her popularity at the time.

The misconception of Pomona as a goddess worthy of a major festival seems to have originated in the nineteenth century, and was propagated especially by poets. William Morris, in his poem entitled "Pomona," refers to her as "the ancient apple-queen." In early Halloween books, Pomona is sometimes mentioned as an influence on Halloween, but the history is vague; for example, in her 1919 *The Book of Hallowe'en*, RUTH E. KELLEY notes, "Not much is known of the ceremonies, but … much may be deduced." By the 1950s and 1960s, Pomona had become nearly as influential to the holiday's history as Samhain. For example, in her 1963 book on Halloween, Lillie Patterson states that Pomona was one of the "greatest" of Roman holidays, and further suggests that "The Romans took their holidays to Britain with them." Although this may be, it is in fact unlikely that the Romans invading Britain would have celebrated a minor nymph, and the Halloween traditions of apples and nuts often ascribed to Pomona are likelier to be Samhain or Celtic holdovers.

Pooka (also puca) — An evil fairy or hobgoblin said to have spent Halloween night contaminating or destroying unharvested crops. This shape-changer was said to have favored the form of an ugly black horse, and is sometimes described as being an animal spirit whose name derives from *poc*, meaning "male goat." In the story "Mac-na-Michomhairle," the pooka is described as a steed that emerges each November Day from a hill in Leinster, and speaks to those it encounters in a human voice; he would describe events destined to occur during the next year. One variety of pooka was the *augh-ishka* (or *each-uisge*), or water-horse, which emerged from the water and would make an exceptional HORSE if it could be caught and kept away from the sight of water; but if one caught sight of water, it would plunge in and tear its rider to pieces at the bottom.

In the story "The Piper and the Puca," a drunken piper is kidnapped by a pooka with long horns who takes him to a feast of FAIRIES, where the pooka is welcomed as

"Puca of November (*na Samhna*)." At the feast (which is attended by hundreds of old women called *cailleacha*), the piper plays and is rewarded with immense riches; when he returns home in the morning, however, the gold coins have become worthless plant leaves.

The pooka supposedly came in various forms, sometimes as a donkey, a horse, or an eagle. If it was kindly spoken to, it would answer questions regarding the events of the coming year.

Pooka was probably derived from the Welsh *pwca*, or goblin, and was sometimes called simply puck (as in the mischievous spirit from Shakespeare's *A Midsummer Night's Dream*).

Popcorn— Favorite American FOOD at Halloween, and also the basis for one FORTUNE-TELLING custom: Pop a dozen popcorn kernels in a wire popper over an open flame; those eventually left unpopped indicate the number of years left before marriage.

Pope *see* **Gregory I**

Pope Day/Night *see* **Guy Fawkes Day/ Night**

Pork Night— Late nineteenth-century American name for GUY FAWKES DAY, when the original appellation of Pope Day had lost its meaning.

Postcards— From about 1900 to 1930 (when telephones had become commonplace enough to replace letters and postcards), sending Halloween postcards was nearly as popular as sending Christmas cards is today. Over 3,000 different Halloween postcards were produced, most depicting the holiday's most popular symbols—PUMP-KINS, WITCHES, GOBLINS— although many also showed the FORTUNE-TELLING methods that were still popular at the time. Today these cards are highly prized COLLECTIBLES, none more so than those manufactured by John Winsch; Winsch cards featuring the artwork of Samuel Schmucker are small masterpieces of art nouveau, combining enchanting women, Halloween symbols, and high quality printing, often with gelatin finishes. Another popular Winsch artist was Jason Freixas, known for his sweet, Kewpie-doll like children. On the collector's market, a single Winsch postcard can command up to $500.

Possibly second only to Winsch was Raphael Tuck. Tuck's cards often carried the slogan "art publisher to their Majesties The King and Queen" (in 1866 he was granted the title by Queen Alexandra of Saxony), and Tuck's cards were so popular that just after the turn of the twentieth century there was an entire club made up of Tuck card collectors. Tuck's artists included Francis Brundage, although the queen of postcard artists was probably Ellen Clapsaddle. Born in New York State in 1856, Clapsaddle worked as a portrait and landscape artist before finding work with the International Art Publishing Company in New York, then Wolf Brothers

Pumpkin-headed vegetable people flee a witch in this Raphael Tuck postcard.

in Germany. Clapsaddle often signed her postcards, which feature beautiful children or exquisitely rendered Halloween scenes; contemporary collectors will pay high prices for cards that feature Clapsaddle's name and art.

Dr. Bernhardt Wall's postcard art was among the most colorful and sometimes surreal, featuring grinning anthropomorphic vegetable people, and boys apparently trapped in JACK-O'-LANTERNS. Cards produced by Gottschaulk, Dreyfuss and Davis tended to feature Scottish motifs, with tartan designs, Scottish emblems such as thistles, and Scottish sayings (mainly "AULD LANG SYNE").

Pranking

Pranking— Pranking has long been one of the most common Halloween activities; in fact, pranking is usually thought to have originated along with the belief that evil spirits roamed the land on Halloween night (since pranksters could engage in mischief and ascribe it to these spirits). Halloween pranking probably originated in Ireland, and then crossed the Atlantic with the Irish who fled the Potato Famine in the mid–1840s. In America, pranking figured prominently on Halloween from the late nineteenth century on, and is still found (albeit in a reduced form) today.

In Ireland, where Halloween is celebrated for several weeks prior to October 31 by RHYMING and collecting fuel for BONFIRES, pranks were often practiced on the night of Halloween, after PARTIES (which included such traditional activities as BOBBING FOR APPLES and storytelling). In older times, typical Irish pranks might include clogging a chimney with cloth or CABBAGES, or shaving only half of a goat's beard; pranking is still practiced today, but tends to be more benevolent, including

such activities as clipping cabbage leaves to a neighbor's clothesline. Pranks in Ireland might also include FIREWORKS, especially "bangers" or rockets. Even though some Irish pranking seemed destructive (such as pouring diesel oil on a potato field, or digging up an entire field of cabbages), they might also involve a sense of Robin Hood-style redistribution of goods, with pranks being played on those thought to be most miserly and greedy. Stolen cabbages might also be thrown at the houses of those who were too poor to get them in any other way.

In *Folklore of the Ulster People*, Sheila St. Clair describes an amusing prank perpetrated by her father as a lad: On Halloween he climbed up the chapel BELL rope and severed all but the last few strands. The next morning when the sexton tried to ring the bell, the rope fell to the floor, leaving him to summon his flock by cycling through the village ringing a handbell borrowed from the school.

Scottish Halloween pranksters developed several unique practices, including BURNING THE REEKIE MEHR and sham window-smashing, in which one prankster struck a window with his hand while the other smashed a bottle against the side of the house, creating the aural illusion of a window being smashed.

Typical American pranks might include

A 1916 postcard showing two boys carrying peashooters, engaged in pranking.

hitching cows to a carriage instead of horses, so that when the driver pulls out his whips, the cows throw the carriage; disassembling wagons and carriages and rebuilding them on top of barn roofs; moving GATES, tie posts, ladders and small pieces of machinery about during the night; tying gates or even front doors shut; stealing welcome mats; throwing dirt or FLOUR on porches; soaping windows; or the ever-popular outhouse-tipping. Throwing EGGS, a traditional activity, is still so popular that egg orders are doubled in many U.S. markets come Halloween time (in fact some store owners refuse to sell eggs to kids during this time); one dangerous stunt involved filling eggshells with chemical hair remover, resulting in children with bald spots showing up on the first day of November.

At the beginning of the twentieth century, as urban and suburban areas expanded and the country became ever more industrialized, American Halloween pranking moved into cities and became more destructive: Strings were tied across sidewalks to make passersby trip, windows and lighting fixtures were smashed, and small fires were set. One Halloween, an orchestrated group of boys broke into every car on a street, taped the horns down and then locked the doors. By 1925, cities like Chicago were instituting large-scale plans to thwart pranking; many cities had success by enlisting the pranksters themselves to patrol with police on Halloween night or fix up damages on the following day.

Minneapolis instituted a Hallowe'en party plan in 1934 in an effort to control pranking, or "rowdyism." They successfully reduced damage by Halloween pranksters by two-thirds within two years. Y.M.C.A., Y.W.C.A., Boy Scouts, Girl Scouts, Campfire Girls and Volunteers of America were organizations that sponsored events to entertain 25,000 children on Halloween, and approximately 6,000 private parties for children were held.

In 1933 and 1934, mobs of boys aged 10

Chart shows average indices of Hallowe'en trouble in Minneapolis during years 1931-1933, preceding the introduction of the Hallowe'en Party Plan, as compared with years 1934-1936, when Party Plan was in effect.

1937 chart showing facts about destructive pranking in Minneapolis

to their early twenties broke out in riots and destruction on Halloween in a number of major American cities. Streets were barricaded with debris and flooded by open fire hydrants; automobiles were overturned; buildings were torched or wrecked; and telephone poles were sawed down. A 1933 report on Halloween in Minneapolis that year refers to gangs of "hoodlums" and notes that "for hours they roamed the city, overwhelming the police by sheer force of numbers." For many American cities the "Black Hallowe'en" of 1933 was the most destructive night in their history. Determined to prevent another catastrophic Halloween from happening, cities like Minneapolis formed committees to deal with the problem. Within a year "boy trouble" police calls on Halloween dropped from an average of .31 per 1000 people to .17. An average of 372 streetlights had been replaced in 1931–3, but in 1934 only 250 were replaced. One boy that year was held for trial on disorder charges as compared to 17 after "Black Hallowe'en." Businesses donated money to civic activities, and the Minneapolis PTA sent letters to all parents, suggesting the following:

1. Conduct a party or other social affair in your home and join with the young people in having a good time.
2. Assert parental authority to keep aimless children off the streets.
3. Entertain the family at theater parties.
4. Encourage the young people to attend community parties being held under responsible leadership.
5. Talk over the problems in your family circle and ask for intelligent and sportsman-like cooperation. Suggest that we observe a Will Rogers kind of Hallowe'en — one in which everybody has a good time and which hurts nobody.

The problems of destructive Halloween pranking were further exacerbated by the severe economic restraints imposed by the Great Depression. One mother of five wrote:

"As so many parents are unemployed or earning so little money that they cannot afford these extras, we have tried to work out a plan whereby the children will have a good time but will not be deprived of some necessity later on because of it. Six mothers and fathers have gone together for this party, each furnishing an equal share."

Boys 14 to 16 were encouraged to find activities out of town, such as barn parties or campfires. Although COSTUMES were encouraged, MASKS were not (for fear of causing "rowdyism").

Other cities, such as Freehold, New Jersey, came up with novel events for children such as a town-wide window decorating contest, in which merchants donated their display windows on Halloween night and children were provided with poster paints and chalks, with prizes awarded to the best displays.

Although most cities were able to discourage pranking somewhat, by the 1940s—during the World War II years, when the country was already rationing many things—pranking had come to be seen as not just mildly destructive but downright unpatriotic. In 1942, in fact, Chicago tried to abolish Halloween just to control pranking.

Apparently unbeknownst to the Chicago authorities, a far more effective way of controlling destructive Halloween pranking had already appeared in some parts of the country: TRICK OR TREAT. Although contemporary children are virtually unaware of the genuine implied threat in this phrase, in its early days the ritual consisted of homeowners inviting pranksters in and entertaining them with cider, DOUGHNUTS, POPCORN and other treats. The purchase of food was thought to be a bargain compared to the costs sometimes involved in post–Halloween clean-up and repair.

Thus, by the 1950s, Halloween pranking had decreased in popularity; in some areas pranking began to take place on a separate night, usually October 30, referred to as MISCHIEF NIGHT (or, mainly in Detroit, DEVIL'S NIGHT, where it became known for its widespread arson). There were still reports of pranking, however; in 1972 one Halloween prank include knocking out the power at a trailer court. It was also popular in some rural areas to place or even throw stuffed dummies into roads, creating a heart-pounding hazard for drivers. In more urban areas, pranks involving manure in burning bags placed on porches and strewing toilet paper through trees (or "t.p.-ing") continue to be practiced.

One of the most unusual American Halloween customs involves an elaborate form of pranking in the village of Danbury, New Hampshire: A tremendous pile of junk — old cars, bathtubs, barrels, etc. — appears in the center of the town common during the night. The townspeople have become so accustomed to this odd practice that few attempts have been made to try to stop it; one lawman who did attempt to investigate was burned in effigy.

In "Halloween in America: Contemporary Customs and Performances," JACK SANTINO says: "Traditional pranks … are playful, yet 'practical' reminders (as in 'practical jokes') of the winter that lies ahead." He also draws a connection with ALL FOOLS' DAY as the two days of acceptable pranking, and notes that they lie on almost opposite ends of the calendar.

Although pranking continues into the twenty-first century, the practice has also led to some of the uglier Halloween incidents over the last two decades. Halloween in New York City in 1989 resulted in 67 arrests for assault. In 1989, one man was killed and nine injured when a group of costumed men stormed a homeless camp in New York while shouting "Trick or treat." In 1990 a group of costumed men raped a Boston woman. And in 1999 Brandon Ketsdever, 17, was shot to death in Buena Park, California, while trying to steal a plastic pumpkin from homeowner Pete Tavita Solomona (Solomona was eventually convicted of manslaughter).

Progressive Parties *see* **House-to-House Parties**

Protestant Reformation Day—MARTIN LUTHER nailed his 95 theses to the door of the castle church in Wittenberg, Germany on October 31, 1517 (a day he chose because he knew the church would be heavily visited that day). This day is observed by all Protestant denominations, and is also often marked by special services on the last Sunday of October (or Reformation Sunday). This day may also explain why Halloween continued to be celebrated within Protestant circles, where ALL SAINTS' DAY was denounced as Catholic or papist.

Psalm Caking— Variation of SOULING practiced at Great Marton, Lancashire. In celebration of ALL SOULS' DAY, young people went from house to house and recited "psalms" at each stop, receiving small cakes in return — hence the name "Psalm caking." The name may have been derived from "sal-mass," the name of the service given on November 2nd.

Puca *see* **Pooka**

Pumpkin Patches— Pumpkin patches are a popular form of HALLOWEEN ATTRACTION, and as such are considered "agri-

Two children enjoy a visit to a pumpkin patch (photograph circa 1930)

tainment" or "agri-tourism" along with CORN MAZES and HAYRIDES. Pumpkin patches may be simple seasonal roadside stands where customers purchase pumpkins, or "PYO" (pick your own) pumpkin farms, which may include other attractions and which offer urban dwellers the chance to interact with rural farm life. As with corn mazes and hayrides, pumpkin patches have become an important source of revenue for many farmers, with these seasonal attractions bringing in $30-$40 million in revenues annually.

Pumpkin Pie— Once a popular dish at Halloween (as well as THANKSGIVING). This 1932 recitation by Lenore K. Dolan is called "Gifts":

> October gives us Hallowe'en
> And Hallowe'en gives us fun;
> If I had lots of Pumpkin pies
> I'd gladly give you one.

Pumpkins— When carved into JACK-O'-LANTERNS, pumpkins are probably the single most popular symbol of Halloween. Part of the *Cucurbitaceae* family, which includes squash, melons and cucumbers, pumpkins are native to the Americas, and were a key food in the diets of early natives (several pumpkin dishes are still found in Mexican DAYS OF THE DEAD festivities). Pumpkins range in size from the "Baby Boo" to the "Atlantic Giant," which can reach over 1,000 pounds (the largest pumpkin on record in 2009 was grown by Ohio teacher Christy Harp and weighed 1,725 pounds). Pumpkins are harvested in September and October.

Pumpkins are important in Halloween FOOD, GAMES, CELEBRATIONS, and even FOR-

TUNE-TELLING practices. In an American divination, the surface of a pumpkin was randomly carved with alphabet letters; fortune-seekers were then led blindfolded to the pumpkin, where the letters they touched, poked with a pin, or pointed at foretold their true loves' initials. Party games using pumpkins might include guessing how many seeds were inside, or throwing an apple stem into an open pumpkin from a short distance away. Hosts of these same parties might feed their guests with roasted pumpkin seeds and PUMPKIN PIE.

Pumpkin patch at Forneris Farms, Mission Hills, California

Pumpkin festivals are held all over the United States and Canada around Halloween time. Some, such as the Circleville Pumpkin Show in Ohio, extant since 1903, emphasize tradition; the New Hampshire Pumpkin Festival boasts sheer numbers (over 17,000 pumpkins featured); or at the Great Jack-o'-lantern Festival in Vermont, art is the thing, with a team of about 10 artists carving some of the most unique pumpkins around (try a 700-lb. recreation of the sinking of the *Titanic*). In Sycamore, Illinois, the week before Halloween is celebrated with various pumpkin activities, including awards for the best pumpkins, a pumpkin-pie contest, an eating contest, and a pumpkin parade.

A few recent Halloween CELEBRATIONS have featured an event known as "pumpkin hurling" (or "punkin chunkin"), in which the idea is to design a contraption which can hurl a pumpkin farther than anyone else's. The record probably stands at 4,491 feet, or more than a half-mile. One such event in Wilmington, Delaware, drew an estimated 45,000 spectators and raised $35,000 for charity. Another strange event was held in New York in 1997: the World's First Pumpkin Regatta, with three competitors each piloting 800-lb. pumpkins equipped with small boat motors; the annual Windsor Pumpkin Regatta in Nova Scotia boasts an 800 meter course and has been held annually since 1999 (home decorating maven Martha Stewart attempted to enter the race in 2005, but was delayed from entering Canada because of her recent incarceration). And Delta, Pennsylvania, is home to an underwater pumpkin-carving contest.

Teenagers in Springfield, Vermont, have managed to combine a number of different Halloween symbols and Halloween-related activities—pumpkins, PRANKING, and gathering materials for a BONFIRE—into one elaborate Halloween night prank: For weeks before they collect pumpkins, then on Halloween night they load them all into a pickup truck, drive the truck to the top of a hill overlooking Main Street, and open the tailgate.

The town is said to be "ankle deep in orange mush" for some time.

As possibly the most popular symbol of Halloween for the last century, it is to be expected that pumpkins figure prominently in Halloween COLLECTIBLES, but it is curious how many of these collectibles feature anthropomorphic characters (although other vegetables such as CORN and squash also show up occasionally). There are literally hundreds of pumpkin-headed characters in CANDY containers, POSTCARDS, wall decorations, table centerpieces, TOYS, CANDLES and more. In fact, there's even one book almost solely dedicated to these pumpkin-head collectibles (*More Halloween Collectibles: Anthropomorphic Vegetables and Fruits of Halloween* by PAMELA APKARIAN-RUSSELL). In "The Folk Assemblage of Autumn: Tradition and Creativity in Halloween Folk Art," JACK SANTINO notes that carved pumpkins usually provide the heads for HARVEST figures (like SCARECROWS) in most yard displays.

In the delightful short story "The Pumpkin Giant" from her 1892 collection *The Pot of Gold*, Mary Wilkins-Freeman suggests the origin of pumpkins: When a young man kills the evil "Pumpkin Giant," the creature falls to the ground in his potato field, and by next spring the field is covered with vines and pumpkins. Although the king forgets to knight the hero for killing the giant, one taste of "Giant's head pies" earns the hero his knighthood.

Punkie Night— A Halloween-like celebration held at one village (Hinton St. George, in Great Britain). Punkie Night, celebrated on the fourth Thursday in October, commemorates an event which supposedly occurred over a century ago, when all the men in the village went to a fair at the neighboring borough of Chiselborough and didn't return. Their wives went to the fields, where they pulled and hollowed out mangolds (a crop grown for cattle feed, also known as a foliage beet or a "mangel-wurzel") and used the vegetables as lanterns to light their search for their missing men. Nowadays, children celebrate the evening by carving their mangolds (called "punkies"), and going from house-to-house singing traditional songs. Two children are crowned Punkie King and Punkie Queen, and there are punkie decorating contests. Punkie Night is also recorded at Horton and at Lopen, where the date is sometimes confused with November 5 (Guy Fawkes Day or Bonfire Night). The typical Punkie Night rhyme is:

> It's Punkie Night tonight
> It's Punkie Night tonight
> Give us a candle, give us a light
> It's Punkie Night tonight.

In another version, Adam and Eve are mentioned, and in yet another version a threat is made of a "fright" coming if no candle or light is given.

Unlike American jack-o'-lanterns, the decorations on punkies don't cut all the way through the vegetable — the interior contents are scooped out and the flesh is peeled away to allow the candle inside to glow through the punkie.

Purgatory— In the Catholic religion, Purgatory is an afterlife realm wherein souls do fiery penance for their sins (those unconfessed at the time of death) in order to achieve entry into Heaven. In many Catholic areas (especially in Ireland), it was believed that the doors of Purgatory were opened to release the spirits on Halloween night to return to their homes (in some areas, for just one hour, while other areas held it to be forty-eight hours, including All Saints and All Souls Days). In a slight variant, souls were said to be released from Purgatory for their journey to Heaven on this night, and they might choose to pass by their homes. Since the Protestant faiths don't include belief in Purgatory, returning souls on Halloween night could only be evil spirits.

Purgatory Field— The site of one of the most unusual Halloween fire customs. The field is located near Gosmore, U.K., and on Halloween night there men once assembled in a circle at midnight, one burning a large fork of straw while the rest prayed for the souls of departed friends. The dead were released on this one night from the pains of purgatory, but only so long as the straw continued to burn.

Q

Quarter Days— In the Celtic tradition (and in modern Neo-Pagan practices), Halloween (or Samhain) is one of the four quarter days, or days which divide the year into four quarters, roughly corresponding to the seasons. In the Celtic calendar these day were Imbolc (February 1), Beltane (May 1), Lughnasad (August 1) and Samhain (November 1); each of these days was marked by a *ceann féile*, or major festival. However, in later calendars the quarter days more closely correspond to the solstices and equinoxes, so that Halloween is no longer a quarter day. In Scotland, Martinmas is a quarter day, celebrated on November 11 (which, according to the old Julian calendar, was November 1, or Samhain).

In some areas of Ireland, the quarter days were known as Great Days, and were defined as Halloween, Christmas, Easter, and St. Patrick's Day. Some Irish also celebrated "Set Times" at Halloween, Easter, and Christmas.

One quarter-day superstition involved

changelings, or fairy children left in place of kidnapped human children: One solution for those who believed their child was not their own was to dig a grave in the FIELDS at the next quarter-day, and place the fairy child there until next morning, at which time the parents returned to find their real child in the grave instead.

Rabbit's Foot— Although the rabbit's foot is a well-known form of good luck, to be truly fortunate it must be a true rabbit's foot (not a hare's foot) obtained from a white rabbit slain at MIDNIGHT in a GRAVEYARD on Halloween; it must also be the right hind foot.

Radio *see* **War of the Worlds**

Ragweed *see* **Ben-Weed**

Rain— In one American belief, rain on Halloween was thought to foretell good fortune, and was even celebrated with this rhyme:

> Felicity for you!
> Felicity for me!
> For rain on Hallowe'en
> Forebodes Prosperity!

Raisins— Raisins are a popular Halloween fruit, whether used in Halloween GAMES (including SNAPDRAGON), or, more recently, as giveaways for TRICK OR TREAT. In one game called "The Raisin Race," a raisin was threaded onto the middle of a string about a yard long, and two players then began chewing on opposite ends of the string; whoever could reach the raisin first would be the first to be married.

Rake— Several Halloween FORTUNE-TELLING methods involve a rake. For example: The fortune-seeker would go out to a haystack on Halloween night with a rake, and walk around the stack THREE times while raking and reciting:

> Round and round and round I go,
> That my future husband I may know.
> Tall or short let him be,
> This Hallow E'en I must him see.

Around the stack will walk your future intended.

In a slight variation of this custom, an unmarried young person took a rake, went to a rick and walked around it NINE times, saying, "I rake this rick in the DEVIL's name." At the ninth time, the WRAITH of the future spouse would appear to take the rake.

Another rake divination involved ASHES: Rake the ashes in the HEARTH smooth, then search them the next morning for tracks, from which it may be judged whether anybody in the household will die before the next Halloween.

Ratches, Gabriel *see* **Spectre Huntsman**

Rattletrap (also horse fiddle or ratchet)— Probably the most popular type of Halloween NOISEMAKER, this TOY (which was originally a homemade folk toy, and was later mass produced in both wood and tin, first in Germany then in the United States) consists of a handle holding a star-shaped wheel; a

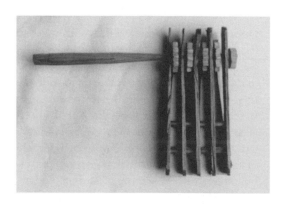

Vintage rattletrap noisemaker

frame around the wheel holds a thin spring leaf, which strikes the wheel repeatedly as the frame is swung around the wheel, creating a delightfully horrible racket.

Recitation— A popular form of Halloween entertainment for children practiced during the 1920s and 1930s. These are small rhyming performances for a solo performer, usually consisting of just one or a few short rhyming stanzas. An example is this recitation by Lenore K. Dolan (from *Handy Helps for Halloween*) for a small boy, entitled "A Brave Boy":

> I'm not scared at Hallowe'en —
> That is I'm not scared much;
> I don't believe in witches
> In ghosts or goblins or such.
>
> The wind holds no terror
> For a stout heart like mine;
> I do not fear the moaning made
> By the swaying of the pine.
>
> Still I never venture forth
> When Hallowe'en comes around;
> I think it best to stay at home
> Where I am safe and sound.

Red— Red is a color believed in some places to protect from evil spirits and WITCHES, so it was worn on Halloween. ROWAN branches which still had their red berries attached were thought to be very protective. *See also* COLORS.

Reformation— Period of religious turmoil which followed the Renaissance and resulted in Western Christendom being split between the Protestant and Catholic faiths. The Reformation officially began on October 31, 1517, when MARTIN LUTHER presented his 95 theses on indulgences (although there is no date for the end of the Reformation, the major changes it started took place for about the next century). In Britain, the Reformation took official hold with the passing of the Act of Restraint of Appeals by Parliament in 1533, followed by the Act of Supremacy in 1534, which gave ultimate power to the monarch over the Church. Part of the Reformation was to protest certain Catholic Church practices which were believed to be

superstitious, and so ALL SAINTS' DAY and ALL SOULS' DAY celebrations were severely affected. For example, in England both Henry VIII and his daughter Elizabeth I abolished the ringing of BELLS at this time, and the echoes of the Reformation finally led to Parliament's 1647 ban on all festivals except GUY FAWKES DAY. Because of the date of the beginning of the Reformation, October 31 was also celebrated as PROTESTANT REFORMATION DAY.

Remembrance Day— Held in U.K. on November 11, in honor of those who died in war. November 11 is also the date of MARTINMAS and OICHE SHEAN SHAMHAIN ("Old Halloween Eve").

Retailing— Halloween retailing on a national scale probably began about 1900 with the B. Shackman company of New York, an import/export firm that may have been the first to bring German Halloween decorations to the United States. By 1909, when Dennison's introduced the first of their famed BOGIE BOOKS (which they began to revise annually in 1912), the Dennison company had become a leading retailer of Halloween goods, including decorations, costumes, and various paper goods. Another early manufacturer of paper goods, the Beistle company, joined the Halloween market in the teens. Products produced during this time (which also included cut-out decorations, paper lanterns, candy containers, and party favors) are now much sought-after COLLECTIBLES.

However, Halloween retailing didn't become big business until the 1990s, when Halloween purchases began to lean more toward adult items and home decorating. Although the reasons for this boom are difficult to trace, some retailers attribute the increased adult interest over the last 20 years in Halloween costuming to analogous increased interest in such popular media fantasies as *Star Wars*, *Star Trek* and *The Lord of the Rings*. Because of this increase in adult interest, in the mid–1990s companies began to rethink their Halloween strategies, changing the notion of a "candy occasion" to a "season experience." This meant that products such as orange and black Rice Krispies, similarly-colored Oreo cookies, and contests for free trips to Alcatraz (Barq's root beer) flooded the market place; in the case of the Oreos, demand increased production of the cookies by 50 percent. Coors made horror movie-show hostess Elvira its Halloween mascot, and seasonal sales increased 10 percent.

The Halloween retailing boom has also produced companies and stores dedicated solely to Halloween merchandise. The seasonal Spirit Halloween stores (which operate only between Labor Day and Halloween)

This 1953 ad for Old Gold cigarettes shows one of the more politically incorrect uses of Halloween retailing.

started in 1983, had 63 retail outlets when they were acquired by Spencer Gifts in 1999, and were up to more than 700 stores by 2009. The stores sell costumes, decorations, and other seasonal Halloween items only. The Spirit chain has even advocated for officially moving Halloween to the last Saturday in October, citing (among other things) a 30% increase in sales when the holiday falls on a weekend.

By 1996 Halloween retailing was up to 2.5 billion yearly (by 2000, that figure had become six billion, an amount that would be repeated at the end of the decade), with the increase attributed largely to the spending of nostalgic baby boomers (and a surge in "family values"). Retailers were happy, since Halloween took up the slack time traditionally experienced between "Back to School" and CHRISTMAS. Halloween had replaced Easter to become the second-biggest holiday for home decorating (behind Christmas), and was in the top five sales days for beer, surpassing St. Patrick's Day. It had also become the nation's third-biggest party day, rivaling Super Bowl Sunday and New Year's Eve. One out of three adults typically attends a Halloween PARTY, and more than 50 percent of American homes decorate for the holiday. Adults spend more than $200 on a COSTUME, and $50 for a child's outfit. In 2001, consumers spent an average of $45 per household on Halloween items. The fastest-growing segment of Halloween retailing is home decorating, which generated close to a billion dollars in 2001. In a survey of where consumers purchased their Halloween goods, 57.1 percent responded with discount department stores (as compared to 70 percent of households with children), 27.8 percent listed drug stores, 22.6 percent chose Halloween or party supply stores, and 20 percent listed fabric stores.

According to a survey conducted by the International Mass Retail Association in 1999, nearly 82 percent of Americans purchased some item for Halloween. About 30 percent bought costumes; 29 percent bought decorations; 14 percent bought party supplies and 13 percent bought cards. The top five items mentioned on respondents shopping lists were, in order of importance, adult costumes, CANDY, decorations, children's costumes and books (which probably include horror fiction in addition to "how-to" books on celebrating the holiday).

However, the economic downturn in the last few years of the 2000s also led to less spending on Halloween. Consumers in 2009 were expected to spend an average of $56.31 on the holiday, down from $66.54 in 2008. Young adults (in the 18 to 24 age range) were most impacted by the recession — 2008's average expenditure of $86.59 was expected to drop to $68.56. Spending in all areas—costuming, candy, decorations, and even haunted house visits— were expected to decline.

Despite its high figures in decorating and costume sales, Halloween still ranks sixth in overall holiday retailing, mainly because — unlike holidays like Mother's Day, Father's Day, and of course Christmas—it doesn't involve expensive gifts.

Rhyming (also known as begging)— In Ireland, Halloween rhyming is the closest equivalent to the American custom of TRICK OR TREAT. Rhyming starts several weeks prior to Halloween (September is considered too early), and does not occur on the actual night of Halloween. Probably descended from MUMMING traditions, rhyming involves a very simple COSTUME (usually a trash bag or a parent's oversized clothing), a MASK, and a rhyme delivered door-to-door in exchange for APPLES, NUTS or, most commonly, COINS. Children typically don't carry bags or containers, and they may be refused (especially if the house they visit has already been visited that night by a number of children). The children will usually ask "Anything for Halloween?" or they may perform a more complicated rhyme such as:

> Halloween is coming and the geese are getting fat.
> Please put a penny in the old man's hat.
> If you haven't got a penny, a ha'penny will do.
> If you haven't got a ha'penny, then God bless you,
> And your old man, too!

(The rhyme above has apparently adapted to inflation, as some recent reports have replaced "ha-penny"—a coin that no longer exists—with "fiver," meaning a five-pound note). In some parts of Ireland the word "Christmas" is inserted in place of "Halloween" in the above rhyme, and rhyming is performed at CHRISTMAS, not Halloween.

Another popular Halloween rhyme usually involved the lines:

> It's money I want and I money I crave,
> If you don't give me money, I'll sweep you all to your graves.

This rhyme often included a mention of "Mr. Funny" or "Johnny Funny," a character who was specifically designated to collect money. Some participants have explained that part of the importance of Halloween rhyming was that it allowed them to save up enough money to buy FIREWORKS for Halloween night; and some have suggested that the rhymers' costuming was to emulate the "wee folk," or FAIRIES, who were thought to be active on that night.

Roads— In some areas, roads were to be avoided on Halloween, because of the spirits and FAIRIES abroad on the night.

In parts of Britain the following saying was once popular:

Hallowe'en will come, will come,
Witchcraft will be set agoing,
Fairies will be at full speed,
Running in every pass.
Avoid the road, children, children.

Rome, Ancient *see* **Feralia; Lemuria; Parentalia; Pomona**

Rosemary—FORTUNE-TELLING dreams could be provoked on Halloween night by placing a sprig of rosemary and a silver sixpence beneath the pillow (a variant from Derbyshire specified a crooked sixpence and rosemary); a young person could then be assured of seeing his or her future spouse in DREAMS that night.

Roses— In one FORTUNE-TELLING method, a young woman took two long-stemmed pink roses to bed with her on Halloween night

A 1909 postcard showing a classic Halloween fortune-telling custom using roses.

(speaking to no one on the way). At her bedside she knelt, named one of the roses for herself and one for her lover, twined the stems together, and then (while gazing intently at the rose designated for her lover) she spoke the following:

Twine, twine, and intertwine
Let my love be wholly mine.
If his heart be kind and true,
Deeper grows his rose's hue.

If the color of the rose darkened, her lover would remain faithful; but if it grew paler, her lover was untrue. *See also* FLOWERS.

Rowan (also mountain ash, wittern, whitty, wiggen, quicken and quickbeam)—Rowan is a popular protection against FAIRIES, WITCHES and other evil spirits on Halloween, and may date back to Celtic lore. In "The Wood of Dubhros," one rowan tree puts out berries that will grant unshakable health to whomever eats them. They also grant the feeling of the liveliness of wine and the satisfaction of mead, that any old person of a hundred years would be young again, and that any young girl would grow into a beauty.

As a protective charm (used in Britain), branches of the rowan tree (sometimes called "witch posts" or "witch-wood") were placed over doors on Halloween; the best protection is a branch with its RED berries still attached.

Another custom involves driving livestock between rowan branches (or through a hoop of rowan) to protect them from evil forces on Halloween. Highlanders of Strathspey used to force all their sheep and lambs to pass through a hoop of rowan on ALL SAINTS' DAY and BELTANE, as a means of warding off witches and fairies. A twig of rowan might also be tied to the tails of cattle with red THREAD to keep them safe from witches, and there was even a Scottish Halloween rhyme that ran:

"Rowan tree and red thread
To gar the witches dance their dead."

In other words, rowan tree and red thread could cause witches to dance until they died.

Rowan trees in GRAVEYARDS helped the dead to slumber peacefully. A witch who is touched with rowan will instantly be dragged off to Hell by the DEVIL. A cross made of rowan was recommended for travelers out on Halloween.

In *Forty Years in a Moorland Parish*, J. C. Atkinson describes a very particular method used for acquiring rowan to be employed as magical protection: The rowan must be cut on St. Helen's Day with a household knife, and it must be cut from a tree which the cutter has never seen before or even known about. After cutting, it must be carried home along a different path than the one used to arrive at the rowan.

Russia *see* **Festival of the Radunitsa**

S

Sage— In one FORTUNE-TELLING custom, on ALL SAINTS' EVE a young woman must go alone into the garden at MIDNIGHT, and pluck a sage leaf for each toll of the clock, up to NINE; then she will either see the face of her future husband or a COFFIN. The Welsh version says simply that the girl must go at midnight on Halloween to strip the leaves from a branch of the sage bush, and she'll see an apparition of her future husband.

St. Agnes' Eve— The night before St. Agnes' festival day, held January 21. Regarded as the patron saint of young girls, St. Agnes has been venerated as a virgin since the fourth century, but early legends of her martyrdom vary and little is certain about either the date or manner of her death (though it is often given as A.D. January 21, 304) A second feast used to be kept in her honor on the octave day, January 28. Like Halloween, St. Agnes' Eve was a time of divination for young unmarried girls in England and Scotland. FORTUNE-TELLING customs included DUMB CAKES, reading of DREAMS, HEMP SEED sowing, etc. One popular divination involved sowing grain while reciting a poem:

> Agnes sweet and Agnes fair,
> Hither, hither, now repair;
> Bonny Agnes, let me see
> The lad [or lass] who is to marry me.

A few similar divinations were also practiced on St. Faith's Day (October 6).

John Keats wrote the lovely poem "The Eve of St. Agnes," which includes this mention of St. Agnes' Eve fortune-telling customs:

> They told her how upon St. Agnes' Eve,
> Young virgins might have visions of delight...
> If ceremonies due they did aright,
> As, supperless to bed they must retire...

The Armenians acknowledge St. Sarkis on this same date, and practice similar forms of divining a future spouse.

St. Andrew's Day— Christian day celebrated on November 30. This is the day of the martyrdom of St. Andrew, and the only Apostle's day said to be observed on such an anniversary. It's a day for reunion of Scotsmen (who claim St. Andrew as their patron), but also includes many practices that are similar to those conducted on Halloween. In England, evil spirits were once driven from houses with noise on this day. In Germany young maidens practice Halloween-like FORTUNE-TELLING to determine the nature of their future husband: They strip themselves naked, and recite a prayer to St. Andrew. In "Tabletalk," MARTIN LUTHER describes this practice, noting that the maids must strip themselves naked and utter the prayer "*Deus, Deus* *meus, O Sancte Andrea, effice ut bonum pium acquiram virum; hodie mihi ostende qualis sit cui me in uxorem ducere debet"* ("God, my God, O Saint Andrew, bring it about that I may obtain a good affectionate husband; show me today what manner of man it is that shall lead me to the altar"). Another German custom bears a striking resemblance to many Halloween divinations: In a tub or basin of pure WATER are floated little foil cups, each inscribed with the names of those present. If two cups move towards each other and finally cling together, those two whose names are inscribed will be lovers. However, some cups are also marked as priests, and marriage can be expected only when two cups unite with a priest's.

St. Just Feast— The St. Just parish in Cornwall holds a yearly two-day celebration (commemorating the dedication of the parish church) on the Sunday nearest to ALL SAINTS' DAY. The celebration begins on Sunday with church services and a procession, and continues on Sunday with feasting, drinking, and games. Young people would often come into town from miles around on Saturday night, spend money on drink and courting, and leave on Tuesday morning. Festivities concluded with a street fair on Monday evening.

St. Swithin's Chair— In his 1814 historical novel *Waverley; or, 'Tis Sixty Years Since,* SIR WALTER SCOTT offers a song which tells of a curious legend involving "St. Swithin's Chair," a "projecting peak of an impending crag," located in Scotland near Loch-Veolan. The first few stanzas describe how "on Hallow-Mass Eve the Night-Hag will ride" (the "Night-Hag" mentioned here is probably an OWL), and the song goes on to describe this charm:

> He that dare sit on St. Swithin's Chair,
> When the Night-Hag wings the troubled air,
> Questions three, when he speaks the spell,
> He may ask, and she must tell.

The song is a fragment, but tells the tale of a lady who attempts the charm to learn the fate of her husband, who has been at war for three years; but one of the novel's characters mentions that, when the baron returned from the wars, the lady was found "clay-cold upon the grounsill ledge."

In the late 1920s this rhyme was occasionally performed as a Halloween party game: An armchair was filled with blocks or stones to make it uncomfortable, and a hostess dressed as a witch stood beside the chair to answer questions.

Salt— In one Halloween FORTUNE-TELLING tradition, after eating a spoonful of salt a woman would walk BACKWARDS down the cellar stairs, carrying a CANDLE in one hand (or a glass of WATER) and a MIRROR in the other; at the bottom of the stairs, the mirror would reveal the face of her future husband. In some variations, the fortune-seeker was instructed to hold the salt in her mouth and repeat a chant, trying not to swallow the salt:

> Looking glass, I hope to see
> The one who is my destiny!
> Ask him now to give a sign
> That some day he will be all mine.

On the Isle of Man, a girl took a mouthful of water and two handfuls of salt, then sat down at a door; the first name she heard mentioned would be that of her future husband. In another curious test, women filled their mouths with water, their right hands with salt, then ran around the block; those who completed the circuit were assured that the next name they heard would be that of their future husband. An Irish tradition involved scattering salt in the four corners of a room while reciting:

> Salt, salt, I sow thee until eternity
> That in my first sleep I may see
> The boy that is ordained for me.

A number of divinations center on eating salt at bedtime: Take three doses of salt two minutes apart, then go to bed backwards, lie on the right side, and do not move until morning. This charm will cause DREAMS that foretell important events. More typical was one that suggested eating a cake of FLOUR, suet and salt just before bed; this would invoke a dream of the future husband coming to offer a drink of water.

In South Uist and Eriskay (the Outer Hebrides), a cake of common meal and a great deal of salt (called *bonnach salainn*) is eaten at Halloween to induce dreams that will reveal the future. After eating the cake, no water may be drunk and no word uttered. This ritual could also be performed by eating a salt HERRING (bones and all) in THREE bites; in some versions, the girl must then walk backwards to bed.

A particularly grim Manx divination called for each member of a household to fill a thimble with salt on Halloween night, and then empty it onto a plate before retiring. In the morning, if any heap of salt had fallen, that person would die within the year.

An American-Irish folklore custom suggests that salt rubbed into the hair on Halloween will provide protection from FAIRIES.

Samhain (variations: *Saman, Samain, Samonios, Samuin, Samhuin, Samhuinn, Samhtheine, Sainfuin, La Samon, La Samhin, Sham-in, Saimhain, Samhein, Oiche Shamhna,Taman*; also known as *Nos Calan Gaeaf* (Welsh); pronounced "sow-en") — The Celtic NEW YEAR'S festival (and the first day of *Gemred*, or winter) and arguably the single biggest influence on the contemporary celebration of Halloween.

It is a popular misconception that Samhain was the name of a Celtic god of the dead worshipped on the evening of October 31; a 1934 Halloween book refers to Samhain as "patron of the field" (although the same book later refers to "Saman, lord of death"); sometimes the word TAMAN is used instead to refer to a Lord of Death. The "Lord of Death" definition of Samhain began in the 18th-century, as part of the work of Charles Vallancey. Vallancey was a British surveyor who spent nearly 40 years in Ireland and wrote extensively about the island's language, history,

and folklore. Vallancey believed that the Celts worshipped a deity called "Samhan" who "at this season called the souls to judgment"; Vallancey also wrote that "Samman [sic] was named BALSAB, or Dominus mortis, for Bal is lord, and Sab death." Vallancey's ideas were reiterated by the Rev. Thomas Dudley Fosbroke in his popular 1825 book *Encyclopaedia of Antiquities* (there has also been conjecture that some early historians may have confused the word "Samhain" with the name "Samana," an ancient Hindu deity). However, most historians discredited Vallancey almost immediately — the *London Quarterly Review* in 1818 stated that Vallancey "wrote more nonsense than any man of his time."

In reality, there was probably no single god worshipped on this day, and the CELTS had no "god of the dead." Likewise, after Vallancey it was commonly stated that on this night "the lord of death gathered together all the souls of all those who had died in the passing year and had been condemned to live in the bodies of animals, to decree what forms they should inhabit for the next twelve months" (from RUTH EDNA KELLEY's *The Book of Hallowe'en*, 1919); but beyond Vallancey's suppositions there is no evidence to support this idea, either. Samhain translates as "summer's end"; in Gaelic, *Lá Samhna* is the name given to the first of November, and *samhradh* is the name for summer. In Celtic tradition, Samhain was the greatest of four *ceann féile*, or chief festivals (or QUARTER DAYS) held by the Celts (the others were Imbolc — later St. Brigid's Day — on February 1, BELTANE or Beltene on May 1, and Lughnasad on August 1, when first fruits were celebrated). All Celtic festivals were associated with either agriculture or livestock; Beltane (when crops were planted and livestock put out to pasture) and Samhain (when the livestock were brought in for the winter) were the main calendar points, and Imbolc (associated with the lactation of ewes) and Lughnasad (a midsummer celebration) marked three-month points in between.

Surprisingly little is known of the actual rites and activities of Samhain, since the Celts kept oral rather than written histories; in fact, there is no indication that mainland European Celts celebrated the day at all, and it may have been a festival originally celebrated only by the Irish Celts. What is recorded about Samhain is found largely in the vernacular literature of the Celts, which was first recorded by monks and so is usually thought to be somewhat colored by Christian interpretation.

For the Celts, Samhain (the celebration of which is mentioned in the Celtic mythology as lasting for THREE days before and three days after the actual day itself) probably began with bringing the livestock in from the fields for the winter; the hardiest were kept as breeding stock, while the weakest were slaughtered, partly to provide provisions for the winter and partly because it was difficult to provide feed for animals in the winter months. This tradition of slaughtering livestock at Samhain time carried on in many parts of Britain; for example, until the 1930s most villages in the Wiltshire area had an official pig-killer who was always extremely busy at this season. The last of the HARVEST— BARLEY, APPLES, OATS, wheat, TURNIPS— was also brought in at this time (the Celts may have shared the later Irish belief that any crops left out after November 1 were rendered inedible by malicious spirits or FAIRIES).

The rest of Samhain was devoted to a mix of political and religious activities. A great assembly of the five Irish provinces was held at Tara (or Teamhair, sometimes also called *Druim Cain*, the beautiful ridge; *Liath Druim*, the grey ridge; and *Druim na Descan*, the ridge at the outlook). Tara was the seat of the high kings of first the crude Firbolgs, then later the great Tuatha de Danaan; the Samhain festivities held there included HORSE races, markets, political discussion, feasting and drinking (some folklorists have stated that the Samhain assembly may have lasted over a fortnight, and was celebrated only every three years). In one Celtic myth the young hero FINN MacCUMAL, goes at Samhain time to the assembly and encounters a law that

Romantic nineteenth-century depiction of the type of ritual the Druids might have practiced on Samhain.

states that no one there may raise a quarrel or bring a grudge against another as long as the gathering goes on. Samhain feasts were often held on the shores of lakes (bodies of WATER such as wells, lakes and rivers were held in great reverence by the Celts); for example, THE DREAM OF ANGUS occurs on the shore of Loch Bel Dracon. On the evening of October 31 (since the Celts reckoned time by nights instead of days, their actual Samhain may have been the evening of October 31), all fires were extinguished, and then the DRUIDS, or priests, enacted a ritual in which a new fire was kindled on the hill of TLACHTGA (about 12 miles from Tara). Embers from this fire were distributed to each home (which paid a tax to the king in return) to start their own fires anew. Historical tradition has it that debts were paid on this day and duties honored (a tradition which was continued in the later celebration of MARTINMAS); any who refused to do so might be excommunicated (a fate which also awaited any who had dealings with those already excommunicated).

Samhain's most significant aspect, however, was probably not political but spiritual. The Druids would have performed sacrifices on this night, hoping to propitiate the gods into gifting their people with a mild winter; sacrifices may have included human offerings, perhaps even the infamous "wicker man" described by Roman historians—a large man-shaped figure made from wicker, in which sacrificial animals and people were caged and then burned (other accounts suggest that the Druids sacrificed black sheep on this night). The Celts, who often dug ritual pits, may have placed seed in such shafts or pits on Samhain, to ensure fertility come spring (when some of the seed was removed for sowing and replaced with a second offering). On this date the Dagda and the Morrigan (chief male and female deities) copulated to ensure crop and animal fertility for the coming year (one variant of this tale describes the Morrigan as having one foot on either side of a river). In some versions of this

myth the goddess, an old hag by year's end, is revitalized by the union, becoming young and beautiful again.

As the border between two years, it was believed that Samhain was a night when the entrances to the Otherworld were open, and the spirits of the dead could roam free. The dead were commemorated (there were also similar activities at Lughnasad), and it was customary to put food out for spirits returning home. The dead, however, could also be malicious tricksters, like non-human supernatural entities, and so Samhain Eve was a night to stay indoors. The Celtic vision of the afterlife was largely benevolent: One description of Annwn (the Otherworld) was "Court of Intoxication," since it was a place where heroes feasted and drank with beautiful women and sometimes fought; but it could also be fraught with danger, since mortals entering the realm of the Otherworld might come across horrific monsters, and were often condemned to stay, never aging, until they tried to return to their own land, where they died instantly.

The Celts had a rich mythology, in which Samhain figured prominently. It first appeared when the Tuatha de Danaan (or the Celts' gods and goddesses) took Ireland from the Firbolgs; the Tuatha de Danaan were then beset by the nightmarish Fomorians, maimed monsters who each had only one leg or one arm and were led by an evil giant and his mother. The Fomorians demanded a ritual tribute each Samhain of two-thirds of the Tuatha de Danaan's CORN, milk, and children. The Tuatha de Danaan battled against the Fomorians, and although the monsters were largely defeated they still roamed the Irish countryside, spoiling corn, milk, fruit and fish. Finally one Samhain night the Morrigan and Angus Og drove the last of the creatures from Ireland, and the Fomorians returned to their kingdom from beyond the sea.

Some Samhain myths center on legendary feats, such as Finn's slaying of the murderous Aillen, or NERA leading an army into the Otherworld on a quest for a great crown; others involve meetings between mortal men and women of the *sidhe* (fairies). In this latter vein is the tale of Fingin Mac Luchta, who is visited by a BANSHEE (fairy woman) every Samhain who tells him all the precious things to be found in the royal strongholds of Ireland, as well as prophecies for the coming year. These meetings between mortal man and fairy woman are not always romantic, though: In the one story set at the CRUACHAN of Connaught, Cailte and Cascorach the Musician meet an old man who turns out to be Bairnech, steward to the King of Ireland. Bairnech tells them that every year at Samhain a woman comes out of the hill of the *Sidhe* of Cruachan and brings away NINE of the best cattle from every herd. Since it is Samhain night, Cascorach goes to the door and kills the banshee with his spear.

Another Samhain story emphasizes the involvement of Druids with the holiday: On Samhain Eve Dathi, king of Ireland (from A.D. 405 to 428) was at *Cnoc-nan-druad* ("the Druids' Hill," now Mallaroe); he ordered his Druid to forecast the events of the coming year. The Druid went to the summit of the hill, spent the night there and returned at sunrise, only to address Dathi as King of Erin (Ireland) and Alban (Scotland). He thus correctly predicted Dathi's conquering expedition to Alban, Britain and Gaul.

Another tie between Druids and Samhain was the idea of *fe-fiada*, a spell that some believed the Druids cast on fairies to render them invisible throughout the year; only on Samhain was this spell lifted.

One of the most frightening (and one of the oldest) Samhain stories is found in the *Dinnsenchus* in the *Book of Leinster*. It tells of how King Tigernmas (who ruled Ireland around 939 B.C.) and many of his people were destroyed by some mysterious force as they worshipped an idol (given as Cromm Cruach) on Samhain Eve; they may have been destroyed by vengeful Druids, who were angry that Tigernmas had turned away from them.

When the Julian calendar was replaced by the Gregorian calendar in the mid-eighteenth century British Isles, it essentially created two Samhain celebrations, with November 11 henceforth being known as OÍCHE SHEAN SHAMHAIN, or "Old Samhain Eve," and November 12 as *Lá Shean Shamain*, or "Old Samhain Day." Most customs and beliefs regarding Samhain and Halloween transferred to the "new" October 31 or November 1, while in most areas November 11 came to be celebrated as Martinmas.

Although Samhain was largely incorporated into the Christian holidays of ALL SAINTS' DAY and ALL SOULS' DAY, it has been celebrated from Celtic times under its original name in certain areas of Ireland. It is also celebrated as Samhain by some contemporary WICCA, NEO-PAGAN and Neo-Druid groups.

Samhanach— A Scottish name for the dreadful BOGIES that were abroad on Hallowe'en, stealing babies and committing other monstrous crimes.

Samhnag (also *Samhnagan*; *Samh-nag*; *Savnag*)— In the British Isles, Halloween CELEBRATIONS once included a special BONFIRE, called the samhnag, at each household. At Fortingall in Scotland, the samhnag was a communal effort and was built on the mound called *Carn nam Marbh*, "The Mound of the Dead." Local legend has it that this mound contains the CORPSES of plague victims, and a stone set atop the mound was called the *Clach a' Phlaigh*, "the Plague Stone." Once the bonfire was lit, the entire community joined hands and danced about it; later, boys held leaping contests over the remains of the fire. The last samhnag was built in Fortingall in 1924, and was supposedly stopped because local groundskeepers were upset with the brush being stripped from the hillsides, leaving no cover for game.

The samhnag was called COEL COETH in Wales. In the Highlands of Scotland, children vied to see who could make the biggest samhnag. Samhnags were typically made of ferns, PEAT and other fuels. Sometimes a circle of stones was placed around the fire, and each stone was named one for a person in the family. When the fire burned out, families returned home to hold Halloween PARTIES. The next morning they returned to the remains of the bonfire and examined the stones; if any were misplaced or if FOOTPRINTS were visible nearby, that person would not live out the year.

Santino, Jack (1947–)— American folklorist whose body of work has significantly enhanced both the historical and sociological understanding of Halloween over the last 20 years. Santino was born and raised in Boston and the surrounding New England areas, and always had both an appreciation for autumn and an interest in myth and legend. While still working on his Ph.D. in folklore and folklife from the University of Pennsylvania, Santino was hired to work for the Smithsonian Institution's annual Festival of American Folklife in Washington, DC. In 1983 he left Washington and accepted a faculty position in the Department of Popular Culture at Bowling Green State University, where he continues to teach.

Santino's professional interest in Halloween began in the 1970s when he noticed an increase in adult participation in the holiday. His first work on the subject, "Halloween in America: Contemporary Customs and Performances" appeared in *Western Folklore* in 1983, and established his goal of showing that contemporary culture (and Halloween) deserved to be seriously studied. His 1986 article "The Folk Assemblage of Autumn: Tradition and Creativity in Halloween Folk Art" discussed the increased interest in home decorating for Halloween, and coined the term "folk assemblage." He lectured publicly on the subject at the Library of Congress and produced a flyer on Halloween that is still in print and in use at the Archive of Folk Culture. His cover-feature article on Halloween for *Natural History* magazine in 1983 led to the publication of two books: *Halloween and*

Other Festivals of Death and Life (this collection of works was edited by Santino and was the first academic book devoted to Halloween), and *All Around the Year: Holidays and Celebrations in American Life*. In 1991 he received a Fullbright Research Grant to study Halloween in Ireland for 11 months, and in 1998 he published *The Hallowed Eve: Dimensions of Culture in a Calendar Festival in Northern Ireland*. Currently, Santino coordinates an annual conference: Holidays, Ritual, Festival, Celebration, and Public Display at Bowling Green State University and elsewhere.

Satan *see* **Devil**

Scadding the Peas— A Halloween FORTUNE-TELLING game, in which a lone bean was placed among many peapods. After the vegetables were boiled and served, whoever got the bean among the PEAS was assured good luck.

Scarecrows— The popularity of scarecrows as a Halloween symbol is something of an anomaly, since scarecrows are not practical in late October, when crops have already been harvested. However, their association with HARVEST remains (in fact they're often referred to simply as "harvest figures"), and they also offer the opportunity to use other Halloween icons, since they often feature JACK-O'-LANTERNS for heads (in fact the entire figure — whose body may consist of an old plaid shirt and jeans stuffed with leaves, and cornstalk arms— may be called "jack-o'-lantern").

Perhaps the most popular tale of scarecrows is Nathaniel Hawthorne's "Feathertop"; even though the story itself is set in late May, it includes many Halloween elements and has been adapted to Halloween on several occasions (including the children's PANTOMIME "The Straw Phantom" by Dorothy Brewer Blackall). In the original story a skilled witch, Mother Rigby, wants to create a scarecrow for her cornfield, but she becomes so enamored of her PUMPKIN-headed

Contemporary Halloween scarecrow toy figure

creation that she endows it with life and sends it off to town, to win the hand of fair Polly Gookin. Her plan nearly succeeds until Feathertop catches a horrifying glimpse of himself in a mirror, and races back to Mother Rigby, throwing away the magic pipe that gives him life and dooming himself to existence as merely the witch's scarecrow.

A common word for scarecrow in the north of England is "bogle," which is also sometimes used for BOGIES.

Schneider, Stuart — Stuart Schneider is an American collector and author whose 1995 book *Halloween in America: A Collector's Guide* was the first book published on Halloween COLLECTIBLES; the book is now credited with tremendously increasing interest in and the value of Halloween collectibles. In 2001, Schneider published a second book on Halloween, *Halloween: Costumes and Other Treats*, which is the most extensive book to date on Halloween COSTUMES. Schneider, who has written on a variety of other collectible subjects including space memorabilia and fluorescent minerals, also runs a popular Halloween website, "The Halloween Museum" (found at wordcraft.net), where he documents some of his work as a "home haunter" and sells various vintage Halloween pieces.

Scott, Sir Walter (1771–1832) — Prolific Scottish novelist best known for *Ivanhoe*, *Rob Roy* and the Waverley novels. Scott was also a collector of regional folklore, and, along with ROBERT BURNS (whom he met in 1786), is one of the best sources of Scottish Halloween beliefs. Many of his novels (especially *The Monastery*) refer to Halloween SUPERSTITIONS and FORTUNE-TELLING customs, including "ST. SWITHIN'S CHAIR." In 1802 and 1803 he published his three-volume collection *Minstrelsy of the Scottish Border*, which included such classic ballads as TAM LIN.

Sea — In coastal areas of Normandy, one Halloween SUPERSTITION involves a ghostly sailing vessel that appears on Halloween; the vessel is one that was lost at sea the year before, and whose lost souls haven't received enough prayer to find rest. The ship moors at the dock, but vanishes by morning light. It is also believed to be bad luck to sail on this night; those who are foolish enough to try fishing on it might see their doppelganger or duplicate aboard the ship, and risk drawing in human remains with their nets. In other parts of France, it is believed that corpses can be seen in the hollows of the waves at this time.

In Wales, one belief is that at CHRISTMAS, Easter and Halloween all those who have drowned in the sea come up to ride over the waves on white HORSES, and hold amazing revels.

Second Sight — Most cultures believe that some people possess the ability to sense GHOSTS or supernatural entities. This power is sometimes called "second sight" (or clairvoyance). In some areas that celebrate Halloween, those who possess second sight are said to easily see numerous spirits on both Halloween and CHRISTMAS Eve. In Scotland, a child born at SAMHAIN was said to be gifted with *an dà shealladh*, "The Two Sights," or second sight; a child born on Christmas was believed to have the power to see spirits and to command them. Second sight was also known as *taisch* or *taishitaraugh*, and those who possessed it were referred to as *taibh-sear*. It was also believed that the seventh child of the same sex born in succession would possess it. In America, some believe that those born on Halloween can recall and interpret DREAMS.

In *Folklore in America*, Tristram P. Coffin and Hennig Cohen record an African-American who was born with a caul and believed he could see ghosts on ALL SAINTS' DAY (he also reportedly had the gift of prophecy).

In 1909, Thomas Ratcliffe reported this from Derbyshire: "In respect of a woman who was born on Hallow E'en night, on the stroke of MIDNIGHT, it was said that she would have certain knowledge of coming events, especially those in connection with her own family. Regularly, when birthnight came round, she was perturbed and, as people who knew said, 'the spirit was on her.'"

In his novel *The Monastery*, Sir Walter Scott refers to a character, Mary Avenel, who had second sight: "Being born on All-hallows' Eve, she was supposed to be invested with power over the invisible world."

Shadow—One European SUPERSTITION holds it is bad luck to glimpse your shadow by the light of the MOON on Halloween.

Shirts—Shirts figure in several Halloween FORTUNE-TELLING customs involving attempting to learn the name of one's future spouse. One Norfolk custom is unusual since it centers on men: Men practicing this ritual sat in a circle around a pitchfork stood upright and on which was placed a clean white shirt; if their lovers were faithful, it was believed the women would enter in silence before MIDNIGHT and take away the shirt.

However, probably the most common fortune telling method involving shirts—often referred to as "the wetting of the sark sleeve"—involved dipping the sleeve of one's shirt in WATER, then waiting to see if one's beloved would appear to help dry the shirt.

Shoes—Several Halloween FORTUNE-TELLING customs involve shoes. In one Scottish highland divination, the fortune-seeker takes a shoe by the tip and throws it over the house, then observes the direction in which the toe points as it lies on the ground on the other side, for that indicates the direction in which the shoe hurler is destined to go soon. If the shoe falls with the sole up, it is very unlucky. In a variation of this custom, the shoe need be tossed over a shoulder only.

Another divination involving shoes on Halloween directs a young unmarried woman to go up to her bedroom secretly, take off her shoes and place them at right angles to each other, then recite:

> I cross my shoes in the shape of a T,
> Hoping this night my true love to see.
> Not in his best or worst array,
> But in the clothes of everyday.

If she looks over her right shoulder, she'll see her true love appear.

An anonymous 1923 rhyme runs:

> Turn your boots toward the street,
> Leave your garters on your feet,
> Put your stockings on your head—
> You'll dream of the one you're going to wed.

In an American fortune-telling game, each girl stood exactly NINE feet from a paper black CAT, took off her left shoe, and hurled it at the target. If she successfully knocked it down, it foretold good luck for the coming year.

Shoes also figure in at least one protective ritual: ASHES from a BONFIRE (kindled with "need-fire," or friction) are placed inside the shoes as a charm against evil forces.

Shoney (or Shony)—A sea-god in ancient Lewis (in Scotland), who was traditionally offered a cup of ale at Halloween by a man who waded into the evening sea and intoned, "Shoney, I give you this cup of ale hoping that you will be so kind as to give us plenty of sea-ware [seaweed] for enriching our ground the ensuing year." Afterwards, those gathered returned to the church, had a short period of silence, then adjourned for a night of wild revelry. There has been some suggestion that "Shoney" is derived from SAMHAIN, but there is no evidence to support this idea.

Shrove Tuesday *see* **Mardi Gras**

Shrubbery— An American FORTUNE-TELLING belief centers on pulling up a piece of shrubbery on Halloween night; if it is still green by MIDSUMMER'S EVE, it signifies a prosperous coming year.

Shuma Sashti ("Skeleton Day")— Name given to ALL SAINTS' DAY by Native American residents of Laguna, New Mexico. They celebrated the day by taking food to the cemetery (the best PUMPKINS, melons and sheep), where CANDLES were set out on graves (see DAYS OF THE DEAD for similar customs). Boys would also beg for food, calling out, "Sare'mo, sare'mo!"

They tell a story about a young man told by his mother to bring in the two fattest lambs for Shuma Sashti; after he objected, he fell sick for two or three days, until a medicine-man restored him. On recovering, he reported that he had been with the dead.

Sieve— Several Halloween FORTUNE-TELLING customs involve sieves. In one, an odd number of keys are placed into a sieve, which is then carried to the barn, where they must be shaken *tuaitheal*, or with a lefthand turn; the destined one will come and put the odd key right. Another custom involved shaking three silver COINS in a sieve before a MIRROR at MIDNIGHT, in order to see the future reflected in the mirror.

Sieves were also sometimes associated with WITCHES, who might ride them instead of BROOMS (when King James I of England's wedding plans were frustrated by sea-borne witches they were said to have ridden in sieves and caused storms by tying human body parts to CATS which were cast into the sea).

Skeleton Day *see* **Shuma Sashti**

Skeletons— Skeletons and skulls are traditional Halloween symbols. Their association with Halloween may stem partly from the Black Death which rampaged through Europe from 1347 to 1351, claiming as much as a quarter of the continent's population; in the wake of the Black Death, skeletons and other death imagery were popularized largely through depictions of the "Danse Macabre," which showed human figures being led off by skeletal depictions of Death. These images first began appearing in the fifteenth century and were soon popular throughout Europe.

In Mexican DAYS OF THE DEAD celebrations, skeleton imagery — which includes sugar skulls and small skeleton figures — may have derived from the pre–Columbian Aztec

This vintage Halloween bridge tally card uses a skeleton to embody the holiday.

celebrations of MICCAILHUITONTLI and MIC-CAILHUITL.

Sketlets— Scottish Halloween ritual similar to the American TRICK OR TREAT; children masquerade as spirits on the prowl for FOOD.

Sluath (sloo-ah)— Scottish word for the "Host of the Dead," whose feet never touch the earth, and who appear at dusk on Halloween, drifting on the WIND. The Sluath might be met at other times as well, and would leave those who encountered them bruised and soiled.

Snails— One of the more unusual Halloween methods of FORTUNE-TELLING involves placing a snail on a plate or in the hearth ASHES on Halloween, and leaving it there overnight; in the morning the initials of the future beloved can be read in the resulting slime trail. Sometimes it is specifically mentioned that a basin or dish must be placed over the snail, to keep it from crawling away.

Snap-Apple Night— English name for Halloween, referring to a variation of BOBBING FOR APPLES in which an APPLE is hung on a string which is then tied overhead, often on one end of a stick with a CANDLE attached to the opposite end. Anyone who can successfully bite the apple will have a happy life (although a variant belief is that whoever bites the apple first will be first to wed). The Scots occasionally replaced apples with treacle scones or sweets smeared with jam, giving the game an extra element of stickiness.

Snapdragon— Late nineteenth-century Halloween

FORTUNE-TELLING GAME in which half a pint of brandy or alcohol was poured into a dish and ignited; SALT was then thrown on the flames to add an eerie color to the fire (for that reason, the game was occasionally known simply as "the ghostly fire"). Next, NUTS, figs, small fruits, RAISINS, etc. were thrown into the flames, and whoever could retrieve the most items ("a brand from the burning") from the flames would meet his or her true love within the year (an 1894 party book implies that snapdragon was a game played mainly in the Southern part of the United

1908 postcard depicting "Snap-Apple"

This antique engraving shows several Halloween games (including snap-apple).

States, since "in many Southern families there is a great bowl used for snapdragon or the christening punch"). In a variation, printed fortunes were wrapped carefully in tin foil and placed in the fire, so that players might retrieve their own fortunes. One's fortune might also be told by the type of fruit that was snatched (i.e., a Mediterranean fig might indicate a future spouse from that area of the world). Sometimes players first dipped their fingers into a bowl of ice water, so that any heat from the flames was lessened.

Snotching Night—Welsh name for Halloween, derived from "snatching an apple," or playing snap-apple (in which an APPLE and a lit CANDLE are suspended on opposite ends of a stick hung from the ceiling, and contestants must try to bite the apple and not the candle).

Snowbirds—Snowbirds seen in Ireland on Halloween were an early sign of winter's approach.

Soul Cakes—Special CAKES and BREAD baked for ALL SAINTS' DAY and ALL SOULS' DAY were popular in virtually all areas which celebrated these days, but they may have been most favored in Britain, where there were also rituals attendant upon receiving and distributing these cakes.

The origin of the custom may have been charitable—the cakes were probably first baked and given to the poor on All Souls' Day, possibly in return for their services in saying prayers for the cake-givers' deceased kin. An English book from 1511 called *The Festyvall* contains the line, "We rede in olde tyme good people wolde on All halowen days bake brade and dele it for all crysten soules." Later, the poor begged money to buy the cakes, and the more they could buy, the luckier they would be. Soul-cakes were usually flat and round, and made from ingredients including milk, eggs, and spices. The cakes were also sometimes described as "seed cakes" or "fruit cakes."

In the English village of Antrobus (Cheshire), a traditional MUMMING play is performed by "Soul-Cakers" each Halloween, and for two weeks thereafter. A number of versions of these plays have been recorded, but they most commonly concern a fight (played out with real metal swords) between King George and the Black Prince. When King George fells the Black Prince, the wounded man's mother (played by a man) wails for a "quack doctor"; the quack doctor enters, and goes through a series of comic mishaps trying to restore the injured prince. In some variations of the performance, Beelzebub appears just before a "Wild Horse" (or hobby horse, sometimes referred to as "Old Hob") enters (played by a man carrying an actual horse skull, specially painted for the play), and a driver delivers a final speech while trying to control the horse (in some variants the horse has been badly maimed, and the driver asks money from the audience for the horse). Although some soul-caking plays ask for soul-cakes from the audience, others include lines such as, "All that we are souling for is your ale and strong beer." These soul-caking plays are so beloved around the Cheshire area that one participant (Wilfred Isherwood) referred to souling as "our religion." Many of the items used in the souling performances (which may also include solo song performances before and after the play) date back over a hundred years. The horse skulls in particular are often very old, and must be carefully guarded from rival souling "gangs," who may try to destroy them. Children are sometimes very frightened by the soulers because of the horse skulls (see also BELSNICKLING, another mumming custom that is very frightening to children).

The souling mumming play is obviously a variant of the traditional CHRISTMAS custom of the "hodening," a mumming play that was also performed house-to-house with a horse's skull ("hodening" is thought to be derived from the name of the Norse god Odin, and the hodening play may have origins in the Norse practice of sacrificing a horse to Odin at the winter solstice). In both the Christmas hodening and the November souling, a demonic character called "the Hob" was sometimes in the cast.

In Shropshire and other areas, it was common to pile the boards high with soul cakes on Halloween, and every visitor to the house was expected to take one. In Lancashire and Herefordshire, a customary greeting was:

> God have your Saul,
> Beens and all.

The response to the greeting was the gift of a soul cake.

In Staffordshire cakes were called Soulmass or simply "somas" cakes. In East Yorkshire, bakers gave "saumas loaves" (small square buns with currents on top, including one which was supposed to be kept in the house during the following year for good luck) to their customers on November 2. One woman in Whitby was said to have owned a soul-mass loaf that was about 100 years old.

In Lancashire, children begged house-to-house on All Saints' Day, saying: "For God's sake, a so' loaf." They were then given small round cakes, containing a few seeds and impressed with the "butter-print" (a small wooden stamp used in marking pats of butter) of the farm.

In Aberdeen, Scotland, soul cakes— which were given away to visitors throughout the day — were baked by each house and were called "dirge-loaves."

Soul-Mass Day— Another name for ALL SOULS' DAY (November 2). A soul-mass is a mass for the soul of one deceased. *Mirk's Festival* from about 1450 mentions this name for the day, noting "…aftyr All-halowday ys euermor Sowlemasse-day." Hiring-fairs called Soul-mass hirings were sometimes held on November 2, and "Soul-mass cake" or "Soulmass loaf" was another name for SOUL CAKES.

Souling (also a-souling)— Visiting custom commonly carried out in parts of England on ALL SAINTS' DAY and ALL SOULS' DAY, re-ported as early as the fourteenth century. The "soulers" visited house-to-house, sang a song, and collected food, drink or whatever was offered to them; the practice originated to help redeem souls trapped in PURGATORY, but eventually lost much of its original intent.

Souling was traditionally performed on All Souls' Eve, rather than the day itself; in Cheshire, children often went souling on the morning and afternoon of All Souls' Day, begging fruit, cakes, and money, while older people (often farm servants) went begging in the evening for beer or money. A typical version of the souling song runs:

> Soul, soul for a souling cake
> I pray you, missus, for a souling cake
> Apple or pear, plum or cherry
> Anything good to make us merry
> Up with your kettles and down with your
>   pans
> Give us an answer or we'll be gone
> Little Jack, Jack sat on his gate
> Crying for butter to butter his cake
> One for St. Peter, two for St. Paul
> Three for the man that made us all.

A simpler version is the line, "A Soule-cake, a Soule-cake, have mercy on all Christen soules for a Soule-cake." In Shropshire, they offered this song:

> Here's two or three hearty lads, standing
>   hard by,
> We are come a-souling, good nature to try,
> We are come a-souling, as well doth appear,
> And all that we soul for is ale and strong
>   beer.
> Go down to your cellar, and there you shall
>   find
> Both ale, beer, and brandy and, best of all,
>   wine;
> And when we have got it, O then you shall
>   see,
> And when we have drunk it, how merry
>   we'll be.
> I pray, my good mistress, don't tarry to spin,
> Look for a jug to draw some drink in,
> And when you are drawing, don't let your
>   heart fail,
> But draw us a jug of your bonny brown ale.

A variation of this song is sometimes performed by the Antrobus (Cheshire) soulers (see SOUL CAKES); the Cheshire souling rhyme usually adds lines blessing the "the master of this house, and the mistress also," and sometimes also asks for blessings on the children, the livestock, the hired servants, and the property itself.

When begging for money, the song typically included these lines:

> "The lanes are very dirty,
> My shoes are very thin;
> I have a little pocket
> To put a penny in."

The music accompanying these lyrics was sometimes described as pre-Reformation church music, although in one instance it was said to be so similar to a march by Handel that some believed Handel had based his music on the old folk tune.

Soul-cakes were the usual item requested during souling, but in some areas the soulers asked for APPLES, with this variation of the song:

> Soul, soul, a soul-cake;
> Apple or pear, plum or cherry,
> Any good thing to make us merry.
> Up in your kettles, down in your pans
> Give us an answer and we'll be gone.
> Put your hand in your pocket,
> Pull out your keys,
> Go down in the cellar,
> And draw what you please.
> Soul, soul, for an apple or two,
> If you have no apples, pears will do.

In Staffordshire, soulers began the ritual by assembling in the parish church for a special All Souls' Day service; then, dressed in black and sometimes ringing small BELLS, they visited local homes, singing a version of the typical souling song which emphasized charity and included these lines:

> So give us a cake, for charity's sake,
> And our blessing we'll leave at your door.

In Monmouthshire, the soulers were poor and were given "dole bread."

In some areas, the soulers were accompanied by a hobby horse and practiced more traditional MUMMING (and may have also accompanied themselves on such musical instruments as the concertina); in other locales, the soulers blackened their faces.

Although souling was frequently described as being practiced by children, an observer in South Staffordshire in 1857 described the soulers as old women dressed in gray or black cloaks and bonnets who repeated these couplets:

> "Here we be a-standing round about your
>   door,
> We be come a-souling, an' we bin very poor…
> Remember the departed for holy Mary's sake,
> And of your charity, pray gi' us a big soul-
>   cake."

Souling customs may have faded from areas like Shropshire as those districts became more prosperous.

In Wales, souling evolved to become a tradition in which the poor went about begging *Bara Ran*, or "dole-bread" on All Souls' Day; this custom survived until the first half of the nineteenth century. In modern Britain, the "cakin" or "kaking" song remains popular.

Like mumming, GUISING, RHYMING and BELSNICKLING, souling may be one of the ancestors of the contemporary American ritual of TRICK OR TREAT.

Sowens — A dish made of oatmeal; usually served with milk, it is served with butter instead as a traditional Scottish Halloween supper. In ROBERT BURNS's "Hallowe'en," it caps the evening's festivities:

> Till butter'd so'ns, wi' fragrant lunt,
> Set a' their gabs a-steerin;
> Syne, wi' a social glass o' strunt,
> They parted aff careerin
> Fu' blythe that night.

("Lunt" is steam or smoke; "strunt" is liquor)

An Irish variant of "sowans" is described as potato cakes and BOXTY. In parts of Scotland, sowens was also eaten at CHRISTMAS and HOGMANAY.

Sows— Several Halloween traditions mention frightening "black sows." For example, some BONFIRE customs end with boys fleeing the last of the fire while shouting out "the cutty black sow take the hindmost." This proverb is from Cardiganshire:

> A cutty black sow
> On every stile,
> Spinning and carding
> Every Allhallows's Eve.

("Cutty" means short-tailed)

In Welsh, the cutty black sow is called *hwch du gwta*, and is believed to be at large on Halloween. The house-to-house ritual of MUCK OLLA may also be based on a legend of a demonic sow or boar.

In Celtic myth, DREAMS on SAMHAIN may be invoked by eating a heavy meal of the flesh of a red pig.

Spectre Huntsman— Known also as Herne the Hunter and Gabriel Ratches, this macabre figure is typical of British GHOSTS and GOBLINS who were said to be especially active on Halloween. The Spectre Huntsman was an ungodly hunter who was condemned to lead the chase till Judgment Day; his baleful hounds could be heard on Halloween. He is also the subject of SIR WALTER SCOTT's poem "Wild Huntsman."

In the West Country "the Wild Hunt" can be heard through West Coker, near Taunton, on Halloween Night. Witnesses have described black horses and 20 or 30 black hounds.

In some areas these are actually thought to be FAIRIES (compare to the host described in TAM LIN). Alexander Montgomerie describes the "Scottish Fairy Rade":

> In the hinder end of harvest, on allhallow-
>   even,
> Quhen our good neighboures doth ryd, if I
>   reid rycht,
> …with mony elrich Incubus was rydand that
>   nycht.

One legend involving the spectre huntsman tells the fate of Lady Sybil of Bernshaw Tower, who sells her soul to the DEVIL in exchange for supernatural powers. Her suitor, Lord William of Hapton Tower, is dismayed with her rejection of his proposals, and finally goes to see Mother Helston, a famous Lancashire witch. She tells him to go hunting on the next All-Hallow's Eve to win his bride. He does, and his dogs pursue a milk-white doe, which is actually Lady Sybil transformed. The hunt is unsuccessful until the dogs are joined by Mother Helston's familiar, a hound, and Lady Sybil is caught. They're married shortly thereafter, but Lady Sybil continues her diabolical ways, and while once transformed into a white CAT her paw is cut off by a miller. She soon thereafter begins to decline, and on her deathbed the priest manages to cancel her contract with the devil; although Lady Sybil dies in peace, her ghost is said to still haunt Bernshaw Tower, where on the Eve of All Hallows the hound and the white doe are joined by the spectre huntsman.

Spiders— Although spiders are generally more feared in Western culture than CATS, BATS or OWLS, they have very little association with Halloween, and are seen only in a few COLLECTIBLES and decorations (mainly cobwebs applied to yard decorations and HAUNTED HOUSES).

There are no SUPERSTITIONS or FORTUNE-TELLING customs employing spiders on Halloween, but there is one Halloween party GAME, entitled "Web of Fate," which uses a spider web, in the form of brightly-colored strings strung up about a room and interwoven. At a signal, each guest takes an end of a string and begins winding it until meeting with whomever holds the opposite end. The first lady and gentleman to finish will be the first to be married; should two members of the same sex meet, they are destined to be bachelors or old maids forever.

Spirit Nights— A Welsh description of Halloween, MIDSUMMER'S EVE and May Eve. Halloween was the weirdest of the TEIR NOS YSBRYDION, or "Three Spirit Nights."

Spooky World— Spooky World is billed as "America's Halloween Theme Park." Currently located in Litchfield, New Hampshire, Spooky World runs throughout the month of October and draws 100,000 visitors annually. Started by David Bertolino (who says he loves Halloween for TRICK OR TREAT and humor, not horror) in 1991 as a haunted HAYRIDE, in 2004 Bertolino sold Spooky World and went into producing plays. After moving several times, in 2010 Spooky World joined with haunted attraction Nightmare New England at the current New Hampshire location. Spooky World/Nightmare New England's central attractions are its seven elaborate HAUNTED HOUSES, most recently including the "Raven's Claw Cemetery," "The 3D Freak Show," "House of Eternal Darkness," "Sleep Stalkers," and "Torment." Spooky World also boasts restaurants, the Monster Midway, Zombie Paintball, sports entertainment like go-karts, and special events (in 2002 Bobby "Boris" Pickett appeared live to perform his Halloween classic "Monster Mash"); and celebrity appearances (past celebrities have included Alice Cooper, Elvira, wrestling stars, and even Jerry Springer). Each year Spooky World (which in the past also included museums and a notorious live animal display in which hundreds of live mice and rats ran over a live actor) is a destination point for haunted house and Halloween aficionados from around the globe; in fact one fan was so dedicated she even went into labor while waiting in line to receive an autograph from an actor who had appeared in *The Texas Chainsaw Massacre*. Spooky World has also been featured in *Playboy* and on Jay Leno's *The Tonight Show* (when performer Tiny Tim was married on a Spooky World stage in 1996).

Stampy— Another traditional Irish Halloween FOOD, stampy is a sweet cake made

Chad Lundy as "Nosferatu" presides over Spooky World's "House of Fangs" (photo courtesy of Spooky World)

from potatoes, flour, sugar, caraway seeds and cream.

Stiles— Stiles could be places to fear on Halloween: In Cardiganshire a BOGIE sits on every stile on November Eve, and in Wales the spirits of the deceased could be found on every stile and at every CROSSROAD. The Welsh also had an adage about seeing "a cutty black SOW on every stile" during Halloween.

Stock— In Irish fairy lore, a stock is a kind of changeling, a false fairy child substituted on Halloween night for a real human child. A stock would wither and soon die. At other times the human child would be replaced with a fairy which might not even be a fairy child — it might be a tiny old man who never grew older or changed. Parents who had been deceived might have a chance of getting their own child back on QUARTER DAYS.

IRON was one protection against fairies, and an iron piece was sometimes placed in infants' cribs on Halloween night, to protect them from being taken and replaced by stocks.

Straw— In one Irish FORTUNE-TELLING custom, girls went to the CORN (OATS) stacks on Halloween night and pulled out a straw with their teeth; if the top pickle was present, the future husband would be a young man; but if missing, the husband would be a widower.

In another divination, a straw drawn from the thatch on Halloween was examined in hopes of finding a HAIR, since the color would indicate the hair color of one's future spouse.

Strawboys — In parts of Ireland, the "Strawboys" attacked the homes of families who kept their daughters from the company of boys (although they sometimes also launched offensives against persons whom they simply disliked for some reason); they also stole food from kitchens, stuffed up chimneys, unhinged GATES, etc. This PRANKING activity was typically enacted on Halloween, St. Brigid's Day or MAY DAY, although Strawboys might also appear at a wedding to demand a final dance with the bride. Their name derives from the suits of white STRAW they wore (their faces were usually blackened or hidden beneath homemade masks). The Strawboys, who were led by a Captain who directed them, were always Catholic; Protestants didn't participate.

Sulphur — One British custom was to throw sulphur onto a Halloween HEARTH in the belief that the resulting smoke and blue fire would keep WITCHES from entering a household through the CHIMNEY.

Summer Solstice — See also MIDSUMMER'S EVE. The Hopi Indians in America held a holiday for the dead on this day.

Superstitions — Most holidays are rife with superstitions, and certainly Halloween is no exception. Certain common superstitions, such as a black CAT indicating bad luck (or good luck, in most of Europe) take on particular meaning on Halloween. In most superstitions specific to the holiday, the death of a family member is predicted; for example, to hear CROWS near the house on Halloween afternoon, or to do LAUNDRY on Halloween (especially to wash a sheet, since it bears a resemblance to a funeral shroud) are both deadly omens. For more superstitions, see

BLACKBERRIES, CLOTHES, CORPSES, COWS, DEATH, DIGGING, EARRINGS, FAIRIES, FALLING STAR, GHOSTS, GRAVEYARDS, GUY FAWKES DAY/NIGHT, HORSES, LAUNDRY, MIDNIGHT, MOON, WALKING, WATER, WEATHER, WHITE HARE, and WIND.

Syncretism — The *Oxford English Dictionary* defines syncretism as "attempted union or reconciliation of diverse or opposite tenets or practices, esp. in philosophy or religion"; however, syncretism has a long history as a controversial practice within the Catholic Church, a practice which attempted to meld existing pagan traditions with Christianity and resulted in the contemporary holidays of Halloween and DAYS OF THE DEAD.

Pope GREGORY I was the first leader of the Church to promote the practice of co-opting existing pagan holidays, temples, and practices, in his letter of A.D. 601 to Mellitus. Syncretism is probably what eventually led the Catholic Church to establish the date of November 1st for ALL SAINTS' DAY, thus replacing the Celtic holiday of SAMHAIN. Syncretism also frequently resulted in an existing religion's pantheon of gods being replaced by the Catholic saints. Mary Andrade, in writing about the history of Day of the Dead, has suggested (in regards to attempts to co-opt the Mayan religion) that "Saint John replaces *Chac*, the god of rain; Virgin Mary takes the place of *Ixchel*, and so on."

Historians and anthropologists have also suggested that syncretism may have been less successful when missionaries in South America attempted to replace indigenous peoples' beliefs in and rituals surrounding death. Celebrations like the Mayan XANTOLO (which even specifies that the cross used in table decorations must be green, to represent the *ceiba* tree, which was sacred to Mayan beliefs) owe more to their pre-Columbian predecessors than to All Saints' Day/ALL SOULS' DAY, and the skulls and depictions of death which are prevalent in virtually all Day of the Dead celebrations are unquestionably held over from the earlier religions' "cult of the dead."

T

Tam Lin— Popular Scottish Halloween ballad told in many forms, some plainly drawing on pagan sources while other versions incorporate such Christian iconography as the BIBLE and holy water. In its most primitive form, the ballad tells the story of Janet, the lovely young daughter of a lord, who goes to the forbidden area of Carterhaugh (a real location near Selkirk in Scotland), where she meets the handsome young Tam Lin. She returns to her father pregnant, and assures him that none of his knights is the father of her child. She goes back to Carterhaugh to ask Tam Lin if he is fairy or mortal, and he tells her that he is a noble mortal who fell from his horse while hunting one day and was captured by the Queen of the FAIRIES. Tam Lin tells her that every seven years the fairies pay a tribute to Hell, and he is afraid this year he will be the sacrifice; then he adds:

> But the night is Halloween, lady,
> The morn is Hallowday,
> Then win me, win me, an ye will,
> For weel I wat ye may.
>
> Just at the mirk and midnight hour
> The fairy folk will ride,
> And they that wad their true-love win,
> At Miles Cross they maun bide.

Tam Lin then tells Janet how she will recognize him, and warns her that the fairy folk will not give him up so willingly: Once Janet has him in her arms, he will be transformed into a newt, a snake, a bear, a lion, and last a burning coal (or brand of iron in some versions), at which point Janet must wrap him in her green mantle and hurl him into a well. Janet succeeds and Tam Lin is freed, but the griefstricken Queen of the Fairies hurls a final curse at Janet.

The first time the ballad was recorded was 1729, and many other versions have been recorded from all over Scotland. The locations and families named in the most popular version of the ballad all refer to real place names and families; in fact, the region that serves as the overall setting holds the home of SIR WALTER SCOTT, who recorded a version of "Tam Lin" (sometimes called "Tamlane") in his book *Minstrelsy of the Scottish Border*.

Not only have versions of "Tam Lin" been recorded by such modern groups as Fairport Convention and Steeleye Span, but it has also served as the basis of contemporary fantasy fiction and, in its most curious retelling, as the basis of the 1971 film *The Ballad of Tam Lin* (which is set in England in the "swinging sixties").

The story of "Tam Lin" is echoed in Irish stories in which fairies steal family members on Halloween, but other family members lose courage when the fairies transform the victims. Usually blood is found on the ground the morning after, indicating that the fairies have killed the victim in revenge.

Taman— Popular Irish and Celtic name which is occasionally mistakenly used in place of SAMHAIN. In the culture of the CELTS, a *taman* was a lower-rank *fili*, or poet, who had committed ten stories to memory (the highest rank, *ollam*, knew 350 stories), A popular 20th century belief was that Samhain was the name of a Celtic "Lord of Death," and Taman is most frequently used to replace Samhain in this respect, although it is also occasionally applied in reference to the Celtic New Year's celebration on November 1st. A few authors have even suggested that Samhain was the Celts' October 31st celebration, while Taman was the feast celebrated on November 1st, but this seems to be nothing but an amalgamation of errors and fact.

Tansey Feast— An 1829 account of ALL SAINTS' DAY from Walkington, in the East Riding of Yorkshire, notes that the church there was dedicated to All Saints, and the annual feast of dedication was called the "Tansey Feast." Tansey may refer to a plant which provides a bitter sap once used in making puddings and cakes.

Tattie Bogles— A Scottish Halloween custom, a tattie bogle is a potato SCARECROW.

Tea Leaves— This popular FORTUNE-TELLING method was often used on Halloween. The grounds of tea or coffee are poured into a white cup and shaken about, so as to spread them over the surface. The cup is reversed to drain away the liquid, and then examination is made of what is left. Long, wavy lines denote vexations and losses; straight ones foretell peace, tranquility and long life. Human

Vintage Halloween postcard illustrating reading of tea leaves.

figures are usually good omens, announcing love affairs and marriage. Circular figures indicate money; if the circles are connected by straight, unbroken lines, there will be delay but all will resolve itself. Squares foretell peace and happiness; oblong figures, family discord; curved, twisted or angular ones are signs of stress and irritation. Letters signify the initials of a future spouse. Placement in the cup is also to be considered; for example, a clover shape indicates good luck, coming sooner if nearer the top of the cup. An anchor, if at the bottom of the cup, denotes success in business; if at the top, love and fidelity; but if in a thick or cloudy part, inconstancy. The serpent is always the sign of an enemy, and if in the cloudy part gives warning that great prudence will be necessary to ward off misfortune. The COFFIN portends news of a death or long illness. The dog, at the top of the cup, denotes true and faithful friends; in the middle, that they are not to be trusted; at the bottom, they are secret enemies. The lily at the top foretells a happy marriage, but at the bottom, anger. A letter signifies news; if in the clear area, very welcome news; surrounded by dots, a remittance of money; but if hemmed in by clouds, bad tidings and losses. A heart near it denotes a love letter. A single tree portends restoration to health; a group of trees in the clear, misfortunes which may be avoided; several trees wide apart, promise that your wishes will be accomplished; if encompassed by dashes, it is a token that your future is in its blossom, and only requires care to bring to maturity; if surrounded by dots, riches. Mountains signify either friends or enemies, according to their situation. The sun, moon and stars denote happiness and success. The clouds, happiness or misfortune, depending on whether they are bright or dark. Birds are good omens, but quadrupeds, with the exception of the dog, foretell trouble and difficulties. Fish imply good news from across water. A triangle portends an unexpected legacy; a single straight line, a journey. The figure of a man indicates a speedy visitor; if the arm is outstretched, a present; when the figure is very distinct, it shows that the person will have a dark complexion, and vice versa. A crown near a cross indicates a large fortune, resulting from death. Flowers are signs of joy, happiness and peaceful life. A heart surrounded by dots signifies joy, occasioned by the receipt of money; with a ring near it, approaching marriage.

There were even special china tea cups produced expressly for the purpose of tea-leaf reading; called "The Cup of Knowledge," such a cup would have small symbols printed around its interior. Today these cups are very prized by collectors.

Teanlay— Name for Halloween recorded in the 19th century in the Lancashire area of England. The name is related to *teanlas*, sometimes employed as a name for BONFIRES, and was used by the same residents who lit bonfires in PURGATORY FIELD as a means of helping to secure the release of departed loved ones from PURGATORY.

Teine Eigen— Word for Halloween BONFIRE. In Mull it was made by turning an oaken wheel over NINE oaken spindles, suggesting Druidic origins (since both oak and the number nine were highly prized among the CELTS and their DRUIDS).

Teir Nos Ysbrydron— The "THREE Spirit Nights" in Wales; Halloween was the weirdest (the others were the eve of MAY DAY and MIDSUMMER'S EVE).

Terrorism *see* **Greysteel**

Thanksgiving— American holiday held the last Thursday in November; Thanksgiving not only shares a time of year (fall) and certain foods (PUMPKIN PIE) with Halloween, but one Thanksgiving tradition may have led directly to the beloved Halloween ritual of TRICK OR TREAT.

Thanksgiving was originated by Governor Bradford, the first governor of Massachusetts Colony, in gratitude for the plentiful harvest of 1621 (he first proclaimed the day on December 13). The colonists were joined by the local Native Americans, who brought venison to the feast (which already included turkeys shot by the Pilgrims). Beginning with 1684, the festival became a formal and annual one in Massachusetts. Thanksgiving gained in popularity because of the Puritan dislike of CHRISTMAS, which the colonists considered to be "Popish mummery"; but it was a Mrs. Sarah J. Hale who undertook writing letters to the governors of all states suggesting that Thanksgiving be held on the last Thursday of November. By 1859 the governors of all but two states had agreed with her.

In late nineteenth-century New York, there was a house-to-house begging ritual practiced at Thanksgiving that bears a striking resemblance to trick or treat. Children (sometimes described as impoverished children) donned COSTUMES and went house-to-house, asking "anything for the poor" or "anything for Thanksgiving," and received NUTS, fruits, or other small foods. The costuming may have been a survival of GUY FAWKES DAY (which had largely died out in the United States by the end of the eighteenth

Raphael Tuck postcard for Thanksgiving which strangely employs Halloween icons and colors.

century); the children dressed chiefly as clowns, Yankees, Irishmen, kings, washerwomen and courtiers. The small beggars were assembled into companies with names such as "Square Back Rangers," "Slenderfoot Army," and "Original Hounds," and presented a parade through New York's streets. Although these groups had permits, they were typically joined by thousands of costumed and painted boys who had no such permits. These "ragamuffin parades" were in practice as late as 1885, although individual incidents of Thanksgiving begging were recorded up until almost 1930. Curiously, Thanksgiving begging practices seemed to fade out at almost the same time that Halloween trick or treat was first being practiced, suggesting that the Halloween custom supplanted the earlier Thanksgiving practice.

Thread— In one Canadian FORTUNE-TELLING custom, a thread is held over a lamp on Halloween; the number that can be counted slowly before the thread parts is the number of years before the one who counts will marry.

In an American game, a couple at a Halloween party was given a length of thread to pull with this rhyme:

> Pull the thread, oh, man and maid,
> To test the love between you;
> If it break easy, love is weak;
> If not, 'tis strong, I ween you.

Three— The number three has particular significance in Halloween divination, as does the number NINE (being three times three). Although the Christian religion has an association with three (the Holy Trinity), the use of the number three in many Halloween divinations is probably a holdover from CELTIC beliefs. All odd numbers were significant in early Irish and Celtic customs, but the number three was especially important. Celtic iconography features three-faced or three-headed deities (the Morrigan was a triad of war goddesses), triple-horned bulls, and even male figures with three phalli. Celtic heroes such as CUCHULAIN were often linked with

three (Cuchulain has tri-colored hair and three faults— he is too brave, too young and too handsome).

Three and nine (along with 13) also figure prominently in American witch lore, with three or nine often being the number of items required to create a protective charm. Spells or FORTUNE-TELLING customs involving APPLE PARINGS, BARLEY, BRIAR THORN, CANDLES, CHURCHES, CORN winnowing, DREAMING STONES, EGGS, FEATHERS, HAIR, HERRING, KNOTS, LUGGIE BOWLS, MIRRORS, the MOON, NUTS, OATS, PEAT, RAKES, SALT, SIEVES, WALNUT trees, WATER, WILLOW trees, and YARN all include rituals which must be performed three times.

Three-Legged Stool *see* **Crossroads**

Ticktacks— This traditional folk toy was a favorite NOISEMAKER at Halloween time, when it was applied to the exteriors of windows by boys engaged in PRANKING. The toy consists primarily of a notched wooden spool attached to a wooden handle; a string was wound about the spool, then the toy was placed against the window of an unsuspecting household. When the string was pulled, the ticktack created a terrifying cacophony, but caused no actual damage to the glass. Apparently ticktacks were an endangered species by 1936; this excerpt (to be performed by a boy with a ticktack) from the exercise "Halloween Friends" by Lenore K. Dolan indicates that ticktacks were one more of the Halloween pranks that authorities were anxious to stamp out:

> I carry a ticktack,
>   Which is out of date;
> Boys have more fun
>   In other ways of late.
> At Scout meeting or club
>   New sports they learn;
> So away from ticktacks
>   They now have turned.

However, Helen Ramsey's 1946 poem entitled "Ticktack's the Thing" suggests that ticktacks had taken on more of a harmless meaning by then, and offers them as a comparison to TRICK OR TREAT in this stanza:

> Folks come running to the window,
> When they hear that zing! zing! zing!
> Trick or treating isn't in it.
> Ticktack. That's the thing.

Tindles (also teanlas, tinley) — A Northern English tradition of building fires on hillsides at Halloween, supposedly to symbolize the ascent to heaven of souls in PURGATORY. An account from 1784 notes that these BONFIRES were lit "in the evening of the second of November," by "boys and girls," and the intention was to "light souls out of purgatory."

Tlachtga (also Tlactga) — A place in Ireland where some legends claim SAMHAIN fires were rekindled each year for all of Ireland. Tlachtga was named for the daughter of Mog Roith; Tlachtga was a patroness of druid skills who came from the East with magical artifacts, then died giving birth to three sons (each conceived by a different father). Tlachtga is now known as the Hill of Ward near Athboy, County Meath.

According to some historians, on Samhain Eve the DRUIDS assembled there for the Festival of the Fire of Tlachtga. They burnt sacrifices to the gods in the fires of Tlachtga, and it was made obligatory (to disobey was a punishable offense) to extinguish all the fires of Ireland on that eve. The Irish people were allowed to kindle no fires of their own, but rather must re-start their fires with embers from Tlachtga. The Tlachtga fires were started by *teine-eigin*, or "forced fire" (sometimes also called "need-fire") — the friction caused by rubbing two dry pieces of wood rapidly together (some accounts state that it must be pieces of sacred oak that were used). For each new fire lighted from it the King of Munster was to receive a tax of a *sgreball*, or three pence.

In A.D. 433, St. Patrick challenged the Celtic king Laoghaire and his Druids by lighting the paschal or Easter fires on top of the hill of Slane against tradition and the king's command; however, Laoghaire was so impressed with Patrick's dedication to his purpose that he allowed him to continue on his mission unhindered.

The lighting of Samhain fires on Tlachtga is similar to a Russian custom, in which villages near Moscow extinguished all fires on the eve of the first of September (which was the Russian New Year from 1348 to 1700), and the following sunrise the fires were rekindled by wise men and women, who chanted incantations and invocations while creating new fires. In many parts of Russia a funeral ceremony was performed by girls on this day: They made small COFFINS of TURNIPS and other vegetables, enclosed flies or other insects and buried them with a great show of mourning. Also, this first week of September was when peasants predicted what the coming winter would be like, judging by the abundance of gossamer webs.

Tobacco — The Irish might leave tobacco out with food near the HEARTH for ghostly visitors on Halloween. In some counties snuff or a pipe of tobacco was laid on the grave itself.

Toussaint — French name for ALL SAINTS' DAY. La Toussaint took place on November 1st, and was followed by Le Jour des Morts (ALL SOULS DAY) on the 2nd. A 1916 article on Toussaint calls it "the most impressive holiday of the entire year" in France, and describes how "the streets are thronged with people, mostly in mourning, carrying wreaths of immortelles..." Written during World War I, the article is accompanied by a drawing of a grieving mother who tells her child they can only mourn his dead soldier father, slain on a distant battlefield, "on my heart."

Toys — As with any holiday that is celebrated in part by children, Halloween has its own history of generating unique toys. Aside from NOISEMAKERS — which were often as charmingly decorated and painted as any toy — early Halloween toys included jack-in-the-boxes, jumping jacks, and pull-toys (the latter were usually cast in plastic and also

Contemporary Halloween toys

tons could be used, ominous sounds might be created by fans or cowbells, and the guideline might even be wired to deliver a mild electric shock. Sometimes the trail ended in an AUTOPSY room, where boys received a few last chills before being ushered into a party. The "Trail of Terror" was usually the climax of a party, since it generated considerable excitement and might deter children from participating in quieter events.

Modern "Trails of Terror" are usually outdoor haunted attractions.

Trena Samna—Irish for "the three days of SAMHAIN"; in a number of Celtic stories, Samhain was said to last for three days (although the length of the festival was also given as three days before and three days after Samhain).

Trees—An old British saying for the Halloween season ran: "Set trees at Allhallontide and command them to prosper; set them after Candlemas and entreat them to grow." *See also:* ACORN; HAWTHORN; OSIER; ROWAN; WALNUT; WILLOWS

Trick or Treat—Favorite American Halloween ritual in which costumed children move from house to house, using the phrase "trick or treat" to beg CANDY or other small gifts. Although trick or treat—which has come to refer to the overall practice—is probably the single most popular and beloved element of contemporary Halloween CELEBRATIONS, it is also a ritual whose origins are little known and often misunderstood. It bears some resemblance to other Halloween rituals of the past, including "SOULING" (in which beggars celebrated ALL SOULS' DAY by moving from house-to-house offering up small prayers and carols in exchange for food), "MUCK OLLA" (an Irish custom in which groups demand tribute to "Muck

served as candy containers). Dolls in particular have long been popular at Halloween, and include both commercially made figures and FOLK ART creations. Commercially made dolls have included specially-designed Halloween Kewpie dolls, "troll" dolls, and Barbie dolls (Mattel has manufactured Halloween Barbie dolls every year since 1997). Over the last decade, as Halloween RETAILING has exploded, so has the availability of Halloween toys, which now include everything from rubber balls containing jack-o'-lantern heads to Halloween-themed "Smurf" toys; and TIM BURTON's *The Nightmare Before Christmas* has produced literally hundreds of Halloween toys and dolls. Early toys and dolls (especially the whimsical plastic pull-toys) are now valuable COLLECTIBLES.

Trails of Terror—An early forerunner of the popular contemporary Halloween HAUNTED HOUSE, "Trails of Terror" reflected an era in which houses were large enough to host an indoor attraction, which typically wound through a basement or cellar. Usually a rope was hung overhead as a guideline through a series of darkly lit rooms, and crepe paper and strips of fur were hung to brush against guests' faces as they made their way along. Costumed "creatures" might jump out suddenly from around corners, and doors were blockaded to create only one confined path. Phosphoric paint to simulate glowing skele-

Vintage trick or treat bag

Olla," a legendary boar), Scottish "SKETLETS," COLUM KILL in Ireland, and RHYMING in Britain. Trick or treat also has similarities to non–Halloween practices, such as begging "a penny for the Guy" on GUY FAWKES DAY, "MUMMING" (a costumed performance offered in exchange for food or money), BELSNICKLING (a CHRISTMAS house-to-house masked begging ritual), or the late nineteenth- and early twentieth-century custom of GUISING as a beggar and going house-to-house on THANKSGIVING. It is even tempting to trace it back to Celtic mythology, which included tales of supernatural beings demanding a tribute of food and drink on SAMHAIN (the Celtic precursor to Halloween); yet trick or treat is both uniquely American and, in its true, present form, less than a century old.

Many parents are fond of telling their children that trick or treat stems from an an-cient practice of dressing in costume to scare off GOBLINS or the DEVIL (a service which homeowners are apparently grateful enough for to provide payment), but trick or treat probably has far more practical origins. In the nineteenth and early twentieth centuries, Halloween was still celebrated principally by adults, who engaged in Halloween PARTIES typically involving FORTUNE-TELLING, GAMES and specific FOODS. Children and adolescents, however, often engaged in their own special Halloween activity: PRANKING. At first confined mainly to rural farmhouses, by the early twentieth century Halloween pranking had spread to America's cities, where it evolved into something less innocent than soaping windows or pushing over outhouses: Street lamps were smashed, windows were shattered, and fires were set. This destructive pranking reached a peak with the "Black Hallowe'en" of 1933, when major U.S. cities experienced unprecedented amounts of costly mayhem. In response to "Black Hallowe'en," some cities created committees to find outlets to channel this youthful Halloween zest; these committees were successful in controlling pranking by offering carefully organized events and suggestions to homeowners. Note these lines from the 1936 EXERCISE "A Model Halloween" by Virginia R. Grundy (after descriptions of a Halloween party involving fortune-telling and games):

> The kind of fun you offer us
> Is better than the rowdy fuss
> Some children make on Halloween,
> While they indulge in mischief mean.

Events included large-scale costume parties, TRAILS OF TERROR (an early form of the HAUNTED HOUSE), and HOUSE-TO-HOUSE PARTIES, in which groups of children went from one house to another in their neighborhoods, engaging in a different game or treat at each house. Apparently urban dwellers had learned what rural farmers already knew: The pranksters could be bought off with offerings of food and fun.

Trick or treat's use of COSTUMES may

also have evolved from pranking. This 1930s RECITATION by Ada Clark entitled "My Wish" suggests the use of costuming in pranking activities:

> I wish that you folks could have seen
> Us boys and girls on Halloween,
> For, dressed as ghosts in purest white,
> And horrid witches black as night,
> We all went strolling here and there
> And laughed when people stopped to stare.
> We carried jack-o'-lanterns gay
> That blinked at all who came our way.
> Oh, yes, I wish you could have seen
> Us boys and girls on Halloween!

A 1921 report from Medford, Oregon, notes that costuming and going house-to-house were activities limited to younger children (while older children were pranking): "The younger element had great fun dressed as spooks, goblins, or fairies, parading the streets and every now and then timidly sneaking upon a porch and ringing a door bell, or peering in windows with false faces on. Many carried lanterns made out of pumpkins with grotesquely carved faces." It is also interesting to speculate that the later popularity of plastic and tin JACK-O'-LANTERNS as trick or treat goody collectors may have sprung from this earlier custom of frightening passersby with glowing pumpkin faces.

In these begging rituals that immediately preceded true trick-or-treating, children sometimes offered other spoken solicitations. A 1920 magazine article quotes a group of costumed youngsters demanding "Nuts! Nuts! We want nuts!," while the phrase "Eats or Soap" was recorded in Des Moines, Iowa, as late as 1939 (the phrases "Anything for Hallowe'en?," "Anything

for the goblins?," and simply "Handout!" have also been recorded).

Although trick or treat-like activities were reported as early as 1920, these begging endeavors and house-to-house parties didn't completely evolve into the contemporary trick or treat (which includes the actual phrase "trick or treat") until the 1950s, when the custom finally was spread throughout the country. Strangely, one of the earliest media mentions of "trick or treat" occurs in a 1927 newspaper from Alberta, Canada. A small story headlined "'Trick or Treat' is Demand" draws a direct line between pranking and trick or treat (and makes no mention of costumes): "Hallowe'en provided an opportunity for real strenuous fun. No real damage was done except to the temper of some who had to hunt for wagon wheels, gates, wagons, barrels, etc., much of which decorated the

A group of trick or treaters, circa 1960 (photograph courtesy of Brett Thompson).

front street. The youthful tormentors were at back door and front demanding edible plunder by the word 'trick or treat' to which the inmates gladly responded and sent the robbers away rejoicing." A 1934 article from Portland, Oregon, suggests that trick or treat had already taken hold there: "Other young goblins and ghosts, employing modern shakedown methods, successfully worked the 'trick or treat' system in all parts of the city." A 1937 article discussing trick or treat mentions that some children have started to carry bags to hold all of their treats. Likewise, a 1939 magazine article entitled "A Victim of the Window-Soaping Brigade?," notes that the treats were eaten on the premises. Author Doris Hudson Moss suggests inviting "Trick-or-Treaters" into the house for cider, DOUGHNUTS and other treats (although she also advises putting away the fine glass and silver!); she also recommends telling the young guests "no trick," and notes that only some of her young guests were in costume. Finally, she is also pleased to note that her windows remain unsoaped and her house is intact the next morning. Although Moss refers to the "…age-old Halloween salutation of 'Trick-or-Treat'," by the 1940s the phrase was still not in common use throughout the country. Elizabeth Hough Sechrist's popular 1948 book *Heigh-Ho for Halloween* makes no mention of trick or treat, although it does discuss the problem of destructive pranking; on the other hand, 1946's *The Hallowe'en Festival Book* does mention trick or treat (trick or treat would have been more difficult during the years of World War II, when resources were lean and tensions high). Early trick or treat practices often included trying to guess the youngsters' true real names and inviting them into the house, but as communities grew and fewer suburbanites knew their neighbors, this practice subsided in favor of the contemporary practice centered on the front door. Houses and apartments now customarily put out lit jack-o'-lanterns and other decorations to indicate their participation, and candy became the treat of choice (although treats have never been confined to candy—toothbrushes, coins, and popcorn have all been offered, and one 1959 record distributor even gave out 45 rpm singles he was overstocked on). By the 1950s, when the country had settled into new prosperity and comfort, Halloween and trick or treat had undergone some of the same commercialization as Christmas—costumes, for instance, were no longer handmade, but sold in small boxes and often based on favorite characters from film and television (DEVILS, SKELETONS and WITCHES have always been staples of the trick or treat costume, reflecting Halloween's origins as a commemoration of the dead and its later Christian association with evil forces). Pillowcases were replaced by mass-produced trick or treat bags and plastic jack-o'-lantern buckets, and decorations were now made out of foil, bakelite and plastic.

Perhaps most interesting of all the commercially-made Halloween items were the NOISEMAKERS. These colorful (and loud!) ratchets, rattles, bells and horns became part of the trick or treat ritual, with revelers using them to announce their arrival at each house. Although urban legend has it that noisemakers originated to drive away evil spirits, again their actual usage and origin has more to do with institutionalized pranking.

Sociologists have suggested that trick or treat's enduring appeal lies in its inversion of social norms: Halloween became the one night of the year when children were in power and adults were subordinate (note the decline of adult Halloween parties and celebrations from the 1930s to the 1970s). In this view, noisemakers took on special significance as a sort of totem of the child's power over the adult.

A few sociologists have also seen trick or treat as little more than training for future consumers in a capitalist culture. In his 1959 article "Halloween and the Mass Child," Gregory P. Stone queried trick or treaters as to what trick they would pull if denied their treat; most responded simply that they didn't know, and the few who offered a suggestion for a trick ("I'd probably go home and get some sand or something and throw it on your porch") were obviously inexperienced in pranking. By 1959, the phrase "trick or treat" itself had lost its original connotation, as a genuine threat of mischief.

The 1950s also added another new facet to trick or treating, when in 1950 a few children collected $17 during their trick or treating which they donated to UNICEF. Although this practice continues today, parental concerns over trick or treating have caused a gradual decline in UNICEF's Halloween revenues.

In 1964, trick or treat was dealt a blow from which it has been slow to recover, when a New York housewife was arrested for passing out poisonous ant-buttons to trick or treaters; by 1967 there were rumors of APPLES with concealed razor blades being handed out as treats. Although these URBAN LEGENDS had virtually no basis in fact, they inaugurated a new Halloween fear: that trick or treating children were in danger. Hospitals began to offer free Halloween X-RAYS of goodies, and parents were urged to dispose of any unwrapped candies, for fear of poison (although other urban legends circulated regarding candy being laced with LSD). Towns began to enforce curfews on Halloween, and some banned trick or treating altogether. In the wake of this new panic, large-scale parties reappeared to replace trick or treating; children were also urged to trick or treat in shopping malls and ZOOS instead of neighborhood streets. Some areas made stronger attempts to control the trick or treat custom; for example, in 1993 an Ohio town set aside Saturday, October 23 from 1 to 3 P.M. as the official time for trick or treating. Given the concurrent rise of Halloween PARADES and costume balls, it might be said that adults had decided to take the holiday back for themselves.

However, trick or treating was evidently too well-loved to die, and seems to be gaining again in popularity, continuing in its tra-

ditional form (give or take a trip to the hospital x-raying unit); in 1999, 92 percent of America's children engaged in trick or treating, and during the recent Halloween of 2000, Americans spent $1.9 billion on candy. In fact, Halloween is now the number two retail holiday, just behind CHRISTMAS. Haunted houses, the descendants of the "Trails of Terror," are more popular than ever, with many neighborhood houses now offering trick or treaters a good-natured thrill with their piece of candy. Trick or treat has even spun off its own variants, including a college campus practice of "trick or drink" (in which dorm residents go from room to room demanding "trick or drink"). Churches opposed to the celebration of Halloween have sometimes offered "trunk or treat" parties, where children are offered treats from the trunks of cars parked in a church parking lot.

Trick or treat is an adaptable custom, and has always reflected the culture around it. Spacemen costumes, for example, were popular during the 1960s; the 1980s saw a renewed interest in movie characters, with the massive successes of the *Star Wars* films and the slasher movie cycle started in 1979 by JOHN CARPENTER's *Halloween*; and in the aftermath of the devastating terrorist attacks on America that occurred on September 11, 2001, firefighters and police were the costumes of choice. And treats are no longer confined simply to candy: In 1987 a Canadian man gave out stocks to his first hundred trick or treaters (but he put an end to the practice when the stocks took an abrupt downturn).

Outside of the United States, children have occasionally engaged in Halloween masked begging with other verbal formulae as well: In Nova Scotia, the practice started after World War I with this recitation:

Tramp, tramp, tramp, the boys are marching,
We are the witches at your door.
If you will not let us in
We will bash your windows in
And you'll never see us goblins any more.

In Great Britain, children have a similar (though not as popular and widespread) tradition, in which they'll beg "money for the King, money for the Queen." In Ireland, RHYMING is still popular.

In Saskatchewan, adults practice a form of trick or treat which is very similar to Belsnickling: They dress up in costumes and go house-to-house (usually via car); at each house the residents try to guess their identities, and offer food and drink. This can continue all night until dawn, and, as with Belsnickling, identity-guessing may continue long after Halloween has ended.

Turning the Devil's Stone— Just outside the churchyard in Shebbear, Devon, lies a large stone which was supposedly accidentally dropped by the DEVIL, or possibly moved there to keep it from being used in the church foundation at nearby Henscott. Each year on the eve of November 5 (GUY FAWKES NIGHT) at 8 P.M., the BELL-ringers sound their bells, then a crew of men use crowbars to turn the stone over, since it would be unlucky not to do so (one year when they were short of men —1940, during World War II — the turning was neglected, and the war news

became so appalling that the practice was continued the next year).

Turnips— In Ireland and Scotland, where the PUMPKIN is not a native plant, large turnips (or "swedes") have often been utilized to create JACK-O'-LANTERNS and other Halloween decorations. Some Irish Halloween celebrants have even mentioned making a string handle to carry their carved-out, grinning turnip lanterns with them during Halloween PRANKING (others attach it to a stick and carry it overhead). Unlike the American jack-o'-lantern, the turnip lantern is not cut all the way through; rather, after slicing off the top and scooping out most of the inside of the turnip, a design is carved lightly in the face (this is also the practice in carving "punkies" on PUNKIE NIGHT). In Scotland, at least one traditional GUISING rhyme centers on turnip lanterns:

> Hallowe'en a nicht o' tine!
> A can'le in a custock.
> A howkit neep wi' glowerin' een
> To fleg baith witch and warlock

("Howkit neep" refers to the turnip lantern; to "fleg" is to frighten.)

UNICEF— UNICEF is an acronym for United Nations International Children's Emergency Fund. UNICEF was created by the United Nations General Assembly in 1946 to help children after World War II in Europe, and in 1953 it became a permanent part of the United Nations system, with the ongoing goal of helping impoverished children in developing countries. In 1950 an American volunteer couple, the Reverend Clyde Allison and his wife Mary Emma, convinced a few neighborhood children to collect money for UNICEF instead of candy on

Halloween night, and with the $17 collected that year the popular "Trick or Treat for UNICEF" fund-raiser was born. This charitable practice continued to grow until 1967, when President Lyndon B. Johnson named October 31, 1967 as National UNICEF Day. By 2001, the program had raised more than $105 million, and in the 2002 campaign McDonald's U.S. restaurants distributed 20 million of the traditional orange "Trick or Treat for UNICEF" collection boxes in October, more than doubling the previous reach of the program. In 2004, the program expanded to include online fundraising forms, and in 2005 a record was set when U.S. kids raised $18.25 million, much of which went to help the Indian Ocean tsunami and Hurricane Katrina disaster victims. In 2010, Trick or Treat for UNICEF celebrated its 60th anniversary.

United Nations *see* **UNICEF**

Urabon *see* **Bon Festival**

Urban Legends— Urban legends are modern, orally-transmitted tales. As a holiday which serves in part as a commemoration of the dead, it is certainly no surprise that Halloween in the late twentieth- and early twenty-first centuries had its share of urban legends. By far the most celebrated, of course, is the poisoned candy or razor-blade-hiding-in-the-apple tale. This may have started with a case in 1964, in which housewife Helen Pfeil gave packages containing dog biscuits, steel wool and arsenic-laced ant-poison buttons to teens she thought were too old to be trick or treating; the razor blade motif surfaced in 1967. In their oft-quoted study "The Razor Blade in the Apple: The Social Construction of Urban Legends" (1985), Joel Best and Gerald T. Horiuchi examine 76 cases of "Halloween sadism" which occurred between 1959 and 1984, and came up with startling facts: Of those 76 cases (which covered 15 American states and two Canadian provinces), only 20 reported injuries (the most serious of which required 11 stitches), and only two deaths resulted. In 1970, five-year-old Kevin Toston died after swallowing heroin, but police traced the drug to a stash in his uncle's house, not Halloween candy; in 1974, eight-year-old Timothy Mark O'Bryan died of cyanide poisoning after eating Halloween candy, but police later determined his own father had tampered with the candy. The trend peaked twice, in 1982, when Halloween took place a month after seven people died from swallowing poisoned Tylenol pills; and the first time in the period covering 1969–1971 (there were 31

cases during this time), when Best and Horiuchi suggest that a combination of growing threats to children (including drug use), fear of crime, and increasing mistrust of others combined to fuel the Halloween sadism rumors. As an urban legend, that of the anonymous Halloween psycho hiding razor blades in APPLES or poisoning TRICK OR TREAT candy combines two popular themes, those of danger to children and contaminated food.

Poisoned CANDY took a new twist in 2001, when Halloween occurred not only after the terrorist attacks of September 11, but also after several people died of anthrax poisoning by terrorists. Again, although fears were heightened, there were no genuine anonymous cases of Halloween sadism recorded.

Another popular 2001 legend inspired by the 9/11 terrorist attacks circulated largely via e-mail and reported that "my friend's friend was dating a guy from Afghanistan" until September 6, at which point he disappeared. On September 10, she received a letter from her boyfriend begging her not to get on any commercial airlines on 9/11, and not to go to any malls on Halloween. After the events of 9/11, the friend's friend supposedly turned the letter over to the FBI; on October 11, the FBI did its best to debunk the rumor, affirming that the letter described therein was nonexistent.

Another popular Halloween urban legend began in 1968. That year a rumor circulated on college campuses that popular psychic Jeane Dixon had predicted (on a radio show) a maniac stalking a college campus on Halloween. This legend popped up again in 1979 (the Midwest), 1983 (nationwide), 1986 (Central Pennsylvania), 1991 (New England) and 1998 (mainly Michigan); this time the psychic had appeared on a television talk show (usually given as *The Oprah Winfrey Show*) and predicted that, on Halloween, a knife-wielding madman (in some versions of this legend the psycho was described as being costumed as Little Bo Peep) would carve up a dormitory or fraternity. With each new cycle, details are added to indicate specific locales—for example, students at Florida State University claimed that the psychic had indicated that the killer would stalk a U-shaped building on a campus located near a graveyard (which FSU is). When the story arose in 1991, it spread through a number of East Coast colleges and sometimes cited Nostradamus as the source, noting that the murders would occur in a year with an onomatopoeic number (the ever-popular Nostradamus was also claimed to have predicted the catastrophes of 9/11).

The idea that children are kidnapped on Halloween for use in Satanic cult rituals probably started in 1973–4, after a wave of cattle mutilations. By 1975 officials were warning parents to keep younger children inside after dark; by 1988, this urban legend had appeared in at least nine states. A typical example of this story arose in 1990, when it was claimed that one cult was trying to round up one hundred blond and blue-eyed children. In actual fact, the FBI has never confirmed any murder in the US as a sacrifice.

By 1989 some communities had taken these legends seriously enough to ban Halloween because of them. National Guard Units offered free fingerprinting of children the week before Halloween, hospitals offered free X-RAYS of their candy, and children were encouraged to trick or treat at indoor malls and ZOOS instead of on the streets. In his essay "'Safe Spooks': New Halloween Traditions in Response to Sadism Legends," Bill Ellis suggests that "traditional images of ghosts and witches are simply augmented by images of contemporary fears."

More fanciful but perennially popular is the story of the HAUNTED HOUSE that's so frightening it either offers patrons refunds for surviving, or is simply impossible to survive; this legend dates back to at least the 1980s, has been set in nearly every major U.S. city, and typically states that the haunted attraction in question has five levels, each more frightening than the last. Related to this is the story of the Halloween decoration depicting a hanged man which is actually a real man, usually a suicide or murder victim.

Netlore, or the passing of urban legends via the internet and e-mail, has also produced popular Halloween stories, like the tale of a masked wife who seduces her unwitting and unfaithful husband at a Halloween party. More malicious was a 2008 piece of netlore that claimed a local gang would be committing murders on or around Halloween; the number ranged from "31 women" to "14 white people," and the stories typically claimed that the information had come from the local police. In December of that year, police arrested a man named Andrew T. Lazaro for spreading these "false reports."

Victorians— The nineteenth-century Victorians were fond of festivals and CELEBRATIONS, and it is often claimed that the contemporary celebrations of both CHRISTMAS and Halloween are due to them. Although their influence on Christmas is unquestioned (Christmas trees, for example, didn't become popular until 1848, when a photograph was published showing a decorated tree at Windsor Castle), there is little evidence that the British Victorians did much to promote and celebrate Halloween. One widely-mentioned event did speak of Queen Victoria and a Halloween visit to Balmoral, where she witnessed "BURNING THE WITCH." If the late nineteenth-century American upper-middle class can be properly called Victorians, then indeed their contribution to the holiday is rich, since it was this group that, about 1870 (when possibly the earliest magazine article describing a party appeared in *Godey's Ladies Book*), discovered the celebration of the day among the poorer Scots-Irish immigrants, and claimed it for their own. Victorians were also fond of spiritualism and mediumship (practices later debunked by HARRY HOUDINI).

Voodoo (also voudoun, vodou)— Religion combining West African beliefs with Catholicism, practiced originally by African slaves brought to Haiti and eventually to the Southern United States. Practitioners of Voodoo celebrate both ALL SAINTS' DAY and ALL SOULS' DAY (called *Fête Guédé*). A typical Halloween ritual might ask lingering spirits to move on by invoking the help of *Papa Legba*; rituals typically involve chanting, singing, dancing, and offerings. Every year the New Orleans Historic Voodoo Museum hosts an "All Hallows Eve Voodoo Ritual."

Walking— A common SUPERSTITION throughout Europe and the British Isles has to do with walking on Halloween; if you hear footsteps behind you, don't turn to look since you'll see the ghastly sight of a GHOST following you. In a variation of this belief, you're likely to see the specter of Death, a glimpse of which will hasten your own end.

Many FORTUNE-TELLING practices direct an unmarried young person to walk into a room, to a field, or even to a body of WATER. For example, in an American variation of a classic divination involving a MIRROR, a young lady was directed to walk into a room BACKWARD at MIDNIGHT on Halloween, and look over her left shoulder, at which point she would see her future husband.

Walnuts— Walnut trees held a place of honor in some English Halloween traditions, because of the fruit they bore at this time of year. A GAME played at nineteenth-century Halloween PARTIES involved placing a matching seed of some kind (a bean, a pea, etc.) inside two complete walnut shells, then tying the shells shut with ribbon. The shells were divided, one box for men and one for women; upon receiving and opening a shell, the game was to find the member of the opposite sex who had the counterpart seeds.

In another FORTUNE-TELLING game, English walnut half-shells were filled with wax and wicks or small CANDLES, named for members of the party and floated in a large pan or tub of WATER. The movement of these small boats to or away from each other foretold future relationships; the first person whose flame was extinguished would remain unmarried.

In an older English custom, a young man or woman would go to a walnut tree at MIDNIGHT on Halloween and walk around it THREE times, crying out each time. "Let him (her) that is to be my true love bring me some walnuts." The future intended will then be seen in the tree gathering walnuts. In "Thursday, or the Spell" from *The Shepherd's Week*, poet John Gay refers to this custom:

Last Hallow Eve I sought a walnut tree,
In hopes my true Love's face that I might see.
Three times I called, three times I walked apace;
Then in the tree I saw my true Love's face.

An American version of this indicated that a walnut branch could be placed in the living room during a party, and as young men walked around it three times, they repeated this charm:

> At midnight round the walnut tree
> Three times I go; so let me see
> My own true love before me stand,
> With walnuts for me in her hand.

In another nineteenth-century fortune-telling game, small fortunes were written with milk on white paper (compare to the formula for WITCHES' INK), allowed to dry and then placed in empty walnut shells. Each guest at a party would select a shell, and hold the paper above a flame until the fortune was revealed. Here is a typical suggested fortune: "It will be your fate to serve others; but your calling will be a high one. You will never suffer from want or hunger, and many will bless you. There are sorrows in your life, but the closing years will be bright and happy."

An Irish custom used walnut or chestnut shells, which were filled with red, yellow, pink, and green paper (a few were left empty as well). The shells were then sealed together with wax, and after each person at a party had selected one they were hung above a lighted candle until the wax melted and the colors were revealed. Red stood for love; pink, an affectionate nature; green, possession of land; yellow, money; and empty, a life of hard work.

Walpurgisnacht (also Walpurgis Night) — European holiday celebrated on the eve of MAY DAY, or April 30, and named after Walpurga, an eighth-century British nun who went to Germany to found holy houses there, and is the protectress against magic. With Halloween, this is one end of the calendar year in many parts of Europe (see QUARTER DAYS), just as SAMHAIN and BELTANE mark the two ends of the Celtic calendar. In many parts of Europe this was believed to be a night of great evil, as WITCHES held revels on Brocken in the Harz Mountains, stole milk, cast spells on livestock, and brought murrains (plagues), blight and disaster to fields and crops. Houses were purified with juniper and rue as protection; ROWAN was fastened over doors. Dried hemlock, caper spurge, and ROSEMARY were bundled, fastened on poles and made into torches. German farmers put three crosses and herbs over stable doors, and hid broomsticks so that witches couldn't use them; fires were lit around trees, since the smoke would protect the trees from the ravages of evil forces. When BELLS rang on Walpurgisnacht, men carried torches and women banged pots and pans around the village seven times. Witches flying on this night would try to take a bite out of each church bell they passed. BONFIRES were lit, then the ASHES strewn over fields to ward off blight and mildew.

This was also the night of Beltane, and Scots may have enacted old DRUID sacrificial rituals when they burned "The Carline," a "devoted one" who was pelted with eggs and spoken of throughout the year as if dead. The Welsh reenacted sacrifice by sending NINE men (with pockets turned inside out as protection against FAIRIES and witches) to the forest to collect nine kinds of wood for their fires. When the fire was blazing, they drew by lot pieces of light and dark oatmeal CAKE, and those who drew the dark (burned) pieces were required to jump THREE times through the flames.

Girls also practiced FORTUNE-TELLING on this night, with many customs being similar to those practiced at Halloween. In one, the temperament of the future husband could be deduced by keeping a linen THREAD near an image of the Madonna for THREE days, then at MIDNIGHT on Walpurgisnacht it was pulled apart while reciting:

> Thread, I pull thee;
> Walpurga, I pray thee,
> That thou show to me
> What my husband's like to be.

Whether the thread was strong or easily broken, soft or tightly woven, indicated the future husband's disposition.

Walpurgisnacht is mentioned in Goethe's *Faust*, in a sequence where Mephistopheles calls on a WILL-O'-THE-WISP to lead them into the mountains (the Brocken) to view the witches' revels. As Mephistopheles describes it:

They dance, they cook, they drink, make love, and chat.
Now say, where's something better than all that?

War of the Worlds— Undoubtedly the single greatest act of Halloween PRANKING ever perpetrated. On October 30, 1938, Orson Welles and his Mercury Theatre presented their dramatization of H. G. Wells's classic on the Columbia Broadcasting System radio stations across the U.S., and instigated a nationwide panic when listeners took its imitation of news bulletins for the real thing. Although the drama ran for only one hour and was introduced as "a radio play by Howard Koch suggested by the H. G. Wells novel," an estimated 1.2 million people phoned police stations, ran down streets in panic and, in one case, even threatened to take poison to keep from enduring the invasion (fortunately the woman in question here was stopped by her husband). At the conclusion of the broadcast, Welles reassured his audiences that the broadcast had been fictional, calling it "the Mercury Theatre's own radio version of dressing up in a sheet and jumping out of a bush and saying Boo! Starting now, we couldn't soap all your windows and steal all your garden gates, by tomorrow night…" His final words for the evening: "…and if your doorbell rings and nobody's there, that was no Martian … it's Halloween." Over the next few days, Welles and his cohorts were demonized by some, but praised by others, who felt the show aptly demonstrated how unprepared Americans were for a real announcement of war (at the time, Americans were concerned over Hitler's build-up of power in Germany). The show is now a Halloween classic, and has probably been broadcast on some U.S. radio station every Halloween since.

Water— Water is a major component of Halloween FORTUNE-TELLING: APPLES are bobbed in it, LEAD is poured into it, lighted CANDLES are placed to sail on it, and wedding rings are suspended in it; the three LUGGIE BOWLS— with clean water, dirty water and empty— also use water. In her book *Pagan Celtic Britain*, Anne Ross notes that "springs, wells and rivers are of first and enduring importance as a focal point of Celtic cult practice and ritual." Rivers were associated with fertility in Celtic tradition, and the sacred feast of SAMHAIN was often held on the shores of lakes (Celts also threw treasure offerings into lakes), so it is possible that the use of water in Halloween customs is a Celtic survival.

Probably the most popular divination involving water was the Scottish tradition sometimes called "the wetting of the sark sleeve": A young unmarried person would go (although not necessarily alone) to a south-running spring or rivulet, where "three lairds' lands meet," and dip the left

Vintage postcard illustrating the "sark-sleeve" divination.

shirt sleeve into the water (another version states that the shirt must be dipped silently in "a dead and living ford," meaning a ford which has been crossed by a funeral). This person would then retire to bed in sight of a fire, having hung the wet sleeve before the fire to dry. He or she would then lie awake, and sometime near MIDNIGHT an apparition (or FETCH) of the future beloved would come and turn the sleeve, as if to dry the other side of it. A variant of this custom suggests that a nightdress be washed THREE times in running water; another said that the water should be brought "from a well which brides and burials pass over." In another version, the shirt or other linen item was to be hung up at 11 P.M. and turned once by the girl at half-past, then her future husband's apparition would appear at midnight. It was also possible that a girl might see a COFFIN (sometimes described as dripping blood, indicating death by accident) instead of a future husband. Usually bread and butter were set out as well, and after turning the garment the husband would take a bite of the food before departing. In some variations the garment had to be washed in south-running water. Some have suggested that this custom may have originally been Scandinavian, since a similar custom was supposedly used to lure the Norse goddess Freya to assist in love divination.

The Americans also have a version of the "sark sleeve": On Halloween night a girl would wash and dry an undergarment BACKWARDS, then sit down before the stove backwards without speaking; if she was meant to marry, she would see her future husband come down the steps. If she was not to marry, she would see a black CAT come down the steps, followed by four men carrying a coffin. In a frightening Irish ghost story, the fetch of the husband would enter by the front door and leave by the back; in one old farmhouse, a foolish girl performed this ritual without remembering that her home had no backdoor. When the apparition of the husband was trapped in the house, it was revealed to actually be the DEVIL, and the family suffered

various misfortunes until they all died (at which point their house was considered to be haunted).

A variation of this custom stated that a wet sheet hung in front of the fire on Halloween would show a vision of the future mate.

Modern practitioners of WICCA practice a cousin of this custom called the DREAMING STONES, in which three small stones are plucked from a boundary stream after dark, and placed under the pillow at home to induce dreams which will offer guidance.

In one especially amusing tradition, a fortune seeker would fill his or her mouth with water and WALK around the house or block without swallowing or spilling a drop; the first person of the opposite sex met was the future spouse. In an Irish variation, a young unmarried woman must acquire the mouthful of water from a stream where two townlands border, then she must go to the first house, listen at the doorway, and the first male name will be that of her future husband. One person describing this custom mentioned that girls had a tendency to go only to households where they had an interest in some young male kin. In a variation, the young person had to fill the mouth with water and the right hand with SALT.

An American custom suggested that a glimpse of the face of one's future spouse could be obtained by looking into a spring with a lightwood torch at midnight on Halloween; a fortune-seeker reluctant to go out after dark could approach the spring in the daylight hours while carrying a broken EGG in a glass. Pouring some of the spring water into the glass would disclose images of both the future husband and the children the couple would have. Another version of this stated that looking into the well at 11 o'clock on Halloween Day would reveal one's future. In the Midwest, the custom was to lie on Halloween on one's back by a well with a MIRROR held over the head, positioned to show the bottom of the well; this would reveal the image of the future spouse in the mirror. In an Illinois variant, a girl must go to a spring on Halloween and take a mouthful of water, then return home walking backwards and get into bed backwards. She would swallow the water, and would then DREAM of her future husband coming to give her a drink; as with a DUMB CAKE ritual, this must all be accomplished in silence.

In another popular divination, questioners would write the names of their love interests on small pieces of paper. The papers were rolled into individual bits of dough made from FLOUR and water, and then placed into a tub of water; the first name to rise up would be that of the future mate.

One particular divination method involved going to bed on Halloween night with a glass of water nearby, in which floated a small sliver of WOOD. During the night the sleeper would dream of falling from a bridge into a river and being rescued by the future husband or wife.

Water also figured in one WEATHER divination: A stake placed upright at the junction of two streams on ALL SAINTS' DAY would forecast the winter weather.

Water also had certain protective powers on Halloween. In Orkney, they have a special "forespoken water" which is sprinkled on sick livestock or on boats when fishing is bad, especially at Halloween (they might also apply a cross of tar to the boats). In Wales, old women went to the parish holy well on ALL SOULS' DAY and washed their eyes in the water, in the belief that this would help their eyesight retain its strength.

One SUPERSTITION involving water also involved FAIRIES: It was thought to be bad luck to throw out water on Halloween night, since the water might hit returning souls or even fairies (who could be angered by the act). It was helpful to call out "*Seachain*" ("beware") or "*Chughaibh an t'uisce*" ("water towards you") as a warning. In Grey County, Ontario (Canada), it was believed that anyone who threw out dirty water on Halloween would see the DEVIL.

In many areas, bowls or jugs of water were also left out on Halloween or All Souls' Eve for returning souls to quench their thirst from. *See also* HOLY WATER.

Weather— Because Halloween represents the onset of winter, there are several FORTUNE-TELLING customs involving the weather. One belief was that the weather could be foretold by looking at the MOON on Halloween evening. Another Halloween weather belief (from the *Shepherd's Calendar*) held that if a chip cut from a "beach tree" [*sic*] was dry, the winter would prove to be warm. In Sussex, they had this saying regarding the weather:

> If ducks do slide at Hallowtide,
> At Christmas they will swim.

A variation referred to MARTINMAS instead:

> If there's ice at Martinmas will bear a duck,
> There'll be nothing after but sludge and muck.

There was sometimes a short spell of warm weather around Martinmas called "St. Martin's Little Summer." Shakespeare uses the name ALL-HALLOWN SUMMER in a reference from *Henry IV Part One*. In Germany they said, "ALL SAINTS' DAY brings the second summer," and further noted, "All Saints' summer lasts three hours, three days or three weeks." In Sweden, warm weather at this time was called "the All Saints rest." In Italy, they held this belief: "If All Saints find the weather disturbed, they settle it; but if they find it fine they unsettle it"; a variant of this from Lombardy ran, "If All Saints unsettle the weather, All Souls set it to rights again."

If it rained on ALL SOULS' DAY, Dalmatians noted: "The dead are weeping."

There are several aphorisms regarding All Saints' Day and HARVEST, like this one:

> On the first of November, if the weather hold clear,
> An end of wheat-sowing do make for the year.

There were also several SUPERSTITIONS involving the WIND on Halloween; most of these (such as the belief that wind soughing against your window on Halloween night predicts your death within the coming year) were eerie and concerned death.

Wedding Ring— A wedding ring suspended from a silken cord in a goblet of water could foretell a future mate on Halloween night; as the string-holder went through the alphabet, any time the ring struck against the glass indicated one of the future beloved's initials. A variant from Cornwall stated that the ring be strung on a length of cotton by a maiden, who would then say, "If my husband's name is to be — let this ring swing." Another Halloween game also used a wedding ring, and is recalled in this 1937 poem "The First to Wed":

A wedding ring is hung up in a doorway,
   This wedding ring is hung up by a string;
Just twelve feet back there stands a lovely
   maiden
   Who points a pencil at the hung up ring.
With cautious step she moves on toward the
   doorway
   She dare not let the pencil rise or fall.
She aims to slip it first straight through the
   trinket
   For then she soon will hear Dan Cupid's
   call.

Wedding rings were also the most common tokens baked into BARM BRACK, BOXTY, BREAD, CAKES or other Halloween FOODS that might contain small FORTUNE-TELLING tokens.

Welles, Orson *see* **War of the Worlds**

Wheat— A popular seasonal saying was: "Sow wheat from Michaelmas to Hallontide." *See also:* CORN.

Whistle Wassail Night— Name for Halloween sometimes used by children in northwest Shropshire, who practiced SOULING on October 31st with this rhyme:

"Whistle, wassail,
Bread and possel,
An apple or a pear,
A plum or a cherry,

Any good thing to make us merry.
One for Peter, one for Paul,
Three for the man who made us all.
So up with the kettle and down with the pan,
Give us an answer and we'll be gone."

White Hare— One SUPERSTITION suggests that a maiden who has died of a broken heart will come back as a white hare to haunt her betrayer; the white hare will follow him everywhere but be invisible to all others, and will cause his death on some Halloween.

Wicca (also The Craft, The Old Religion, witchcraft) –Wicca is a neo-pagan practice, and as such is polytheistic and animistic. Although Wiccan beliefs are divergent (some practitioners don't consider it to be a religion), most Wiccans worship a Mother Goddess and her male counterpart, a Horned God. Many believe the theory espoused by Margaret Murray in her book *The Witch-Cult in Western Europe*, that contemporary Wicca or witchcraft is the descendant of an ancient fertility religion which was forced to go underground to survive. Modern Wicca is usually considered to have been inaugurated in 1951 by Gerald Gardner, who claimed to have been initiated in a system practiced by persecuted but benevolent WITCHES for centuries.

The Old English *wicce* (probably stemming from a root word meaning either "to know" or "to turn aside") eventually became the word "witch," and modern practitioners of witchcraft returned to this root word when seeking a new name for themselves (although many still prefer the more traditional "witch"). Wiccans celebrate eight "sabbats," including Halloween or SAMHAIN (paradoxically, newer covens tend to use Samhain, while older covens still use Halloween). Halloween is also one of the four High Holidays, or Greater Sabbats (or QUARTER DAYS), and is sometimes called "The Great Sabbat," since it is commonly held to be the most important holiday of the year. It is most often recognized as the New Year, but is also called Ancestor Night (other Wiccan names for

Halloween are Day of the Dead, and Shadowfest or Strega); the day may also be referred to as Third Festival of Harvest (the first two are Lughnasad on August 1 and Fall Equinox on September 21). Wiccans believe that on this night the Goddess (in her "crone" form) enters the Underworld, where the God reigns as Lord of Death and Rebirth; the God is reborn at the Winter Solstice, and he rules as the Bright Lord or Oak King until the Summer Solstice, when he impregnates the Goddess and becomes the Dark Lord again. Modern covens occasionally echo this structure by letting the High Priest oversee the coven beginning on Samhain, with rulership returned to the High Priestess at BELTANE. Some Wiccans also believe that on this night they enter the dreamtime, and can remember past lives.

With such an important holiday, Witches often hold two distinct celebrations: First, a large Halloween party for non–Wiccan friends is often held on the previous weekend; and then a coven ritual is held on Halloween night itself, late enough so as not to be interrupted by trick or treaters. A Wiccan Halloween sabbat ritual usually involves a CAULDRON (which may be sprinkled with incense), a High Priest and a High Priestess, an invitation to the dead to visit with their loved ones in the coven on that night, and a reaffirmation of life. The ritual is followed by feasting and partying (during which one coven member designated as "the LORD OF MISRULE" may carry out some PRANKING and mischief).

Wiccans use many of the symbols of Halloween in their Halloween or Samhain rituals. For example, JACK-O'-LANTERNS may be placed at the four points of a magick circle (symbolizing Air, Water, Earth and Fire) and lit at the beginning of the ritual; they are also believed to be welcoming beacons for visiting souls. Wiccans display images of GHOSTS and SKELETONS to celebrate their belief in reincarnation, and cauldrons can be used to hold incense during a Samhain ritual. APPLES may be buried by Wiccans on Halloween to honor and nourish the souls of the dead. Wiccans also utilize particular Halloween herbs (mugwort, allspice, broom, catnip, deadly nightshade, mandrake, oak leaves, sage and straw), Halloween incense (heliotrope, mint, and NUTMEG), Halloween stones (all black stones, especially obsidian), Halloween plants (allspice, apples, catnip, gourds, mugwort, and sage), Halloween oils (basil, camphor, clove, frankincense, lilac, yarrow, and ylang-ylang), and Halloween teas (angelica, apple, catnip, Indian hyppo, sage and valerian; these teas are often drunk just before a Sabbat ritual).

In 1970, the Witches International Craft Associates received a permit from the Parks Department of New York City to hold a "Witch-in," which was held in Sheep Meadow and attended by more than a thousand. In 1999, about two hundred Wiccans and other pagans gathered at Halloween in Washington, D.C., "to show society who we are and what we really do," said Helen Roper, president of the Blessed Be Pagan Unity Inc.; and to correct the misconception that witches worship the DEVIL. They conducted a drumming ritual in honor of the ancestors at the Jefferson Memorial, a Samhain ritual, *Tambor to Oguan*, a Santeria service honoring Orisha, god of the forests and hard work, and a Radical Faeries ritual, performed by a gay men's group.

Wiccan ideas have been adopted by feminist groups as well, some of whom celebrate Samhain or Halloween with an emphasis on female spirituality.

Will-o'-the-Wisp (also spunky)— Like the JACK-O'-LANTERN, the will-o'-the-wisp (also known as *teine sith*, or "fairy light") is an enigmatic light glimpsed in bogs or swamps. These lights are occasionally thought to be the ghosts of unbaptized infants (the same explanation is sometimes given for PIXIES). Will-o'-the-wisp shares many trickster legends (a great deal of which are set on Halloween) in common with jack-o'-lantern, even though in reality these bobbing lights are a natural phenomenon known as *ignis fatuus* (meaning "foolish" or "false fire").

In the traditional Irish tale "The Three Wishes," Billy Dawson is a young rogue whose father apprentices him to a blacksmith. Billy eventually marries an equally reprobate wife, and descends ever lower into poverty and dissolution. One day he allows an old beggar to warm himself at the forge, and in gratitude the beggar — who is actually St. Moroky — grants him three wishes. Billy wishes for a hammer at the forge that no one can stop using until Billy releases them; an armchair that releases none who sit in it until Billy commands; and a purse that will open to none but Billy. For a while Billy uses these tricks to extort money from unwary neighbors, but eventually they catch on and he finds himself so broke that he calls upon the DEVIL. The devil appears and offers him an immense amount of money, but says he'll return for Billy in seven years. Billy spends the money in five, and is forced to return to blacksmithing, where the devil finds him at the end of the seven years. Billy persuades Old Nick to help hammer a last horseshoe, and the devil falls prey to Billy's enchanted hammer. Billy leaves him hammering for a month, then forces the devil to grant him more money and another seven years. Again, the money is gone in five, and this time Old Nick returns to find Billy fighting with his wife.

When Satan tries to protect Billy's wife, she surprises him with a blow that drives him back into the magic armchair. Billy takes advantage of the Devil's captivity to torture him by twisting his nose impossibly out of shape with heated tongs, and once again the devil grants him money and seven more years. As before, the money is gone before the seven years; this time the devil is wary of Billy, and tries to trick him by turning himself into a coin that he knows Billy will spot and pick up. Billy does, and once inside Billy's purse Satan announces himself, but Billy tells him he's trapped in the purse. Billy proceeds to place both purse and coin on the forge and sledgehammer them until the devil screams for mercy, which Billy grants only when the devil gifts him with twice as much money and the promise to never return. When Billy finally dies, he finds himself turned away from heaven, and so he turns to hell. Once informed that his old adversary Billy Dawson is at the gates, the devil is so alarmed that he runs to the gates and orders his men to keep them barred. Billy tries to shove his nose through the bars, and the devil tweaks his nose, which is set eternally aflame. Left with no other option, Billy wanders the earth with his flaming nose and beard tangled with wisps of hay, seeking bogs and fens into which he can cool his burning proboscis. Hence his name — "Will o' the Wisp" — and the relationship of bogs and fens.

Willows — One Halloween FORTUNE-TELLING custom dictates that a maiden take a willow branch (or wand) in her right hand (although it was a ball of YARN in some versions), leave the house unseen, and run around the house THREE times while reciting, "He that is to be my goodman, come and grip." On the third circuit the FETCH of the future husband would appear and take the other end of the willow.

In an American Halloween game, girls were given hoops made of willow and told to step through them while the hostess recited:

> The first to go through the willow hoop
> Will be the first to wear a gold one.

Willow sprigs and branches are also used in the Chinese festival CH'ING MING, and some modern WICCA practices also suggest the use of willow wands.

Wind — Several SUPERSTITIONS concern wind: For example, wind blowing over CORPSES on Halloween night will speak the future to those brave enough to listen. Wind soughing against the window on this evening predicts your death within the year. Wind at a CROSSROADS predicts events from the coming year.

In some parts of England people took CANDLES to the bottom of the garden on Halloween night to see which way the wind blew, for it would remain in that quarter for three months. If an easterly wind set in, it foretold sickness during the coming quarter.

Wind was also used to predict the WEATHER, as demonstrated in this adage:

Where the wind is at Hollandtide — that is,
All Saints — it will remain most of the winter.

In Cumberland, it was believed that whatever quarter a bull faced when laying down on Halloween, from that quarter the wind would blow through most of the coming winter.

Wishing— Closely connected to Halloween FORTUNE-TELLING customs were Halloween wishing rituals. For example, this Scottish Halloween night practice: Write your wish on a piece of paper and roll it up, then place it on the fire. If it burns up immediately, your wish will be granted, but if it chars and remains half-burned, you will be disappointed.

Witchcraft *see* Wicca

Witches— Not to be confused with WICCA and the modern practice of witchcraft, the idea of "witches" in connection with Halloween invariably refers to the stereotypical conception of a withered hag in league with the DEVIL, practicing her malicious arts with the help of a CAULDRON, a familiar (typically a black CAT), and an olio of herbs and strange animal parts. Or, from George William Douglas's *American Book of Days* (1937):

The witches held a party on Hallowe'en and the women, who seemed like other people during the rest of the year, but had sold their soul to the devil, would put a stick in their beds anointed with the fat of murdered babies. This would change itself into their likeness and they would fly up the chimney on a broomstick attended by black cats. They met the devil at a place arranged by him to which he rode on a goat. They drank out of horses' skulls and danced in a circle from west to east, or widdershins ... the devil played a bagpipe for the dancing and the revelers were

lighted by a torch between the horns of the goat. When the torch was burned out the witches gathered the ashes which were supposed to be especially potent in incantations.

The word "witch" originally comes from the old English word *wicce*, meaning "one who practices magic"; the root of *wicce* was probably either "to know" or "to turn aside." How witches came to be so strongly associated with Halloween is unclear; some scholars have suggested that witches represent early pagan worshippers, just as the devil and his demons are transformed pagan gods.

Although witchcraft is mentioned in the Bible in both the Old and New testaments, many early Church figures were opposed to the idea of its existence, including St. Hippolytus and St. Chrysostom; about the ninth century, the "Canon Episcopi" denounced the claims of witches to be able to fly. In 1258 Pope Alexander IV forbade the Inquisition to deal with cases of witchcraft unless they were related to heresy, but later theologians argued that witchcraft was a form of heresy because it involved a pact with the devil, and from 1398 on the Inquisition was given jurisdiction over such cases. In 1484 two German inquisitors (Heinrich Kramer and Jacob Sprenger) obtained a bull from Pope Innocent VIII giving them jurisdiction over witchcraft, and in 1487 they printed the bull at the front of their witch-hunting manual, *Malleus Maleficarum* (*"Hammer of Witches"*), so that it appeared to be officially sanctioned. From that point on, witch-hunting became a frenzy throughout Europe; witchcraft trials reached their height between 1580 and 1630. Probably about 50,000 were executed for this alleged crime, although some have also suggested the number was in the millions. In England, the worst persecution occurred during 1645–6, when the activities of the notorious witch-finder Matthew Hopkins led to 200 executions. Witch-hunting had basically ended by 1750; the last legal execution took place in Switzerland in 1782.

Halloween was supposedly one of the

four great witch festivals days: May Eve (April 30), called Roodmas or Rood Day in Britain and WALPURGISNACHT in Germany; NOVEMBER EVE (October 31), called in Britain Allhallow Eve; Candlemas (Feb. 2) and the Gule of August (August 1), called LAMMAS in Britain; all were, of course, celebrated at the stroke of MIDNIGHT. Testimony delivered during a witches trial in Aberdeen described typical witches' Halloween activities as including music-playing and dancing "wnder the conduct and gyding of the Dewill present withe you, all in company, playing befoir yow on his kynd of instrumentis."

Witches were greatly feared on Halloween, as seen in this saying from South Uist and Eriskay:

Hallowe'en will come, will come,
Witchcraft will be set agoing,
Fairies will be at full speed,
Running in every pass,
Avoid the road, children, children.

One British custom was to place food outside on Halloween for witches, since it was thought to be better to placate them with food rather than risk being the target of their spells.

Witches were supposedly capable of transforming themselves into any number of animals; one British folk tale tells of the killing of three Halloween witches, one in the form of an OWL, one a mouse and one a jackdaw. Another belief is that by injuring or killing a witch's familiar or imp, one would injure or kill the actual witch. Witches would stop mills, put boulders before ploughs, ride upon the ocean winds and upset fishing boats, and cause sickness in humans and livestock.

In Britain, a protection against witches was to plait pitchforks with burning STRAW and wave them overhead to singe the BROOMS of lurking witches. In Lancashire it was believed that witches gathered on Halloween at the Malkin Tower, a ruined and desolate farmhouse in the forest of Pendle. To keep them at bay, it was necessary to carry a lighted CANDLE about the fells from 11 to 12 on Halloween night; the witches would try to blow out the candles. Beggars went house-to-house, offering their services to "LEET THE WITCHES." In Scotland, witches were banished by waving torches and chanting the following:

This is the night of Halloween.
All the witches to be seen,
Some of them black, and some of them green,
And some of them like a randy quean.
Halloween we fear will come.
Witchcraft will be done by some.
Burn your brand and let us see
Confusion to the witches be!

(Black witches were those who had sold themselves to the Devil, and so were evil; green witches were good. A child's version of the above rhyme substitutes the pleasantly nonsensical "Some of them like a turkey bean" for the fourth line.)

Although witches are no longer feared on Halloween, they have remained a popular

These two vintage Halloween noisemakers show two different ideas of Halloween witches.

Halloween icon; not only are witches among the most popular COSTUMES each Halloween, but witches are even the subject of the most popular Halloween rhyme in England:

> We're witches of Halloween —
>   Woo-oo
> The ugliest you've ever seen —
>   Woo-oo
> We fly around at night
> And give you such a fright,
> We're witches of Halloween —
>   Woo-oo
> We're witches of Halloween —
>   Woo-oo
> Our faces are crooked and
>   green — Woo-oo
> We have black pointed hats
> And wicked witches' cats,
> We're witches of Halloween — Woo-oo

Titled simply "Witches of Halloween" (and originally composed by Cynthia Raza), this rhyme was popularized through its use on the BBC-TV program "Words and Pictures."

In America, Salem (once the home of the most widely-known American witch trials) is now a popular destination point on Halloween, and boasts a number of events as part of its Halloween CELEBRATIONS.

A prosaic American folk saying is that "On Halloween, witches ride their broomsticks to brush cobwebs off the moon."

Witches' Ink— An ink made of milk, strained lemon juice, baking soda and water; the ink is invisible until the white paper it is written on is held to heat. One early twentieth-century Halloween party GAME involved slips of paper on which fortunes were written in witches' ink. The fortunes were often amusing couplets, such as this example:

> You'll be a missionary and learn to sing and
>   shout,
> But cannibals will eat you, and finish you,
>   no doubt.

Withering Day— Like Winter's Day, this Finno-Ugrian day was celebrated in mid–October (the 14).

Nineteenth-century engraving showing the Salem witch trials.

Wood— One popular FORTUNE-TELLING custom involved floating a small sliver of wood in a glass of water by one's bedside on Halloween night, then reciting these lines just prior to sleeping:

> Husband mine, that is to be,
> Come this night and rescue me.

This would supposedly invoke Halloween DREAMS of falling from a bridge and being rescued by one's future intended.

A few different types of wood — including ROWAN and WILLOW— were also thought to have special powers on Halloween.

Wraith— Wraith can refer to the spirit of either a dead person (like a GHOST) or a living person (a FETCH). A report from the secretary of the Commonwealth in 1691 noted: "What the Low-countery Scotts calls a Wreath, and the Irish Taibhshe or Death's Messenger." Wraiths would also appear to relatives to warn of sickness or death, and were sometimes also called a *sith* (which is similar to a word for FAIRIES, *sidhe*). In their aspect as the spirit of a person still living, wraiths figure into the many Halloween FORTUNE-TELLING customs in which a young unmarried person is granted a look at his or her future intended.

X-rays — In light of fears of razor blades in APPLES (see URBAN LEGENDS), in the 1970s many hospitals began to offer free x-rays of children's TRICK OR TREAT candy, and positioned themselves as the last stop on Halloween night. Despite the fact that the American Association of Poison Control noted that x-rays could not detect poison or drug-laced candies (adding that hospitals might also be opening themselves up to litigation involving children injured by eating x-rayed CANDY), the practice has become what author Bill Ellis refers to as a new custom (in his paper "'Safe Spooks': New Halloween Traditions in Response to Sadism Legends"). In fact, hospitals have worked to make the practice entertaining for children, by having the staff dress in costume, by decorating the hospitals, and by offering the x-rays plates to children as Halloween souvenirs.

Xandu Ya — DAYS OF THE DEAD celebration from the Mexican state of Oaxaca, practiced by the Tehuanos (descendents of the Zapotecs). The holiday begins on October 30th, with memorial altars to deceased loved ones; anyone who has died within the previous year must have been dead at least forty days prior to the start of the festival. As in other Mexican Day of the Dead celebrations, dead children are remembered on October 31st, with adults following on November 1st and 2nd. The preparation of food offerings (atole, tamales) is shared by neighbors, as are the altars, which take the form of stepped pyramids. The altar, which includes a photo of the deceased as well as food and flowers, is called the All New Saints altar. The Tehuanos believe the deceased souls return during *Xandu Ya* as butterflies; the first night is celebrated with music and fireworks. In some houses the pyramidal altar is replaced with the traditional Zapotec *biquie*, a floor-to-ceiling offering of foods and flowers set up beneath two arching banana trees. Neighbors visit house-to-house offering small donations of money in exchange for ceremonial foods, and visits to the cemeteries are also conducted.

Xantolo — DAYS OF THE DEAD celebration found in the lush central Mexican states of San Luis Potosi and Hidalgo, and considered the region's most important festival. Huastecan members of the ancient Tenek tribe (relatives of the Mayans) celebrate *Xantolo* (a name derived from the Nahuatl language version of the Latin *Sanctorum*, or saints) beginning on October 28th, as bakers prepare special breads and family members who died in accidents are remembered. *Xantolo* continues on with a remembrance of children who died without receiving baptism (on October 30th), deceased children (October 31st), and continues through November 2nd celebrating dead adult loved ones (in some areas of the state, November 3rd becomes a day of ritualized cleaning and prayer offering to mark the end of *Xantolo*). Arches are a significant part of *Xantolo* decorating, and may be constructed both over an altar and at the entrance to a home; visits to cemeteries occur typically during the day, and music and dance (with the dancers usually in MASKS) also figure into *Xantolo*. However, this is one of the few areas in Mexico in which candy skulls do not typically appear during Day of the Dead celebrations.

Some areas of San Luis Potosi also celebrate the *Ochavario*, a period of eight days when the spirits are believed to still be present and food offerings are made throughout this time. The *Ochavario* usually ends on November 9th, when it is believed that the spirits depart, but in some areas it continues as long as November 30th.

Yann Postick—A Halloween folk tale from Brittany tells of Yann Postick, who ignored the duties of offering prayer for the dead on ALL SOULS' EVE and instead spent the night carousing in the tavern. At MIDNIGHT he drunkenly passed the CROSSROADS calvary, took the wrong turn and came upon a hearse drawn by coal-black steeds. Since the hearse blocked his path, Yann Postick shouted at it, and heard in response: "I seek Yann Postick." Suddenly Yann was engulfed in a shroud by the hideous "washerwomen of the night," who commanded him to wring it out. The more he struggled the tighter the shroud wrapped around him, while the washerwomen shrieked, "Forever we must wash our linens, in the rain, the snow and the wind. Cursed be he who forgets to pray for his dead." Then Yann saw their faces: They were his mother, wife and sister. The next day Yann was found dead, and at his burial the CANDLES continually blew themselves out. Yann was buried in unconsecrated ground.

Yarn—The most common Halloween FORTUNE-TELLING method involving yarn directed a young woman to throw blue yarn into a LIME-KILN in order to find out the name of her future husband. However, given the increasing scarcity of lime-kilns, over time the custom evolved to the point where the girl was simply required to throw the yarn out of a window on Halloween; while holding one end of the thread, she then rewound it while saying the *Pater Noster* backwards, and, upon looking outside, she would see her future husband. In one very particular variant, the yarn must be blue wool which has been teased, carded and spun by the fortune-seeker from the fleece of a male lamb, and the words "Wha hauds on to my clue's end?" must be spoken. Some versions of this custom specify that it must be performed at MIDNIGHT, while others state that the yarn must be wound back in "widdershins," or against the course of the sun. In another variation, the girl needs to simply roll the ball of yarn out a door and down some steps on Halloween.

In Wales, two girls made a LADDER of yarn without breaking it from the ball, threw it out the window, then wound the yarn back. This was done THREE times, and as the yarn was wound back the girls would see their future husbands climbing the ladder.

Vintage postcard showing colonials practicing a yarn divination.

An American version specifies that the yarn custom must be practiced around a barn, an old house or a cellar on Halloween; the girl would throw the yarn into the structure, then wind it back while repeating:

I wind, I wind, my true love to find,
The color of his hair, the clothes he will wear,
The day he is married to me.

The shade of the girl's future husband would appear to wind with her.

In another variation, a girl would walk around the outside of her home unwinding a ball of yarn while repeating:

Whoever will my husband be
Come wind this ball behind of me.

One fortune-telling custom dictated that a maiden take a ball of yarn in her right hand (although it was a WILLOW branch in some versions), leave the house unseen, and run around it three times reciting, "He that is to be my goodman, come and grip." On the third circuit the FETCH of the future husband would appear and take the other end of the yarn.

Upon occasion these fortune-telling methods could fall victim to PRANKING; for example, one tale told of a man who once hid in a barn on Halloween, since he knew a young lady would be visiting there at midnight with her yarn. When she threw the yarn in, he called out the name of a man the girl hated. The girl became very ill, and recovered only when assured it was a joke.

Blue yarn in particular is specified in most of these customs, and blue yarn also appears in some WITCHES' spells.

Yew— A ritual from Herefordshire specified that a young girl who wanted to see her future husband in DREAMS on Halloween should place beneath her pillow a sprig of yew from a tree growing in a churchyard in which she'd never been before.

Yue Laan (also known as the Festival of the Unforgotten Dead or Hungry Ghost Festival)— In the nineteenth century this Chinese celebration was sometimes referred to as the "Chinese ALL SOULS' DAY." It is held on Moon 7, Day 15, which is either July 15 or August 15 in the Western calendar; souls from the Buddhist and Taoist purgatory roam the earth on this day. In some areas of China it was known as the *Chieh Tsu*, or "Receiving Ancestors Festival." In most areas the festival lasted three days.

Yue Laan was similar to the Western ALL SAINTS' DAY observances in that it consisted mainly of honoring the familial dead, and visiting and decorating their graves. In the Chinese tradition, FAMILIES clean and decorate tombs (although most have already done this at the earlier CH'ING MING), where offerings of food and paper money (as well as other paper items, such as paper clothes or even paper vehicles) are burned. At home, wine is poured over the altar and firecrackers are lit to dispel evil spirits. The beggars of the afterlife are also offered something, and the local deity receives three dishes of food, three cups of wine, three incense-sticks, two candles, and three packets of paper money. At the conclusion, the family feasts together in the ancestral hall of the clan, and finally the head of the family puts paper money and other items in a basket and burns it at the door, saying "Goodbye, go quickly." The festival originally ended with burning lamps on lakes, but this practice was banned by the government as superstitious. Children were generally kept indoors at this time, to keep them safe from both GHOSTS and the poor.

In Formosa the feast in honor of the dead was once conducted in a different fashion: The food was tied in rows on great cone-like structures of bamboo poles, often as high as 50 or 60 feet. After the food had been offered to the spirits, it was offered to a vast mob who fought each other in their efforts to climb the structures. After the structures collapsed and deaths resulted, the practice was banned in 1894.

The Taiwanese call this day "opening of the gates of Hell." A banquet-sacrifice called *phó-to* must be prepared for the wandering souls. The Gates of Hell are open until the 30th, which is the birthday *of Te-châng ông*, the Buddhist saint who presides over the infernal regions and tries to release the suffering souls from torment. Figures of the generals *Fan* and *Hsieh*, guardians of the entrance to Hell, are placed around for protection. Ghosts without families have rites conducted for them on these days: Food is laid out before each house, and incense and paper money are burned. Lanterns are floated on rivers, and processions with lanterns along river banks lead the souls of those who drowned to their final resting places.

In Vietnam, the *Trung Nguyen* ("Wandering Souls' Day") is the second-largest festival (after *Tet*). This is the best day for priests and relatives to secure amnesty for souls in purgatory; on this day, the gates of hell are opened, and souls fly out, unclothed and hungry, so paper clothing is burned for them along with paper money.

Z

Zoos— Zoos in many cities throughout North America have become the focal points of civic Halloween CELEBRATIONS geared especially toward children aged 11 and younger. As an alternative to TRICK OR TREAT (which many parents believe to be dangerous) or HAUNTED HOUSES (generally deemed too intense for younger children), zoos offer a wide variety of Halloween activities for children. Many cities host "Boo at the Zoo" events, which typically include free CANDY, face painting, midway-style games, and educational events.

Oklahoma City Zoo's "Haunt the Zoo" will soon celebrate its twentieth anniversary, and is probably the largest Halloween ZOO event, taking place over six days and involving 900 volunteers (plus zoo staff). With over 30,000 guests each year, "Haunt the Zoo" is one of the zoo's biggest earners. Other zoos, such as Baltimore's, emphasize scary animals, including bats, snakes and owls; the zoo's two African elephants also participate in a "pumpkin smash" every year. The Louisville Zoo claims to host "The World's Largest Halloween Party," with a "trick or treat route" for costumed youngsters. New York City's zoo strives to offer activities for small-fry too young to take part in the city's Greenwich Village PARADE festivities.

Zuni *see* **Ahoppa Awan Tewa**

Appendix I
Chronology of Halloween

3000 B.C.— Egypt is united under one ruler (the pharaoh), hieroglyphic writing invented

1500 B.C.— Unknown Egyptian priest writes *The Book of the Dead*

1200–750 B.C.— "Proto Celtic" (Urnfield) civilization of the Bronze Age, throughout Europe.

939 B.C.— First record of Samhain occurs during reign of King Tigernmas (26th king of Ireland); he and many of his people are slain while worshipping an idol on Samhain

753 B.C.— Founding of Rome

750–300 B.C.— Golden Age of Greece

279 B.C.— The Celts suffer a devastating defeat at Delphi and move north and west in greater numbers

55 B.C.— Caesar invades Britain

45 B.C.— Julian calendar goes into effect

A.D. 1— Christ is born; the Christian era begins

A.D. 8— Ovid is exiled, never finishes the *Fasti* (Feralia and Lemuria still observed in Rome at this time)

A.D. 43— Claudius begins conquest of Britain

A.D. 51— The British leader Caratacos is taken by the Romans; Britain is conquered

A.D. 100–400— Ireland remains unconquered by the Romans, and now is the age of the Celts recorded later on (with Samhain celebrations at Tlachtga, etc.)

306–407— St. Ephrem Syrus and St. Chrysostom celebrate a feast similar to All Saints' Day

313–325— Christianity becomes the official religion of Rome

317— St. Martin is born

400–500— Christianity spreads through Ireland

538— According to legend, Festival of the Spirits (or Yue Laan) is first celebrated in China

601— Pope Gregory writes letter to Abbot discussing Catholic response to pagan temples and rituals

609— Boniface IV consecrates the Pantheon, sets All Saints' Day to May 13

657— First recorded celebration of Bon Festival in Japan

680— Christian Third Council of Constantinople tries to abolish bonfires

731–741— Pontificate of Gregory III, who moves All Saints' Day to November 1

742— Church condemns practice of "need-fire" as a pagan custom

800–1100— Christian monks set down Irish and Celtic sagas

827–844— Pontificate of Gregory IV, who orders universal observance of All Saints' Day

998— Odilon institutes All Souls' Day on November 2

999–1003— Pontificate of Silvester II, who approves All Souls' Day

1200— About this time the "Horseshoe and Hobnail Service" begins

1300–1400— All Souls' Day is placed in official books of Western Church

1471–1484— Pontificate of Sixtus IV, who adds octave to All Saints' Day

1487— *Malleus Maleficarum* is published; witchhunts begin in earnest

1493— *Festivall* mentions celebrating Halloween with "good frendes"

1509 and 1603— Henry VIII and daughter Elizabeth I both abolish bell-ringing on Halloween

1511— *Festyvall* mentions giving of "brade" to the poor on Halloween

1517— On October 31 of this year Martin Luther begins the Reformation

1548— First appearance of the poem "Tamlane"

1555— Ordinance passed in Scotland prohibiting the use of Lords of Misrule

1582— Gregorian calendar goes into effect in parts of Europe, shifting dates by 11 days

1584 — Alexander Montgomerie's "Flyting Against Polwart" appears

1585 — First report of guising at Halloween

1605 — On November 5 Guy Fawkes is apprehended; Gunpowder Plot is exposed

1606 — Guy Fawkes is executed; Parliament declares November 5 a holiday

1627 — Northumberland record book records bell-ringing on Guy Fawkes Day

1629 — Bulstrode Whitelocke oversees a festive Halloween gathering in Britain

1647 — Parliament bans all festivals except Guy Fawkes Day

1729 — First recording of the ballad of *Tam Lin*

1740s — First reports of Mexican celebration of Days of the Dead

1751 — Gregorian calendar accepted in England

1766 — Royal Criminal Chamber tries to limit Mexican Days of the Dead festivities

1772 — Thomas Pennant records Scottish Halloween celebrations

1782 — Last legal execution for witchcraft takes place in Switzerland

1785 — Robert Burns writes "Hallowe'en"

1786 — Charles Vallancey publishes mistaken interpretations of Samhain

1799 — *Statistical Account of Scotland* notes Halloween bonfires are attended only by children

1801 — Matthew Lewis publishes his Halloween ballad "Bothwell's Bonny Jane"

1814 — Sir Walter Scott publishes his novel *Waverley*, which includes the Halloween song "St. Swithin's Chair"

1820 — Washington Irving publishes "The Legend of Sleepy Hollow" and "Rip Van Winkle"

1833 — Guy Fawkes celebrations are abolished in America; Scottish explorer J. E. Alexander describes Halloween as a day for children

1841 — First mention of sugar skulls in Days of the Dead celebrations

1845 — Arthur Cleveland Coxe's book *Halloween, a Romaunt, with Lays* is published

1846–1852 — Potato famine in Ireland; many Irish immigrate to America

1847 — Officials in Lewes try to limit Guy Fawkes Day celebrations; compromise is reached

1859 — Special service for Guy Fawkes Day is excised from the *Book of Common Prayer*

1860 — Areas of Lincolnshire ban shooting on Guy Fawkes Day

1868 — Guy Fawkes pranking is banned in Guildford

1870 — First American mention of a Halloween party in *Godey's Lady's Book*

1876 — A *New York Times* article suggests Halloween's "glory ... has departed"

1885 — Magazine article has one of first mentions of jack-o'-lanterns used at Halloween

1889 — Vassar College holds a Mother Goose-themed Halloween party

1895 — Magazine article argues that May Day should become as popular in U.S. as Halloween

1898 — First Halloween book published (*Hallowe'en: How to Celebrate It*, by Martha Russell Orne)

1900 — Serious Halloween retailing begins in America with the B. Shackman Company

1902–1904 — Lady Gregory's collections of Celtic mythology are published

1904 — African American poet Charles Frederick White publishes "Hallowe'en"; the character Jack Pumpkinhead first appears in *The Marvelous Land of Oz*; "Halloween Night at the Seminary" becomes first Halloween film

1907 — Hatherleigh holds its first annual Guy Fawkes Carnival

1909 — Dennison begins publishing *Bogie Books*

1912 — Merchants in Danville, Illinois, begin hosting a yearly Halloween costume contest for children

1914 — James Joyce publishes *Dubliners*, which includes his Irish Halloween story "Clay"

1915 — Pope Benedict XV gives priests permission to say three masses on All Souls' Day; Sir James Frazer publishes 12-volume third edition of *The Golden Bough*

1916 — Dennison makes first commercially-produced Halloween costumes (from disposable paper); Toussaint is called "the most impressive holiday of the entire year" in France

1920 — Anoka, Minnesota, begins its Halloween celebrations; Prohibition commences, and adult Halloween celebrations begin to decline

1924 — A storage room in the Biltmore Estate is converted to the "Halloween Room"

1926 — Harry Houdini dies on Halloween

1927 — The phrase "trick or treat" is used with Halloween pranking in Alberta, Canada

1929 — Arthur Ford utters the key phrase during the yearly séance to contact Houdini

1931 — 7-year-old Truman Capote's Halloween party is protested by Ku Klux Klan; first animated Halloween film ("Toby the Pup in Halloween") is released

1933 — Destructive pranking causes some American cities to call Halloween this year "Black Hallowe'en"

1938 — Finnie's Club in Chicago begins yearly Halloween masquerade ball for "Female Impersonators"; National Magic Day on October 31st is instituted; Orson Welles airs "The War of the Worlds"

1939 — Robert Bloch publishes "The Cloak"; one of the earliest mentions of "trick or treat" appears in Doris Hudson Moss's article "A Victim of the Window-Soaping Brigade?"

1942 — Chicago tries to abolish Halloween because of destructive pranking

1944 — *Arsenic and Old Lace* and *Meet Me in St. Louis* become the first two major feature films to include Halloween scenes

1950 — Children first trick or treat for UNICEF; trick or treat is now widespread throughout U.S.

1951 — Modern Wicca begins

1952 — Disney releases the Donald Duck Halloween cartoon "Trick or Treat"

1955 — All Saints' Day octave (eight day observance) is suppressed by the Catholic Church

1962 — Bobby "Boris" Pickett releases "Monster Mash"

1964 — First recorded incident of tampering with trick or treat candy on Halloween

1966 — *It's the Great Pumpkin, Charlie Brown* debuts

1967 — First record of the "razor-blade-in-the-apple" urban legend

1968 — Campus massacre urban legends set on Halloween begin circulating

1969 — "Dies Irae" is no longer obligatory for All Souls' Day masses; Agatha Christie's *Hallowe'en Party* is published

1971 — Mexican government begins to promote Days of the Dead to tourists

1972 — Ray Bradbury publishes *The Halloween Tree*

1973 — Ralph Lee starts Greenwich Village Halloween parade; Knott's Berry Farm starts annual "Knott's Scary Farm" haunted attraction

1976 — "The Paul Lynde Halloween Special" airs

1977 — *Star Wars* is released, creating more adult interest in Halloween costuming

1979 — John Carpenter's *Halloween* is released

1981 — Nova Scotia begins its Halloween "Mardi Gras" celebrations

1982 — Steven Spielberg's *E.T.* is released

1983 — The seasonal Spirit Halloween stores first appear

1984 — Pamela Apkarian-Russell begins publishing *Trick or Treat Trader*

1988 — Alan Moore's *V for Vendetta* is published

1989 — Outbreaks of violence reported on Halloween in New York and in Boulder, Colorado's "Mall Crawl"; in New York, a group of costumed youths attack a homeless camp while shouting "trick or treat"

1990 — Lesley Bannatyne's book *Halloween: An American Holiday, An American History* is published

1991 — David Bertolino opens Spooky World

1993 — Tim Burton's *The Nightmare Before Christmas* is released

1995 — Stuart Schneider's *Halloween in America: A Collector's Guide* is published

1996 — Mexican clerics try to ban Halloween; Nova Scotia ends Halloween "Mardi Gras" celebrations; boom in U.S. Halloween retailing puts holiday second only to Christmas, with $2.5 billion spent

1997 — "The World's First Pumpkin Regatta" is held in New York; Mattel introduces annual Halloween Barbie doll

1998 — The first of J. K. Rowling's Harry Potter books is released

1999 — 17-year old Brandon Ketsdever is shot in Buena Park, California, for trying to steal a plastic Halloween pumpkin decoration; headstones are defaced in a Jewish cemetery in Milford, Connecticut, on Halloween; International Association of Haunted Attractions (IAHA) forms; annual Windsor Pumpkin Regatta in Nova Scotia begins

2000 — Justin Rudd's "Haute Dog Howl'oween Parade" for pets begins in Long Beach, California

2001 — In the wake of 9/11 terrorist attacks, a new urban legend circulates, warning people not to go to malls on Halloween; 185 students arrested after staging fake lynchings at Halloween party; Halloween retailing tops $6 billion; Disneyland starts seasonal transformation of "Haunted Mansion" ride into a *Nightmare Before Christmas* attraction

2002 — George Ratliff's documentary *Hell House* is released

2005 — Pamela Apkarian-Russell opens Castle Halloween Museum

2006 — Norman Partridge's *Dark Harvest* is published

2007 — Rob Zombie releases "reboot" of John Carpenter's *Halloween*

2008 — Michael Dougherty's *Trick 'R' Treat* is released; urban legend circulates on internet claiming local gangs will commit murders on Halloween night

2009 — Police in New Jersey issue warnings and curfews on night before Halloween; Guinness Book of World Records awards the title of "Largest Walk-Through Horror House" to Cutting Edge in Fort Worth; Halloween attraction industry grosses over $1 billion; Halloween retail spending declines slightly because of recession

2010 — Chris Stevens of New Richmond, Wisconsin, grows the largest pumpkin on record (1,810.5 lbs.)

Appendix II
Halloween in Literature and the Arts

The list below represents some of the short stories, novels, poems, films, television shows, comic books and songs that have either used Halloween or have become important in the celebration of Halloween (or related holidays like Guy Fawkes Day/Night). It is by no means a comprehensive list (children's Halloween books alone could fill up most of a book), nor is it intended to be a serious critical overview. It merely provides a brief look at how Halloween has been used by writers and other artists, and how these works in turn have affected the ways in which we celebrate Halloween. The list is presented in chronological order.

"Tamlane" (1548) — "Tamlane," a Scottish poem which tells of a young fairy prince and the brave woman who rescues him on Halloween night, is possibly the oldest surviving mention of Halloween in any work of fiction or poetry. It first appeared in 1548's *Complaynt of Scotland*, and has been adapted dozens of times since, most famously by Sir Walter Scott for his 1802 collection *Minstrelsy of the Scottish Border*.

"Flyting Against Polwart" (1584) by Alexander Montgomerie — More properly entitled "Montgomeries Answere to Polwart," this Scottish poem (which is actually a playful attack on one of Montgomerie's contemporaries) includes a frequently quoted description of Halloween as the night "when our good neighbors do ride" (the poem includes lengthy descriptions of fairies and other creatures).

The Shepherd's Week (1714) by John Gay — Gay's "mock pastoral" includes "Thursday, or the Spell," a section recording various forms of love divination; it is both the earliest work of art to make considerable use of these customs (including the burning of nuts), and one of the most frequently-quoted works in non-fiction books about Halloween.

"Hallowe'en" (1785) by Robert Burns — Possibly the single most influential work on Halloween ever written, Burns's long poem describes an eighteenth-century Scottish Halloween celebration in detail (including many different fortune-telling customs), and is often cited in studies of both folklore and Halloween. Written in Scottish dialect, the poem describes a group of young people who engage in divination practices involving nuts, hemp seed, corn (oats), apples and barley; most of the attempts at learning about future spouses end in unexpected and amusing ways. The poem depicts a Halloween celebration that is simultaneously mysterious, bawdy and frantic, and it remains a key source in our understanding of the history of the holiday.

"Tam O'Shanter" (1790) by Robert Burns — This poem tells the story of Tam O'Shanter, "That frae November till October,/Ae market-day thou was na sober." One night the drunken Tam sets off for home in a dreadful storm; upon finding himself near the haunted area of Kirk-Alloway, he stumbles across a witches' revel, presided over by "Auld Nick" himself. Tam's presence is unnoticed until he makes the mistake of shouting out a compliment to the dancing, and the festivities cease instantly. Tam finds himself now the prey in a diabolical hunt, and his faithful (and sober) steed Maggie heads for a nearby bridge, since the fiends cannot cross running water. The lead witch is so close behind them that she grabs hold of Maggie's tail, and pulls it out completely as Maggie makes it over the bridge. "Tam O'Shanter" makes no direct reference to Halloween (although in the line mentioned above it does seem to indicate that the new year begins on November 1), but its use of witches, the devil and a spooky ride have made it a Halloween favorite for generations.

"Bothwell's Bonny Jane" (1801) by Matthew G. Lewis— Lewis, the author of the Gothic classic *The Monk*, penned this imitation of a traditional ballad while residing at Bothwell Castle in Scotland. The poem tells of a young maiden, Jane, who is found sobbing by a monk after she's promised in marriage to Lord Malcolm. She confesses to the monk that

This metal tobacco tin shows Tam O'Shanter riding furiously to escape the witches (lower right).

she's in love with a young peasant, and the monk agrees to help her elope with the young man. On Halloween, the monk takes her to the river Clyde, then reveals that he is in love with her himself. Holding a knife to her neck, he forces her into a boat, but a storm arises and the ferryman tells the monk he must either throw Jane overboard or risk sinking with the boat. The monk does as instructed, and the ferryman is revealed to be a terrible demon that drags the monk down. Now, on every Halloween, legends say "that still the ferryman-fiend is seen/To waft the monk and bonny Jane." The poem originally appears in Lewis's collection *Tales of Wonder*, and has been reprinted numerous times since.

"The Legend of Sleepy Hollow" (1820) by Washington Irving—Perhaps the most popular Halloween story of all time, "Sleepy Hollow" contains no direct reference to the holiday, but nevertheless captures both the pastoral and macabre sides of the season. It tells the story of Ichabod Crane, a gangly schoolteacher with a fondness for Cotton Mather's *History of New England Witchcraft*, who comes to the little Dutch American town of Sleepy Hollow. Ichabod falls for the lovely young Katrina Van Tassel, but his rival for her affections is the handsome, boisterous Brom Van Brunt, nicknamed "Brom Bones." Kristina's father holds a party one "fine, autumnal day," when Ichabod dreams of wooing Katrina; but after a night of ghost stories—many about the Headless Horseman, the ghost of a Hessian soldier who

supposedly haunts the area—Ichabod is apparently spurned and rides home, dejected. Making his way through the dark night, Ichabod remembers the ghost stories at the party, and encounters the Headless Horseman, who begins to pursue him. The frightening chase ends when the spectre apparently hurls its head at Ichabod, but all that is found the next morning is a shattered pumpkin. Ichabod is never seen in Sleepy Hollow again, and Brom Bones, who marries Katrina after Ichabod's disappearance, is "observed to look exceedingly knowing whenever the story of Ichabod was related." The story has been filmed several times, most famously by Disney in 1949, and by Tim Burton (under the title *Sleepy Hollow*) in 1999.

"Rip Van Winkle" (1820) by Washington Irving—Set, like Irving's "The Legend of Sleepy Hollow," in a small Dutch enclave near the Hudson River, this classic tale tells the story of henpecked Rip Van Winkle, who, on "a fine autumnal day" (a favorite phrase of Irving's) sets out hunting with his trusty dog Wolf. Rip climbs high into the Catskill Mountains, and meets a man who calls him by name to help lug a heavy keg of liquor. Rip follows the man into a mountain glade where he encounters an astonishing group of folks dressed in archaic clothing, playing games. Rip is ordered to serve these strange beings, but can't resist sampling their liquor. He soon falls into a heavy sleep, and awakens to discover that his dog has vanished, his gun decayed, and his beard grown over a foot. He returns to his house, but it seems to have been abandoned long ago; he heads for the nearby village, but discovers that it, too, has changed. He finally realizes that he has slept for 20 years, during which time his wife has died and his children grown. A few of the villagers whisper stories of the long-dead explorer Hendrick Hudson, who, along with his crew, supposedly haunts the mountains, appearing once every 20 years. Like "Sleepy Hollow," "Rip Van Winkle" never directly mentions Halloween (which was probably still largely unknown in America when the story was written), but it has remained a Halloween favorite.

"Young Goodman Browne" (1835) by Nathaniel Hawthorne — Undoubtedly the most famous supernatural tale of early American witchcraft ever written, this Halloween favorite tells of Young Goodman Brown of Salem, who one night leaves Faith, his wife of three months, on a mysterious nocturnal errand. In the deeps of the forest he meets an older man, who is revealed to be the devil in disguise. As Goodman Brown plans to return to his wife and his sanctity, he discovers that many of his apparently–Christian neighbors and authorities are already in league with the dark forces; Brown's own will crumbles when he hears his wife being carried away by the worshippers of evil. He follows the voices to a witches' gathering, where the devil delivers a sermon which concludes with the pronouncement that "Evil is the nature of mankind." Just as the devil is about to baptize the unfortunate young newlyweds, Goodman Brown calls upon God, and instantly the congregation vanishes. Brown returns to his village, but can't stand the sight of the villagers, even though he knows the entire witch gathering may have been nothing but a dream he had while sleeping in the forest. He spends the rest of his life despising the company of both neighbor and wife.

"Halloween" (1842) by Arthur Cleveland Coxe — Coxe was an Episcopal bishop who was most well-known for his collection *Christian Ballads*, first published in 1840 and reprinted numerous times since. He first published his lengthy poem "Halloween" privately in 1842, but in 1845 it was published by H. S. Parsons in a book titled *Halloween, A Romaunt, with Lays, Meditational and Devotional*. Running 95 stanzas, the poem is largely a description of the glories of Heaven and Christ, although it does include a few lines that paint a colorful picture of Halloween ("'Tis the night — the night/Of the grave's delight/And the warlocks are at their play!"). The small volume is interesting mainly for being the first book-length work to bear the title "Halloween" (with no apostrophe).

"The Black Cat" (1843) by Edgar Allan Poe — Although "The Black Cat" contains no obvious reference to Halloween, its continuing popularity as a seasonal tale is due, of course, to its use of one of Halloween's classic symbols, the black cat. It tells the story of a man who begins life as an animal lover, who dotes especially on his black cat Pluto (even though his wife "made frequent allusion to the ancient popular notion which regarded all black cats as witches in disguise"). Unfortunately he becomes an alcoholic, and turns his increasingly evil temper on his cat, first gouging out one of its eyes, then finally hanging it. Later, experiencing both guilt and grief, he takes in another black cat, but soon comes to loathe it. One day he tries to destroy the cat with an axe, but when his wife tries to stay his hand he murders her instead. Since the murder has been committed in the cellar, he decides to wall his wife's body up behind the recently-plastered walls, and for a few days he seems to have eluded detection. But during the last police visit to the cellar, in his arrogance he raps on the very wall behind which rests the corpse, and a horrible shriek is heard. The police knock down the wall to discover the decaying corpse of his murdered wife — with the black cat perched on her head, wailing its fury at having been walled up in the makeshift tomb.

The Return of the Native (1878) by Thomas Hardy — Hardy's classic includes one of the earliest descriptions of a provincial Guy Fawkes celebration, and also explores the meaning of bonfires, and the wild, pagan joy they seem to produce.

"Ken's Mystery" (1883) by Julian Hawthorne — Julian was the son of Nathaniel, and was also a writer, who never lived up to his father's legacy (and who unfortunately wound up in fraudulent schemes which damaged his reputation and earned him a year in the Atlanta penitentiary). "Ken's Mystery," however, is considered a minor classic in the canon of vampire literature, as it combines Irish lore, vampires, and Halloween.

Cuchulain of Muirthemne: The Story of the Men of the Red Branch of Ulster (1902) and *Gods and Fighting Men: The Story of the Tuatha de Danaan and of the Fianna of Ireland* (1904) both by Lady Gregory — Isabella Augusta, Lady Gregory, was also a playwright and co-founder (with William Butler Yeats) of the Irish Literary Theatre, but she's most well-known now for her work as folklorist. These two books comprise the most popular collection of Celtic mythological tales, which probably originated from 800 B.C. to A.D. 500. Included here are a number of evocative tales centering on Samhain, Halloween's Celtic precursor; the eeriest is the story of Nera, a warrior who goes forth on Samhain, and first encounters a talking corpse before following a fairy army through the Hill of Cruachan and into the fairy world.

"Halloween Night at the Seminary" (1904) — Produced by the Edison Manufacturing Company in 1904, this short (featuring cinematography by the legendary Edwin S. Porter) may be the first appearance of Halloween on film. A bum interrupts a group of young ladies trying various Halloween divination rituals, including descending the stairs backwards; one of the girls mistakes the tramp for her future husband, then he's thrown out when she realizes her mistake. The girls continue their Halloween hijinks, bobbing for apples and finding a ring in a plate of flour, but when they're interrupted by a young man, they push him into the bobbing tub and pour the flour on him. This was the first of a number of Halloween shorts produced during the silent film era, and was followed a year later by American Mutoscope and Biograph's "Halloween," shot by G. W. "Billy" Bitzer.

"Hallowe'en" (1908) by Corporal Charles Frederick White — White was an African-American poet and soldier who served with distinction in the Spanish-American War. His collection *Plea of the Negro Soldier and a Hundred Other Poems* provides this poem, which is both an eloquent description of an early 20th-century Halloween celebration (centering on pranking boys), and a rare look at the holiday from the point-of-view of an African-American writer.

"Clay" from *Dubliners* (1914) by James Joyce — In this short story, we celebrate an urban Irish Halloween with Maria, "a very, very small person" who works in a laundry. After sharing tea and barmbrack with her co-workers (who tell her every year that she'll get the ring, even though she never does), Maria sets off for a Halloween party, stopping on the way to buy some cakes (since "they would be sure to have plenty of apples and nuts"). The party is full of games and children, nuts and port wine; at one point a variation of the luggie bowls are set out, including a saucer holding a prayer-book. Maria is blindfolded and led to the saucers, but she touches clay, and one of the adults present is angry at the children for putting that saucer out. When Maria is told to try again, she finds the prayer-book. The party ends when Maria sings a song, which causes her friend and host Joe to cry.

"Theme in Yellow" (1916) by Carl Sandburg — This brief poem set "on the last of October" captures a child's love of Halloween, without ever using the name itself. It describes how the color yellow appears throughout America at this time of year, in cornfields and in pumpkins, and it ends with the lines:

> I am a jack-o'-lantern
> With terrible teeth
> And the children know
> I am fooling.

"The Very Old Folk" (1927) by H. P. Lovecraft — Lovecraft, the most famous American horror writer of the first half of the 20th century, is most well-known for his cycle of "Cthulhu Mythos" stories, but he also penned this, surely one of the strangest Halloween stories ever written. Told in the form of a dream Lovecraft himself had on Halloween night, the story is a period piece set in a distant province of the Roman empire on the "Kalends of November." When a nearby barbarian tribe called the Miri Nigri begin a strange ceremony as the eve approaches, the Romans lead a military expedition into the hills to stop them, and instead fall prey to terrible ancient gods called up to wreak vengeance.

"Toby the Pup in Halloween" (1931) — Produced by Charles Mintz, this is probably the first animated short to feature Halloween. Toby the Pup and his girlfriend are holding a Halloween party, which is invaded by ghosts and goblins; Toby saves the party by pretending to crow like a rooster, sending all the spooks running from what they think is approaching daylight. Two years later, "Betty Boop's Hallowe'en Party" (directed by Dave Fleischer) offered virtually the same plot — Betty's Halloween party is crashed by Halloween spirits — but included even more Halloween imagery, with scarecrows, corn fields, jack-o'-lanterns, Halloween decorations, bobbing for apples, and snap apple.

All Souls' Night (1933) by Hugh Walpole — Walpole, a well-regarded 20th-century novelist descended from Horace Walpole, whose 1764 classic *The Castle of Otranto* gave birth to Gothic literature, wrote what is now generally regarded as the first Halloween-themed story collection. The 16 stories in *All Souls' Night* make little specific mention of the holiday, but all utilize some Halloween-themed element, whether it's autumn weather, saints, or ghosts. The story "The Oldest Talland," about witches, is probably the most well-known story from the collection.

"All Souls'" (1937) by Edith Wharton — Although known mainly as the author of such classic American novels as *Ethan Frome* and *The House of Merriment*, Wharton was also a gifted creator of ghost stories, including this one, which is regarded as one of her finest. "All Souls'" is about an isolated Connecticut house called Whitegates, and the house's widowed mistress, Sara Clayburn. On one particular All Souls' Eve, Sara encounters a strange woman approaching the house, and the next morning awakens to find the house mysteriously deserted by the five servants who work there. Eventually Sara ties the mysterious visitor in with Agnes, an aging servant originally from the Hebrides, and realizes the staff has fallen prey to dreadful superstition. Wharton also wrote a poem entitled "All Souls,'" which is a lovely and moody seven-stanza description of the evening (Wharton uses "All Souls" instead of "All Hallows," although she plainly refers to the "last day of October").

"The War of the Worlds" — Originally aired on October 30, 1938, this notorious Halloween prank begins with a famous line delivered by Orson Welles: "We now know that in the early years of the twentieth century this world was being watched closely by intelligences greater than man's and yet as mortal as his own." What follows over the next hour is a series of clever news bulletins documenting the arrival of a meteorite in rural Grovers Mill, New Jersey; soon the "meteorite" opens and reveals a monstrous Martian which kills the onlookers with a heat ray. Within moments the monster has wiped out nearly 7,000 soldiers and is laying waste to the eastern seaboard; soon more Martian "tripods" are spotted, and major cities are being evacuated. After the hero, Professor Pierson, meets another survivor who wants to steal the Martian technology to make himself an emperor, he returns to the streets of New York where he finds that the Martians are all dead, felled by simple earth bacteria. Presented by Welles, co-producer John Houseman and Welles's renowned Mercury Theatre, this live broadcast created a panic, as millions around the country took it for actual reports of an alien invasion, despite an introduction and commercial breaks. The broadcast concluded with Welles reminding his listeners that "it's Halloween."

"The Cloak" (1939) by Robert Bloch — This classic vampire tale is generally regarded as one of the first important works of short horror fiction dealing with Halloween. A man, Henderson, goes to a mysterious costume shop on Halloween and purchases a vampire's cloak — and in this case clothes make the man (or the vampire), as Henderson strides into an upper-crust costume party and finds he has an insatiable desire to sip the blood of the rich partygoers. As usual with Bloch, the story has a twist ending. Bloch mocks the costume choices of the wealthy, noting that "most people at costume parties gave vent to suppressed desires." The story has been reprinted numerous times, most recently in the collection *The Early Fears*.

Hallowe'en (1941) by Leslie Burgess — Borrowing liberally from Daphne du Maurier's 1938 classic *Rebecca*, this Gothic novel tells of a young bride, Claire, who is taken to live in her husband's remote Scottish castle; the castle was supposedly once the site of a great fight on Halloween, and the novel's plot builds to a tense climax in the castle on Halloween night. The book is chiefly interesting for being the earliest novel to both center its action on Halloween and to refer to the holiday in its title; it also includes some quaint passages in which the hero's mother reminisces about Halloween celebrations of her youth ("'I mind when I was young, the village ladies used to come to the houses begging for the fire. 'Gi'e's a peat tae burn the witches,' they used to say.'").

Arsenic and Old Lace (1944) — Frank Capra's film adaptation of Joseph Kesselring's comedic Broadway megahit moves the play's setting from September to Halloween, and in the process Capra created one of the most beloved Halloween family films. *Arsenic and Old Lace* opens with credits over Halloween graphics, and a card upfront confirms that the date is Halloween. We soon meet Mortimer Brewster (Cary Grant), a famed bachelor who is marrying his longtime sweetheart Elaine (Priscilla Lane). Unfortunately, Mortimer's honeymoon plans go awry when he discovers that his two sweet, dotty old aunts are serial killers, and his criminally insane brother (Raymond Massey) has just returned home to hide out with his sidekick Dr. Einstein (Peter Lorre) in tow. The films includes one interesting pre–trick-or-treat scene, as the two elderly aunts hand out goodies (including an entire jack-o'-lantern) to costumed children, who beg but never actually say "trick or treat." The film preceded the release of *Meet Me in St. Louis* by approximately two months, so it stands as the first feature-length motion picture to put Halloween on prominent display.

Meet Me in St. Louis (1944) — Vincente Minnelli's idealized musical about the Smith family in 1903 America, based on the novel by Sally Benson, features a long section set during Halloween. The two younger girls Tootie and Agnes blacken their faces with a charred marshmallow and head out costumed as ghosts to play pranks — they ring doorbells and throw flour in the faces of the adults who answer. The two girls meet a costumed gang of kids creating a bonfire out of stolen gates and carts. Adventurous five-year-old Tootie (played by Margaret O'Brien) takes on the job of pranking on the sinister Braukoffs, and after she completes the daring prank, she is finally allowed to participate in adding fuel to the bonfire. Later, when the Smith family hears Tootie screaming, they at first fear she has been hit by a streetcar, but it turns out Tootie's cut lip is due to a prank she played when she and sister Agnes placed a fake body on the trolley tracks. Although *Meet Me in St. Louis* is chiefly remembered for its performance by a young Judy Garland, it is also one of the earliest depictions of Halloween featured in a major Hollywood film.

All Hallows' Eve (1945) by Charles Williams— Considered the best of the early novels to center on Halloween, Williams's dark fantasy focuses on a group of Londoners surrounding "Simon the Clerk," a mage. Events build to the title evening, encountering along the way ghosts, magical rituals, and strange creatures. Williams was a member of the legendary group the Inklings, which also included J. R. R. Tolkien (*The Lord of the Rings*) and C. S. Lewis (*The Chronicles of Narnia*); unlike those two writers, Williams wrote entirely for adults, and he remains highly regarded among scholars of the fantasy genre.

"The October Game"(1948) by Ray Bradbury— A dissatisfied husband oversees a Halloween party in the basement, where the lights are turned off and various "body parts" are passed hand-to-hand in the dark. Toward the end of the game, the man's wife guesses the truth: that he has murdered their young daughter in an ultimate act of cruelty to the wife. The story ends with the line: "Then ... some idiot turned on the lights." "The October Game" is probably the most famous— and genuinely horrific— Halloween short story to deal specifically with the holiday.

"Trick or Treat" (1952)— It was a clear sign that trick or treat was here to stay when Disney based this popular Donald Duck cartoon around it. Directed by Jack Hannah, the short features Donald playing tricks on his three trick-or-treating nephews, until a witch helps the boys out by placing Donald under various spells.

"Shock Theater" (1958)— In 1958 Universal packaged 52 of its classic (and some not-so-classic) horror films under this umbrella title, and released the package to television stations across the country. That same year saw the publication of the first issue of the magazine *Famous Monsters of Filmland*, and what author David J. Skal calls "Monster Culture" was born. Although none of

Bela Lugosi in the title role of Universal's *Dracula*

the Universal films makes real use of Halloween, the films swiftly became holiday favorites, and over the next decade, Halloween gained new popularity thanks in no small part to the rediscovery of *Frankenstein*, *Dracula*, *The Wolf Man*, *The Creature from the Black Lagoon*, *The Mummy*, and the multitude of sequels, spinoffs and lesser creatures. Universal horror movie masks became bestsellers at Halloween, and the trick or treat experience often included a horror movie at the end of the night. "Monster Culture" also led to the popularity of the horror-show host, and characters such as Zacherley, Ghoulardi, Vampira, and, finally, Elvira, generated their own Halloween costumes and merchandise. "Monster Culture" also heavily influenced Halloween haunted houses, with many haunters such as Cortlandt B. Hull providing Halloween exhibits which painstakingly recreated scenes from the Universal horror films.

"Monster Mash" (1962) by Bobby "Boris" Pickett and the Crypt-Kickers— This novelty song can almost be described as the official Halloween anthem (or perhaps the "Jingle Bells" of Halloween). The song describes a party featuring Dracula, Frankenstein, the Wolf Man, and other creatures of the night, all delivered in a Boris Karloff impression that Pickett first used to win first prize in a Massachusetts talent contest (where he performed the song "Little Darlin'" in the inimitable Karloff tones). After the record was turned down by four major labels, producer Gary Paxton had it privately pressed and hand-delivered the single to radio stations all over California. The song was number one in the *Billboard* charts for two weeks in October 1962, and 40 years later is still played on radio stations all over the country every Halloween. The song was once performed by Karloff himself, on the television show *Shindig*.

It's the Great Pumpkin, Charlie Brown (1966)—This animated perennial holiday favorite was the second *Peanuts* animated holiday special (following 1965's *A Charlie Brown Christmas*), and remains popular nearly 40 years later. Written by Charles M. Schulz and directed by Bill Melendez, *Great Pumpkin* is about Linus's belief that Halloween has its own Santa Claus, a mythical character called the Great Pumpkin, who rises each Halloween out of the pumpkin patch he thinks is "most sincere," and flies through the night delivering toys to good children. While the other kids are out trick or treating (during which Charlie Brown, in a badly made ghost costume, gets nothing but a bag of rocks), Linus and Charlie Brown's sister Sally wait in the pumpkin patch, but the only thing to appear is Snoopy, who is pretending to be a World War I flying ace working his way through the trenches. In the end, Linus is undeterred and already planning his next year's vigil in the pumpkin patch. The special also spawned a very successful tie-in book, first published in 1967 and still in print (in a "35th Anniversary" edition).

Star Trek, "Catspaw" (aired October 26, 1967)—This episode of the original *Star Trek* series has the distinction of being the most well-known example of Halloween playing a major part in a work of science fiction with a futuristic setting (which precludes *E.T.*). Scripted by the remarkable Robert Bloch (whose Halloween credits alone span nearly 30 years), the story concerns a routine visit to a mysterious planet which goes horribly wrong when a crewman turns up dead. Captain Kirk, Mr. Spock and Dr. McCoy follow the trail from the dead man to a planet of witches, black cats, castles, magicians and skeletons, all controlled by two mysterious aliens named Sylvia and Korob. After comparing their surroundings to both Halloween and trick or treat ("you'd be a natural," Kirk quips to the pointy-eared Vulcan Spock), the *Enterprise* crew realizes that Sylvia and Korob have created all this from the human subconscious, in the mistaken belief that their visitors would find it comforting. When Sylvia turns on both the humans and Korob, she forces the Captain to destroy the device that has given the aliens their powers of illusion, and in the end she and Korob are revealed to be two tiny, dying, very alien lifeforms. Despite an obviously limited television budget, Bloch and director Joseph Pevney manage to combine distinctly opposite themes and iconography—horror and science fiction, Halloween and the distant future, rayguns and magic wands—to create a unique blend of genres.

Hallowe'en Party (1969) by Agatha Christie—Featuring Christie's beloved detective Hercule Poirot, this novel uses Halloween as a key element in a classic "who-dunnit" mystery plot. During preparations for a Halloween party just outside of London, a teenaged girl claims to have once witnessed a murder; later she is found drowned in the galvanized tub used in bobbing for apples, and mystery writer Ariadne Oliver goes to her friend Hercule Poirot to help solve the murder. Christie describes a classic English Halloween party: Aside from the deadly bobbing for apples, there is a decorating competition (involving miniature broomsticks), fortune-telling with mirrors for the girls (while the boys, some in disguise, sneak into the reflections!), and snapdragon (which one character describes as being "really more a Christmas festivity"). The novel also contains an apple motif: The house wherein the murder occurs is called "Apple Trees," and Poirot always associates apples with his friend Mrs. Oliver.

The Ballad of Tam Lin (1971)—Based loosely on the classic Scottish Halloween ballad, this was the only film directed (very stylishly) by actor Roddy McDowell. The milieu is moved to the "swinging '60s," with Ava Gardner as Michaela Cazaret, an imposing and fabulously wealthy woman who vies for the affections of Tom Lynn (Ian McShane) with the young Janet (Stephanie Beacham). Although the film omits any mention of Halloween (or fairies), it does include the ballad's animal transformations in the grand finale (now a by-product of an hallucinogenic drug).

The Halloween Tree (1972) by Ray Bradbury—Bradbury's book is less a novel and more an extended valentine to his favorite holiday, Halloween. A group of small-town American boys is costumed and ready to trick or treat, but when their friend and leader Pipkin is mysteriously absent, they find themselves at the center of a grand adventure to track down their missing friend. Their journey begins at the town's haunted house, which now sports a tree full of glowing pumpkins— a Halloween tree — and a whimsical owner named Carapace Clavicle Moundshroud. When Moundshroud discovers that the boys are ignorant about the history of Halloween, he takes them back into the past, where he shows them cavemen, ancient Egypt, Samhain, the Roman invasion of Britain, witches, Notre Dame, and Mexico's Day of the Dead; all the while the boys chase Pipkin's spirit. Finally at the end, the boys save Pipkin and gain an understanding of Halloween in the process. In book form, Bradbury's richly-written story is accompanied by Joseph Mugnaini's exquisite illustrations. *The Halloween Tree* was also made into an animated television special in 1993.

The Exorcist (1973)— While the plot of William Peter Blatty's memorable tale of demonic possession probably doesn't even need to be described, what must be mentioned is director William Friedkin's inclusion of a nod to Halloween in his film version: In fact, the film opens (after the prologue set in Iraq) on Halloween, as we discover when the possessed child's mother, actress Chris MacNeil (played by Ellen Burstyn), walks home from her day on the set and passes several gleeful trick-or-treaters. Friedkin's decision to include this reference is interesting on several points: Most obviously, of course, it foreshadows the evil events to come; but the scene also sets up a false sense of momentary happiness (Chris smiles to herself at the costumed, jack-o'-lantern-carrying children). The allusion also establishes a psychological question regarding Chris's own child, Regan: Why isn't she out with the other children? Although brief references to Halloween occasionally appear in other horror films, they usually take the form of jokes (i.e., Lamberto Bava and Dario Argento's 1985 *Demons*, in which a boy holds a cursed mask to his face and shouts out "Trick or treat!"). *The Exorcist* remains unique in its adroit use of a brief reference to the holiday.

The Paul Lynde Halloween Special (1976)— Until its 2007 DVD release, this comedic variety special was considered lost, although much sought after by fans. Lynde— mostly known for his snide comebacks on the game show *Hollywood Squares*— gets to sing, dance, and exchange jokes with guests Margaret Hamilton (for the first time reprising her legendary performance as *The Wizard of Oz*'s Wicked Witch), Billie Hayes ("Witchie-poo" of the cult television series *H.R. Pufnstuf*), and rock group KISS, making their network television debut here with three (lip-synched) performances. The show begins with a tribute to trick or treat, and includes witches, outrageous costumes, neon pumpkins, and other Halloween imagery that are rendered as kitsch and have contributed to the special's status as a camp gem.

Halloween (1979)— John Carpenter and Debra Hill's immensely successful independent thriller began the slasher-movie cycle of the 1980s, and spawned a whole new classic holiday character: The Halloween maniac. The film opens in 1963, with a prologue in which a small boy, dressed in his Halloween clown costume, knifes his sister to death before being discovered by his parents. Sixteen years later the boy, Michael Myers, is now an adult mental patient who escapes the asylum where he is being held. His psychiatrist, Dr. Loomis, tries to convince authorities that he believes Michael is headed back to his hometown of Haddonfield, Illinois, but they don't believe that Michael — who hasn't spoken in 15 years— is dangerous. In Haddonfield, the town is gearing up for Halloween evening. Laurie Strode is a brainy, virginal teenager who will spend her night babysitting. As Laurie entertains her young charge with pumpkin-carving and horror movies, she is unaware that Michael Myers has already struck, murdering several of Laurie's friends at the house across the street. The demented killer, wearing a cheap Halloween mask stolen from a local store, finally stalks Laurie throughout a two-story house; although Laurie is resourceful and manages to injure Michael, he seems unstoppable, at least until Dr. Loomis appears and empties his gun into the killer. Although Loomis has saved Laurie from Michael's rage, the killer's body — apparently shot dead by Dr. Loomis— is gone by the movie's ending, leaving Michael's demise uncertain. In addition to single-handedly creating an entire new sub-genre, that of the mad slasher horror film, *Halloween* also made a star of Jamie Lee Curtis, whose performance as Laurie Strode helps to elevate the film above the horde of imitators that were to come after it.

Halloween III: Season of the Witch (1982)— Certainly *Halloween III* ranks as one of the oddest sequels of all-time, not only because of the often-surreal images and bizarre plot twists of the movie itself, but also because it features none of the characters or situations from the other films in the series (except as scenes glimpsed on background televisions). The first *Halloween* employed the standard iconography of modern Halloween — pumpkins, costumes, haunted houses— but this sequel attempts to examine the historical (Celtic) traditions behind the holiday.

Halloween III: Season of the Witch

liott, a suburban California boy who befriends a lost alien (whom he at first mistakes for a "goblin"). E.T. spends his time under Elliott's care building a device to communicate with his home planet, which is put into effect on Halloween night (after trick or treating, which strangely occurs in broad daylight). Although Spielberg at first uses Halloween to create an atmosphere of fantasy (and, for the baby boomers in his audience, nostalgia), traditional Halloween symbols such as jack-o'-lanterns later become symbols of menace, as mysterious government agents close in on the extra-terrestrial. Although Elliott's mother is dressed in costume, Spielberg clearly uses Halloween's popularity as a children's holiday, emphasizing his themes of the innocence and trust of children. The film even created a popular new Halloween candy in "Reese's pieces" (which Elliott feeds to E.T.).

Day of the Dead (1985)—The third film in George Romero's zombie series almost seems to knowingly riff on *Night of the Living Dead*'s seasonal popularity by opening with a scene in which a woman lovingly gazes at a calendar opened to October and illustrated with a glowing photo of a pumpkin patch; we see by the date that it is Halloween. Suddenly the woman's reverie is cut short when the wall around the calendar erupts with hands, and the woman awakens from her nightmare. She is Sarah, a member of an elite scientific team attempting to halt the zombie holocaust that has now apparently destroyed the world. Sarah's team is at odds with its own protectors, a group of soldiers being whittled away by zombies and desperation. As the tensions between the two groups escalate, Sarah realizes that the scientists' experiments—even those involving "Bub," a thinking zombie—are destined for failure. When one soldier, maddened by injury, opens the protected complex to the zombies, Sarah and two others just barely manage to escape. In the end,

Conal Cochran is an Irish-American business mogul whose company, Silver Shamrock, has become the leading manufacturer of Halloween masks. A small-town doctor whose patient has been mysteriously murdered joins with the dead man's daughter to track down the secrets behind Silver Shamrock, and eventually they uncover the truth: Cochran is actually an ancient Celt who has equipped each mask with a small chip off a block from Stonehenge, and on Halloween night a television signal will activate the masks, killing millions of children in a huge Samhain sacrifice. The film concludes with a montage of children trick or treating throughout the United States and the suggestion that Cochran's evil scheme will succeed.

E.T. (1982)—There may be no greater testament to Halloween's popularity than the significant role the holiday plays in one of the most successful films of all time. Stephen Spielberg's beloved science fiction fable tells the story of El-

Day of the Dead

Sarah has found apparent sanctuary on a tropical island, and as she marks days off a calendar we see that it is now November 4, meaning that she and her two companions have survived both Halloween and All Souls' Day — or the Day of the Dead.

Trick or Treat (1986) — This uneven thriller and minor entry in Halloween cinematic history is notable for one thing: It may be the only film to exploit Halloween's supposed Satanic side. Main character Eddie is an introverted young victim of bully abuse who lives for heavy metal music. His idol is Sammi Curr, a heavy metal rock singer who dies in an apparent black-magic ritual near the film's beginning. When a local DJ (played amusingly by Kiss lead singer Gene Simmons) gives Eddie a copy of Sammi's final recording, Eddie takes it home, plays it backwards and resurrects the vengeful Sammi. Sammi's goal is to unleash his powers to their fullest on Halloween night, and take vengeance on the school where he was so often bullied as a child himself. The film throws in a fundamentalist preacher who condemns rock music (played by Ozzy Osbourne), but never seems to decide whether to become a black comedy or a horror film (it is especially unsuccessful in the latter attempt, featuring — until the climax, that is — the lowest body count of any horror film made in the 1980s).

Beauty and the Beast, "Masques" (originally aired 10/30/1987) — This romantic fantasy television series involved a "beauty," Catherine (Linda Hamilton), who falls in love with a noble, leonine beast, Vincent (Ron Perlman). Because of his disturbing appearance, Vincent lives in a secret community deep beneath the streets of New York City, and rarely ventures topside. In this Halloween episode, Vincent attends a Halloween party to meet an author he admires; after some political intrigue, the episode ends with Catherine taking advantage of Halloween's ability to render Vincent invisible, and showing him around New York. The episode used Halloween as a vehicle for tolerance and acceptance.

V for Vendetta (1988) — This 10-issue comic book written by Alan Moore (with art by David Lloyd) must be the only comic book to make considerable use of Guy Fawkes and the holiday that bears his name. The story opens on November 5, 1997 as a lone anarchist — who dresses in a Fawkes costume — blows up the Houses of Parliament in his first offensive against the fascist regime ruling this nightmarish version of Britain. Moore proposes a future (forward from 1988, remember) in which privacy, cultural diversity and art are all things of the past; the anarchist has escaped from a concentration camp, intent on succeeding where Guy Fawkes failed. Moore references both the classic Guy Fawkes begging rhyme (forgotten in this future), and the evening's traditional fireworks, which are wondrous to this London's stifled citizens. The graphic novel series was adapted into a 2006 feature film of the same name, starring Hugo Weaving as "V" and Natalie Portman as "Evey," the young woman whom V attempts to mentor.

The Nightmare Before Christmas (1993)— Tim Burton's whimsical stop-motion animation fantasy-musical is probably the greatest expression of love for a holiday (actually two holidays) ever put on film. The film is rich in Halloween imagery, yet manages to create its own new icon for Halloween in Jack Skellington, the Pumpkin King. The story begins in Halloween Town, as Jack (accompanied by his ghost dog Zero) broods over being stuck in one holiday forever; even the attentions of Sally, a strong-willed Frankenstein-like heroine, can't lift his spirits. Then, one day, Jack stumbles on a doorway to Christmas, and instantly seizes on the idea of using the denizens of Halloween Town to provide this year's Christmas. Of course Jack's plan goes badly, and in the end he realizes he is happy to lead the yearly Halloween celebrations. With songs by Danny Elfman (formerly of the rock band Oingo Boingo), *Nightmare* features a supporting cast of mad scientists, boogeymen, vampires, werewolves, maniacs, trick or treaters and other assorted things that go bump in the night, all installed in the gothic, skewed, headstone-laden realm of Halloween Town. The film not only became an instant cult favorite, it also provided a wealth of new Halloween collectibles, and, beginning in 2001, even led to a Christmas redecoration of Disneyland's famed "Haunted Mansion" attraction.

The Crow (1994)— Based on a comic book series by James O'Barr, this stylish thriller by director Alex Proyas spawned sequels, a television series and novels, and will also forever be remembered as the final film made by Bruce Lee's charismatic young son Brandon Lee (who died during the filming as a result of an accident involving a supposedly-blank gun). However, the film has a special standing within the history of Halloween-related cinema for another reason: It is the only major feature film (aside from its own sequels) to focus on the October 30 tradition from Detroit of "Devil's Night." The story features a gang of thugs who use "Devil's Night" as a cover for their own nefarious activities, such as extortion, rape and murder. After they kill two young people, Shelly Webster and Eric Draven (Lee), Draven's spirit is brought back to earth exactly one year later by a crow. Draven resurrects, gifted with supernatural ability, and sets out to exact revenge one-by-one on his killers. The film captures a completely unique (and utterly hellish) vision of a modern urban landscape, and because of its late–October setting, there are occasional glimpses of pumpkins, Halloween posters and even a group of trick-or-treaters, all of which Proyas seems to use knowingly to contrast the more innocent traditions of Halloween with the violent history of Devils' Night.

Buffy the Vampire Slayer (1996–2003)— No other horror-themed television series has used Halloween as many times as creator Joss Whedon's highly-praised series, or with such unique inversions. Its first Halloween episode was in its second season: "Halloween" aired on October 27, 1997, and established the amusing idea that Halloween is the one night out of the year when vampiric and demonic activity is quiet. When Buffy and her friends get inducted into assisting trick-or-treaters on Halloween night, little do they know that the costumes they have purchased are cursed, with the end effect being that they actually become the characters they portray. Unfortunately, Buffy has dressed as a colonial maid, and is now a shrinking violet with none of her slayer abilities or powers, leaving her small town of Sun-

The Nightmare Before Christmas (photograph by Joel Fletcher)

nydale to be overrun by transformed goblins and monsters.

Season Four featured the episode "Fear, Itself," in which a haunted house set up by a local fraternity really does become a haunted house when the frat boys inadvertently add a powerful occult symbol to the decorations. The haunting begins with a twist on the classic Halloween game, when a girl thrusts her hand into a bowl of peeled grapes that are supposedly eyeballs — only to discover that they are really eyeballs. (This episode also began with an amusing joke on the practice of renting scary videos for the night — Buffy's friend Xander is dismayed to find out that his copy of *Phantasm* is actually Walt Disney's *Fantasia*.)

Season Six had "All the Way," in which Buffy's younger sister Dawn runs off on Halloween to engage in pranking with some older kids, but is caught by a sinister old man named Kaltenbach. When Kaltenbach is revealed to be nothing but a lonely retired toymaker, Dawn realizes the evil force is not the old man but is instead her date for the evening.

Harry Potter and the Sorcerer's Stone (1998) by J. K. Rowling —

Buffy the Vampire Slayer

This first volume in Rowling's massively popular series (which spawned six sequels, films, merchandising, and even an amusement park) not only introduced the world to the heroic young Harry Potter and the secret world of wizards, but also established Halloween as an important date in Harry's world. Each Halloween, the wizarding school of Hogwart's gifts its students with a Halloween feast, which takes place in the Great Hall, is also attended by ghosts, and features enchanted decorations ("A thousand live bats fluttered from the walls and ceiling..."). The Harry Potter franchise has created an entire cottage industry of Halloween costumes and accessories (including broomsticks, wands, and robes), and the Castle Halloween Museum in West Virginia boasts a large display of Harry Potter collectibles in addition to its main focus of Halloween items.

Dragonfly (1999) by Frederic S. Durbin — Originally published by Arkham House in a small edition (4,000 copies), this novel has since been reprinted in mass market paperback, was a finalist for the International Horror Guild award, and has garnered a sizable following for its lyrical blend of young adult fantasy and Halloween mythology. It follows ten-year-old "Dragonfly," who's been hearing strange sounds from the basement of her uncle's funeral home. On Halloween night her uncle sends a friend, Mothkin, down to the basement, and Dragonfly impulsively follows. She finds an impossibly long stairway that leads them to the secret underground world of Harvest Moon, where the sky is lit by a giant glowing jack-o'-lantern and the ruler is a tyrant named Samuel Hain. On her travels through Harvest Moon, Dragonfly encounters hordes of gypsy cats, a village called Hallowe'en Town, vampires, and a kindly werewolf named Sylva.

October Dreams: A Celebration of Halloween (2000) edited by Richard Chizmar and Robert Morrish — This anthology of Halloween fact and fiction is probably the best collection ever offered of actual Halloween-themed horror fiction; it is nicely rounded out with Halloween memories from horror authors (including Ray Bradbury), "A Short History of Halloween" by Paula Guran, Gary Braunbeck's "'First of All, It Was October...': An Overview of Halloween Films," and Stefan Dziemianowicz's "Trick-or-Read," a comprehensive overview of horror fiction covering Halloween. Included in this collection is the award-winning short story, "Gone," by Jack Ketchum, in which a lonely woman and former pre-school teacher whose three-year old child has been missing for years tries to reconnect with her love of children by engaging in trick or treat giving, but the only three children who come to her door offer a terrible message about her daughter's whereabouts before disappearing into the night. In the series of 30 "My Favorite Halloween Memory" pieces, several writers cite Halloween as having been a major influence on their eventual vocation as horror writers.

"Mr. Dark's Carnival" (2000) by Glen Hirshberg — Originally published in the anthology *Shadows and Silence* and reprinted several times since (including in Hirshberg's 2003 collection *The Two Sams*), this acclaimed and multiple award-nominated novella explores the psychology and history of the Halloween haunted attraction. Set in a Montana city that celebrates Halloween on a grand scale every year, the novella tells of a legendary haunted house that may or may not be urban folklore. When college professor David Roemer receives a flyer with directions to Mr. Dark's Carnival, he and his girlfriend Kate follow the trail to a bleak location on the snowy Montana plains, where they are divided and led into a haunted house that combines traditional haunting techniques with strangely mundane images, suggestions of carnage, and pieces of local history (especially those centering on the notorious 19th century judge/executioner Albert Dark). The novella also mentions trick or treat, Halloween parties, and a home yard haunt that employs live spiders and cockroaches.

Donnie Darko (2001) — Richard Kelly's quirky drama about a boy with serious psychological problems takes place in October and includes a countdown to October 30, the day when Donnie believes the world will end. Donnie, who is in therapy, refuses his heavy prescription drugs and experiences visions of a demonic rabbit who exhorts him to various criminal acts, both petty and serious (arson). Donnie becomes obsessed with an archaic theory of time travel, which he knows will somehow intersect with an airplane crash that has already occurred. The film's climax takes place on October 30, at a Halloween party when costumes and masks lead to mistaken identities and tragic consequences. In the film's epilogue, Donnie's demonic rabbit friend is revealed to actually have been a mask created by his sister's boyfriend. The film uses Halloween to emphasize weird occurrences and Donnie's dark and dangerous state of mind.

The Orangefield Cycle (2001–2009) by Al Sarrantonio — Sarrantonio is an American editor and horror author who is perhaps best known for a series of Halloween-themed short stories and novels set in the fictitious east coast town of Orangefield (so named because of its spectacular pumpkin crops). In the first Orangefield story, "Hornets" (which originally appeared in the 2001 anthology *Trick or Treat: A Collection of Halloween Novellas)*, horror author Peter Kerlan writes a bestselling children's story called *Sam Hain and the Halloween That Almost Wasn't,* while dealing with the Halloween appearances of the fearsome Samhain, the Celtic Lord of Death. In 2002, Sarrantonio extended the saga with the first novel, *Orangefield*, in which Samhain controls various citizens in Orangefield and steers them towards an apocalyptic Halloween. Sarrantonio continued the cycle through the novels and stories *Hallows Eve* (2004), *The Pumpkin Boy* (2005), *The Baby* (2006), *Halloweenland* (2007), and "All Souls Day" (2009). Sarrantonio also edited 2010's anthology *Halloween: New Poems.*

Hell House (2002) — George Ratliff's award-winning documentary focuses on the design, construction, and operation of a "hell house," or Christian haunted house, in Cedar Hill, Texas. The film not only follows the lives of various members of the evangelical church producing the attraction, but it also provides the only in-depth look at a "Hell House" available anywhere. Ratliff presents a largely unbiased point of view as he shows scenes from the Hell House horrifically depicting date rape, AIDS, abortion, and of course Hell.

I Luv Halloween (2005–2008) by Keith Giffen (writing) and Benjamin Roman (art) — This graphic novel series originally appeared as three separate black and white volumes, then was colorized and collected into a single "Ultimate Twisted Edition" in 2008. Offering up what must be the most irreverent look at Halloween on record, the series follows the adventures of a group of trick-or-treating boys, with each volume offering a different twist: In volume 1, leader Finch's little sister Moochie endangers his trick-or-treating by creating havoc throughout the town; in the second volume, Halloween occurs during a zombie outbreak; and in the final volume, the kids contend with an alien invasion during Halloween. *Publishers Weekly* reviewed the series favorably, noting: "Full of ghoulish tricks, *I Luv Halloween* is a seasonal treat that the not easily offended will thoroughly enjoy."

Dark Harvest (2006) by Norman Partridge — This award-winning short novel was originally published in a limited edition by Cemetery Dance and later published in paperback by Tor, and was named one of *Publisher's Weekly* "100 Best Books of 2006." Set in a small town in 1963, it follows the October Boy, a pumpkin-headed living legend, as he is hunted by the town's young men; the winner gets a ticket out of town ... or so the boys are told. Partridge's acclaimed book (which won the Bram Stoker Award and was a finalist for the World Fantasy Award) is rich in Halloween iconography but also dissects the American dream and the myth of the small town.

Halloween (2007) — Filmmaker/musician Rob Zombie "rebooted" the *Halloween* franchise with this remake of Carpenter's classic. Zombie, who wrote and directed, extended the original's story by focusing more on killer Michael Myers' childhood, showing the boy as the product of a stripper mother and abusive stepfather. Zombie retained most of the plot and Halloween imagery of the original film, and (in what is becoming a trademark for him)

Cover of Al Sarrantonio's 2009 "Orangefield" book *Halloweenland* (courtesy of Cemetery Dance)

packed his cast with character actors from 1970s and 1980s horror films, including Malcolm McDowell (who plays Dr. Loomis, the psychiatrist played by Donald Pleasance in the original version), Dee Wallace, Richard Lynch, Udo Kier, etc. Two years later Zombie also wrote and produced a sequel, *Halloween II*.

Trick 'r Treat (2008) — Writer/director Michael Dougherty's well-reviewed anthology film features four interwoven Halloween stories that each explore some different aspect of the holiday: In one, a man (Dylan Baker) who is actually a serial killer teaches his son to carve jack-o'-lanterns;

in the second, a shy girl (Anna Paquin) arrives for a party in the woods only to discover a deadly secret; the third centers on a group of trick-or-treaters who get more than they bargained for when they follow an urban legend; and in the last, a holiday-hating old man (Brian Cox) encounters "Sam," a Halloween spirit with a misshapen head that looks like a rotting pumpkin. Dougherty's film (which won the Audience Award at the 2008 Screamfest and the Silver Audience Award at 2009's Toronto After Dark Film Festival) spawned toys (depicting Sam) and a graphic novel.

Bibliography

Acland, Abigail. *The Tam Lin Pages*, www.tam-lin.org

Addis, M. E. Leicester. "A Modern May Day," *Frank Leslie's Popular Monthly*, Vol. XXXIX, No. 5, May, 1895.

Addy, Sidney Oldall. *Household Tales with Other Traditional Remains*. London: David Nutt in the Strand, 1895.

Adler, Margot. *Drawing Down the Moon: Witches, Druids, Goddess Worshippers, and Other Pagans in America Today*. Revised and expanded edition. New York: Penguin and Arkana, 1997.

Alexander, Captain J. E. *Transatlantic Sketches, Comprising Visits to the Most Interesting Scenes of North and South America, and the West Indies*. Philadelphia: Key and Biddle. 1833.

Allibone, S. Austin. *A Critical Dictionary of English Literature and British and American Authors*. Philadelphia: J. B. Lippincott. 1891.

Ambrosi, Marietta. *When I Was a Girl in Italy*. Boston: Lothrop, Lee and Shepard, 1906.

"Ancient Customs Which Prevail in the County of Northumberland; with Conjectures Concerning Them," *The Universal Magazine: New Series*. Vol. XX, No. CXX, November, 1813.

Andrade, Mary J. *Day of the Dead in Mexico: Through the Eyes of the Soul: Michoacan*. 3rd ed. San Jose: La Oferta Review Newspaper, 2003.

_____. *Day of the Dead in Mexico: Through the Eyes of the Soul: Oaxaca*. 2nd ed. San Jose: La Oferta Review, 2002.

_____. *Day of the Dead in Mexico: Through the Eyes of the Soul: Puebla, Tlaxcala, San Luis Potosi, Hidalgo*. San Jose: La Oferta Review, 2002.

_____. *Day of the Dead in Mexico: Through the Eyes of the Soul: Yucatan*. San Jose: La Oferta Review, 2003.

Andrews, Alexander. *Long Ago: A Journal of Popular Antiquities*. London: F. Arnold, 1873.

Anoka: Halloween Capital of the World. www.anokahalloween.com

Apkarian-Russell, Pamela. *Collectible Halloween*, Atglen, PA: Schiffer, 1997.

_____. *Halloween: Collectible Decorations and Games*. Atglen, PA: Schiffer, 2000.

_____. *More Halloween Collectibles: Anthropomorphic Vegetables and Fruits of Halloween*. Atglen, PA: Schiffer, 1998.

Arkins, Diane C. *Halloween: Romantic Art and Customs of Yesteryear*. Gretna: Pelican, 2000.

Ashley, Leonard R. N. *The Amazing World of Superstition, Prophecy, Luck, Magic and Witchcraft*. New York: Bell, 1988.

Atkinson, J. C. *Forty Years in a Moorland Parish*. London and New York: Macmillan, 1891.

Bailey, Cyril. *Phases in the Religion of Ancient Rome*. Berkeley: University of California Press, 1932.

Bailey, Helen Miller. *Santa Cruz of the Etla Hills*. Gainesville: University of Florida Press, 1958.

Baker, Anne Elizabeth. *Glossary of Northamptonshire Words and Phrases*, Vol. 2. London: John Russell Smith, 1854.

Baker, Margaret. *Folklore and Customs of Rural England*. London: David and Charles, 1974.

Balderston, Robert R. and Margaret, *Ingleton, Bygone and Present*. Skipton: Edmondson, 1888.

Bannatyne, Lesley Pratt. *Halloween: An American Holiday, an American History*. New York and Oxford: Facts on File, 1990.

_____. *A Halloween How-To: Costumes, Parties, Decorations, and Destinations*. Gretna: Pelican, 2001.

Barber, Edward, and P. H. Ditchfield, *Memorials of Old Cheshire*. London: George Allen and Sons, 1910.

Barbour, John Gordon. *Unique Traditions Chiefly of the West and South of Scotland*. London: Hamilton, Adams, 1886.

Barrett, W. H. *More Tales from the Fens*. London: Routledge and Kegan, 1964.

Barth, Edna. *Witches, Pumpkins, and Grinning Ghosts: The Story of the Halloween Symbols*. New York: Ticknor and Fields, 1972.

Baum, L. Frank. *The Marvelous Land of Oz*. Chicago: Reilly and Britton, 1904.

Bauman, Richard. "Belsnickling in a Nova Scotia Island Community," *Western Folklore*, Vol. 31, No. 4 (October 1972): 229–43.

BBC — Northern Ireland. www.bbc.co.uk/northernireland/

Becerra, Hector, and David Pierson. "Scarier Than Usual Holiday," *Los Angeles Times*, November 1, 2001: B3.

Beck, Ervin. "Rhymes and Songs for Halloween and Bonfire Night," *Lore and Language*, Vol. 4, No. 2 (July 1985): 1–17.

Beesley, Colin. "The American Hobo," The University of Leeds, University College of Ripon and York St. John, 2006.

Behan, Michele. "The Hair-Raising Prices of Dennison's Bogie Books," *BookThink*, http://www.bookthink.com/0106/106beh1.htm

Belk, Russell W. "Carnival, Control, and Corporate Culture in Contemporary Halloween Celebrations," In *Halloween and Other Festivals of Death and Life*, edited by Jack Santino. Knoxville: University of Tennessee Press, 1994.

Benton, Caroline French. *Easy Entertaining*. Boston: The Page Company. 1917.

Best, Henry. *The Farming and Account Books of Henry Best*, Vol. 33. Durham: Surtees Society, 1857.

Best, Joel, and Gerald T. Horiuchi. "The Razor Blade in the Apple: The Social Construction of Urban Legends," *Social Problems*, Vol. 32, No. 5 (June 1985): 488–99.

Black, William. "A Halloween Wraith" *Harper's New Monthly Magazine*, Vol. LXXXI, No. 486 (November 1890).

Blackburn, Bonnie, and Leofranc Holford-Stevens. *The Oxford Book of Days*. Oxford: Oxford University Press, 2000.

Bladen, W. Wells. *Notes on the Folk-Lore of North Staffordshire*, London, 1901.

Bladey, Conrad Jay. *Bonfire Prayers, Customs, Recipes, Songs, and Chants for Guy Fawkes Day*. Linthicum, MD: Hutman Productions, 2000.

_____. *The Irish Customs of November Night, or Samhain, or Halloween*. Linthicum, MD: Hutman Productions, 1999.

Blain, Mary E. *Games for Hallowe'en*. New York: Barse and Hopkins, 1912.

Bloch, Robert. *The Early Fears*. Minneapolis, MN: Fedogan and Bremer, 1994.

Borten, Helen. *Halloween*. New York: Thomas Y. Crowell, 1965.

Bourque, Nicole. "Eating Your Words: Communicating with Food in the Ecuadorian Andes," *An Anthropology of Indirect Communication*, edited by Joy Hendry and C. W. Watson, London: Routledge, 2001.

Bowker, James. *Goblin Tales of Lancashire*. London: W. Swan Sonnenschein, n.d.

Bradbury, Ray. *From the Dust Returned*. New York: William Morrow, 2001.

_____. *The Halloween Tree*. New York: Alfred A. Knopf, 1972.

_____. *Long After Midnight*., New York: Alfred A. Knopf, 1986.

_____. *Something Wicked This Way Comes*. New York: Simon and Schuster, 1962.

Brand, John. *Observations on Popular Antiquities*. London: Chatto and Windus, 1913.

Brandes, Stanley. "The Day of the Dead, Halloween, and the Quest for Mexican National Identity," *Journal of American Folklore*, Vol. 111, No. 442 (Fall 1998): 359–80.

Brasse, Denise. "He's Got Spirit: Spencer Gifts CEO Talks Halloween, CIT and Retail Careers," http://blog.nrf.com/2009/10/23/hes-got-spirit-spencer-gifts-ceo-talks-halloween-cit-and-retail-careers/

Braunbeck, Gary A. "'First of All, It Was October…': An Overview of Halloween Films," In *October Dreams: A Celebration of Halloween*, edited by Richard Chizmar and Robert Morrish. Baltimore: Cemetery Dance, 2000.

Bray, Mrs. *The Borders of the Tamar and the Tavy*, Vol. I. London: W. Kent, 1879.

Brewer's Dictionary of Phrase and Fables. In Bibliomania: Free Online Literature and Study Guides. http://www.bibliomania.com/2/3/255/frameset.html

Briggs, Katharine. *British Folktales*, New York: Pantheon, 1977.

_____. *The Fairies in Tradition and Literature*. London: Routledge and Kegan Paul, 1967.

Brunvand, Jan Harold. *The Baby Train and Other Lusty Urban Legends*. New York and London: W. W. Norton, 1993.

Bulfinch, Thomas. *Bulfinch's Mythology: The Age of Fable*. In Bulfinch's Mythology. http://www.bulfinch.org/

Burgess, Leslie. *Hallowe'en*. New York: G. P. Putnam's Sons, 1941.

Burne, Charlotte Sophia. *Shropshire Folk-Lore: A Sheaf of Gleanings*. London: Trubner, 1883.

Burns, Alice Hale. *Hallowe'en at Merryvale*. New York: New York Book Co., 1916.

Burns, Robert. *Robert Burns: Selected Poems*. Edited by Carol McGuirk. London: Penguin, 1993.

_____. *The Works of Robert Burns*. Edited by James Currie. New York: William Borradaile, 1826.

Burt, Edward. "Letters from a Gentleman in the

North of Scotland" (1754). In *Beyond the Highland Line: Three Journals of Travel in 18th Century Scotland: Burt, Pennant and Thornton*. Edited by A. J. Youngson. London: Collins, 1974.

Burton, Thomas. *The History and Antiquities of the Parish of Hemingborough*. York: Sampson Brothers, 1888.

Bye-Gones Relating to Wales and the Border Counties 1899–1900. Oswestry and Wrexham: Woodall, Minshall, Thomas, 1900.

Cadigan, Lisa C., and Vicki Duckett. "Halloween at the Zoo: A Spooktacular Idea," *Communique*, October 2001: 6–7.

Campanelli, Dan, and Pauline Campanelli. *Halloween Collectables: A Price Guide*. Gas City, IN: L-W Books, 1995.

Campbell, Alan, and David S. Noble. *Japan: An Illustrated Encyclopedia*. 2 vols. Tokyo: Kodansha, 1993.

Campbell, Helen. *The American Girl's Home Book of Work and Play*. New York and London: G. P. Putnam's Sons, 1894.

Campbell, John Gregorson. *Superstitions of the Highlands and Islands of Scotland*. Glasgow: James MacLehose and Sons, 1900.

_____. *Witchcraft and Second Sight in the Scottish Highlands*. Glasgow: MacLeod, 1902.

Carey, George. *A Faraway Time and Place: Lore of the Eastern Shore*. Washington, D.C.: Robert B. Luce, 1971.

Carley, Rachel. *A Guide to the Biltmore Estate*. Asheville, NC: Biltmore Company, 2001.

Carmichael, Elizabeth, and Chloë Sayer. *The Skeleton at the Feast: The Day of the Dead in Mexico*. Austin: University of Texas Press, 1991.

Carpentier, Gary, and Louise Carpentier. *Halloween Postcards: A Pictorial Catalog of Over 3,000 Old Postcards in Color with Valuation Guide*. 2nd ed. Golden Valley, MN: G & L Postcards, 2003.

Castle Halloween, www.castlehalloween.com

Catholic Online. www.catholic.org

Chafets, Ze'ev. *Devil's Night and Other True Tales of Detroit*. New York: Random House, 1990.

Chambers, R. *Chambers's Book of Days*. 2 vols. Philadelphia: J. B. Lippincott, 1879.

Chase, Richard. *American Folk Tales and Songs*. New York: Dover Publications, 1971.

Chavez, Jerry R. *Haunted House Halloween Handbook*. Jefferson, NC: McFarland, 1997.

Chizmar, Richard, and Robert Morrish. *October Dreams: A Celebration of Halloween*. Baltimore: Cemetery Dance, 2000.

Christie, Agatha. *Hallowe'en Party*. New York: Dodd, Mead, 1969.

Clynes, Tom. *Wild Planet! 1,001 Extraordinary Events for the Inspired Traveler*. Detroit: Visible Ink Press, 1995.

Coffin, Tristram P., and Hennig Cohen. *Folklore in America*. Garden City: Doubleday, 1966.

Cohen, Hennig, and Tristram Potter Coffin. *The Folklore of American Holidays*. 3rd ed. Detroit: Gale Research, 1987.

"Consumers Greet Halloween with Enthusiasm," *About.com*. retailindustry.about.com/library/bl/q4/bl_nrf101001.htm

Cordingly, David. *Under the Black Flag: The Romance and the Reality of Life Among the Pirates*. New York: Random House, 1996.

Cossins, James. *Reminiscences of Exeter Fifty Years Since*. 2nd ed. Exeter: William Pollard, 1878.

Cox, J. Charles, editor. *Memorials of Old Derbyshire*. Derby: Bemrose, 1907.

Coxe, Arthur Cleveland. *Hallowe'en, A Romaunt, with Lays, Meditative and Devotional*. Hartford: H. S. Parsons, 1845.

Coxe, William. *A Historical Tour Through Monmouthshire*. 2nd ed. Brecon: Davies, 1904.

Crawford, Ann Cadell. *Customs and Culture of Vietnam*. Rutland, VT: Charles E. Tuttle, 1966.

Cromek, R. H. *Remains of Nithsdale and Galloway Song*. Paisley: Alexander Gardner, 1880.

Cross, F. L., and E. A. Livingstone, editors. *The Oxford Dictionary of the Christian Church*. 3rd ed. New York: Oxford University Press, 1997.

Crump, William D. *The Christmas Encyclopedia*. Jefferson, NC: McFarland, 2001.

Cullen, James Bernard. *The Story of the Irish in Boston*. Boston: James B. Cullen, 1889.

Cumbow, Robert C. *Order in the Universe: The Films of John Carpenter*. 2nd ed. Lanham, Maryland and London: Scarecrow, 2000.

Cunliffe, Barry. *The Ancient Celts*. Oxford and New York: Oxford University Press, 1997.

Curott, Phyllis. *Book of Shadows: A Modern Woman's Journey into the Wisdom of Witchcraft and the Magic of the Goddess*. New York: Broadway Books, 1998.

Dana, Olive E. "A Halloween Party: An Occasion Pleasantly Remembered," *Good Housekeeping*, October 11, 1890.

Davies, J. C. *Folklore of West and Mid-Wales*. Aberstwyth: Welsh Gazette Offices, 1911.

Davis, Hubert J. *The Silver Bullet and Other American Witch Stories*. Middle Village, NY: Jonathan David, 1975.

"The Decadence of Halloween," *New York Times*, November 1, 1876.

Dégh, Linda. *Legend and Belief: Dialectics of a Folklore Genre*. Bloomington: Indiana University Press, 2001.

Dennison's Bogie Book. Framingham, MA.: Dennison Manufacturing, various years.

Denton, Clara J. *Creepy Hallowe'en Celebrations*. Dayton, Ohio: Paine, 1926.

Derry City Council. www.derrycity.gov.uk

"Detroit Citizens Help Deter Devil's Night Fire," *Student Publications Inc., Kansas State University*. www.spub.ksu.edu/issues/v100/fa/n052/ap-DevilsNight-11.3.html

Dillon, Myles. *The Cycles of the Kings*. London: Oxford University Press, 1946.

Dolan, Lenore K. *Handy Helps for Hallowe'en*. Dayton, Ohio: Paine, 1932.

Douglas, George Bart. *Scottish Fairy and Folk-Tales*. London and Felling-on-Tyne: Walter Scott, ca. 1920.

Douglas, George William. *The American Book of Days*. New York: H. W. Wilson, 1937.

Dracula Tour of Transylvania. www.dractour.com

Dugdale, Sir William. *The Antiquities of Warwickshire*. London: John Osborn and Thomas Longman, 1730.

Dunwich, Gerina. *The Pagan Book of Halloween*. New York: Penguin/Compass, 2000.

_____. *The Wicca Book of Days*. Secaucus, NJ: Carol Publishing, 1995.

Durbin, Frederic S. *Dragonfly*. Sauk City: Arkham House, 1999.

Dyer, T. F. Thiselton. *British Popular Customs: Present and Past*. London: George Bell and Sons, 1900.

Dziemianowicz, Stefan. "Trick-or-Read: A Reader's Guide to Halloween Fiction." In *October Dreams: A Celebration of Halloween*. Edited by Richard Chizmar and Robert Morrish. Baltimore: Cemetery Dance, 2000.

Edwards, H. *A Collection of Old English Customs, and Curious Bequests and Charities*. London: John Bowyer Nichols and Son, 1842.

Eichler, Lillian. *The Customs of Mankind*. Garden City, New York: Doubleday, Page, 1924.

Elliott, Helen. "Hallowe'en," *Godey's Lady's Book and Magazine*, Vol. 81, No. 485 (November 1870): 439–443.

Ellis, Bill. "'Safe' Spooks: New Halloween Traditions in Response to Sadism Legends," In *Halloween and Other Festivals of Death and Life*. Edited by Jack Santino. Knoxville: University of Tennessee Press, 1994.

Ellis, Peter Berresford. *The Celtic Empire: The First Millennium of Celtic History 1000 B.C.–51 A.D.* London: Constable, 1990.

Emery, David. "Halloween Campus Massacre '98." In *Urban Legends and Folklore on About. com*. urbanlegends.about.com/library/weekly/aa102898.htm

_____. "Halloween Terror Attacks on Malls, 10/31/01." In *Urban Legends and Folklore on About. com*. urbanlegends.about.com/library/blmall-terror.htm

The Encyclopaedia Brittanica. 14th ed. London and New York: Encyclopaedia Brittanica, 1929.

Evans, Arthur Benoni. *Leicestershire Words, Phrases, and Proverbs*. London: English Dialect Society, 1881.

Evans, E. Estyn. *Irish Folk Ways*. London: Routledge and Paul, 1957.

Evans-Wentz, W. Y. *The Fairy Faith in Celtic Countries*. New York: Carol Publishing, 1990.

Faivre, Abel. "The Day of the Dead," *The Outlook*, December 6, 1916.

Farrar, Janet, and Stewart Farrar. *Eight Sabbats for Witches*. Custer, Washington: Phoenix Publishing, 1981.

Feldman, Ellen. "Halloween," *American Heritage*, Vol. 52, No. 7 (October 2001): 63–9.

"Female Impersonators Cavort at 'Fashionable' Chicago Ball," *Jet*, November 14, 1957.

Fergusson, R. Menzies. *Rambling Sketches in the Far North and Orcadian Musings*. London: Simpkin, Marshall, 1883.

Festivals.com. www.festivals.com/01-10-october/halloween/events.cfm

"Firemen Halt a Halloween School Blaze," *Des Moines Register*, November 1, 1939.

Fishwick, Henry. *A History of the Parish of Kirkham*. Manchester: Chetham Society, 1874.

Flavier, Dr. Juan M. *My Friends in the Barrio*. Quezon City: New Day, 1974.

Fletcher, Richard. *The Barbarian Conversion: From Paganism to Christianity*. New York: Henry Holt, 1998.

Foote, Monica. "Userpicks: Cyber Folk Art in the Early 21st Century," *Folklore Forum* 37.1, 2007.

Fortier, Alcee. *Louisiana Studies*. New Orleans: F. F. Hansell and Brothers, 1894.

Fowler, W. Warde. *The Roman Festivals of the Period of the Republic: An Introduction to the Study of the Religion of the Romans*. London: Macmillan, 1899.

Fraser, Antonia. *Faith and Treason: The Story of the Gunpowder Plot*. New York: Nan A. Talese/Doubleday, 1996.

Frazer, Sir James George. *The Golden Bough: A Study in Magic and Religion*, Vol. 13., 3rd ed. London and Basingstoke: Macmillan, 1913.

"Full Moon Will Be Rare Halloween Treat," *Los Angeles Times*, October 31, 2001: A22.

Gaer, Joseph. *Holidays Around the World*. Boston: Little, Brown, 1953.

Gainer, Patrick W. *Witches, Ghosts and Signs: Folk-*

lore of the Southern Appalachians. Grantsville, WV: Seneca Books, 1975.

Galembo, Phyllis. *Dressed for Thrills: 100 Years of Halloween Costumes & Masquerade.* New York: Harry N. Abrams, 2002.

Garnett, Henry. *Portrait of Guy Fawkes: An Experiment in Biography.* London: Robert Hale, 1962.

Gay, John. *The Shepherd's Week.* London: Ferd. Burleigh, 1714.

Glassie, Henry. *All Silver and No Brass: An Irish Christmas Mumming.* Philadelphia: University of Pennsylvania Press, 1983.

_____. *Irish Folktales.* New York: Pantheon, 1985.

_____. *Passing the Time in Ballymenone.* Philadelphia: University of Pennsylvania Press, 1982.

Goethe, Johann Wolfgang von. "Goethe's Faust," www.levity.com/alchemy/faustidx.html

Goldsmith, Oliver. *The Vicar of Wakefield. Bibliomania: Free Online Literature and Study Guides.* www.bibliomania.com/0/0/24/52/frameset.html

Goodrich, S. G. *Johnson's Natural History, Comprehensive, Scientific and Popular.* New York: A. J. Johnson, 1868.

Goodrich-Freer, A. "More Folklore from the Hebrides," *Folklore,* Vol. XIII (1902): 29.

Graham, Eleanor. *Happy Holidays: Stories, Legends and Customs of Red-Letter Days and Holidays.* New York: E. P. Dutton, 1933.

Grannis, Kathy. "As Economy Impacts Halloween, Americans Get Creative," National Retail Federation, http://www.nrf.com/modules.php?name=News&op=viewlive&sp_id=790

Gray, Steven. "Can Detroit Prevent a Return of 'Devil's Night'?" *Time* Magazine, October 30, 2009.

Green, Marian. *A Harvest of Festivals.* London and New York: Longman, 1980.

Green, Miranda J. *Dictionary of Celtic Myth and Legend.* New York: Thames and Hudson, 1992.

Greenleigh, John, and Rosalind Rosoff Beimler. *The Days of the Dead/Los Días de Muertos.* San Francisco: Pomegranate, 1998.

Gregor, Rev. Walter. *Notes on the Folklore of the North-East of Scotland.* London: Stock for the Folk-Lore Society, 1881.

Gregory, Dick. "My Answer to Genocide," *Ebony,* October 1971.

Gregory, Lady Isabella Augusta. *Lady Gregory's Complete Irish Mythology.* London: Chancellor Press, 2000.

Greif, Martin. *The Holiday Book: America's Festivals and Celebrations.* New York: Universe Books, 1978.

Gresham, William Lindsay. *Houdini: The Man Who Walked Through Walls.* New York: Holt, Rinehart and Winston, 1959.

Griffin, Robert H., and Ann H. Shurgin, editors. *The Folklore of World Holidays,* 2nd ed. Detroit and London: Gale Research, 1999.

Gundaker, Grey. "Halloween Imagery in Two Southern Settings," In *Halloween and Other Festivals of Death and Life.* Edited by Jack Santino. Knoxville: University of Tennessee Press, 1994.

Guthrie, E. J. *Old Scottish Customs Local and General.* London: Hamilton, Adams, 1885.

Haggerty, Bridget. "An Irish Hallowe'en," *Irish Culture and Customs.* www.irishcultureandcustoms.com/articlep1061.html

Haining, Peter. *Hallowe'en Hauntings.* London: William Kimber, 1984.

Hale, Virginia. "Jack-ma-Lanterns." In *The Silver Bullet and Other American Witch Stories.* Edited by Hubert J. Davids. Middle Village, NY: Jonathan David, 1975.

Halliwell, James Orchard. *A Dictionary of Archaic and Provincial Words, Obsolete Phrases, Proverbs, and Ancient Customs, from the Fourteenth Century,* Vol. I. London: John Russell Smith, 1847.

The Hallowed Haunting Grounds. www.hauntinggrounds.org

"Halloween and Official Houdini Seance Houdini's Haunted House," www.microserve.net/~magicusa/seance.html

"Halloween Gang Initiation," http://www.snopes.com/crime/gangs/halloween.asp.

"Hallowe'en Is Observed by Medford Boys," *Medford Mail Tribune,* November 1, 1921.

Hallowe'en Parties: Decorations, Favors, Games and Stunts. Framingham, MA: Dennison's, 1935.

"Halloween Pranks Keep Police on Hop," *Oregon Journal,* November 1, 1934.

"Halloween 'Trick or Treat' Supplants Old-Time Raids," *The Oregonian,* November 1, 1937.

"Halloween Unmasked 2000," from *Halloween* DVD. Anchor Bay. ASIN: 6035546789, 2002.

Hamper, William, editor. *The Life, Diary, and Correspondence of Sir William Dugdale.* London: Harding, Lepard, 1827.

Hampson, R. T. *Medii Aevi Kalendarium,* Vol. I. London: Henry Kent Causton. 1841.

Hand, Wayland D. *Popular Beliefs and Superstitions from North Carolina,* Vol. VI. Durham: Duke University Press, 1961.

Hardin, Terri. *A Treasury of American Folklore: Our Customs, Beliefs, and Traditions.* New York: Barnes and Noble, 1994.

Hardy, Dr. James, editor. *Denham Tracts: A Collection of Folklore by Michael Aislabie Denham,* Vol. 2. London: Folklore Society, 1895.

Hardy, Thomas. *The Return of the Native.* London: Smith, Elder, 1878.

Harland, John, and T. T. Wilkinson. *Lancashire Folk-Lore: Illustrative of the Superstitious Beliefs and Practices, Local Customs and Usages of the People of the County Palatine.* Manchester: John Heywood, 1867.

_____, and _____. *Lancashire Legends, Traditions, Pageants, Sports, &c. With an appendix containing a rare tract on the Lancashire Witches....* London: George Routledge and Sons, 1873.

Harris, Joel Chandler. *Uncle Remus: His Songs and His Sayings.* New York: D. Appleton, 1880.

Hatch, Jane M. *The American Book of Days.* 3rd ed. New York: H. W. Wilson, 1978.

Haunted Attraction Magazine. www.hauntedattraction.com

Haunted House Association. "Haunted Fast Facts," http://www.hauntedhouseassociation.org/haunted_attraction_information.htm.

Hawthorne, Julian. *David Poindexter's Disappearance and Other Tales.* New York: D. Appleton, 1888.

Hawthorne, Nathaniel. *Mosses from an Old Manse.* 2nd ed. Boston: Ticknor and Fields, 1854.

Hazeltine, Mary Emogene. *Anniversaries and Holidays: A Calendar of Days and How to Observe Them.* Chicago: American Library Association, 1944.

Heiser, Charles B., Jr. *Of Plants and People.* Norman: University of Oklahoma Press, 1985.

Henderson, William. *Notes on the Folk-Lore of the Northern Counties of England and the Borders.* London: W. Satchell, Peyton, 1879.

Herskovits, Melville J., and Frances S. Herskovits. *Trinidad Village.* New York: Alfred A. Knopf, 1947.

Heslop, Richard Oliver. *Northumberland Words,* Vol. I. London: English Dialect Society, 1892.

Hetrick, Lenore. *The Giant Hallowe'en Book.* Dayton, OH: Paine, 1934.

Hirshberg, Glen. *The Two Sams.* New York: Carroll and Graf, 2003.

The Hold Life Has: Coca and Cultural Identity in an Andean Community. Washington and London: Smithsonian Institution Press, 1988.

Hole, Christina. *English Folklore.* London: B. T. Batsford, 1940.

Holland, Robert. *A Glossary of Words Used in the County of Chester.* London: English Dialect Society, 1886.

Holmberg, Carl B. "Things That Go *Snap-Rattle-Clang-Toot-Crank* in the Night: Halloween Noisemakers." In *Halloween and Other Festivals of Death and Life.* Edited by Jack Santino. Knoxville: University of Tennessee Press, 1994.

"Home Matters," *The Vassar Miscellany,* Vol. XIX, Number 1, October, 1889.

"Hostility Greets Students at Black School in White Area of Detroit," *New York Times,* December 2, 1992.

"The Houdini Seances—MagicTricks.com: Magic, Magicians and Magic History," www.magictricks.com/houdini/seancehistory.htm

Huffstutter, P. J. "It's not corny—Midwest maze is a fall tradition," *Los Angeles Times,* October 23, 2009.

Hull, Eleanor. *Folklore of the British Isles.* London: Methuen, 1928.

Hume, Carina. "Ghost Supper," *Northern Express,* http://www.northernexpress.com/editorial/dining.asp?id=2123

Hunter, George McPherson. *When I Was a Boy in Scotland.* Boston: Lothrop, Lee and Shepard, 1920.

Hurston, Zora Neale. *Mules and Men.* Philadelphia: J. B. Lippincott, 1935.

Hutchinson, William. *The History of the County of Cumberland,* Vol. I. Carlisle: F. Jollie, 1794.

Hutchison, Ruth, and Ruth Adams. *Every Day's a Holiday.* New York: Harper and Brothers, 1951.

Hutton, Ronald. *The Pagan Religions of the Ancient British Isles: Their Nature and Legacy.* Oxford: Blackwell, 1991.

Hyde, Douglas. *Beside the Fire: A Collection of Irish Gaelic Folk Stories.* London: D. Nutt, 1890.

International Association of Haunted Attractions. www.iahaweb.com

Irish, Marie, *Hallowe'en Fun.* Syracuse, NY: Willis N. Bugbee, 1927.

_____. *Hallowe'en Merrymakers.* Syracuse, NY: Willis N. Bugbee, 1930.

Irving, Washington. *The Sketch Book of Geoffrey Crayon, Gent.* In *Project Gutenberg.* ftp://ibiblio.org/pub/docs/books/gutenberg/etext00/sbogcl10.txt

Irwin, Elizabeth A. "A Witches' Revel for Hallowe'en," *Good Housekeeping,* October 1908.

Johnson, F. Roy. *Legends and Myths of North Carolina Roanoke-Chawan.* Murfreesboro, North Carolina: Johnson Publishing, 1971.

Johnson, W. Branch. *Folktales of Provence.* New York: Frederick A. Stokes, 1928.

Jones, Fran, and Doris Baker. *The Folklore of Hertfordshire.* Totowa, NJ: Rowman and Littlefield, 1977.

Jones, Prudence, and Nigel Pennick. *A History of Pagan Europe.* London/New York: Routledge, 1995.

Joyce, James. *Dubliners.* London: Grant Richards, 1914.

Joyce, P. W. *Old Celtic Romances*. London: Kegan Paul, 1879.

_____. *A Social History of Ancient Ireland*. 2 vols. London: Longmans, 1903.

"Justin Rudd's Haute Dog Howl-oween Parade," http://www.hautedogs.org/howloween.html.

Keating, Geoffrey. *The History of Ireland*. 3 vols. London: Irish Texts Society, 1902.

Kelley, Ruth E. *The Book of Hallowe'en*. Boston: Lothrop, Lee and Shepard, 1919.

Kennedy, Peter. *Cheshire Soulcaking Plays*. (CD). Folktrax-107, 1975.

_____. *Traditions of Guernsey and Sark*. (CD). Folktrax-213, 1975.

_____, editor. *Voices of Children*. (CD). Folktrax-298, 1978.

Kerridge, Roy. *Bizarre Britain: A Calendar of Eccentricity*. New York: Akadine Press, 1998.

Kightly, Charles. *The Customs and Ceremonies of Britain*. London: Thames and Hudson, 1986.

Kinealy, Christine. *This Great Calamity: The Irish Famine 1845–52*. Boulder, Colorado: Roberts Rinehart Publishers, 1995.

Klavans, Nancy. "A Halloween Brunch: The Affirmation of Group in a Temporary Community." In *"We Gather Together": Food and Festival in American Life*. Edited by Theodore C. Humphrey and Lin T. Humphrey. Ann Arbor and London: UMI Research Press, 1988.

Koch, Howard. *The Panic Broadcast*. New York: Little, Brown, 1970.

Krythe, Maymie R. *All About American Holidays*. New York: Harper and Bros., 1962.

The Ku-Klux Klan Hearings Before the Committee on Rules, House of Representatives. Washington: Government Printing Office, 1921.

Kugelmass, Jack. "Imagining Culture: New York City's Village Halloween Parade." In *Feasts and Celebrations in North American Ethnic Communities*. Edited by Ramon A. Gutierrez and Genevieve Fabre. Albuquerque: University of New Mexico Press, 1995.

Kuhn, Alvin Boyd. *Hallowe'en: A Festival of Lost Meanings*. Elizabeth, NJ: Academy Press.

Laing, Gordon J. *Survivals of Roman Religion*. New York: Cooper Square Publishers, 1963.

Leather, Ella Mary. *The Folk-Lore of Herefordshire*. Hereford: Jakeman and Carver, 1912.

Leland, Charles Godfrey. *Gypsy Sorcery and Fortune Telling*. New York: Charles Scribner's Sons, 1891.

Leodhas, Sorche Nic. *Twelve Great Black Cats and Other Eerie Scottish Tales*. London: The Bodley Head, 1972.

Leonard, Jack, Louise Roug, and Meg James. "Buena Park Teen Slain Over a Plastic Pumpkin," *Los Angeles Times* (Orange County edition), Oct. 20, 1999: 1.

Lewis, Matthew G. *Tales of Wonder*. London: J. Bell, 1801.

_____. *The Life and Correspondence of M. G. Lewis*. London: Henry Colburn, 1839.

Limburg, Peter R. *Weird! The Complete Book of Halloween Words*. New York: Bradbury, 1989.

Lindahl, Carl, John McNamara and John Lindow. *Medieval Folklore: A Guide to Myths, Legends, Tales, Beliefs, and Customs*. Oxford and New York: Oxford University Press, 2002.

Linton, Ralph, and Adelin Linton. *Halloween Through Twenty Centuries*. New York: Henry Schuman, 1950.

Lists and Links. www.listsandlinks.com/calendar holidays.html

Lloyd, Gladys. *Hallowe'en Pranks and Parties*, Franklin, Ohio: Eldridge Entertainment House, 1927.

Loftus, Major Charles. *My Life from 1815–1849*, Vol. I. London: Hurst and Blackett, 1877.

Long, George. *The Folklore Calendar*. London: Phillip Allan, 1930.

Lys, Claudia de. *A Treasury of American Superstitions*. New York: Philosophical Library, 1948.

Macgregor, Alexander. *Highland Superstitions*. Bruceton Mills, WV: Unicorn, 1994.

Mackenzie, Alexander. *Historical Tales and Legends of the Highlands*. Inverness: A. & W. Mackenzie, 1878.

"Magic Week," *The Gulf Coast Magicians Guild*, http://www.gulfcoastmagicians.com/magic week.htm.

Markale, Jean. *The Pagan Mysteries of Halloween*. Translated by Jon Graham. Rochester, VT: Inner Traditions, 2001.

Matthews, Caitlin, and John Matthews. *Encyclopaedia of Celtic Wisdom*. Dorset: Element Books, 1994.

Maxwell-Stuart, P. G. *Chronicle of the Popes: The Reign-by-Reign Record of the Papacy from St. Peter to the Present*. London: Thames and Hudson, 1997.

Mayorga, Margaret. *One-Reel Scenarios for Amateur Movie-Makers*. New York: Samuel French, 1938.

McKinley, James C., Jr. "Wilding Youth and Homeless: A Blood Feud," *New York Times*, November 3, 1990.

McNeill, F. Marián. *Hallowe'en: Its Origin, Rites and Ceremonies in the Scottish Tradition*. Edinburgh: Albyn Press, 1970.

_____. *The Silver Bough*, Vol. 3. Glasgow: William MacLellan, 1956.

Merilatt, Bianca. "Mall Crawl Memories," *Cam-*

pus Press. http://bcn.boulder.co.us/campus press/1997/oct3097/mall103097.html

Milton, John. *Paradise Lost*. In *Project Gutenberg*. ftp://ibiblio.org/pub/docs/books/gutenberg/ete xt91/plboss10.txt

Minneapolis Halloween Committee. *Halloween Fun Book*. Minneapolis: Minneapolis Halloween Committee, 1937.

_____. *Halloween Fun Book Revised Edition*. Minneapolis: Minneapolis Halloween Committee, 1951.

The Miscellany of the Spalding Club, Vol. I. Aberdeen: Printed for the Club, 1841.

"Mississippi Whites Start Fund for Slain Negro, 15," *Jet*, Nov. 19, 1959.

Montgomerie, Alexander. *The Poems of Alexander Montgomerie* (edited by James Cranstoun). Edinburgh and London: William Blackwood and Sons, 1887.

Morin, Monte. "Killer of Pumpkin Thief Found Guilty," *Los Angeles Times*, May 25, 2002: B1.

Morton, Lisa. *A Hallowe'en Anthology: Literary and Historical Writings Over the Centuries*. Jefferson, NC: McFarland, 2008.

Moss, Doris Hudson. "A Victim of the Window-Soaping Brigade?" *American Home*, Vol. 22 (November 1939), 48.

Mulpezzi, Frances M., and William M. Clements. *Italian-American Folklore*. Little Rock: August House, 1992.

Murray, Margaret Alice. *The Witch-Cult in Western Europe: A Study in Anthropology*. London: Oxford University Press, 1921.

Nagle, Betty Rose. *Ovid's Fasti: Roman Holidays*. Bloomington: Indiana University Press, 1995.

Napier, James. *Folk Lore: Or, Superstitious Beliefs in the West of Scotland Within This Century*. Paisley: Alex. Gardner, 1879.

Newell, William Wellis. "The Ignis Fatuus, Its Character and Legendary Origin," *Journal of American Folk-Lore*, Vol. 17, 1904: 39–60.

O'Connor, Anne-Marie. "Day of the Dead Crosses Borders," *Los Angeles Times*, October 31, 1998: 1.

O'Dónaill, Niall. *Foclóir Gaeilge-Béarla*. Baile A'tha Cliath: Richview Browne and Nolan, 1977.

O'Donoho, Denis. "The Irish Peasants—Halloween" *The Dublin Penny Journal*, October 25, 1834.

Oliver, George. *The History and Antiquities of the Town and Minster of Beverley*. Beverley: M. Turner, 1829.

_____. *History of the Holy Trinity Guild at Sleaford*. Lincoln: Edward Bell Drury, 1837.

Orne, Martha Russell. *Hallowe'en: How to Celebrate It*. New York: Fitzgerald, 1898.

Osgood, Cornelius. *Village Life in Old China: A Community Study of Kao Yao Yunnan*. New York: Ronald Press, 1963.

O'Sullivan, Humphrey. *The Diary of Humphrey O'Sullivan*. 4 vols. Irish Texts Society, 1930–1933.

Ovid. *Metamorphoses*. Translated by A. D. Melville. Oxford and New York: Oxford University Press, 1986.

"Pagans Unite for a Day in the Sun," *Los Angeles Times*. October 31, 1999: 15.

Palmer, Kingsley. *The Folklore of Somerset*. London: B. T. Batsford, 1976.

Parkinson, C. Northcote. *Gunpowder, Treason and Plot*. London: Weidenfeld and Nicolson, 1976.

Partridge, Norman. *Dark Harvest*. Baltimore, MD: Cemetery Dance, 2006.

Patterson, Lillie. *Halloween (A Holiday Book)*. Champaign, IL: Garrard, 1963.

Pennant, Thomas. *A Tour in Scotland and a Voyage to the Hebrides 1772*. Chester: John Monk, 1774.

"Photos of Mock Lynching at Halloween Party Leads to Suspensions at White Auburn U. Frats," *Jet*, Dec. 3, 2001.

The Picayune's Guide to New Orleans 6th Edition. New Orleans: Picayune, 1904.

Pickering, David. *Cassell Dictionary of Superstitions*. London: Cassell, 1995.

Pinkerton, Charlene. *Halloween Favorites in Plastic*. Atglen, PA: Schiffer, 1998.

Pleck, Elizabeth H. *Celebrating the Family: Ethnicity, Consumer Culture, and Family Rituals*. Cambridge and London: Harvard University Press, 2000.

Plimpton, George. *Truman Capote*. Aylett, VA: Ancher, 1998.

Pointer, John. *Oxoniensis Academia: Or, the Antiquities and Curiosities of the University of Oxford*. London: S. Birt and J. Ward. 1749.

Porter, John. *History of the Fylde of Lancashire*. Fleetwood and Blackpool: W. Porter and Sons, 1876.

Prochaska, Suzanne. "Halloween Barbie Dolls," http://www.fashion-doll-guide.com/Hallo ween-Barbie-Dolls.html

Puckett, Newbell Niles. *Folk Beliefs of the Southern Negro*. Chapel Hill: University of North Carolina Press, 1926.

_____. *Popular Beliefs and Superstitions: A Compendium of American Folklore: From the Ohio Collection of Newbell Niles Puckett*. 3 vols. Boston, MA: G. K. Hall, 1981.

"The Pumpkin Effigy," *Harper's Weekly*, November 23, 1867.

Quintanilla, Michael. "Halloween Mutates Into a $2.5-Billion Binge," *Los Angeles Times*, Oct. 28, 1996: 1.

Radford E., and M. A. Radford. *The Encyclopedia of Superstitions*. Edited by Christina Hole. London: Hutchinson, 1961.

Ralston, William Ralston Shedden. *The Songs of the Russian People, as Illustrative of Slavonic Mythology and Russian Social Life*. New York: Haskell House, 1970.

Rampant Scotland. www.rampantscotland.com/ know/blknow halloween.htm

Ramsay, John. *Scotland and Scotsmen in the 18th Century*, Vol. II. Edinburgh and London: Blackwood, 1888.

Ramsey, Helen. *The Hallowe'en Festival Book*. Chicago and Minneapolis: T. S. Denison, 1946.

Randall, Kay, "What's in a Name? Professor Takes on Roles of Romani Activist and Spokesperson to Improve Plight of His Ethnic Group," University of Texas at Austin, http://www.utexas. edu/features/archive/2003/romani.html

Rees, Alwyn, and Brinley Rees. *Celtic Heritage: Ancient Tradition in Ireland and Wales*. New York: Thames and Hudson, 1961.

Reichel-Dolmatoft, Gerardo, and Alicia Reichel-Dolmatoft. *The People of Aritama: The Cultural Personality of a Colombian Mestizo Village*. Chicago: University of Chicago Press, 1961.

Reid, Jane Davidson. *The Oxford Guide to Classical Mythology in the Arts, 1300–1900s*. New York and Oxford: Oxford University Press, 1993.

"Residents and Civic Leaders in Milford Meet to Confront Reports of Bigotry," *New York Times*, November 25, 1999.

Rhys, Sir John. *Celtic Folklore, Welsh and Manx*. 2 vols. Oxford: Clarendon, 1901.

_____. *The Hibbert Lectures on the Origin and Growth of Religion as Illustrated by Celtic Heathendom*. England: Hibbert Lectures, 1886.

Robinson, Philip. "Harvest, Halloween, and Hogmanay: Acculturation in Some Calendar Customs of the Ulster Scots." In *Halloween and Other Festivals of Death and Life*. Edited by Jack Santino. Knoxville: University of Tennessee Press, 1994.

Rocky Point Haunted House. www.rockypoint hauntedhouse.com

Rogers, Charles. *Social Life in Scotland, From Early to Recent Times*. 3 vols. Edinburgh: W. Paterson, 1884–86.

Roman, Benjamin, and Keith Giffen. *I Luv Halloween: Ultimate Twisted Edition*. Los Angeles: Tokyopop, 2008.

Ross, Anne. *The Folklore of the Scottish Highlands*. London: B. T. Batsford, 1976.

_____. *Pagan Celtic Britain*. Chicago: Academy Chicago Publishers, 1996.

_____, and Don Robins. *The Life and Death of a Druid Prince*. Great Britain: Century Hutchinson, 1989.

Rowling, J. K. *Harry Potter and the Sorcerer's Stone*. New York: Scholastic, 1998.

Russe, Jennifer M. *German Festivals and Customs*. London: Oswald Wolff, 1982.

Ryan, Harriet. "Glamour and Gore: Kennedy Kin Accused of Murder," *Court TV* (8/22/01), www. Courttv.com

Sadler, A. W. "The Seasonal Context of Halloween: Vermont's Unwritten Law." In *Halloween and Other Festivals of Death and Life*. Edited by Jack Santino. Knoxville: University of Tennessee Press, 1994.

Sage, Agnes Carr. "Halloween Sports and Customs," *Harper's Young People*, October 27, 1885.

St. Clair, Sheila. *Folklore of the Ulster People*. Cork: Mercier Press, 1971.

Salisbury, Jesse. *A Glossary of Words and Phrases Used in S.E. Worcestershire*. J. Salisbury, 1893.

Santino, Jack. *All Around the Year: Holidays and Celebrations in American Life*. Urbana and Chicago: University of Illinois Press, 1994.

_____. *Hallowed Eve: Dimensions of Culture in a Calendar Festival in Northern Ireland*. Lexington: University Press of Kentucky, 1998.

_____. "The Folk Assemblage of Autumn: Tradition and Creativity in Halloween Folk Art." In *Folk Art and Art Worlds*. Edited by John Michael Vlach and Simon J. Bronner, Logan: Utah State University Press, 1992.

_____. *The Hallowed Eve: Dimensions of Culture in a Calendar Festival in Northern Ireland*. Lexington: The University Press of Kentucky, 1998.

_____. "Halloween in America: Contemporary Customs and Performances," *Western Folklore*, Vol. 42, No. 1. (1983): 1–20.

_____. "Halloween: The Fantasy and Folklore of All Hallows," *American Folklife Center, Library of Congress*. www.loc.gov/folklife/halloween. html, 1982.

_____, editor. *Halloween and Other Festivals of Death and Life*. Knoxville: University of Tennessee Press, 1994.

Sarrantonio, Al. *Orangefield*. Baltimore, MD: Cemetery Dance, 2002.

Saso, Michael R. *Taiwan Feasts and Customs*. Hsinchu, Taiwan: Chabanel Language Institute.

Sawyer, Frederick Ernest. *Sussex Natural History, Folk-Lore, and Superstitions*. Brighton, 1883.

Saxon, Lyle, Robert Tallant, and Edward Dreyer.

Gumbo Ya-Ya: A Collection of Louisiana Folk Tales. Louisiana Library Commission, 1945.

Schauffler, Robert Haven. *Hallowe'en (Our American Holidays).* New York: Dodd, Mead, 1935.

Schnacke, Dick. *American Folk Toys: How to Make Them.* New York: G. P. Putnam's Sons, 1973.

Schneider, Stuart. *Halloween in America: A Collector's Guide with Prices.* Atglen, PA: Schiffer, 1995.

_____, and Bruce Zalkin. *Halloween: Costumes and Other Treats.* Atglen, PA: Schiffer, 2001.

Schulz, Charles M. *It's the Great Pumpkin, Charlie Brown.* Cleveland and New York: World, 1967.

Schwoeffermann, Catherine. "Bonfire Night in Brigus, Newfoundland." In *Halloween and Other Festivals of Death and Life.* Edited by Jack Santino. Knoxville: University of Tennessee Press, 1994.

Sciarappa, William J. and Joseph Heckman. "Growing an 'A-maize-ing' Corn Maze," New Jersey: Rutgers Cook College Resouce Center, 2004.

Scott, Sir Walter. *Lady of the Lake.* In *Project Gutenberg.* digital.library.upenn.edu/webbin/gutbook/lookup?num=3011

_____. *Minstrelsy of the Scottish Border.* http://www.electricscotland.com/history/other/minstrelsy_ndx.htm

_____. *The Monastery: A Romance.* 3 vols. Edinburgh: Longman, Hurst, Rees, Orme, and Brown, etc.

_____. *Waverley; Or, 'Tis Sixty Years Since.* Edinburgh: Archibald Constable, 1814.

Scullard, H. H. *Festivals and Ceremonies of the Roman Republic.* Ithaca, N.Y.: Cornell University Press, 1981.

Searle, Adrian. *Isle of Wight Folklore: The Island's Legends, Customs and Traditions.* Dorset: Dovecote Press, 1998.

Sechrist, Elizabeth Hough. *Heigh-Ho for Halloween.* Philadelphia: Macrae Smith, 1948.

Seton, Susannah. *Simple Pleasures for the Holidays.* Berkeley: Conari, 1998.

Shakespeare, William. *Henry IV Part One.* New York: Washington Square Press, 1964.

_____. *Two Gentlemen of Verona.* New York: Penguin, 2000.

Shipman, Dorothy M., et al. *Jolly Hallowe'en Book.* Syracuse, New York: Willis N. Bugbee, 1937.

Shoemake, Helen Carson, Ada Clark, Julia M. Martin, Mildred Hastings, et al. *Halloween Fun Book.* Chicago: Beckley-Cardy, 1936.

Shuel, Brian. *The National Trust Guide to Traditional Customs of Britain.* Exeter, England: Webb and Bower, 1985.

Simmons, Dave. "Deconstructing Halloween," *Dallas Business Journal,* November 6, 2000: http://dallas.bizjournals.com/dallas/stories/2000/11/06/editorial3.html.

Simpson, Jacqueline. *The Folklore of Sussex.* London: B. T. Batsford, 1973.

_____, and Steve Roud. *Oxford Dictionary of English Folklore.* Oxford: Oxford University Press, 2000.

Sims, Patsy, *The Klan.* Lexington: The University Press of Kentucky, 1996.

Siporin, Steve. "Halloween Pranks: 'Just a Little Inconvenience.'" In *Halloween and Other Festivals of Death and Life.* Edited by Jack Santino. Knoxville: University of Tennessee Press, 1994.

Skal, David J. *The Monster Show: A Cultural History of Horror.* New York and London: W. W. Norton, 1993.

Skinner, Ada M., and Eleanor L. Skinner. *The Topaz Story Book: Stories and Legends of Autumn, Hallowe'en and Thanksgiving.* New York: Duffield, 1928.

Smith, Major H., and Charles Roach Smith. *Isle of Wight Words.* London: English Dialect Society, 1881.

Somers, Frances. "Civilizing Hallowe'en," *Survey Graphic,* November 1937.

Spence, John. *Shetland Folk-lore.* Lerwick: Johnson and Greig, 1899.

Spence, Lewis. *The History and Origins of Druidism.* Rider, 1949.

Spencer, DeShuna. "NAACP Youth and College Division Continues Struggle for Civil Rights," *The Crisis,* Jan.-Feb. 2007.

Spicer, Dorothy Gladys. *Festivals of Western Europe.* New York: H. W. Wilson, 1958.

Steinhauer, Jennifer. "Drop the Halloween Mask! It Might Scare Someone," *New York Times,* October 30, 2009.

Stern, Renee B. *Neighborhood Entertainments.* New York: Sturgis and Walton, 1913.

Stevenson, Burton E., and Elizabeth B. Stevenson, *The Days and Deeds Reader and Speaker.* Garden City: Doubleday, Page, 1912.

Stewart, William Grant. *The Popular Superstitions and Festive Amusements of the Highlanders of Scotland.* Edinburgh: Archibald Constable, 1823.

Stoker, Bram. *Dracula.* In *Dracula: Truth and Terror.* (CD-ROM). Edited by Raymond T. McNally. New York: Voyager, 1996.

Stone, Sir Benjamin. *Sir Benjamin Stone's Pictures: Festivals, Ceremonies, and Customs.* London, Paris, New York & Melbourne: Cassell, 1906.

Stone, Gregory P. "Halloween and the Mass Child," *American Quarterly,* Vol. 11 (1959): 372–79.

Stukeley, Dr. William. *Itinerarium Curiosum or an Account of the Antiquitys and Remarkable Curiositys in Nature or Art*, Vol. I. London: Privately printed, 1724.

Sugimoto, Etsu Inagaki. *The Daughter of the Samurai*. Rutland, VT: Charles E. Tuttle, 1926.

Superville, Denisa R. "Police Issue Mischief Night Warnings," www.northjersey.com, October 29, 2009.

Sutton-Smith, Brian. *The Games of New Zealand Children*. Berkeley: University of California Press, 1959.

Swainson, Rev. C. *A Handbook of Weather Folklore*. Edinburgh and London: William Blackwood and Sons, 1873.

S´wiebocka, Teresa, *Auschwitz: A History in Photographs*, Bloomington and Indianapolis: Indiana University Press, 2003.

Taft, Michael. "Adult Halloween Celebrations on the Canadian Prairie." In *Halloween and Other Festivals of Death and Life*. Edited by Jack Santino. Knoxville: University of Tennessee Press, 1994.

Telford, Mae McGuire, "What Shall We Do Halloween?," *Ladies Home Journal*, October 1920.

"This Week in Black History: October 31, 1900 — Ethel Waters," *Jet* Magazine, November 6, 1995.

Thompson, Frank. *Tim Burton's Nightmare Before Christmas: The Film, the Art, the Vision*. New York: Hyperion, 1993.

Thompson, Sue Ellen, editor. *Halloween Program Sourcebook*. Detroit: Omnigraphics, 2000.

Toor, Frances. *Festivals and Folkways of Italy*. New York: Crown, 1953.

"Tower Hamlets Replaces Guy Fawkes with Bengali Firework Festival," www.thisislondon.co.uk/news/article-23373126-tower-hamlets-replaces-guy-fawkes-with-bengali-firework-festival.do

Train, Joseph. *An Historical and Statistical Account of the Isle of Man*. Douglas, Isle of Man: Mary A. Quiggin, 1845.

"TransWorld Halloween, Costume and Party Show," www.partyplansplus.com/Trans world/transworldrelease.htm

Trevelyan, Marie. *Folk-Lore and Folk-Stories of Wales*. www.red4.co.uk/ebooks/trevfolklore.htm

_____. *A Glimpse of Welsh Life and Character*. www.red4.co.uk/ebooks/glimpse.htm

"'Trick or Treat' Is Demand," *The Lethbridge Herald*, November 4, 1927.

Truwe, Ben. *The Halloween Catalog Collection: 55 Catalogs from the Golden Age of Halloween*. Medford, OR: Talky Tina Press, 2003.

Tuleja, Tad. "Trick or Treat: Pre-Texts and Contexts." In *Halloween and Other Festivals of Death and Life*. Edited by Jack Santino. Knoxville: University of Tennessee Press, 1994.

Turner, Kay, and Pat Jasper. "Day of the Dead: The Tex-Mex Tradition." In *Halloween and Other Festivals of Death and Life*. Edited by Jack Santino. Knoxville: University of Tennessee Press, 1994.

Tusser, Thomas. *Five Hundred Points of Good Husbandry: A New Edition*. London: Lackington, Allen, 1812.

"US Halloween $$$ Figures," *Sightings*. www.rense.com/politics5/hallowfig.htm

Vallencey, Charles. *Collectanea de Rebus Hibernicus*, Vol. III. Dublin: Luke White. 1786.

Van Teslaar, Dr. J. S. *When I Was a Boy in Roumania*. Boston: Lothrop, Lee and Shepard, 1917.

Vaux, James Edward. *Church Folk Lore*. 2nd ed. London: Skeffington and Son, 1902.

Verbeten, Sharon. "Trick or Treat! Halloween Toys," *Toy Collectors Magazine*, http://www.toycollectormagazine.com/index2.php?option=com_content&do_pdf=1&id=97.

Villa, Susie Hoogasian, and Mary Kilbourne Matossian. *Armenian Village Life Before 1914*. Detroit: Wayne State University, 1982.

Vlach, John Michael, "'Properly Speaking': The Need for Plain Talk About Folk Art." In *Folk Art and Art Worlds*. Edited by John Michael Vlach and Simon J. Bronner, Logan: Utah State University Press, 1992.

Vreeland, James M., Jr. "Day of the Dead," *Archaeology*, Vol. 45, no. 6 (November/December 1992): 43.

Wade, Nicholas, editor. *The Science Times Book of Insects*. New York: Lyons Press, 1998.

Wainwright, Martin. "Halifax Mischief Night Gets Out of Hand," *The Guardian Unlimited*. www.guardian.co.uk/race/story/0,11374,657703,00.html

"Wait 'Til the Kids Play 'Em," *The Billboard*, November 9, 1959.

Walpole, Hugh. *All Souls' Night*. London: Macmillan, 1933.

Walsh, William S. *Curiosities of Popular Customs and of Rites, Ceremonies, Observances, and Miscellaneous Antiquities*. Philadelphia: J. B. Lippincott, 1897.

Weiser, Francis X. *The Holyday Book*. New York: Harcourt, Brace, 1956.

West, John O. *Mexican-American Folklore*. Little Rock: August House, 1998.

White, Corporal Charles Frederick. *Plea of the Negro Soldier and a Hundred Other Poems*. Easthampton, MA: Enterprise, 1908.

Whitelocke, R. H. *Memoirs, Biographical and His-

torical, of Bulstrode Whitelocke. London: Routledge, Warne, and Routledge, 1860.

Whitlock, Ralph. *The Folklore of Wiltshire.* Totowa, NJ: Rowman and Littlefield, 1976.

Whitney, Annie W., and Caroline C. Bullock. "Folk-Lore from Maryland," *Memoirs of the American Folklore Society*, Vol. XVIII (1925), 123–135.

Wilkins-Freeman, Mary. *The Pot of Gold.* New York: Lothrop, Lee and Shepard, 1892.

Williams, Charles. *All Hallows' Eve.* London: Faber and Faber, 1945.

Williams, Rynn. *Pumpkins.* New York: Friedman/ Fairfax, 1998.

Williamson, George C. *Guildford in the Olden Time.* Guildford: Woodbridge Press, 1904.

Willis, P. L. "Making the Hallowe'en Spirit Profitable to the City," *The American City*, Vol. XVII, No. 4, October 1917.

Wintemberg, W. J. and Katherine H. "Folk-lore from Grey County, Ontario," *The Journal of American Folk-lore*, Vol. 31, 1918.

Wright, A. R. *British Calendar Customs: England Volume III: Fixed Festivals, June-December Inclusive.* London: The Folk-Lore Society, 1940.

Yeats, W. B., editor. *Fairy and Folk Tales of Ireland.* New York: Macmillan, 1983.

Young, George. *A History of Whitby and Streoneshalh Abbey*, Vol. 2. Whitby: Clark and Medd, 1817.

Index

Numbers in *bold italics* indicate pages with illustrations.